for Ed Finegan,

with friendship and respect,

Jack Hawkins March 1984

Word Order Universals

QUANTITATIVE ANALYSES OF LINGUISTIC STRUCTURE

Under the general editorship of

William Labov (Ed.), *Locating Language in Time and Space*

Thomas E. Toon, *The Politics of Early Old English Sound Change*

John A. Hawkins, *Word Order Universals*

Word Order Universals

John A. Hawkins

Department of Linguistics
University of Southern California
Los Angeles, California

Max-Planck-Institut für Psycholinguistik
Nijmegen, Holland

1983

ACADEMIC PRESS

A Subsidiary of Harcourt Brace Jovanovich, Publishers

New York London
Paris San Diego San Francisco São Paulo Sydney Tokyo Toronto

ACADEMIC PRESS, INC.
111 Fifth Avenue, New York, New York 10003

United Kingdom Edition published by
ACADEMIC PRESS, INC. (LONDON) LTD.
24/28 Oval Road, London NW1 7DX

Library of Congress Cataloging in Publication Data

Hawkins, John A.
Word order universals.

(Quantitative analyses of linguistic structure)
Bibliography: p.
Includes indexes.
1. Grammar, Comparative and general--Word order.
2. Universals (Linguistics) 3. Historical linguistics.
I. Title. II. Series: Quantitative analyses of linguistic structure series.
P295.H34 1983 415 83-3912
ISBN 0-12-333370-9

PRINTED IN THE UNITED STATES OF AMERICA

83 84 85 86 9 8 7 6 5 4 3 2 1

To Anne Dunlea

Contents

3 : *Implicational Universals in Greenberg's Data and the Expanded Sample*

4 : *A Distributional Universal in Greenberg's Data and the Expanded Sample*

5 : *The Diachronic Predictions of Implicational Universals*

6 : *The Diachronic Predictions of Distributional Universals*

7 : *Language Universals and the Logic of Historical Reconstruction*

8 : *The Expanded Sample*

Preface

Twenty years ago, in 1963, Joseph Greenberg's paper "Some Universals of Grammar with Particular Reference to the Order of Meaningful Elements" was published in the first edition of the *Universals of Language*, under his editorship. The impact of this paper has been considerable. Greenberg stated his word order universals using implicational statements, and these paved the way for the discovery of other implicational universals and for the development of a form of universal grammar that I shall label "Typological Universal Grammar." His universals have come to play an important role within theorizing in historical linguistics. They are receiving increasing attention in formal grammar, as different versions of generative grammar have come to include within their goals the setting of parameters on cross-language variation. And they have also influenced descriptive grammar writing, structuring and contributing to the checklist of properties to be researched.

The present book is a contribution to the descriptive data base of Greenberg's original paper, and to the theoretical issues that have emerged in response to these data within the field as a whole. Greenberg was not primarily interested in trying to explain his word order statements, so this will be an important focus of the present volume. I will also devote considerable attention to the role of universals in theories of historical change.

My starting point is the Greenberg data set, which has been expanded. Greenberg used a sample of 142 languages for certain limited co-occurrences of basic word orders, and a 30-language sample for more detailed information. In the Language Index, the 142 have been expanded to some 350 languages. And for between one-third and one-half of these, supplementary data have been collected of the type that Greenberg listed in his 30-language sample. Using the original Greenberg samples and the Expanded Sample, an alternative set of descriptive word order statements is provided. These define all and only the relevant co-occurrences of basic word orders that are attested in the samples, and they predict differences in language frequencies among the attested types. Several descriptive regularities emerge thereby which have gone unnoticed hitherto.

In seeking explanations for these descriptive universals, numerous insights are borrowed from formal syntax, particularly from those versions of generative grammar that try to capture cross-categorial generalizations. To my knowledge, the present volume represents the first in-depth attempt to draw together detailed typological universals on the one hand, and formal syntax on the other. It is argued that wide-scale language comparison can yield certain types of insights for formal grammar which do not emerge when one adopts a single language (or single language family) approach. The insights provided by formal syntax are, however, only part of the explanatory package. In addition, some psycholinguistic considerations involving language processing are explored. I also examine the role that principles of language change can (and cannot) play in explaining synchronic universals. I am unimpressed, however, by the exclusive appeal to innateness of grammatical knowledge as a source of explanation in this context. I hold that some aspects of Universal Grammar probably are innately represented in the human species, but that it is bad methodology to invoke innateness without first exploring more tangible alternative explanations, such as language function, semantics, and language processing, and without seriously investigating other cognitive domains in order to see just how unique a mental activity the acquisition of language is. I prefer a multifactor approach to explanation, therefore, which views descriptive universals as the product of several interacting demands upon linguistic systems. The innateness factor should be a residue, and not an initial assumption, and should be invoked only when other possible explanatory principles have been tried and found wanting, and when other cognitive domains have been properly explored.

In the diachronic chapters of the book, I illustrate how implicational universals can make predictions for the relative timing of changes, as languages move from one type to another. I discuss critically the role that has been assigned to language universals in explaining the chain of changes which frequently follow or accompany the independently explainable shifts in verb position, the so-called "Trigger–Chain Theory," and I propose a less controversial alternative which I feel captures the spirit of this theory while avoiding many of its problems. The consequences of my reformulated universals for historical reconstruction are also explored. Some laws of reconstruction derived from synchronic universals are formulated, and by applying them to Proto-Indo-European the most likely word orders for the parent language turn out to be just the opposite of what is most commonly assumed.

The data and theorizing in this volume have consequences for the notion of a language type itself. I am led to the view that language types are more abstract objects than they are currently assumed to be. A type is here regarded as a family of variant subtypes, each of which obeys certain linguistic regularities and each of which shares at least one "typological indicator" with every other subtype. The Greenbergian VSO/SVO/SOV trichotomy is abandoned.

The book therefore draws on work in numerous traditions and areas of linguistic research (descriptive grammar, generative syntax, semantics, typology, language history, theories of processing) in seeking to understand one of the central relations in syntax: relative order. It is hoped that the conclusions will be of interest to those working in these areas.

Acknowledgments

The present book represents the final product of a research project which I have been pursuing, inter alia, over a ten-year period. The assistance of many individuals over these years has been indispensible in bringing the project to fruition. The most formative influence was a 1974 seminar on Universal Grammar organized at Cambridge University by Ed Keenan, which provided the theoretical and descriptive framework within which some of the ideas could first be developed. In 1975 and 1976 David Kilby and I organized seminars on the same model for students and faculty at Essex University, and in 1978 I organized a similar seminar at the University of Southern California. All these seminars were important in providing part of the data which constitute the Expanded Sample and in giving feedback and ideas.

The first draft of this manuscript underwent considerable revision following detailed and most helpful comments from David Sankoff. I would like to express my gratitude to him for the time and effort that he put into this. I am also grateful to all of the following who have given me comments and reactions to portions of the material presented here: Emmon Bach, Bernard Comrie, Ed Finegan, Paul Friedrich, Talmy Givón, Martin Harris, Dick Hudson, Larry Hyman, Ray Jackendoff, Osvaldo Jaeggli, Ed Keenan, David Kilby, Wolfgang Klein, Winfred Lehman, Pim Levelt, David Lightfoot, Marta Luján, Bill Moulton, William Marslen-Wilson, Elinor Ochs, Barbara Partee, Bob Stockwell, Sandy Thompson, Maner Thorpe, and Lorraine Tyler. I would also like to thank Joseph Greenberg for his encouragement in a venture which owes so much to his own seminal work. Not all of these individuals agree with my conclusions in the different areas of the book, but I have had sufficient positive feedback and encouragement to want to collect together the various strands of my work on word order in book form. I have also benefited from some discussions in print of earlier papers of mine by Neil Smith, Barry Blake, and Theo Vennemann, whose points I have incorporated and, where necessary, responded to.

I would also like to acknowledge in person the individuals who have contributed to the Expanded Sample of this book. A special word of gratitude must go to Maner Thorpe who provided me with information on a very large number of Altaic and Caucasian languages. Other persons that I would like to thank include (in alphabetical order): S. Ali (Khasi), C. Biggs (Brahui), C. Chea (Khmer), B. Comrie (Amharic, Arabic, Czech, Russian, Tamil), J. Durand (Mandarin), A, Duranti (Italian, Samoan), J. Gates (Welsh), L. Hyman (numerous Bantu, Kwa and Mande languages), E. Keenan (Arosi, Motu, Maori, Malagasay), D. Kilby (Evenki, Twi), A. Kim (Korean), E. Kitis (Finnish), G. Mardirrussian (Armenian, Persian), E. Ochs (Samoan), J. Payne (Classical Mayan, Thai, Vietnamese), G. Pullum (Hausa, Hindi, Kiriwinan), C. Randriamasimanana (numerous Indonesian and Oceanic languages), J. Roberson (numerous languages of South East Asia), J. Roberts (Welsh), M. Sanchez (Spanish, Tagalog), N. Saunders (Mandarin), Y. Uchida (Assamese, Chamorro, Japanese, Yuan), K. Williamson (numerous Kwa languages), E. Yarnall (numerous American Indian languages).

The first draft of this book was developed and completed while I was working full-time in the Department of Linguistics, University of Southern California, between 1977 and 1981. The final version was produced in the course of 1982 while I was full-time at the Max-Planck-Institut für Psycholinguistik, Nijmegen. I would like to thank these institutions for their support, both academic and practical, in the course of this research. I have learned a considerable amount from my colleagues, and it has been a privilege to be associated with centers of excellence such as these.

I would like to thank Edith Sjoerdsma (Max-Planck-Institut) for her assistance with typing the manuscript, and Heather Holmback for helping me with the indexes.

Finally, this book is dedicated to Annie. Her love and support were invaluable in seeing it through to completion. The ideas were developed at the same time that we were getting to know each other, and I will always associate this work with her: with two-part harmonies, our walks along the ocean waves, trips up Highway One, the sharing of minds, and the growth of a very special bond.

Abbreviations

A	Adjective
AII	Greenberg's Appendix II
AMS	Adjective – Marker – Standard
AN	Adjective – Noun
AP	Adjective Phrase
Adj	Adjective
AdjAdv	Adjective – Adverb
AdjMS	Adjective – Marker – Standard
AdjN	Adjective – Noun
AdjP	Adjective Phrase
Adp	Adposition
AdpP	Adposition Phrase
Art	Article
Aux	Auxiliary
AuxV	Auxiliary – Verb
Adv	Adverb
AdvAdj	Adverb – Adjective
CCH	Cross-Category Harmony
CN	Common Noun
CNP	Common Noun Phrase
CNPN	Common Noun – Proper Noun
CV	Consonant – Vowel
Comp	Complement
DAH	Doubling Acquisition Hypothesis
DI	Deductive Inference
DN	Demonstrative – Noun

DNP	Determined Noun Phrase
DO	Direct Object
Dem	Demonstrative
DemN	Demonstrative – Noun
Det	Determiner
ENHG	Early New High German
ES	Expanded Sample
FIH	Frequency Increase Hypothesis
GN	Genitive – Noun
Gen	Genitive
GenN	Genitive – Noun
HH	Heaviness Hierarchy
HSP	Heaviness Serialization Principle
IE	Indo-European
IO	Indirect Object
LCV	Logic of Competing Variants
LCGmc	Late Common Germanic
lgs	Languages
MHG	Middle High German
MHIP	Mobility and Heaviness Interaction Principle
MP	Mobility Principle
MV	Main Verb
MVSV	Main Verb – Subordinate Verb
N	Noun
N_o	Object Noun Phrase
N_s	Subject Noun Phrase
NA	Noun – Adjective
NAdj	Noun – Adjective
ND	Noun – Demonstrative
NDem	Noun – Demonstrative
NG	Noun – Genitive
NGen	Noun – Genitive
NHG	New High German
NNum	Noun – Numeral
NP	Noun Phrase
NPoss	Noun – Possessive
NRel	Noun – Relative Clause
NSP	Natural Serialization Principle
NomO	Nominal Object
Num	Numeral
NumN	Numeral – Noun
O	Object

OHG	Old High German
OV	Object–Verb
OVS	Object–Verb–Subject
OSV	Object–Subject–Verb
Obl	Oblique Object
PIE	Proto-Indo-European
PN	Proper Noun
P	Preposition
PNCN	Proper Noun–Common Noun
PP	Prepositional Phrase
PS-rules	Phrase-Structure Rules
Part	Particle
Po	Postposition
Poss	Possessive
PossN	Possessive–Noun
PossPh	Possessive Phrase
Postp	Postposition
PoNMH	Postpositional Noun Modifier Hierarchy
Pr	Preposition
PrNMH	Prepositional Noun Modifier Hierarchy
Prep	Preposition
Q	Quantifier
QuPart	Question Particle
RDI	Reconstruction of Doubling Innovations
RP	Relative Probability
RQ	Relative Quantities
RT	Relative Time
RTH	Relative Time Hypothesis
Rel	Relative Clause
RelN	Relative Clause–Noun
S	Sentence
S	Subject
S-complements	Sentence-complements
SMA	Standard–Marker–Adjective
SMAdj	Standard–Marker–Adjective
SOV	Subject–Object–Verb
SOVnr	Nonrigid Subject–Object–Verb
SOVr	Rigid Subject–Object–Verb
SV	Subject–Verb
SVMV	Subordinate Verb–Main Verb
SVO	Subject–Verb–Object
Spec	Specifier

Su	Subject
T-rules	Transformational Rules
TGG	Transformational Generative Grammar
TVP	Transitive Verb Phrase
UCH	Universal Consistency in History
UCR	Universal Consistency in Reconstruction
V	Verb
VAux	Verb–Auxiliary
VO	Verb–Object
VOS	Verb–Object–Subject
VP	Verb Phrase
VS	Verb–Subject
VSO	Verb–Subject–Object

Further abbreviatory conventions are given in the text itself.

Word Order Universals

1 : *Toward a Theory of Word Order Universals*

1.1 Word Order Variation across Languages

We begin our study by observing that languages appear to vary considerably with regard to word order. Take the position of the verb relative to subject and object. Three common orders are found: SOV, SVO, and VSO, as in (1)–(3) respectively. The orders VOS and OVS, as in (4) and (5), are also found, though in relatively few languages.

(1) SOV (e.g., Japanese)
Taroo ga tegami o kaita.
Taroo letter wrote
'Taroo wrote a letter.' (Kuno 1978:65)

(2) SVO (e.g., English)
Harry hit the dog.

(3) VSO (e.g., Welsh)
Lladdodd y ddraig y dyn.
killed the dragon the man
'The dragon killed the man.' (Comrie 1981:81)

(4) VOS (e.g., Malagasay)
Nahita ny vehivavy ny mpianatra.
saw the woman the student
'The student saw the woman.' (Keenan & Comrie 1977:70)

(5) OVS (e.g., Hixkaryana)
Toto yonove kamara.
man he-ate-him jaguar
'The jaguar ate the man.' (Derbyshire 1977:593)

Such variability extends to other word orders as well. The noun may precede or follow the other constituents of the noun phrase (adjective, genitive, relative clause, etc.). Prepositions in some languages (***in** the house*) correspond to postpositions in others (*the house **in***), and so on.

And yet, within this variation linguists have discerned clear patterns. Nineteenth- and early-twentieth-century German scholars were the first to draw attention to them (see, e.g., Schmidt 1926), and the more recent work of Greenberg, Lehmann, and Vennemann owes a considerable debt to their groundwork. The basic intuition that emerges from the writings of all these authors is the following: Languages tend to place modifying elements either consistently before or consistently after modified elements (or heads). Thus, where a language has direct object modifiers before the verb (e.g., Japanese), it will typically place genitive, adjective, and relative clause modifiers before the modified noun, as in (6)–(8), and noun phrase modifiers before the postposition, as in (9):

(6) *Taroo no ie* (Japanese: GenN)
Taroo 's house

(7) *kono omosiroi hon* (Japanese: AdjN)
this interesting book

(8) *Taroo ga issyoni benkyoosita hito* (Japanese: RelN)
Taroo together studied person
'the person with whom Taroo studied'

(9) *Taroo ga zidoosya de Hanako to Tokyo kara ryokoosita.*
Taroo car by Hanako withTokyo from traveled
'Taroo traveled from Tokyo with Hanako by car.'
(Japanese: NP + Po)

Conversely, consider a language like Samoan (cf. Marsack 1962), in which verb precedes direct object, as in (10).[1] The modifying genitive, adjective, and relative clause now all follow the modified noun, and the language is prepositional:

(10) *Ua iloa e Atamu lana ava o Eva.* (Samoan: VO)
knew Adam his wife Eve
'Adam knew Eve his wife.'

(11) *o le paopao o Tavita* (Samoan: NGen)
the canoe of David

(12) o le teine puta (Samoan: NAdj)

the girl fat
'the fat girl'

(13) *le teine o le sa moe i lona fale* (Samoan: NRel)
the girl who was asleep in her house

(14) *i le potu* (Samoan: Pr + NP)
in the room

This principle of consistent serialization for all modifying in relation to modified elements has proved an invaluable aid in discovering cross-language word order patterns. The basic intuition has been progressively refined over the decades, culminating in the most recent work of Lehmann and Vennemann (to be discussed in Chapter 2), but the word order predictions remain essentially as they were.

One of the aims of this book, however, is to argue that this modifier–modified serialization principle is not quite correct in its present form. Its predictions are too strong. There are lots of OV languages which differ from Japanese in having either NAdj in lieu of AdjN [cf. (7)] or NRel in lieu of RelN [cf. (8)], or both. And there are numerous VO languages with, for example, AdjN rather than NAdj (English is one such language), or postpositions rather than prepositions.

The predictions are also too weak, for there are significant restrictions on co-occurring word orders across languages which are not being captured. As I see it, the central descriptive task in this area is to be able to define the discrepancy between the mathematically possible and the actually attested word order combinations across languages. The mathematics of word order variation allows for enormous numbers of language types. In the examples above, we considered just 6 pairs of word orders: subject–verb; object–verb; genitive–noun; adjective–noun; relative clause–noun; and adposition–noun phrase. If we add just 4 more modifier–modified pairs, we get $2^{10} = 1024$ possible language types. Add just 10 more (and we are still barely scratching the surface of the number of orderings that grammars define on their categories), and we get $2^{20} = 1{,}048{,}576$, that is, over one million language types. Add just 5 more, and we have over 33 million possible language types, and so on.

Clearly, the attested word order co-occurrences amount to just a fraction of the mathematical possibilities. Large numbers of languages share a relatively small set of word order co-occurrences, and the great majority of possible word order types have no exemplifying languages at all. But the modifier–modified generalization, in all its forms, does not succeed in distinguishing between those word order co-occurrences that are never found and those that are.

1.2 What Needs To Be Described and Explained in This Area?

In the light of the considerations raised in the preceding section, the first question we need to address is the following:

(*a*) What are the relatively few word order co-occurrences that languages select from among the mathematical possibilities?

That is, we must attempt to define all and only the attested word order types that can be observed. We must then address the more explanatory question:

(*b*) Why do languages select these rather than other possible co-occurrences?

Greenberg (1966) attacks Question (*a*) by setting up so-called implicational universals. These are generally cross-categorial statements defining which word orders within one category (e.g., S or VP) can be predicted to co-occur with certain word orders in another category (e.g., NP or PP). And they have the logical form 'if a language has some word order *P*, then it will also have word order *Q*'. For example, if a language has VSO, then it also has Prep + NP (rather than NP + Postp). Greenberg was not primarily concerned with Question (*b*), though he acknowledges the explanatory force of the traditional modifier–modified distinction as a significant generalization within the grammars of the world's languages. The work of Lehmann, Vennemann, and others has built upon Greenberg's descriptive statements by refining the explanatory potential of the modifier–modified distinction.

There is another set of facts which needs to be described in the area of cross-language variation, but which has received only indirect attention hitherto, namely, language frequencies. Among the attested word order types, there are very different quantities of languages. Some co-occurrence types are very frequent (e.g., the Japanese type), other are slightly less so, yet others are considerably less so, and some word order types have only a handful of exemplifying languages. This distribution raises the following questions:

(*c*) What are the relative frequencies of languages among the attested word order types?

(*d*) Why do the attested word order types exhibit the varying frequencies that they do?

Distributional regularities will provide an important source of data and of theorizing in this book. It will be argued that their explanation involves intrinsically gradient, rather than absolute, causes.

The existence of word order variation synchronically is compatible with the possibility of word order change historically, as languages move among the synchronically attested word order types. We shall devote considerable attention to diachrony in this book, with the following questions in mind:

(*e*) What can historical principles contribute to the explanation of current synchronic word order variation?
(*f*) How and why do languages change from one word order type to another?
(*g*) What predictions do the synchronic universals of word order make for word order change?
(*h*) What use can be made of the synchronic universals of word order in linguistic reconstruction?

There are other questions that must eventually be addressed within a theory of word order universals. One very important one involves the relationship between basic word order and other properties of the grammar. For example, how does word order interact with case marking, and with extraction, movement, and deletion processes across languages? We shall consider only case marking in this study. The reader is referred to Mallinson and Blake (1981) for a thorough discussion of the relationship between word order type and other such properties of the grammar. Our answers to Questions (*a*)–(*h*) will also be limited, of course, to the sample of word orders and the sample of languages that we have collected.

1.3 Theories of Universal Grammar

Greenberg's (1966) implicational statements defining co-occurring word orders have been referred to here as "universals," as is now common practice among those who work in this area. But the sense in which these statements are universals of language needs to be commented on, by distinguishing two major traditions of research on universal grammar: first, the theory associated with generative grammar and, second, that of "typological universal grammar."

1.3.1 THE CHOMSKYAN PARADIGM

The primary goal of linguistic analysis, advocated in Chomsky (1965) and subsequent publications, is to extract the formal and substantive universals of language from an in-depth study of single languages, typically English, thereby developing a universal grammar. This universal grammar defines the notion "possible human language."

More precisely, Chomsky defines FORMAL universals as those having to do with the form and shape of the grammars of all languages (the various components, rule types, principles of rule interaction, etc); SUBSTANTIVE universals are those having to do with the content of rules (e.g., the syntactic categories or phonological distinctive features to which rules refer). The generative approach is founded on the proposition that by uncovering the basic formal and substantive properties of the grammar of any one language, we discover the universals of language in general. Universals are properties that are shared by all languages, and they are therefore extractable from any one language. By defining these universals as precisely as possible, we distinguish possible human languages (whose grammars incorporate the universals) from impossible ones (whose grammars do not). The universal grammar so defined then provides the general model and descriptive tools that can be applied to the analysis of any language to generate all and only the grammatical sentences of that language, etc.

At an explanatory level, Chomsky argues that his universals are a direct consequence of, and are explained by, certain innate properties of the human mind. It is on the basis of these properties that the newborn child begins to construct a grammar out of the utterances in his linguistic environment. And Chomsky draws a strict distinction between innate properties of the human language faculty, for which in-depth grammatical analysis provides evidence, and psycholinguistic principles derived from observations of language use, involving memory, complexity, processing difficulty, and so on, all of which are assigned to a theory of performance rather than competence.

1.3.2 TYPOLOGICAL UNIVERSAL GRAMMAR

There is a second paradigm of universal grammar, typological universal grammar, which is associated with the names of Greenberg, Keenan, Comrie, Thompson, and many others (see Comrie, 1981, and Keenan, 1978a, for the clearest general statements).

Typological universal grammar is explicitly designed to accommodate the considerable variation observed between languages. Although not denying that there are properties which all languages share (called "absolute" universals), this paradigm focuses primarily on the search for regularities in the ways that languages vary, and on the constraints and principles that underlie this variation. A possible human language is one whose properties fall within the parameters permitted by the variation-defining language universals; an impossible language is one whose properties do not. Classifications of languages made in terms of the properties or property clusters mentioned in the variation-defining statements are then referred to as "typologies." To quote Keenan (1978a): "Universals are characterisations of the regularities in the ways languages may differ from one another. Structures which differ from one another . . . are among the primary objects of study [p. 90]." Keenan's theory of universal grammar includes an inventory of syntactic and semantic primitives in terms of which the grammars of individual languages are to be constructed, a set of descriptive statements defining attested versus nonattested patterns of cross-language variation, and various explanatory principles of language variation. These last include the functional principle, the principle of logical variants, conservation of logical structure, and the principle of semantic dissonance, and they offer semantic explanations for cross-language variation patterns being the way they are.[2]

The chief advantage of this approach lies in its serious attention to diverse languages, and in its formulation of descriptive, typological statements covering major syntactic and semantic properties across languages. It can also incorporate a variety of explanatory considerations in relation to this variation: pragmatic, semantic, and psycholinguistic. For example, in addition to Keenan's semantic explanations, Comrie (1981) gives some plausible pragmatic explanations for diverse language universals. And the reader is referred to Clark and Clark (1977:Chapter 14) for a discussion of explanations for language universals in perceptual and cognitive terms, and to Grosu and Thompson (1977) and Dryer (1980) for explanations in terms of language processing. The typological approach can be seen as building on the tradition of language description established by traditional grammarians, by many nontransformational linguists, and by anthropologists. This tradition has resulted in often excellent descriptions of major portions of many of the world's languages.

1.3.3 EVALUATING THE TWO APPROACHES

Comrie (1981) voices a critique of the generative paradigm which is to be found in varying degrees in the work of most typologists. He argues that one cannot define the notion "possible human language" on the basis of a study of single languages. Rare, but occurring, linguistic possibilities will not be noticed in this way. And many (if not most) universals are of the variation-defining sort, since languages vary throughout their grammars in often radical ways. If one is to define a "possible human language," therefore, one must survey the range of variation patterns across languages, define principled limits on these, and search for regularities underlying, and explanations for, the attested versus nonattested variants.

Single languages underdetermine the range of possible and impossible language types.

Comrie also criticizes the exclusive appeal to innateness as an explanation for language universals. Invoking innate properties of the human mind, for which the only evidence is the putative universals themselves, runs the risk of circularity. One can evaluate the putative universals empirically, but as there is no independent evidence for the innate language faculty, the explanation cannot be subjected to any kind of test, and requires a strong act of faith. Typological explanations for language universals, by contrast, typically appeal to INDEPENDENTLY ESTABLISHED principles of the grammar and of the human cognitive and perceptual apparatus, and are therefore susceptible to empirical test.

However, this issue about the ultimate explanation for language universals may be more methodological than substantive. Typologists cannot reasonably deny the innateness of some aspects of language and language acquisition. They simply prefer to investigate those linguistic universals which *can* be explained in other ways. And for those which cannot, it would be a rather ungenerous typologist who did not take the innateness account very seriously indeed. That is, innateness is a residue, to be invoked when other, more readily observable, explanatory principles fail. Conversely, a generativist who totally excluded the explanatory potential of, for example, language function or language processing, would be guilty of an extreme dismissiveness of the opposite kind, given currently available universal data.

The generative grammarian might reply to Comrie's critique with the following two points.

First, there has been a definite shift of emphasis within more recent generative grammar (cf. Chomsky 1981) toward an approach in which the theory defines parameters on variation, that is, possible and impossible grammars. One (to my mind very promising) example is the X-bar theory of phrase structure (cf. Jackendoff 1977, Lightfoot 1979), which makes predictions for the co-occurring and non-co-occurring phrase structure rules that a grammar can have. Certain grammars are permitted, while other (hitherto permitted) variants are ruled out. The typologist might object here that these variation-defining predictions are still derived from English, and that there has still been no systematic attempt to check the proposed predictions against sufficient cross-language data to justify X-bar theory as a component of any universal grammar. Nonetheless, there *is* an increasing interest in language variation in the generative literature, and an increasing application of generative principles to languages other than English (e.g., Heny 1981, Hale 1982).

Second, the generativist might argue that Comrie's critique is beside the point, as he (along with most other typologists) is typically not addressing the kinds of theoretical questions that generative grammarians address, questions involving formal properties of grammars, rule complexity or markedness, the role of performance in relation to a theory of competence, the interaction between rules and between components, etc.

The question that we need to ask, therefore, is the following: Are there things that the typological method can contribute to the SAME theoretical issues that generative grammarians address? If so, what are they? And, more generally, what exactly does large-scale language comparison yield for a theory of universal grammar that single-language analysis does not?

The present book will attempt to provide some general answers to these questions. And we shall anticipate our conclusions by briefly outlining the method of analysis and its theoretical relevance.

1.4 The Method and Theoretical Relevance of the Present Study

The present study is based on a language sample of some 350 languages, taken from all the major language families of the globe (see Chapter 8 and the Language Index). This sample has incorporated Greenberg's (1966) samples as a starting point (see Chapter 2), and has considerably expanded them. The particular emphasis within these languages is on approximately one dozen word orders consisting of pairs of modifier + head: adjective and noun, direct object and verb, preposition and NP, etc. For five of these pairs I have data from all 350 languages (adjective and noun, genitive and noun, preposition/postposition and noun phrase, object and verb, and subject and verb). For the remainder (demonstrative determiner and noun, relative clause and noun, etc), I have data from between one-third and one-half of the sample. The same methodological problems apply in this work which apply in all large-scale typological studies: Only a limited number of properties (here word orders) can be studied; the grammars upon which we rely are not always dependable; the categories that we study are not always readily comparable across languages (we are heavily reliant upon semantic criteria; see Section 1.5); and some word orders exhibit variant orders (e.g., French *pauvre homme* 'poor man'/*homme pauvre* 'man poor'). In this study we are primarily interested in "basic word orders," and in most cases there is no problem in recognizing these, but sometimes there is (see Section 1.5.1).

I and other typologists (e.g., Mallinson and Blake 1981) believe that such problems are real but solvable. The word orders that I have selected for study are those where grammars are typically most informative and reliable, and where decisions on basic word order and category comparability are clearest. All languages have two-place predicates, possessor–possessed constructions (cf. genitives), restrictive modifiers on nouns which translate English adjectives, whether these appear to be more verblike or nounlike in surface, etc. And to those single-language grammarians who have their doubts about the viability of the typological method, I would say this. In single-language analysis, one recurrent problem is the notion "grammatical sentence of *L*." Native speaker disagreements are not infrequent on this question, and the choice between theories often hinges on questionable data. But this does not detract from the overall viability of the single-language method. There are lots of clearly grammatical, and lots of clearly ungrammatical, sentences in each language, and we try to base our theoretical conclusions on the clearest data possible. So it is too with typology. We strive to build our universals and theories on the clear cases, and to minimize the unclarities as much as possible. Furthermore, as our universals are mostly of the implicational kind (if a language has property *P*, then it also has property *Q*), a language that does not clearly have property *P* is simply irrelevant for, and not a counterexample to, the universal (see Section 1.5.1).

The benefits of the typological methodology are that it contributes to the theory of universal grammar in ways that single-language analysis cannot. We shall enumerate what seem to us the most important ways in which this is so, by anticipating our most general conclusions.

There are two variables in cross-language data which can inform theory construction. The first involves the possible and impossible combinations of properties (here word orders): A single language can attest to the POSSIBILITY of some combination, but only large language samples can motivate its IMPOSSIBILITY. The second involves language numbers. My data are compatible with numerous "frequency hierarchies," defined by "distributional universals of language." Once again, the larger the sample, the less skewed and more representative it will be of the ±5000 currently spoken languages. The values for these two variables are theoretically revealing in the following four ways.

The observed parameters on cross-language variation (e.g., the Prepositional Noun Modifier Hierarchy, Section 3.3.7) reveal patterns which suggest explanations for all and only the relevant grammatical sentences in the relevant languages (cf. Section 3.4). In some cases such explanations are not revealed at all in single-language analysis, in others the class of explanations compatible with single-language analysis can be considerably reduced.

Cross-language frequencies provide a set of relevant data which can inform the construction of a theory of rule complexity (and markedness) in the area of cross-categorial generalizations (cf. Chapter 4). A single language provides sufficient data for the beginnings of such a theory, but cross-language data provide an empirical means of refining it, and of making theoretical decisions which otherwise cannot be made. Current formalisms are compatible with too many possibilities.

The role of processing difficulty (a performance notion) within linguistic theory appears in a new light (Section 3.4.2.1). The kinds of processing considerations that Chomsky used to motivate the irrelevance of performance for the competence grammar of English can now be used to explain the form and functioning of numerous grammatical rules across the world's languages. Processing difficulty also appears to be a gradient notion, with different degrees of processing difficulty reflected in different numbers of languages, all things being equal.

Combinatorial and frequency data also reveal the interaction of explanatory principles, some of them in conflict, which are inextricably intertwined (or one of which is obliterated) in the grammars of single languages. The interplay and relative strength of these principles emerges from the plurality (cf. the interplay between Keenan's logical structures and his Subjects Front Principle, Section 4.3.1).

1.5 On Basic Word Order

Throughout this book we are going to assume the viability of a notion of "basic word order." The basic verb position of English is SVO; the basic adjective position of Japanese is AdjN; the basic genitive position of Samoan is NGen; etc. We are also going to assume that the categories of subject, object, verb, adjective, genitive, noun, adposition, etc., whose basic ordering we are going to study, are comparable across languages. Both assumptions are commonly made in the typological literature, and I believe that they are both reasonable, even though there are some obvious problems. It is my aim to minimize these problems as much as possible: We shall give systematic attention to nonbasic word orders as well, by incorporating them as an essential ingredient into a theory of word order change; we shall not force languages into some basic word order mold where a decision on basicness is problematic; and we shall concentrate on those linguistic categories from among the set first studied by Greenberg (1966) whose cross-linguistic comparability is most straightforward.

The biggest problem for a notion of basic word order is to be found in the ordering of the arguments of the verb at the sentence level. This is typically the locus of considerable word order freedom, and the prevailing opinion is that sentence-level word order freedom is conditioned by pragmatic rules sensitive to old versus new information, topic, focus, etc. (see Firbas, 1971, for a discussion of Czech; Erguvanli, 1979, for Turkish; Bolinger, 1972, for English; Silva-Corvalan, 1982, for Spanish; see also Thompson, 1978, for a discussion of "pragmatic word order languages"). The two arguments of the verb whose relative position to one another, and to the verb, is most fixed are subject and object, and we shall therefore concentrate on these. Within the noun phrase and the adposition phrase, word order freedom is much less extensive, and so most of our detailed word orders will be taken from these categories. The undecidability of basic order is thereby considerably reduced, though not eliminated. Since this is the major objection that can be made to a cross-language study of the type offered here, I shall devote the next subsection to it. I believe that the problem is not as severe as it is sometimes argued to be.

As for the comparability issue, it is, of course, an assumption of all typological work that certain basic linguistic entities are recognizable across languages. This does not imply a sharing of all the relevant properties for the entity in question by all languages. But it does imply a sharing of sufficient properties to allow the equation to be made. It also implies the search for a principled explanation for the variation. For example, are certain properties of subjects more basic than others, and can the cross-language differences be predicted and explained by setting up a hierarchy of essential and nonessential properties (cf. Keenan 1976b) or by linking the variation to other general typological differences? The present book shares with its predecessors the assumption that the categories illustrated in Section 1.1 are recognizable across languages. Some detailed problems are discussed in Mallinson and Blake (1981) involving, for example, the status of subjects in ergative languages and the status of adjectives in languages in which the translation equivalents of English adjectives are either nominal or verbal, there being no morphologically separate class of adjectives. But Mallinson and Blake's overall conclusion is positive. In the final analysis, semantic criteria will suffice to make the cross-linguistic equation.

1.5.1 DOUBLING AND BASICNESS

For the majority of the word orders in this study in the majority of our languages the basicness issue is not problematic, for the simple reason that only one order occurs. English has *this man,* never **man this; in the house,* never **the house in; Harry saw the dog,* never **Harry the dog saw;* and so on. But for at least some word orders in the majority of languages, variants do exist, and the question then arises as to which order, if any, is the "basic" one. For example, English has both preposed and postposed genitives (*the king's castle/the castle of the king*); French has postnominal and prenominal adjectives (*un homme pauvre* 'an impecunious man'/*un pauvre homme* 'an unfortunate man'); German has a minor prenominal relative clause strategy in addition to its postnominal relatives (*die den Mann liebende Frau* 'the the man loving woman'/*die Frau, die den Mann liebt* 'the woman who loves the man'), and the variation in its verb position (OV in subordinate clauses, verb-second or -first in main clauses) is well known.

I am going to use the term "doubling" to describe the situation in which one and the same modifier category (e.g., the adjective) can occur both before and after its head in a given language. And in general I shall follow these three (overlapping) criteria when making a basicness decision:

1. Where one doublet (e.g., NAdj) occurs with greater frequency than the other (AdjN) in attested samples of the relevant language, then, all things being equal, the more frequent doublet is the basic one.
2. Where one doublet (e.g., NAdj) is more frequent within the grammatical system of the language than the other (e.g., the quantity of adjective lexemes that occur postnominally exceeds the number that occur prenominally), then, all things being equal, the grammatically more frequent doublet is the basic one.
3. Where one doublet is grammatically unmarked and the other marked (i.e., a special type of grammatical meaning may be associated with one order of Adj and N, but not the other, over and above their lexical meanings; one word order may not undergo certain general rules that the other does, or may be generated by rules of a more restricted nature; one word order may be the one chosen by exceptional modifiers, whose exceptional status is marked in the lexicon; etc.), then, in all these cases, the unmarked order is the basic one.

In many (if not most) cases, these three criteria suffice to give a clear basicness decision. For example, postnominal adjectives can be argued to be basic in French, because they are more frequent than prenominal adjectives by Criteria (1) and (2). German has both prepositions, as in English, and postpositions (*dem Haus gegenüber* 'the house opposite'), but prepositions are basic by Criteria (1) and (2): The quantity of German adpositions that precede their modifying NPs far exceeds those that follow, both in the grammar and in language use. Similarly, the syntactic rules of German generate postnominal relative clauses more productively than prenominal relatives, and hence NRel is basic by Criterion (3) (see

Chapter 5, Note 14). English verb before subject structures (*rarely did he play a wrong note*) are triggered by a more restrictive set of environments than SVO, and so SVO is basic for the same reason.

However, there will be a residue of cases where no such clear difference in basicness emerges [i.e., two doublets are equally frequent according to (1) and/or (2), equally productive according to (3)], or where two criteria contradict one another. In these cases, no basicness decision can be made, and the languages in question cannot be classified for the relevant basic word order property. For example, I can find no difference in basicness between prenominal and postnominal genitives in English: Sometimes both are possible, as in the example given earlier; sometimes just the postnominal is possible (*the age of reason/*reason's age, the corner of the road/?*the road's corner*), and sometimes just the prenominal (*John's adolescent period/*the adolescent period of John*). And though for German I am much more sympathetic to a deep structure verb-final position (cf. Bierwisch 1963) than to SVO (cf. Huber & Kummer 1974), I do not consider deep structure order of itself a sufficient guarantor of basicness in surface structure within the present more typologically oriented context.

There seems to be a view implicitly held by some linguists that the existence of languages some of whose word orders are of undecidable basicness renders futile, or at least highly problematic, the whole attempt at a basic order typology. But this does not follow for a number of reasons (see also Section 3.3.8).

First, we are going to propose a number of implicational universals of the form 'if a language has some basic word order(s) *P*, then it also has basic word order(s) *Q*'. In the event that some languages do not clearly have basic word order(s) *P*, then no predictions are made for them, as the antecedent property is not satisfied. To take a similar example, the universals of tone are irrelevant for, rather than falsified by, a language that does not have a tone system (cf. Comrie 1981:33).

Second, the undecidability of basic word orders is the exception rather than the rule, when one considers the totality of word orders in all the languages of our sample, and it is limited primarily to the arguments of the verb.[3] Within the noun phrase, for example, doubling structures are much less common than unique orders, and, where they occur, they are generally limited to one or two modifiers: English has a single order for demonstrative determiners (all preposed), numerals (all preposed), (single descriptive) adjectives (all preposed), and relative clauses (all postposed); French has a single order for demonstrative determiners, numerals, genitives, and relative clauses; and German has a single order for demonstrative determiners, numerals, and adjectives (with doubling on the genitive as well as the relative clause). Within the adposition phrase, doubling is extremely rare (though German as we have seen, is an example, as is Mandarin Chinese).

Third, when doubling does occur, it is generally subject to strict grammatical rules which determine the respective syntactic/semantic modifier subclasses which can be preposed or postposed, together with any semantic/pragmatic differences in interpretation resulting from the ordering, all of which facilitate a basicness decision in terms of markedness. For example, German prenominal relative clauses are possible on subjects only (see Keenan & Comrie 1977), with additional restrictions superimposed (see Weber 1971; Chapter 5, Note 14). French prenominal adjectives are limited in number, and often involve a clear difference in interpretation (cf. *un homme pauvre/un pauvre homme* given earlier).

Fourth, I believe that Frequency Criterion (1) is a very sensitive one, and one that we shall be making extensive use of in the historical discussion (Chapters 5–7). Frequency typically reflects grammatical preferences and productivity. And in the absence of detailed grammatical analyses for many of the languages under investigation, it provides the only means we have of determining grammatical preference and productivity, and with it basicness. Changing frequencies in historically successive texts can then provide a sensitive quantification of ongoing changes involving word order doublets, whose syntactic/semantic/pragmatic functions are especially difficult to determine in the absence of native speakers.

Finally, notice that doubling exists in different forms. Thus, to take the example of adjective modifiers, some follow the NAdj pattern, others the AdjN pattern, while yet others occur in either order. In noun phrases containing two such modifiers at the same time, it is therefore possible for doubling to be "simultaneous"; that is, the head is both preceded and followed by modifiers of one and the same category within the same phrase. French *un pauvre homme célèbre* (Adj + N + Adj) 'a poor famous man' and English *Germany's destruction of the city* (Gen + N + Gen) are examples. A particularly interesting case is "identical simultaneous doubling," where preceding and following modifiers are identical. An example is the demonstrative determiner in Malagasay which can "frame" the noun phrase: *ity trano fotsy ity* (Dem + N + Adj + Dem) 'this house white this' (i.e., 'this white house'). A variant of identical simultaneous doubling can also be found with the French negation morphemes, which frame the verb: *Je ne vois pas l'homme* 'I not see not the-man' (i.e., 'I don't see the man'). Another type of simultaneous doubling is "internal simultaneous doubling," where instead of being preceded and followed by two modifiers of the same category, the head is framed by daughter constituents of one and the same modifier category. An example is English adjective phrase modifiers of the type *a higher mountain than Everest* (where *mountain* is the head, and the adjective phrase *higher than Everest* frames the head to left and right — compare *a mountain higher than Everest,* where the adjective phrase follows the head entirely (cf. C. Smith 1961). Further examples are the "internal relative clause strategies" of Keenan and Comrie (1977:65), exemplified in the following sentence from Bambara (an SOV language), in which the relative S frames the head noun *so* 'horse':

(15) *tye ye (ne ye so min ye) san*
man past I past horse which see buy
'the man bought the horse which I saw'

and the 'preposition internal to PP strategy," which is found as a minor adposition ordering variant in Wedauan PPs such as the following (cf. King 1901:90):

(16) *numa au aburuna*
house into small
'into the small house'

The NP ('small house') here frames the adposition within the adposition phrase.

1.6 On the Notion "*X* as a VSO/SVO/SOV Language"

It is common in the literature to see discussions of Chinese as an SVO or SOV language, Arabic as VSO or SVO, and so forth. These discussions typically assume some variant of the modifier–head principle summarized in Section 1.1, and a decision on typological status is made by inspecting the (typically mixed) language in question, to see how many of the universally predicted properties characteristic of each language type are actually present.

This book is going to present a different set of word order universals which, if accepted, will have the following consequences for typological classification:

1. SVO is no longer a type indicator; that is, nothing correlates with SVO in a unique and principled way, according to our evidence. There are, of course, many languages with SVO, but there is no "SVO-type."
2. VSO and SOV are type indicators, but limited ones. Much better and more general type indicators are prepositions and postpositions.
3. The whole notion of a "word order type" becomes more abstract. The set of languages comprising a common type no longer share all of a given set of word order properties. (In fact, they never did this

anyway — there have always been too many exceptions to the modifier – head generalization, whence the problematic status of so many languages!) The set of languages which are considered to belong to a common type (e.g., prepositional languages) may now vary in many (even most) of their basic word orders. But they must all conform to a relatively restricted set of word order subtypes obeying certain general regularities (e.g., the subtypes of the Prepositional Noun Modifier Hierarchy, Section 3.3.7), each of which contains a shared common property functioning as the typological indicator (here prepositions).

These points are discussed more fully in Section 3.5. They will lead us to abandon the typological significance of verb position (VSO/SVO/SOV), advocated by Greenberg (1966).

Notes

1. The position of the subject in Samoan varies. Samoan has both VSO, as in sentence (10) which is like the Welsh example (3), and VOS, as in the following sentence which is like the Malagasay example (4):

(i) *Ua maua le polo e le tama.*
has found the ball the boy
'The boy has found the ball.' (Marsack 1962:105)

In both (10) and (i) the verb precedes both subject and object, with the order of these latter being subject to variation.

2. In order to give the reader some sense of what is involved in these explanations, here are summaries of the relevant principles (as found in Keenan 1978a), along with further references:

The functional principle (cf. Keenan 1974, 1979)
Given a surface structure constituent C and two subconstituents of it, C' and C'', if the meaning (semantic interpretation) of C'' varies as a function of the meaning of C', then the form of C'' may (but need not) vary as a function of the form of C'. The converse, however, fails.

The principle of logical variants (cf. Keenan 1973)
If the meaning difference of two expression types A and B is predictably neutralized in a given logical context, then languages may vary according as expressions of that context contain A or B or either.

Conservation of logical structure (cf. Keenan 1973)
The more the output of a syntactic process ("rule" or "rule complex") corresponds to the semantic representation of that structure, the more productive the process (e.g., it is more productive in languages where the correspondence is better than in those where it is not so good).

The principle of semantic dissonance (cf. Keenan 1978b)
The more semantically dissonant the (semantic) interpretation function for a possible human language, the fewer will be the languages that have such functions.
("By semantically dissonant we mean the extent to which the functions which assign meaning representations to basic [roughly, 'simple'] sentences in the language must be modified to assign representations to more complex, i.e. more 'derived' sentences [Keenan 1978a:119]".)

3. But see Schachter and Otanes (1972) for a discussion of Tagalog in which adjective order is claimed to be essentially free.

2 : *Greenberg's and Vennemann's Universals of Word Order*

Current research on synchronic word order universals has been most influenced by the work of Joseph Greenberg, and by Theo Vennemann, whose work draws extensively on that of Winfred Lehmann. This chapter summarizes and discusses their contributions, as a background to the reformulated word order universals of Chapters 3 and 4.

2.1 Greenberg's Universals

Greenberg's seminal paper "Some Universals of Grammar with Particular Reference to the Order of Meaningful Elements" (1966) is the foundation upon which all subsequent work on word order universals has built. Using a 30-language sample with a wide genetic and areal coverage, Greenberg set up 45 universal statements involving syntax and morphology. The great majority of these are implicational in nature: If a language has some property *P*, then it also has some other property *Q*. Greenberg proposed three universal word order types, Verb + Subject + Object (VSO), Subject + Verb + Object (SVO), and Subject + Object + Verb (SOV), and argued that these different positions of the verb correlate in a principled way with word order patterns elsewhere in the grammar. In a separate appendix, Appendix II, he then gave some basic word order information on a considerably expanded list of the world's languages.

His paper is a landmark in two respects. It established the validity and importance of a new type of universal statement, the implicational universal, thereby setting a precedent for the discovery of other universals of this logical form (e.g., the Accessibility Hierarchy of Keenan and Comrie

1972, 1977; Comrie and Keenan 1979). And it also provided the basis for much subsequent work on word order itself. This subsequent work has gone beyond Greenberg's original paper in three ways: There has been a reformulation of many of the universals; attempts have been made to actually explain the word order patterns which Greenberg discovered but which he presented as observational statements only; and Greenberg's typology has been widely applied in historical theories attempting to explain why word orders change, and as an aid to the reconstruction of protolanguages. The work of Winfred Lehmann and Theo Vennemann exemplifies all three developments and has attracted particular attention.

Fifteen of Greenberg's universals relate verb position to other properties (I retain Greenberg's numbering, adding "a" and "b" where a universal embodies two logically distinct claims; the addition of "-s" means that the universal is "statistical" and admits a limited number of exceptions—all universals without "-s" are nonstatistical, or exceptionless):

(3) Languages with dominant VSO order are always prepositional.

(4-s) With overwhelmingly greater than chance frequency, languages with normal SOV order are postpositional.

(5) If a language has dominant SOV order and the genitive follows the governing noun, then the adjective likewise follows the noun.

(6) All languages with dominant VSO order have SVO as an alternative, or as the only alternative, basic order.

(7) If in a language with dominant SOV order there is no alternative basic order, or only OSV as the alternative, then all adverbial modifiers of the verb likewise precede the verb. (This is the rigid subtype of SOV.)

(10a-s) Question particles or affixes specified in position by reference to a particular word in the sentence almost always follow that word.

(10b) Such particles do not occur in languages with dominant order VSO.

(11a) Inversion of statement order so that verb precedes subject occurs only in languages where the question word or phrase is normally initial.

(11b) Such inversion occurs in yes–no questions only if it also occurs in interrogative word questions.

(12) If a language has dominant order VSO in declarative sentences, it always puts interrogative words or phrases first in interrogative word questions; if it has dominant order SOV in declarative sentences, there is never such an invariant rule.

(13) If the nominal object always precedes the verb, then verb forms subordinate to the main verb also precede it.

(15) In expressions of volition and purpose, a subordinate verbal form always follows the main verb as the normal order except in those languages in which the nominal object always precedes the verb.

(16a) In languages with dominant order VSO, an inflected auxiliary always precedes the main verb.

(16b) In languages with dominant order SOV, an inflected auxiliary always follows the main verb.

(17-s) With overwhelmingly more than chance frequency, languages with dominant order VSO have the adjective after the noun.
(21) If some or all adverbs follow the adjective they modify, then the language is one in which the qualifying adjective follows the noun and the verb precedes its nominal object as the dominant order.
(25) If the pronominal object follows the verb, so does the nominal object.
(41-s) If in a language the verb follows both the nominal subject and nominal object as the dominant order, the language almost always has a case system.

For many of the non-verb-position word orders that are placed in relation to basic verb position in this way (adposition order, genitive order, etc.) Greenberg then gives 10 additional implicational statements. These universals define co-occurrences either between one another or with altogether different word order and morphological properties. They are as follows:

(2a-s) In languages with prepositions, the genitive almost always follows the governing noun.
(2b-s) In languages with postpositions it almost always precedes.
(9a-s) With well more than chance frequency, when question particles or affixes are specified in position by reference to the sentence as a whole, if initial, such elements are found in prepositional languages.
(9b-s) If final, such elements are found in postpositional languages.
(18-s) When the descriptive adjective precedes the noun, with overwhelmingly more than chance frequency, the demonstrative and the numeral do likewise.
(19) When the general rule is that the descriptive adjective follows, there may be a minority of adjectives which usually precede, but when the general rule is that descriptive adjectives precede, there are no exceptions.
(20a) When any or all of the items—demonstrative, numeral, and descriptive adjective—precede the noun, they are always found in that order.
(20b) If they follow, the order is either the same or its exact opposite.
(22a) If in comparisons of superiority the only order or one of the alternative orders is standard–marker–adjective, then the language is postpositional.
(22b-s) With overwhelmingly more than chance frequency, if the only order is adjective–marker–standard, the language is prepositional.
(23a) If in apposition the proper noun usually precedes the common noun, then the language is one in which the governing noun precedes its dependent genitive.
(23b-s) With much better than chance frequency, if the common noun usually precedes the proper noun, the dependent genitive precedes its governing noun.
(24) If the relative expression precedes the noun either as the only construction or as an alternative construction, either the language is postpositional or the adjective precedes the noun or both.
(27a) If a language is exclusively suffixing, it is postpositional.

(27b) If it is exclusively prefixing, it is prepositional.
(40) When the adjective follows the noun, the adjective expresses all the inflectional categories of the noun. In such cases the noun may lack overt expression of one or all of these categories.

Thus a total of 25 of Greenberg's implicational statements involve word order. These 25 statements embody some 34 logically distinct claims. The antecedent *P* property in approximately half these word order implications involves verb position, and many of the consequent *Q* properties are then antecedent or consequent properties in the remaining word order universals. As a result of this overlap, the position of the verb has come to be regarded as an indicator of whole language types, whose constitutive properties are precisely those mentioned in the relevant implicational universals.

Greenberg recognized three basic positions of the verb: VSO, SVO, and SOV. Since the publication of his paper, however, languages with the other logically possible verb positions have been discovered and studied. Greenberg himself (1966:110) drew attention to the existence of a VOS language, Coeur d'Alene. Further examples are Malagasay and Gilbertese (see Keenan, 1978b, and Pullum, 1981, for others), while Fijian, Samoan, and Tongan are best classified as "verb initial" on account of the high frequency of both VSO and VOS (see Hsieh 1976). A language with basic OVS word order, Hixkaryana, is described in some detail in Derbyshire (1977, 1979). Derbyshire and Pullum (1979) and Pullum (1981) document other OVS languages, and they even argue for the existence of a small handful of OSV languages.

It is widely assumed in the literature that Greenberg's universals are primarily "statistical" in nature. This assumption is not justified. I calculate that a total of 56 logically distinct claims are made by his universals; of these, 42 are formulated exceptionlessly and only 14 are statistical.[1] And of the 34 word order claims that have been listed here, 23 are nonstatistical and 11 statistical.

Greenberg's data base will figure prominently in this book, and will form the basis for our Expanded Sample. Both the 30-language sample and Appendix II are impressive for their genetic and areal diversity. The 30-language sample is useful for the breadth of properties investigated, and Appendix II is the biggest single language sample available hitherto giving data on the co-occurrence of the following orders: verb in relation to subject and object, adposition order (i.e., prepositions or postpositions), and adjective and genitive in relation to the noun. I have tabulated in Table 1 those word order properties from the 30-language sample which will be important in this book. Table 2 reproduces Appendix II.[2]

2.2 Discussion of Greenberg's Universals

2.2.1 THE NEED FOR ORGANIZING PRINCIPLES

The work of Greenberg has proved to be truly pioneering in that it has opened up a whole field of research. But like many other original and pioneering efforts, it has raised more questions than it has answered. For example, 16 of his 34 word-order claims relate a disparate variety of non-verb-position word orders to one another, and no clear organizing principle (or principles) is (are) apparent. Why should these word orders regularly correlate rather than others? This question has both an explanatory component (what is the ultimate explanation for these correlations?) and a descriptive component (why did Greenberg find this group of descriptive regularities particularly salient?) In the remaining 18 statements the regular occurrence of VSO or SOV does give some overall structure to the description, but the failure of SVO to yield any significant co-occurrence predictions (see Section 2.2.4) weakens the generality of a verb-based typology. Clearly, descriptive generalizations are to be preferred which range over, and link, as many word order patterns as possible.

2.2.2 DEFINING ALL AND ONLY THE ATTESTED CO-OCCURRENCES

Greenberg's implicational statements are attempts to define co-occurring and non-co-occurring word patterns. To claim that 'if a language has word order *P*, then it also has word order *Q*' is to rule out the co-occurrence of *P* with $-Q$: A language with *P* must have *Q*. But it is in the nature of an implicational claim that any given language does not actually have to have word order *P*, in which case $-P$ may co-occur with either *Q* or $-Q$. One co-occurrence type is therefore ruled out ($*P$ & $-Q$), and three are permitted (*P* & *Q*, $-P$ & *Q*, $-P$ & $-Q$).

The insight Greenberg is using in formulating his implicational universals is that of the 'if . . . then' connective of standard propositional logic (i.e., material implication). The truth table for 'if *P* then *Q*' is:

P	*Q*	$P \supset Q$
T	T	T
T	F	F
F	T	T
F	F	T

The value false is assigned only when the antecedent is true, and the

TABLE 1 : Greenberg's 30-Language Sample: Basic Data on the 30 Languages[(a)]

Language	A V order	B Pr/Po	C NRel/RelN	D NA/AN	E NG/GN	F ND/DN	G NNum/ NumN	H[(b)] AuxV/ VAux	I[(c)] MVSV/ SVMV	J AdjAdv/ AdvAdj	K AdjMS/ SMAdj	L Yes–No Qu. Part.	M Wh-word	N CNPN/ PNCN	O Prefixing/ Suffixing
Basque	SOVnr	Po	RelN	NA	GN	ND	NumN	VAux	MVSV	AdvAdj	SMAdj			PNCN	Suffixing
Berber	VSO	Pr	NRel	NA	NG	ND	NumN		MVSV		AdjMS	Initial	First		Both
Burmese	SOVr	Po	RelN	NA[(e)]	GN	DN	NumN		SVMV	AdvAdj	SMAdj	Final		PNCN	Suffixing
Burushaski	SOVr	Po	RelN	AN	GN	DN	NumN	VAux	SVMV	AdvAdj	SMAdj	Final		PNCN	Both
Chibcha	SOVnr	Po	RelN	NA	GN	DN	NNum	VAux	MVSV	AdvAdj	SMAdj				Suffixing
Finnish	SVO	Po	NRel[(d)]	AN	GN	DN	NumN	AuxV	MVSV	AdvAdj	Both		First	PNCN	Suffixing
Fulani	SVO	Pr	NRel	NA	NG	ND	NNum		MVSV	AdjAdv	AdjMS		First		Both
Greek	SVO	Pr	NRel	AN	NG	DN	NumN	AuxV	MVSV	AdvAdj	AdjMS		First	CNPN	Both
Guarani	SVO	Po	NRel	NA	GN	DN	Both	VAux	MVSV	AdjAdv	SMAdj		First	CNPN	Both
Hebrew	VSO	Pr	NRel	NA	NG	ND	NumN		MVSV	AdjAdv	AdjMS	Initial	First		Both
Hindi	SOVr	Po	NRel	AN	GN	DN	NumN	VAux	SVMV	AdvAdj	SMAdj				Suffixing
Italian	SVO	Pr	NRel	NA[(e)]	NG	DN	NumN	AuxV	MVSV	AdvAdj	AdjMS		First	CNPN	Both
Japanese	SOVr	Po	RelN	AN	GN	DN	NumN[(f)]		SVMV	AdvAdj	SMAdj	Final		PNCN	Suffixing
Kannada	SOVr	Po	RelN	AN	GN	DN	NumN	VAux	SVMV	AdvAdj	SMAdj	Final			Suffixing
Loritja	SOVnr	Po		NA	GN	ND	NNum		MVSV	AdvAdj					Suffixing
Malay	SVO	Pr	NRel	NA	NG	ND	NumN[(f)]		MVSV	AdjAdv	AdjMS		First	CNPN	Both
Maori	VSO	Pr	NRel	NA	NG	DN	NumN		MVSV	Both	AdjMS	Initial	First		Both
Masai	VSO	Pr	NRel	NA	NG	DN	NNum	AuxV	MVSV			Initial	First		Both
Maya	SVO	Pr	NRel	AN	NG	DN	NumN	AuxV	MVSV	AdvAdj			First		Both
Norwegian	SVO	Pr	NRel	AN	GN	DN	NumN	AuxV	MVSV	AdvAdj	AdjMS		First	PNCN	Both
Nubian	SOVnr	Po	Both	NA	GN	DN	NNum	VAux	MVSV		SMAdj	Final		PNCN	Suffixing
Quechua	SOVnr	Po	NRel	AN	GN	DN	NumN	VAux	MVSV	AdvAdj					Suffixing
Serbian	SVO	Pr	NRel	AN	NG	DN	NumN	AuxV	MVSV	AdvAdj	AdjMS		First	CNPN	Both
Songhai	SVO	Po	NRel	NA	GN	ND	NNum		MVSV		AdjMS				Suffixing

Swahili	SVO	Pr	NRel	NA	NG	ND	NNum	AuxV	MVSV	AdjAdv	AdjMS			CNPN	Both
Thai	SVO	Pr	NRel	NA	NG	ND	NumN[f]		MVSV	AdjAdv	AdjMS	Final		CNPN	Prefixing
Turkish	SOVr	Po	RelN	AN	GN	DN	NumN	VAux	SVMV	AdvAdj	SMAdj			PNCN	Suffixing
Welsh	VSO	Pr	NRel	NA[e]	NG	ND	NumN	AuxV	MVSV	Both	AdjMS	Initial	First	CNPN	Both
Yoruba	SVO	Pr	NRel	NA	NG	ND	NNum		MVSV	AdjAdv		Final	First		Both
Zapotec	VSO	Pr	NRel	NA	NG	ND	NumN	AuxV	MVSV	AdjAdv	AdjMS		First	CNPN	Both

[a] Where there is no entry for some language in a particular column, this is either because Greenberg had no available data (e.g., Loritja relative clauses, numerous common noun – proper noun orders) or because the word order property of that particular column is not applicable to that language [e.g., Japanese has no inflected auxiliaries (see Note *b*), many languages do not have question particles at all (see Column L)].

[b] Auxiliary here refers to inflected auxiliary, which is defined by Greenberg (1966) as "one in which a closed class of verbs (the auxiliaries) inflected for both person and number is in construction with an open class of verbs not inflected for both person and number. For example, in English 'is going' is such a construction. This definition . . . excludes the possibility of such a construction in languages in which the verb has no category of person and number (e.g., Japanese) [p. 84]."

[c] Subordinate verb and main verb are limited here to those occurring in expressions of volition and purpose [cf. Greenberg's universal (15)].

[d] Greenberg (1966:90; Note 20) actually lists Finnish as having both constructions. It does, of course, but the prenominal strategy is considerably more restricted than the postnominal one (cf. Karlsson 1972, Keenan & Comrie 1977), so I have listed Finnish as basic NRel.

[e] In Burmese the participle of adjective-verb precedes, and is probably as common as adjective following; and in Welsh and Italian a small number of adjectives usually precede (see Greenberg 1966:108).

[f] But numeral + classifier follows the noun in Japanese and Thai, and either precedes or follows in Malay (see Greenberg 1966:108).

TABLE 2 : Greenberg's Appendix II

Distribution of Basic Order Types	Number of languages
1. VSO/Pr/NG/NA. Celtic languages; Hebrew, Aramaic, Arabic, Ancient Egyptian, Berber; Nandi, Masai, Lotuko, Turkana, Didinga; Polynesian languages and probably other Austronesian languages; Chinook, Tsimshian; Zapotec, Chinantec, Mixtec, and probably other Ote-Mangue languages.	19
2. VSO/Pr/NG/AN. Tagabili and probably other Philippine Austronesian languages; Kwakiutl, Quileute, Xinca.	5
3. VSO/Pr/GN/AN. Milpa Alta Nahuatl.	1
4. VSO/Pr/GN/NA. No examples.	0
5. VSO/Po/NG/NA. No examples.	0
6. VSO/Po/NG/AN. No examples.	0
7. VSO/Po/GN/AN. Papago.	1
8. VSO/Po/GN/NA. No examples.	0
9. SVO/Pr/NG/NA. Romance languages, Albanian, Modern Greek; West Atlantic languages, Yoruba, Edo group, most languages of Benue–Congo group including all Bantu languages; Shilluk, Acholi, Bari, most languages of Chad group of Hamito-Semitic but not Hausa; Neo-Syriac, Khasi, Nicobarese, Khmer, Vietnamese, all Thai languages except Khamti; many Austronesian languages including Malay; Subtiaba.	21
10. SVO/Pr/NG/AN. German, Dutch, Icelandic, Slavonic, Efik, Kredj, Maya, Papiamento.	8
11. SVO/Pr/GN/AN. Norwegian, Swedish, Danish.	3
12. SVO/Pr/GN/NA. Arapesh (New Guinea).	1
13. SVO/Po/NG/NA. No examples.	0
14. SVO/Po/NG/AN. Rutulian and other Daghestan languages in the Caucasus.	2
15. SVO/Po/GN/AN. Finnish, Estonian, Ijo, Chinese, Algonquian (probably), Zoque.	6
16. SVO/Po/GN/NA. Most Mandingo and Voltaic languages, Kru, Twi, Gã, Guang, Ewe, Nupe, Songhai, Tonkawa, Guarani.	11
17. SOV/Pr/NG/NA. Persian, Iraqw (Cushitic), Khamti (Thai), Akkadian.	4
18. SOV/Pr/NG/AN. No examples.	0
19. SOV/Pr/GN/AN. Amharic.	1
20. SOV/Pr/GN/NA. No examples.	0
21. SOV/Po/NG/NA. Sumerian, Elamite, Galla, Kanuri, Teda, Kamilaroi and other southeastern Australian languages.	7
22. SOV/Po/NG/AN. No examples.	0
23. SOV/Po/GN/AN. Hindi, Bengali and other Aryan languages of India; Modern Armenian, Finno-Ugric except Finnish group; Altaic, Yukaghir, Paleo-Siberian, Korean, Ainu, Japanese, Gafat, Harari, Sidamo, Chamir, Bedauye, Nama Hottentot; Khinalug, Abkhaz and other Caucasian languages; Burushaski, Dravidian; Newari and other Sino-Tibetan languages; Marind-Anim, Navaho, Maidu, Quechua.	28
24. SOV/Po/GN/NA. Basque, Hurrian, Urartian, Nubian, Kunama, Fur, Sandawe, Burmese, Lushei, Classical Tibetan, Makasai, Bunak (Timor), Kate (New Guinea), most Australian languages, Haida, Tlingit, Zuni, Chitimacha, Tunica, Lenca, Matagalpa, Cuna, Chibcha, Warrau.	24

Note: Total number of languages = 142; No. with $V_1 = 26$, $V_2 = 52$, $V_3 = 64$; No. with Pr = 63, Po = 79; No. with N_1 (NG/NA) = 51, N_2 (NG/AN v GN/NA) = 51, N_3 (GN/AN) = 40. In calculating the language quantities for each co-occurrence cell I have counted the language families and groups as individual languages only, since Greenberg gives no information on how many members of each group he has actually checked. To assign to these groups any number of languages larger than 1 would give rise to problems in justifying why 2, rather than 3, rather than 4, etc., were assigned.

consequent false. And true is assigned in three cases: when *P* and *Q* are both true; when *P* is false and *Q* is true; and when both are false.

Correspondingly, an implicational universal of word order permits three co-occurrences of word order properties, and rules out one. Consider, for example, Greenberg's (3):

(3) Languages with dominant VSO order are always prepositional; i.e., VSO $\supset$ Pr.

(*P* & *Q*)	VSO & Pr	= attested
(−*P* & *Q*)	−VSO & Pr (e.g., SVO & Pr or SOV & Pr)	= attested
(−*P* & −*Q*)	−VSO & −Pr (e.g., SVO & Po or SOV & Po)	= attested
(**P* & −*Q*)	*VSO & −Pr (i.e., VSO & Po)	= disallowed

This universal can be falsified in one case only: with the discovery of VSO & Po languages.

How successful are Greenberg's implications in defining all and only the word order co-occurrences of his data? Only partly successful, it seems. His universals have more exceptions than necessary, and some typological patterns have been missed which emerge when one attempts to define the balance between attested and nonattested co-occurrences more precisely.

Consider the Appendix II data of Table 2. The following implicational statements are designed to cover these data:

(2a-s) In languages with prepositions, the genitive almost always follows the governing noun.
(2b-s) In languages with postpositions, the genitive almost always precedes the governing noun.
(3) Languages with dominant VSO order are always prepositional.
(4-s) With overwhelmingly greater than chance frequency, languages with normal SOV order are postpositional.
(5) If a language has dominant SOV order and the genitive follows the governing noun, then the adjective likewise follows the noun.
(17-s) With overwhelmingly more than chance frequency, languages with dominant order VSO have the adjective after the noun.

All but (3) and (5) are statistical and admit of a considerable number of exceptions. I calculate that 24 of the 142 entries in Appendix II (=17%) are exceptions to at least one of these universals.[3] And, in addition, in a note on page 107, Greenberg mentions an exception to Universal (3), Papago – Type 7, whose existence was pointed out to him after completion of the paper and which I have inserted into Appendix II as reproduced here in Table 2.

The one universal in this group which is exceptionless is (5). Its logical form is instructive. It is multitermed, being defined on more than two properties, $P \& Q \supset R$, whereas the majority of Greenberg's universals are two termed, $P \supset Q$. In accordance with (5), SOV languages have the following co-occurrence:

SOV languages:	NG & NA:	Types 17 and 21
	GN & NA:	Type 24
	GN & AN:	Types 19 and 23
	*NG & AN:	No examples (potentially Types 18 and 22)

As SOV can co-occur with NG or GN, and with NA or AN, there must evidently be something about *NG & AN coexisting with SOV which explains its total absence. And in order to state this fact and define all and only the attested word order co-occurrences, it is necessary to employ an implicational statement that mentions three properties rather than two.

The exceptions to the other universals may, of course, be an unavoidable fact of life, unless it can be shown that stronger claims with fewer or no counterexamples can be made. In this book I attempt to do this for many of Greenberg's word order properties. Consider just one example at this point:

(17-s) With overwhelmingly more than chance frequency, languages with dominant order VSO have the adjective after the noun.

In Appendix II, 5 languages of Type 2, 1 language of Type 3, and 1 language of Type 7 are counterexamples to this statement, and have *VSO & AN (7 total), while 19 languages have the predicted VSO & NA. But notice that there is an interesting complementarity between SOV and VSO languages with regard to their genitive–noun and adjective–noun co-occurrences: VSO again co-occurs with three out of four noun–modifier combinations in Appendix II (Table 2):

VSO languages:	NG & NA:	Type 1
	NG & AN:	Type 2
	GN & AN:	Types 3 and 7
	*GN & NA:	No examples (potentially Types 4 and 8)

Both verb positions co-occur with the noun-initial combination, NG & NA, and with the noun-final combination, GN & AN. But there is a mirror-image pattern in the noun-medial co-occurrences: SOV allows GN & NA and disallows *NG & AN; VSO allows NG & AN and disallows *GN & NA. An appropriate implicational statement, matching (5) for SOV, would be: If a language has dominant VSO order and the genitive precedes the governing noun, then the adjective likewise precedes the noun.

Hence, by considering both adjective and genitive together, Universal (17-s) can be strengthened from a statistical to an exceptionless statement, defining all and only the attested co-occurrences in Greenberg's data. And in the process a descriptive pattern emerges between SOV and VSO languages, which we shall be analyzing further in Sections 2.4.4 and 3.2. Overall, 8 out of 24 co-occurrence types in Appendix II have no exemplifying languages. Given the wide genetic and areal coverage of this sample (see Note 2), the total absence of such languages would appear to be of some significance. And the purpose of a set of implicational universals, operating collectively, is to define all and only the attested word order co-occurrences in the most revealing, and simplest, manner.

2.2.3 LANGUAGE FREQUENCIES

Another no less significant point of general interest emerges from Appendix II. There is a varied distribution of languages among the 16 basic order types that are attested: four co-occurrence cells have between 19 and 28 entries (Types 1, 9, 23, 24); four have between 6 and 11 entries (Types 10, 15, 16, 21); four have between 2 and 5 entries (Types 2, 11, 14, 17); and four have a single entry (Types 3, 7, 12, 19). In Chapter 4, I shall show that these and other frequency differences in Greenberg's data are principled.

Greenberg made no predictions for such declining language frequencies, though he did make some limited claims about language numbers, in the form of his statistical universals. If a language type is an exception to some statistical universal, it is of necessity a limited distribution type. Statistical implications of the form 'if *P* then *Q* with more than chance frequency' claim, in effect, that the co-occurrence *P* & *Q* is much more frequent than *P* & −*Q*. But as we will argue in Section 4.3.3, statistical implications are not the most appropriate descriptive tool for defining language distributions. The only distributional facts they can capture are those involving high versus low frequencies of co-occurrence. And the data of Appendix II reveal many principled distinctions between large, medium-sized, small, and single-entry types, distinctions that implicational statements are unable to capture. We shall propose instead that implicational universals are appropriate for defining all and only the attested co-occurrences in some language sample, and that they must then be supplemented by an independent distributional universal (the principle of Cross-Category Harmony) defining relative language frequencies.

2.2.4 THE STATUS OF SVO LANGUAGES

There is a striking asymmetry in Greenberg's VSO/SVO/SOV typology. All 15 implicational universals in which the antecedent or consequent property refers to a verb position mention either VSO or SOV, but not SVO. [Universal (6) does refer to SVO—but only as an alternative construction in languages which are VSO.] It transpires that SVO does not correlate with other word order properties in Greenberg's data in a

TABLE 3 : Co-occurrences with Verb Position in the 30-Language Sample

A & B

	VSO	SVO	SOV
Pr	6	10	0
Po	0	3	11

C

	VSO	SVO	SOV
NRel	6	13	2
RelN	0	0	7
Both	0	0	1

D

	VSO	SVO	SOV
NA	6	8	5
AN	0	5	6

E

	VSO	SVO	SOV
NG	6	9	0
GN	0	4	11

F

	VSO	SVO	SOV
ND	4	6	2
DN	2	7	9

G

	VSO	SVO	SOV
NNum	1	4	3
NumN	5	8	8
Both	0	1	0

H

	VSO	SVO	SOV
AuxV	3	7	0
VAux	0	1	8

I

	VSO	SVO	SOV
MVSV	6	13	5
SVMV	0	0	6

J

	VSO	SVO	SOV
AdjAdv	2	6	0
AdvAdj	0	6	10
Both	2	0	0

K

	VSO	SVO	SOV
AdjMS	5	9	0
SMAdj	0	1	9
Both	0	1	0

L

	VSO	SVO	SOV
Initial Question Particle	5	0	0
Final Question Particle	0	2	5

M

	VSO	SVO	SOV
Wh-word first	6	10	0
No such rule	0	3	11

N

	VSO	SVO	SOV
CNPN	2	7	0
PNCN	0	2	6

O

	VSO	SVO	SOV
Prefixing	0	1	0
Suffixing	0	2	10
Both	6	10	1

unique and principled way. It combines properties of VSO and SOV languages, and has none of its own. This can be seen in Table 3, in which I have quantified the number of VSO, SVO, and SOV languages in the 30-language sample having the respective word orders of Table 1. The SVO quantities are generally closer to VSO than to SOV, but SVO is very much a mixed type. Knowing that some unstudied language had SVO word order, little else could be predicted about it with certainty.

Why, then, did Greenberg propose a basic three-way typology in terms of verb position, when one member of the trio, SVO, could guarantee no other word order co-occurrences?[4] The reason must be that VSO and SOV did guarantee regular unique co-occurrences of other word orders. And since VSO and SOV *were* indicators of whole language types, the other very common verb position, SVO, became elevated to basic type status—by default. But to propose a basic type with no type characteristics is unwarranted. If this is a necessary consequence of using verb position to classify the world's languages, it raises the question of whether a verb-based typology is in general desirable. Even the correlations with VSO and SOV are far from perfect, as Table 3 also shows. And many of the correlations that do hold in Table 3 no longer hold in the larger Appendix II data of Table 2 (see, e.g., SOV in relation to adposition order; VSO and SOV in relation to genitive–noun order; VSO in relation to adjective–noun order), or in the Expanded Sample of Chapter 8 (e.g., SVO in relation to NRel).

The discovery of VOS, verb-initial, OVS (and even OSV) languages further reduces the value of a verb-based typology. As far as I can tell, such languages are different types only by virtue of their different verb positions, and these do not appear to correlate with unique sets of word orders elsewhere in the grammar. Thus the major word order properties listed by Keenan (1978b) as typical of VOS languages (prepositions, SVO as alternant, NGen, NRel, NumN, and wh-word first) are typical of VSO and verb-initial languages as well. In Section 3.2.2 we shall reduce all of these languages under a more general "verb-first" type, and will capture thereby certain generalizations that go beyond VSO itself.

However, SVO remains a mixed type, and because it is so, verb position as a whole is not as general or as useful a typological indicator as it appeared to be in Greenberg's initial work. Other word orders will give more general correlations.

2.3 Vennemann's Theory

Theo Vennemann's work on word order is an explicit attempt to reformulate and explain Greenberg's universals, and to integrate them within a historical theory of word order change. The essential ideas upon which he builds were presented in Vennemann (1972), and further elaborated in Vennemann (1974a, 1974b, 1975). More recently (Vennemann 1976, 1977, 1981; Vennemann & Harlow 1977) he has modified his position in certain respects, so it is useful to distinguish the earlier from the more recent work. Sections 2.3 and 2.4 will summarize and discuss the basic theory of Vennemann (1972, 1974a, 1974b, 1975), and Sections 2.5 and 2.6 will do the same for the later modifications.

2.3.1 THE NUMBER OF BASIC VERB POSITIONS AND LANGUAGE TYPES

Vennemann's first innovation is to reduce Greenberg's three-way typology of VSO/SVO/SOV to two basic verb positions: VO or OV. Thus

VSO and SVO are collapsed into one type on the basis of their common V before O order. Vennemann then relates *all* of Greenberg's word order properties to these two verb positions, both those that were already correlated with basic verb position (the group of 15 universals) and those that were not (the group of 10 universals). The result is just two major language types—VO (or V*X*) languages and OV (or *X*V) languages—with verb position determining more word order co-occurrences than in Greenberg's universals. Vennemann acknowledges explicitly that this reformulation derives from Lehmann (1971, 1972a, 1972b, 1973):

> There is now a much better way of presenting [Greenberg's universals] owing to the work of Lehmann. . . . Where Greenberg correlates in the form of universals everything he knows to be correlated statistically, with, however, a basic classification of languages as SOV, SVO, and VSO, Lehmann systematically reformulates the correlations in such a way that everything is correlated to the basic verb position [1974b:344–345].
>
> [Lehmann distinguishes] between verb-final languages ('OV languages') and all others, ('VO languages')—a distinction for which I now prefer the labels 'XV' and 'VX', where 'X' stands essentially for the verb complement [1974a:8].

2.3.2 THE NATURAL SERIALIZATION PRINCIPLE

Vennemann's main concern is to provide an organizing principle for Greenberg's universals with greater explanatory power than Greenberg's descriptive statements. To this end he divides all of Greenberg's "meaningful elements" (direct object and verb, adjective and noun, etc.) into "operator" and "operand" categories on syntactic and semantic grounds, and he proposes that languages serialize all these elements in a consistent order: OV (/*X*V) languages have co-occurrences with the order operator before operand, whereas VO (/V*X*) languages have just the reverse, operand before operator. The two language types therefore exhibit mirror-image contrasts for all operators and operands.

Vennemann (1972, 1974a) illustrates his operator–operand distinction with the following table:

	Operator	*Operand*
I.	(*a*) Object	Verb
	(*b*) Adverbial	Verb
	(*c*) Main verb	Auxiliary
	(*d*) Main verb	Modal
	(*e*) Main verb	Intensional verb
II.	(*a*) Adjective	Noun
	(*b*) Relative clause	Noun
	(*c*) Number marker	Noun
	(*d*) Genitive	Noun

(*e*) Numeral	Noun
(*f*) Determiner	Noun
III. (*a*) Adjective stem	Comparison marker
(*b*) Standard	Comparative adjective
(*c*) Adverbial	Adjective
IV. (*a*) Noun phrase	Relation marker (adposition; i.e., postposition or preposition)
V. (*a*) Indirect object	Direct object
(*b*) Temporal adverbial	Directional adverbial

The criteria for allocating some category to operator or operand status are that "sematically the application of an operator results in a specification of the operand predicate, and, syntactically, that the application of an operator to an operand results in a constitutent of the same general category as that of the operand [1972:5]." In more detail:

> . . . syntactic structures are not co-ordinate constituent structures but rather function–argument structures, as are logical structures. For example, an adjective–noun construction such as *red house* is not seen as a constituent structure $[[red_A][house_N]_N]$ but as a function–argument construction $\{\{red_A\}(\{house_N\})_N\}$ where the adjective is function and the noun is argument: application of *red* to *house* maps the meaning of *house* on the meaning of *red house,* i.e. extensionally speaking, it maps the set of all houses on the set of all red houses. Instead of 'function' and 'argument' the terms . . . adopted are 'operator' and 'operand'. The term 'operator–operand-relationship' covers function–argument relationships in the narrow sense, e.g., 'square-root of', 'father of', but also predicate–term relationships and 'modal operator–proposition' relationships [1974b:346].
>
> The defining criterion (for determining which constituent is operator and which is operand), in addition to the semantic one of the operator specifying the operand, was found in category constancy: In a constituent structure [AB], A is operator and B is operand if the entire construction [AB] is in the same syntactic category as B (except for subcategorization). Thus, an object noun phrase is an operator on a (transitive) verb because the result of its application is an (intransitive) verb and not a noun phrase; a noun phrase is an operator on a preposition, which is a transitive adverb, because the result of its application is an intransitive adverbial rather than a noun phrase; an infinitive is an operator on a finite transitive modal verb because the result of the operation is a finite intransitive modal verb rather than an infinitive; etc. [1974b:347].

Having classified these word order categories as either operators or operands, Vennemann formulates his "Natural Serialization Principle" (NSP): Languages serialize all their operator–operand pairs either operator before operand, or operand before operator, as follows:

$$\{\text{Operator } \{\text{Operand}\}\} \rightarrow \begin{cases} [\text{Operator } [\text{Operand}]] \text{ in OV languages} \\ [[\text{Operand}] \text{ Operator}] \text{ in VO languages} \end{cases}$$

Vennemann thus defines his two language types abstractly. He notes that not all languages are consistent with his schema, and hypothesizes that this is for historical reasons. The inconsistent languages are those which are moving from one type to the other (cf. Vennemann 1974b, 1975). He offers a phonological and morphological explanation for why a language should shift V relative to 0, and he then proposes the Natural Serialization Principle as the source of an analogical pull which brings about the subsequent acquisition of the other operator–operand orderings which are compatible with VO or OV respectively. The inconsistent languages are, therefore, moving toward a target type which is as yet only partially attained (see Section 5.4).

2.3.3 THE THEORETICAL STATUS OF NSP

In the light of Vennemann's more recent modifications, it is important to make explicit the theoretical status of the NSP as it is presented in Vennemann (1972, 1974a, 1974b, 1975).

First, although Vennemann reformulates Greenberg's universals, he makes it clear that he considers his universals to be of the same general type as those employed by Greenberg, namely statistical implicational universals. The only difference involves the number of statements in which verb position has become the antecedent of the implication (which then has consequences for the number of language types that the universals define). Thus, Vennemann explicitly refers to the statistical correlations of his NSP as "Greenberg universals in the Lehmann mode of presentation [1974b:345]," and as "derived Greenberg universals [1974a, p. 10]." Vennemann's, like Greenberg's universals, are explicitly implicational. And as Vennemann considers Greenberg's universals to be predominantly statistical as well, this increases the similarity between the two sets of statements, according to Vennemann: "The importance of [Greenberg's] work . . . [is that] it is statistical . . . and . . . typological-comparative. . . . [Greenberg] relates various positional properties of languages to each other in implicational statements of the character 'If a language has the property *a*, then with more than chance frequency it also has the property *b*' [1974a:7–8]."

Second, Vennemann goes to some length to stress that his NSP is a "theory of basic word order": "With this definition [of the distinction between operators and operands] and the Greenberg universals, there finally was a theory of basic word order, and it can be summarised in . . . one formula. . . . the principle of Natural Serialization . . . [1974b:347]." And as one would expect from such a theory, the universals of word order are claimed to be "explained" by the principle of Natural Serialization (1974a:10).

2.4 Discussion of Vennemann's Theory

2.4.1 STATISTICAL OR NONSTATISTICAL UNIVERSALS?

Vennemann's interpretation of Greenberg's universals as predominantly statistical is not accurate. As mentioned earlier, of the 56 logically distinct universal claims made by Greenberg, 42 are actually nonstatistical, with just 14 statistical. Even the universals of word order, which account for a higher proportion of the statistical statements than the morphological universals, are still predominantly nonstatistical (23 versus 11).

By contrast, all of Vennemann's co-occurrence universals are now statistical, and languages can exhibit varying degrees of consistency with the NSP. The shortcomings of these reformulated universals will be enumerated in the course of this section.

2.4.2 UNILATERAL OR BILATERAL IMPLICATIONS?

Greenberg's 'if *P* then *Q*' universals are unilateral, nonreversible implicational statements. As we have seen, they allow for languages with *P* & *Q*, −*P* & *Q* and −*P* & −*Q* co-occurrences, and rule out **P* & −*Q*. By contrast, a bilateral, reversible implication (corresponding to '*P* if and only if *Q*'), would claim that property *P* guarantees the co-occurrence of *Q*, and property *Q* the co-occurrence of *P*, the effect of which is to disallow the −*P* & *Q* co-occurrence permitted by the unilateral statement:

P	Q	$(P$	$\supset$	$Q)$	&	$(Q$	$\supset$	$P)$
T	T	T	T	T	T	T	T	T
T	F	T	F	F	F	F	T	T
F	T	F	T	T	F	T	F	F
F	F	F	T	F	T	F	T	F

A bilateral implication permits two co-occurrences (*P* & *Q*, −*P* & −*Q*), and is falsified by two (**P* & −*Q*, *−*P* & *Q*).

In Vennemann's operator–operand schema (NSP), the logical status of all of Greenberg's unilateral implications has in effect been changed into bilateral, reversible implications permitting just two co-occurrences, *P* & *Q* and −*P* & −*Q*. Thus *P* & *Q* languages serialize their operator–operand structures in one order, while −*P* & −*Q* languages serialize them in the reverse order. There is no place in this system for the third co-occurrence type permitted by the unilateral implication, −*P* & *Q*.[5]

As a result, any one of the operator before operand word orders should guarantee the co-occurrence of all the others; and any one of the operand before operator orders should do likewise. The position of the verb now loses the special significance that it had for Greenberg as a consequence of its implicational antecedent status in so many unilateral implications. Although SOV does still guarantee the co-occurrence of Po by NSP, Po also guarantees the co-occurrence of SOV; AN guarantees the co-occurrence of GN and Po; GN the co-occurrence of AN, SOV, and so on.

Vennemann's universals are undoubtedly less atomistic and potentially more explanatory than Greenberg's. However, this improvement is at the expense of descriptive power. There are many more exceptions to his predictions, in large part because he has converted unilateral into bilateral implications and is unable to distiguish $-P$ & Q from $*P$ & $-Q$ co-occurrences. The $-P$ & Q co-occurrences are amply attested for Greenberg's universals, whereas $*P$ & $-Q$ co-occurrences are not.

Vennemann does not take into account this change in logical status relative to Greenberg's universals, for he continues to argue as if verb position alone had implicational antecedent status. His language types are labeled V*X* and *X*V; he holds that children acquire verb–object sequences first, and this sets the trend for the other operator–operand structures with are acquired subsequently; and, in his historical theory, a change in verb–object order "triggers" the subsequent acquisition of other implicationally dependent operator–operand structures (see Section 5.4). But, given his synchronic theory (NSP), the diachronic acquisition of, or change in, any one of his operator–operand structures should be able to "trigger" harmonic changes in the others. Each verb position and non-verb-position word order is now both an antecedent and a consequent property in relation to every other word order, within a set of bilateral implications. And Antinucci *et al.* (1979) exploit precisely this property of the theory when they argue that a change in relative clause order, rather than in verb position, triggers subsequent operator–operand reorderings.

By contrast, imagine that we integrated Greenberg's original unilateral implications into Vennemann's scenarios for acquisition and change. Verb position would now be crucial. Given, for example, Greenberg's Universal (3) VSO ⊃ Pr, the emergence of VSO could guarantee the diachronic acquisition of Pr, but Pr could guarantee nothing (as it may co-occur with VSO or −VSO; i.e., with VSO, SVO, or SOV). Hence, Vennemann appears to be assuming that his synchronic universals still have the same logical status that they do in Greenberg's approach, and one consequence of this is that he underrepresents their full consequences for diachrony (see Section 5.4).[6]

2.4.3 OPERATOR–OPERAND ≠ FUNCTION–ARGUMENT

Vennemann explicitly equates his operator–operand relation with the logical function–argument relation.[7] Yet it can readily be shown that the word order generalization for which he is striving and for which he sets up the operator–operand distinction is NOT that of the function–argument relation, but corresponds instead to the more traditional distinction between a modifier and its head.

Keenan (1979) points out that Vennemann's operator–operand constructions are unusual function–argument structures:

> Vennemann (1972) is perhaps the first . . . attempt to systematically correlate word order types with function–argument structure. His approach however is not based on an independently justified logic. He takes for example DNPs [Determined Noun Phrases] as functions with VPs and prepositions as arguments, and their outputs are supposed to somehow have the same category as the argument. But no natural logic treats, for example, *in* and *in the garden* as having the same type of denotation [p. 30].

This criticism is taken into account in Vennemann's more recent work (Section 2.5.1), in which operator–operand and function–argument no longer correspond.

Strong motivation for keeping these two relations distinct comes from Keenan's work in semantics. Keenan (1974, 1979; Keenan & Faltz 1978) gives both logical and linguistic generalizations supporting the assignment of categories to function or argument status, and provides what is, to my mind, the most satisfactory linguistically based discussion of the function–argument relation to date. When he discusses the relation between his function–argument structures and their serialization across languages, however, he is forced to propose a "Dissimilation Principle" (DP): "Functional expressions taking DNPs [Determined Noun Phrases] as arguments and functional expressions taking CNPs [Common Noun Phrases] as arguments tend to serialise on the opposite side of their argument categories [p. 26]." The need for DP emerges from the following statistical correlations:

OV Languages

Argument + function

- Subject (DNP) + VP (e.g., *John sings; John Mary kissed*)
- Object (DNP) + TVP (i.e., transitive verb phrase: X *Mary kissed*)
- DNP + Postposition (e.g., *the garden in*)
- DNP + PossPh (i.e., possessive phrase: *John's father*)

Function + argument
Adjective + CNP (e.g., *tall man*)
Relative Clause + CNP (e.g., *the apple eating man*)
Article + CNP (e.g., *the man; this man*)
Quantifier + CNP (e.g., *every man*)
Numeral + CNP (e.g., *two men*)

VO Languages

Function + argument
VP + Subject (DNP) (*sings John*)
TVP + Object (DNP) (X *kissed Mary*)
Preposition + DNP (*in the garden*)
PossPh + DNP (*the father of John*)
Argument + function
CNP + Adjective (*man tall*)
CNP + Relative Clause (*man who was eating the apple*)
CNP + Article (*man the; man this*)
CNP + Quantifier (*man every*)
CNP + Numeral (*men two*)

Now, although these correlations enable Keenan to capture a serialization principle to the effect that "different functional expressions taking the same class of argument expressions tend to serialize on the same side of their argument expressions [1979:26]," his dissimilation principle actually destroys the generality of the correlation between function–argument structure and word order, and one therefore wonders whether this is the appropriate level of abstract linguistic structure upon which to define a word order serialization principle. I can think of no way of explaining in this approach why CNP- and DNP-arguments should regularly exhibit mirror-image orderings within one and the same language. And, all things being equal, we will prefer a serialization principle that can explain all word orders in terms of one abstract distinction (e.g., between operator and operand) to one whose basic abstract distinction (e.g., between function and argument) forces us to say that some word orders are serialized in one direction, and some in another.

Vennemann's operator–operand schema offers a single generalization. His operators correspond only to those Keenan function categories which take CNPs as arguments. Where Keenan's functions take DNPs as arguments, these functions are the operands for Vennemann, rather than the operators. This can be seen clearly in the following illustrative comparison:

	Vennemann (1972, 1974a)	*Keenan (1979)*
Adjective + CNP	operator + operand	function + argument
Object (DNP) + TVP	operator + operand	argument + function
DNP + Adposition	operator + operand	argument + function

In fact, Keenan's dissimilation principle will need to be modified in order to accomodate additional function–argument serialization facts, such as adverbs in relation to adjectives within the adjective phrase (i.e., phrases such as *extremely interesting* in English). For Vennemann these adverbs are operators on adjectives as operands. Keenan's analysis would agree here by assigning function and argument status, respectively. But since these argument categories are neither CNPs nor DNPs, no ordering predictions are made by the DP. It transpires that the adverb–adjective serialization typically goes with the adjective–CNP serialization (cf. Greenberg 1966:87–88, and Sections 3.3.19 and 3.3.20), that is, function + argument (adverb + adjective) in OV languages; argument + function (adjective + adverb) in VO languages. We can therefore add to our illustrative operator–operand/function–argument comparison as follows:

	Operator–Operand Status	*Function–Argument Status*
Adjective + CNP	operator + operand	function + argument
Adverb + Adjective	operator + operand	function + argument
Object (DNP) + TVP	operator + operand	argument + function
DNP + Adposition	operator + operand	argument + function

Hence, if the operator–operand principle is the significant regularity in the area of cross-categorial word order, the function–argument relation cannot be (and vice versa). Instead, Vennemann's operator and operand categories correspond more to the "modifiers" and "heads of phrase" of traditional as well as more recent linguistic theory.

In the X-bar theory of generative grammar, for example (see Section 4.6, and see further Chomsky 1970, Jackendoff 1977, Lightfoot 1979), and in Emonds' (1976:12–20) base rules, N is the head of the noun phrase, V the head of the verb phrase (or sentence, Jackendoff 1977), A is the head of the adjective phrase, and prepositions are heads of prepositional phrases. These heads of phrases correspond almost exactly to Vennemann's operands, while Vennemann's operators are matched by specifiers and complements within X-bar rules of the form:

a. $\overline{\overline{X}} \rightarrow (\text{Spec } \overline{X})\ \overline{X}$
b. $\overline{X} \rightarrow X \text{ Comp}$

where *X* stands for the head categories N, V, A, and Prep; Comp for the complements of the head categories which enter into the strict subcategorization of the latter (see Chomsky 1965:Chapter 2) such as S, NP, PP, and VP; and (Spec $\overline{\text{X}}$) for the various specifiers of these head categories and their complements—determiners for noun phrases, qualifying and quantifying expressions for adjective phrases, etc. Category constancy is clearly preserved between *X*, the head, and the higher dominating *X*-bar nodes in these rules.[8]

The significant generalization in the area of word order for which Vennemann is striving therefore appears to be that languages serialize their modifier and head categories in a consistent order. With more than chance frequency, OV languages place the modifier before the head across all the phrasal categories (NP, S, VP, AP, PP), giving Det – N and Adj – N, SOV, Adv – Adj, NP – Po, etc., whereas VO languages place the head before the modifier, producing N – Det and N – Adj, VO, Adj – Adv, Pr – NP. But this serialization principle does not overlap with one based on logical function – argument structures, and if these latter are to be employed directly in stating word order universals, some form of dissimilation principle will be needed, as in Keenan's approach.

2.4.4 DEFINING ALL AND ONLY THE ATTESTED CO-OCCURRENCES

Vennemann's universals share the same descriptive weaknesses as the statistical implications in Greenberg's work: They have more exceptions than necessary, and they miss typological regularities which emerge when one tries to define the balance between attested and nonattested word order co-occurrences more precisely.

Taken literally, NSP permits just two co-occurrences of the four operator – operand pairs listed in Appendix II (Table 2):

Operator before operand:	OV & AN & GN & NP + Po
Operand before operator:	VO & NA & NG & Pr + NP

Only 3 of the 24 logically possible co-occurrence types satisfy these two orderings:

Type 1:	VSO & NA & NG & Pr + NP	19 languages
Type 9:	SVO & NA & NG & Pr + NP	21 languages
Type 23:	SOV & AN & GN & NP + Po	28 languages

These three types cover 68 of the 142 languages in the sample (48%). Yet Appendix II contains not 3 but 16 attested co-occurrence cells, the other 13 accounting for the remaining 74 languages (52%). Although Types 1, 9, and 23 are among the four most frequent types (along with Type 24), they amount to less than half the languages of the sample. Of the 74 counterexamples, 50 have one deviant operator – operand order out of the four, and 24 have two word orders of each type. If we were to propose (as Vennemann does) that languages can vary in their degree of consistency, we would say that 68 languages have no inconsistency, 50 have 25% inconsistency, and 24 have 50% inconsistency.[9]

For the 30-language sample, the figures are as follows. Vennemann would predict just two co-occurrences of the following 11 operator–operand pairs:

Operator before operand:	OV & Po & RelN & AN & GN & DN & NumN & VAux & SVMV & AdvAdj & SMAdj
Operand before operator:	VO & Pr & NRel & NA & NG & ND & NNum & AuxV & MVSV & AdjAdv & AdjMS

Of the 30 languages, 7 (23%) have the predicted co-occurrences: Burushaski (OV), Fulani (VO), Japanese (OV), Kannada (OV), Swahili (VO), Turkish (OV), Yoruba (VO); the remaining 23 (77%) are inconsistent. Of these 23, I calculate that 7 would have an inconsistency rate of 1–10%; 3 would have a rate of 11–20%; 5 of 21–30%; 5 of 31–40%; and 3 of 41–50%.[10]

It is difficult to know precisely how to evaluate these figures, given that the NSP is making a "more than chance frequency" claim. What rate of consistency for the operator–operand pairs of any given language will count as satisfying NSP's predictions, and in how many languages must this rate be attained? At the very least, it would seem to be required that the majority of operator–operand orders be serialized consistently in the majority of languages. But what is going to count as a majority in the two cases? Consider the 30-language sample again, measured now in terms of consistency rather than inconsistency rates:

Consistency rate (%)	Language numbers	Total languages above the relevant consistency rate
100	7	7
90–99	7	14
80–89	3	17
70–79	5	22
60–69	5	27
50–59	3	30

The number of languages with 90%+ consistency is only 14, or less than half the sample. A rate of 80% would seem a solid majority figure with respect to consistency, but only 17, or just over half, of the 30 languages, are consistent to this extent. If we go down as far as 70%, we cover 22 of the 30 languages, a sufficient majority perhaps—but 70% consistency is getting very close to 50%, which represents completely random distribution, that is, the relevant languages have half their word orders serialized in one direction and half in the other.

All these figures present a very strong argument against the NSP, it seems to me.[11] The NSP's predictions are both too strong—there are too many exceptions—and too weak—there are distinctions between attested and nonattested language types that it is failing to capture. Vennemann's universals are actually less adequate than Greenberg's. Greenberg's implicational statements are well suited to describing the kinds of three-way typologies illustrated in Section 2.2.2, whereas Vennemann's constantly predict just two productive language types.

Consider again verb position in relation to adjective–noun and genitive–noun order. For OV languages, Vennemann predicts the OV & GN & AN co-occurrence of Types 19 and 23. The exceptions take two forms: Types 17 and 21 have both noun modifiers after the noun, OV & NG & NA; and the only other attested OV type has OV & GN & NA (Type 24), that is, with the adjective alone an exception. There are no OV languages in which the genitive alone is an exception to NSP: OV & NG & AN (potentially Types 18 and 22). Consider next VO languages of the VSO subtype. The predicted noun modifier co-occurrence is: VO & NG & NA (Type 1). The exceptions again take two forms: Either both noun modifiers precede, VO & GN & AN (Types 3 and 7), or only the adjective precedes, VO & NG & AN (Type 2). There are no VSO languages with the genitive alone an exception, VO & GN & NA (potentially Types 4 and 8). In both cases, therefore, if there is going to be just one noun ordering exception it is always the adjective, and never the genitive. The adjective is evidently a more unstable operator relative to its operand than is the genitive, a pattern that generalizes across the two ideal operator–operand types. But NSP is intrinsically unable to differentiate one operator from another in the desired way.

2.4.5 LANGUAGE FREQUENCIES

The distribution of languages across Greenberg's attested types varies considerably. As we have seen, although the three permitted types defined by the NSP are among the four most frequent in Appendix II, the second most frequent type (Type 24) is an exception. And NSP, as currently formulated, makes no predictions concerning the relative sizes of the other attested co-occurrence types.

2.4.6 THE STATUS OF SVO LANGUAGES

The relative position of V and O in VSO and SVO leads Vennemann to collapse these two types into one. But we have seen that SVO languages are typologically ambivalent (Section 2.2.4 and Table 3), though they are more similar to VSO than to SOV (particularly in the frequencies of their co-occurring word orders). Thus, whereas most VSO languages (96% in Appendix II) do indeed have prepositions, as Vennemann predicts, and most SOV languages have postpositions (92% in Appendix II), SVO languages have significant numbers of both (37% are postpositional, 63% prepositional in Appendix II). And a brief glance at Table 3 reveals similar indeterminacies. Hence, SVO is not a type indicator, and collapsing SVO and VSO types has the effect of blurring the typological characteristics of the latter.

2.5 Vennemann's Modifications

Vennemann (1976, 1977, 1981; Vennemann and Harlow 1977) introduces some modifications to the theory outlined in Section 2.3, which we shall now summarize and discuss.

2.5.1 REDEFINITION OF THE OPERATOR–OPERAND RELATION

As of Vennemann (1976), the operator–operand relation is no longer equated with the logical function–argument relation, and "category constancy" is no longer a defining criterion. Operator and operand categories (most commonly referred to now as "specifiers" and "heads," respectively) are defined in relation to an explicit categorial grammar, in the following way:

> Assume that α, of category h, and β, of category k, enter into an asymmetrical construction. If $h = k/k$, then α is an *attribute* of β; and if $k = g/h$ for some category g different from h, then α is a *complement* of β. In either case α is a *specifier* of β, and β is the *head* of the construction [Vennemann 1981:18].

In other words, Vennemann introduces two types of operators/specifiers: attributes and complements. Attributes are exemplified by adverbials in relation to adjectives, or adjectives in relation to nouns, and are like the operators of the earlier theory: Semantically they are function categories, and syntactically they do preserve category constancy. An adverbial or adjective as function, of category h, takes a category k as argument to make a k (which is the meaning of the expression $h = k/k$).

But complements, exemplified by direct object noun phrases in relation to verbs, or noun phrases in relation to prepositions, are now the arguments of their respective functions: A function category k takes an h as argument (e.g., a noun phrase) to make a g ($k = g/h$), where g may be an intransitive verb phrase, prepositional phrase, etc. The operator or specifier h is here an argument and not a function category, and category constancy between the argument and the value of the function is not preserved.

Conversely, the head/operand in an attribute-specifier construction corresponds to the argument of the specifier function (i.e., the rightmost k of k/k); and the head in a complement-specifier construction corresponds to the function that takes the specifier as argument (i.e., g/h).

The difference between attributes and complements as specifiers, and between specifiers (/operators) and heads (/operands), can be seen more clearly in tree-structure form:

(1) $h = k/k$

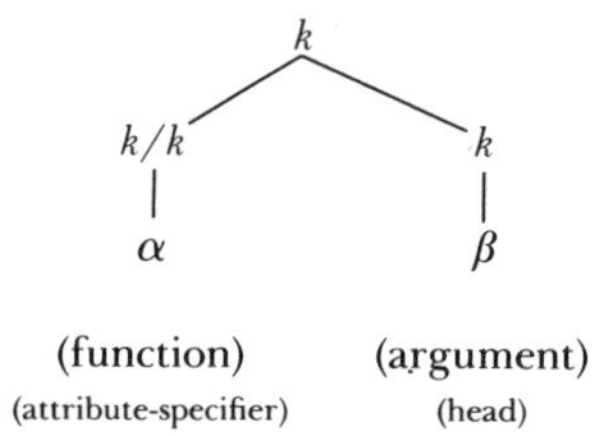

(2) $k = g/h$

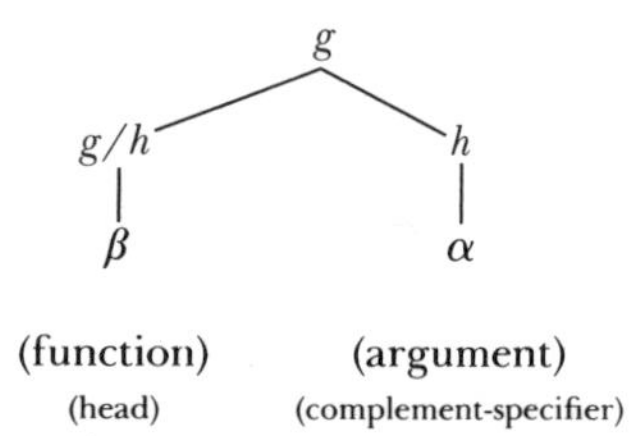

The following are examples of pairs of attribute-specifier + head (*s* stands for sentence, *n* for noun phrase, *c* for common noun):

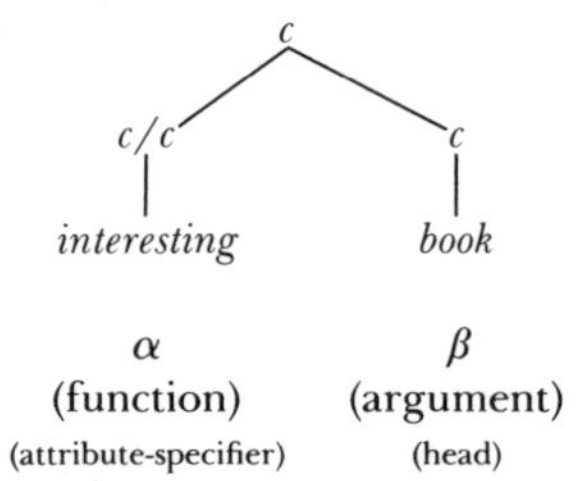

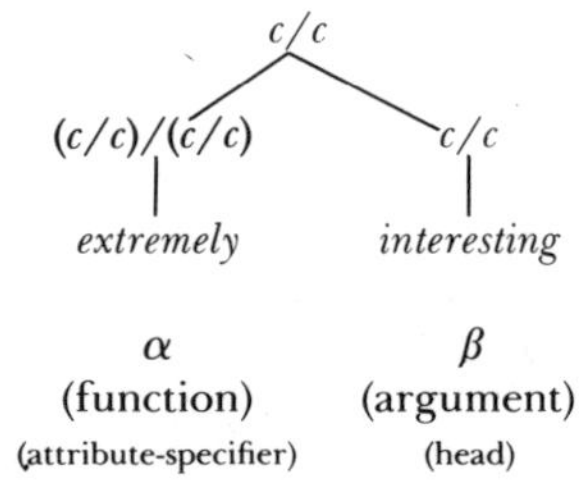

Examples of head + complement-specifier are:

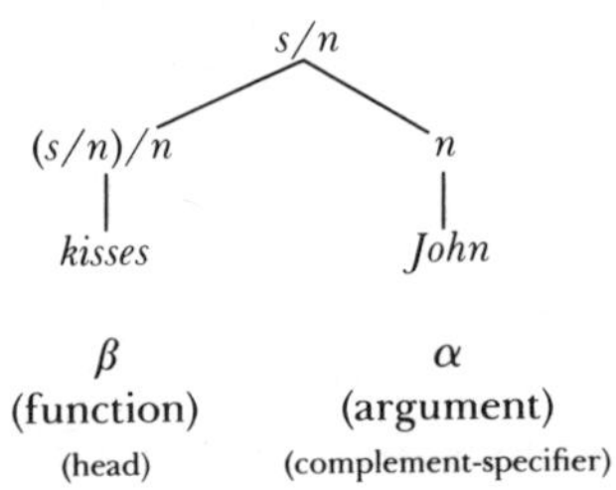

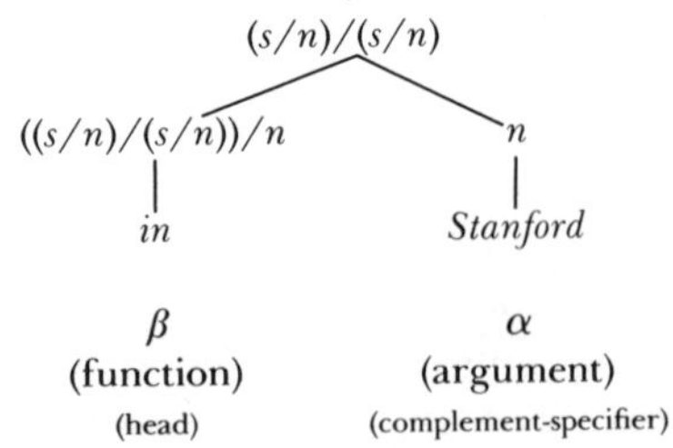

Thus, it appears that where category constancy is preserved between the argument and the value of the function ($h = k/k$), functor and specifier/operator categories overlap, as do argument and head categories. But where category constancy is not preserved between the argument and the value of the function ($k = g/h$), the functor is the head/operand category, and the argument is the specifier/operator category.

The purpose of this redefinition of the operator–operand relation is, in effect, to bring it more into line with current theories of the function–argument relation in categorial grammar and intensional logic. But the class of operator and operand categories defined by (1) and (2) remains essentially as it was before, though with one important difference: Subject NPs, hitherto excluded from both operator and operand status on the grounds that category constancy was not preserved, are now (complement-) specifiers of intransitive verbs, as follows:[12]

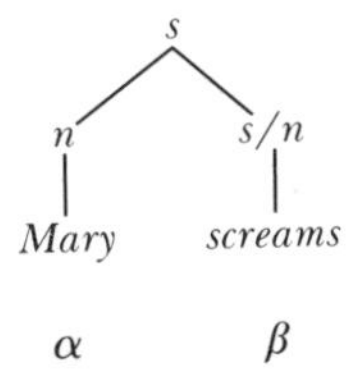

With the addition of the subject relation, the natural serialization principle remains in force in Vennemann's later work, though the terminology has changed: Languages are now consistently "prespecifying" if all specifiers (/operators) precede the head (/operand); and consistently "postspecifying" if all specifiers follow the head. As before, SVO languages are expected to pattern like VSO languages, on account of their common VO order, and to be postspecifying. But as the ordering of subject and verb is clearly prespecifying, Vennemann (1976:630) argues that SVO languages are simply inconsistent with respect to this specifier–head order. And, more generally, complete consistency is now claimed (Vennemann 1981) to be a typological ideal, rather than a universal requirement on language co-occurrences, and languages may or may not attain the ideal, or may attain it in varying degrees. Vennemann's recent theory thereby introduces a clean division between typologies and universals.

2.5.2 TYPOLOGIES VERSUS UNIVERSALS

Vennemann (1981) poses an important question: "What is a linguistic typology supposed to achieve?" In the course of his discussion, he proposes that typologies and universals should be kept clearly distinct from one another; he recasts the theoretical status of his NSP compared to the original theory (Section 2.3.3); and he abandons his earlier view of the role of NSP in historical change (Section 2.3.2).

Vennemann distinguishes two types of universals. The first includes "grammatical universals," having the form " 'for all *L*: *A*(*L*)', where *L* is a variable ranging over the set of all language systems, and *A* is a predicate —basic or defined, simple or complex—of the language of the theory of which these universals form a part [1981:3]." Implicational universals of this type take the form " 'for all *L*: if *B*(*L*), then *C*(*L*)'." Universals of this first variety "can only occur as part of a general grammatical theory [p. 4]."

The second type Vennemann explicitly equates with Greenberg's statistical universals, that is, cases of " 'near-universal', 'universal preference', 'unmarked case', 'natural case', and 'instances of more than chance frequency' [p. 5]." As an illustration he cites Greenberg's universal (17-s): With overwhelmingly more than chance frequency, languages with dominant order VSO have the adjective after the noun. And he comments: "Such insights do not, in my opinion, belong to grammatical theory at all but should be accommodated in a separate theory, a theory of linguistic preferences including grammatical naturalness or markedness [p. 5]."

Vennemann admits to being perplexed about what the purpose of a linguistic typology is, but he suggests that it is useful, as a starting point, to distinguish three types of typologies, which he proceeds to define: classificatory typologies, ideal typologies, and graduating typologies. Only the first two need concern us here.

A classificatory typology partitions the totality of languages by placing each language into one of the disjoint, nonempty classes of the typology. For example, the predicates 'permits only *CV* syllables' and 'does not permit only *CV* syllables' divide all the languages of the world into two disjoint nonempty classes. But the predicates of an ideal typology are idealizations only: Some languages may indeed be disjointly partitioned into a finite number of types defined by these predicates, while some, possibly all, languages match none of the ideal predicates, and remain outside the partitioning. The example that Vennemann gives of an ideal typology is the natural serialization principle, reformulated as summarized in Section 2.5.1.

It should be clear that Vennemann is changing the theoretical status of his NSP.[13] The serialization principle of the earlier theory was explicitly equated with language universals of the second type (i.e., Greenberg-type statistical preferences), and was claimed to be a theory of basic word order (cf. Section 2.3.3). It has now become an "ideal typology," distinct from either of the two universals that Vennemann discusses. And Vennemann now claims that "typologies are not theories or alternatives to theories. The field of linguistic typology . . . is nothing but a branch of applied theoretical linguistics [p. 24]." "Applied theoretical linguistics applies (parts of) theories of language but—by definition—does not produce any [p. 15]." The purpose of an ideal typology is, according to Vennemann, a purely practical one: "Ideal typologies are . . . like Daniel Jones' system of cardinal vowels: They have a purely orientative function [p. 13]."

Finally, Vennemann (1981) withdraws his earlier position that his serialization principle can explain word order changes occurring subsequent to a shift in verb position. As this principle is now an "ideal typology," it can have only a descriptive and orientational function in talking about historical word order changes. And, although linguistic universals have a role to play in defining "reconstructed possible languages," ideal typologies can have no such function.

2.6 Discussion of Vennemann's Modifications

2.6.1 FUNCTION–ARGUMENT OR CATEGORY CONSTANCY?

The operator–operand distinction of Vennemann's earlier theory was defined semantically in terms of the function–argument relation, and syntactically in terms of category constancy. We observed in Section 2.4.3 that the operator–operand distinction does not in fact match the function–argument relation, but is closer to the modifier–head distinction of traditional and more recent syntactic theory. The result is that the two defining criteria of the operator–operand distinction in the original theory were actually at variance with one another.

In attempting to resolve the contradiction, Vennemann tries to have the best of both worlds. Operators and operands are now defined in terms of function–argument structures of the more usual kind. But in contrast to the approach of Keenan, the modifier–head relation still finds a place within his theory, and it is still this relation, rather than the function–argument relation, which is claimed to be the primary generalization for determining word order serialization.

In effect, Vennemann's revision amounts to a dissimilation principle. Those specifiers (or modifiers or operators) which are function categories of the form k/k, he labels attributes; those which are arguments of some function whose application yields a category distinct from that of the argument itself (g/h), he calls complements. Function–argument structures are then claimed to serialize in one direction if the function category is an attribute specifier and the argument is head, and in the other direction if the function category is head and the argument is a complement specifier. The difference between the two types of function–argument structures is precisely whether category constancy is preserved between the argument and the value of the function. It is preserved in the case of k/k, but not with g/h. The definitions of attribute and complement, and of specifier and head, thus guarantee that function–argument structures are divided into two types. And a word order principle defined in terms of specifier–head ordering (just as before) effects dissimilar serializations for these two types of structures in just the right ways: All specifiers and heads are claimed to be serialized in a uniform direction in consistent languages.

But although Vennemann's account is observationally adequate as a predictor of statistical word order correlations, it is unsatisfactory in at least two respects. First, the crucial specifier–head generalization is now quite arbitrarily defined. Vennemann lists the two types of function–argument structures, $h = k/k$ and $k = g/h$, and simply declares by fiat that heads will be argument categories in the former case and function categories in the latter. But there is nothing that all heads now have in common, in terms of which they can be consistently defined. And the proposed mapping between argument and head on some occasions, and function and head on others, is arbitrary. Why should the assignments not be the exact opposite of this? Why should arguments and heads not always correspond? etc. No principled reasons are offered for these assignments, and as far as I can tell none are available.

By contrast, category constancy IS preserved for all head categories within a modifier–head theory such as the X-bar theory. Compare the following X-bar structures with their corresponding function–argument trees in Section 2.5.1: $_{\bar{\bar{\mathrm{N}}}}(_{\bar{\bar{\mathrm{A}}}}(\textit{interesting})\ _{\bar{\mathrm{N}}}(_{\mathrm{N}}(\textit{book})))$, $_{\bar{\bar{\mathrm{A}}}}(_{\bar{\bar{\mathrm{Adv}}}}(\textit{extremely})\ _{\bar{\mathrm{A}}}(_{\mathrm{A}}(\textit{interesting})))$, $_{\bar{\bar{\mathrm{V}}}}(_{\bar{\mathrm{V}}}(_{\mathrm{V}}(\textit{kisses})\ _{\bar{\bar{\mathrm{N}}}}(\textit{John})))$, $_{\bar{\bar{\mathrm{P}}}}(_{\bar{\mathrm{P}}}(_{\mathrm{P}}(\textit{in})\ _{\bar{\bar{\mathrm{N}}}}(\textit{Stanford})))$. In each case the head category is the one whose status remains constant within its phrase (V within $\bar{\bar{\mathrm{V}}}$ etc.). Hence, category constancy can provide a principled syntactic generalization and criterion for distinguishing modifiers from heads in a consistent way. But by using the categorial grammar format, category constancy is not preserved between dominating and dominated categories in phrases of the type *kisses John* and *in Stanford*, and so it can not serve in any general definition of the notion "head of phrase".

In a nutshell, the problem is that the one criterion that could be given for defining modifier versus head consistently, category constancy, is not available in a function–argument theory, because the heads of a modifier–head theory do not all preserve category constancy in their corresponding function–argument structures. As a result, there is no nonarbitrary definition available for the very entity which is claimed to be all-important for word order prediction.

The second problem with Vennemann's revision involves the fact that he is proposing what amounts to a dissimilation principle. As such it is open to the same kind of objection that we raised in Section 2.4.3: why should the presence or absence of category constancy in a function–argument structure result in opposite word order serialization, any more than the DNP or CNP status of an argument should? To argue that the specifier or head status of the different function or argument categories provides the motivation for opposite ordering merely brings us back to our first point: These notions are not satisfactorily defined within the context of Vennemann's theory.

More generally, to say that some function–argument structures serialize in one direction, and some in another in one and the same language, is to admit that there is no single unifying generalization that unites surface word order facts with these hypothesized abstract structures. Given another theory, therefore, whose hypothesized abstract structures avoid this "some do it one way, some another" claim in favor of a single generalization, then this latter is to be preferred. Either the dissimilation theory is defining its serialization principle on the wrong level of abstract structure (i.e., the relevant level may be independently motivated, but it is not the level upon which word order predictions should be defined). Or, less benignly, the nature and composition of the relevant abstract structures themselves are placed in doubt.

The dissimilation theorist can avoid this conclusion by arguing that all things are not in fact equal. More precisely, he can argue that there ARE good reasons why function–argument structures typically serialize in both directions in one and the same language. But if this argument is to be convincing, two forms of justification need to be given for what is in effect a nonregularity. On the one hand, a generalization must be offered unifying each dissimilarly ordered set of function–argument structures, for example, the CNP versus DNP status of the argument. In addition, some reason must be given for why these particular generalizations should result in opposite orderings for the relevant function–argument structures. Unless opposite ordering can be motivated in some way, a dissimilation principle provides a less adequate account of word order than does a theory whose abstract structures permit a uniform generalization. This latter theory can explain all word orders in the relevant language type by demonstrating that they are all instances of the same abstract structural type. Therefore, it can be argued, they can be expected to serialize in the same direction in the simplest, unmarked case. But the dissimilation theories proposed so far can only distinguish between two sets of function–argument structures, and from the point of view of word order, a crucial explanatory step is still missing: Even if we grant the existence of two such sets of function–argument structures, why do they result in the (opposite) word orders that they do? This question has not received a satisfactory answer, either in Vennemann's work or in Keenan's. Nor is it answered in Flynn (1982), where similar function–argument-derived generalizations are proposed.

In sum, Vennemann's attempt to combine function–argument and modifier–head generalizations within the same theory no longer leads to internal contradiction. But I would argue that the very mismatch between these generalizations still has a number of undesirable consequences, and that a general and explanatory theory of word order cannot accommodate both these notions in the way that Vennemann proposes. Specifically, there is no nonarbitrary and consistent definition available for the very entity which is claimed to be all-important for word order prediction, the modifier–head relation. And a criterion which could have been used for this purpose within a different theory, category constancy, is employed for the less general, and much more questionable, task of effecting a dissimilation between function–argument structures.

2.6.2 TYPOLOGY AND UNIVERSALS

Vennemann (1981) is right to draw attention to the fact that typologies and universals are not equivalent. He is, however, too extreme when he asserts: "It seems to me to be one of the few demonstrable things about the concept of a typology of languages that if it is to have any value at all, it has to remain completely distinct from . . . the study of universals [p. 2]." Comrie's (1981:Chapter 2) discussion of the relation between typology and universals is, I believe, nearer the mark. Comrie begins by paraphrasing what is, in effect, the Vennemann position:

> At first sight, the study of language universals and the study of language typology might seem to be opposites, even in conflict with one another: language universals research is concerned with finding those properties that are common to all human languages, whereas in order to typologize languages, i.e. to assign them to different types, it is necessary that there should be differences among languages. The contrast can thus be summed up as one between the study of the similarities across languages and the study of the differences among languages [p. 30].

But then he goes on to show that there is, in fact, no such conflict. In particular, implicational universals are inherently variation defining. If the implication is unilateral, three out of four mathematically possible language types are permitted (Section 2.2.2); if it is bilateral, two of the four are permitted (Section 2.4.2). The formulation of language universals, and the definition of language types, therefore amount to the same thing in these cases.

But there are cases where typologies and universals are distinct from one another. For example, once it is established that all languages have some single property, such as vowels, we are dealing with a universal statement and not a typology, as the class of languages of which the predicate 'presence of vowels' is true would include all languages, and the class of which 'absence of vowels' is true would be empty.

Conversely, there may be typologies for which there are no corresponding universal statements, or at least only trivial universals of the form: for all *L*: *A*(*L*) *or B*(*L*) *or C*(*L*) . . . , where *L* is a variable ranging over all languages. For example, Comrie (1978) establishes a useful typology of case-marking systems as "Nominative-Accusative," "Ergative-Absolutive," "Neutral," and "Tripartite." This seems to me a plausible candidate for a typology and not a universal.

Typologies and universals are therefore not equivalent. But some universals, notably those of the implicational variety (which constitute the primary descriptive mechanism in the statement of word order universals hitherto), are simultaneously typology defining. Vennemann's claim that "typologies of languages . . . cannot be either true or false but have to be evaluated by different criteria . . . e.g. 'useful', 'adequate', 'revealing' [1981:15]" seems therefore to be a reasonable characterization of those typologies which are not defined by universals. But where there are universal regularities awaiting formulation and explanation, as in the area of word order, a retreat to ideal typologies is unwarranted.

2.7 Overview

It should be clear from this chapter that Greenberg is to be credited with the collection of an impressive body of data, and with the formulation of a large number of word order universals. Vennemann, following Lehmann, has proposed a general organizing principle for these word order universals, which has some explanatory value. However, this principle has more exceptions than does the original body of universals proposed by Greenberg, and in his more recent work Vennemann no longer claims that his principle has much descriptive power. There are also interesting differences in language frequencies that are not being accounted for. Is it possible to improve on Vennemann's principle, or to find some alternative principles which will have both descriptive and explanatory power?

The major purpose of this book is to search for such principles. By proposing empirically more adequate descriptive generalizations, I hope to demonstrate that there are profound constraints on the co-occurrences of word orders across the languages of the world. In Chapter 3 it is observed that there is a large discrepancy between the mathematically possible and the actually attested word order co-occurrences, and some exceptionless implicational universals are formulated defining all and only the attested co-occurrences in Greenberg's data. Some principles are then proposed which collectively explain why the implicational universals define the word order co-occurrences that they do. In Chapter 4 it is demonstrated that differences in language frequencies can be predicted by a nearly exceptionless "distributional universal," which we state by adapting and reformulating Vennemann's NSP. In subsequent chapters, these synchronic universals of word order are argued to play an important role in predicting historical word order changes, and in reconstructing protolanguages.

Notes

1. The following implicational universals are formulated as *nonstatistical* (i.e., exceptionless) by Greenberg, relative to his data base (cf. Greenberg 1966:110–113 for a summary of all the universals; again, "a" and "b" subscripts refer to logically distinct claims): (3), (5), (6), (7), (8), (10b), (11a), (11b), (12), (13), (15), (16a), (16b), (19), (20a), (20b), (21), (22a), (23a), (24), (25), (26), (27a), (27b), (28), (29), (30), (31), (32), (33), (34a), (34b), (35a), (36), (37), (38), (40), (43), (44), and (45). The following are *statistical* (admitting of a limited number of exceptions): (2a-s), (2b-s), (4-s), (9a-s), (9b-s), (10a-s), (17-s), (18-s), (22b-s), (23b-s), (35b-s), (39-s), and (41-s). The only universals not included in these two lists are three nonimplicational ("unrestricted") universals: (1-s), (14), and (42). The result is 56 logically distinct universal claims, of which 42 are nonstatistical and 14 statistical.

2. Many of the entries in Greenberg's Appendix II refer to whole families (e.g., Celtic, Bantu, Dravidian), and the individually named languages are genetically diverse, with the result that the majority of the world's language families are represented. In a seminar on word order which I organized at the University of Southern California in the spring of 1978, one of the collective projects was to check as many as possible of these entries, particularly the families and groups, and to add to the sample. The findings are incorporated in the Expanded Sample of Chapter 8, which also gives a genetic classification of all the languages in the sample. Our research provided strong confirmation for the implicational patterns which we originally derived from Appendix II and which are given in Section 3.2. However, we did find that some of Greenberg's Appendix II entries should be reclassified among already attested types. The following changes have been incorporated into the Expanded Sample, but are left unaltered in Table 2, which reproduces Greenberg's original classification:

Type 9: Modern Greek should be Type 10 (cf. Greenberg's own 30-language sample in Table 1).

Type 9: "Almost all" should replace "all Bantu languages" (Tunen and Bandem are Type 17—Larry Hyman, personal communication; Dugast 1971).
Type 14: "Rutulian and other SVO Daghestan languages in the Caucasus" should be Type 15 (Maner Thorpe, personal communication; Bokarev 1967a).
Type 15: Ijo should be Type 23 (Givón 1975; Larry Hyman, personal communication).
Type 23: Abkhaz should be Type 24 (Maner Thorpe, personal communication; Bokarev 1967a).

In addition, for various entries the verb, adposition, or adjective order turn out to be of undecidable basicness, for example:

Type 10: German has both SOV and SVO orders (Section 5.3.5).
Type 15: Mandarin Chinese also has both SOV and SVO, as well as both prepositions and postpositions (Li & Thompson 1975, Hou 1979).
Type 16: Nupe is both pre- and postpositional (Larry Hyman, personal communication).

Such entries have accordingly been removed from the Expanded Sample. Our Expanded Sample would further permit us to delete the word "probably" before: Type 1 "other Austronesian languages"; Type 2 "other Philippine Austronesian languages"; and Type 15 "Algonquian." Finally, Papago (VSO & Po) has been entered into Appendix II as reproduced here. This language is mentioned by Greenberg in a note on p. 107, although not included in his Appendix as such. Ed Keenan has confirmed for me (personal communication) on the basis of his work on verb-first languages that VSO & Po is indeed an existing, though limited, type. Its occurrence is in fact predicted by the existence of languages of the opposite type: SOV & Pr (Types 17 and 19). The limited distribution of both VSO & Po and SOV & Pr languages, and the slighty larger quantity of the latter, are predictable by our principle of Cross-Category Harmony (Chapter 4).

3. The exceptions to (2a-s) include one language of Type 3, three languages of Type 11, one language of Type 12, and one language of Type 19 (= 6 total). The exceptions to (2b-s) include two languages of Type 14 and seven languages of Type 21 (= 9 total). The exceptions to (4-s) include four languages of Type 17 and one language of Type 19 (= 5 total). The exceptions to (17-s) include five languages of Type 2 and one language of Type 3 (= 6 total). Altogether, 24 distinct languages are exceptions to at least one of these universals.

4. Actually, SVO does co-occur invariably with NRel, and predominantly with AuxV in Table 3 [C and H respectively], but even here SVO shares these co-occurrences with VSO, and so has no unique characteristics of its own. Furthermore, the correlation with NRel no longer holds exceptionlessly in the Expanded Sample of Chapter 8: 60 SVO languages have NRel but 4 have RelN.

5. For a small number of universals Greenberg does, in effect, propose a two-way, rather than a three-way, typology. Sometimes, one unilateral implication, $P \supset Q$, is matched by a second whose logical form is $-P \supset -Q$. These two unilateral implications between them amount to a bilateral implication defining just two language types, P & Q and $-P$ & $-Q$, as $(P \supset Q)$ & $(-P \supset -Q)$ is logically equivalent to $(P \supset Q)$ & $(Q \supset P)$. Three clear examples are the following (I give the co-occurrence quantities from the 30-language sample alongside each):

			Pr	Po
(2a-s)	Pr $\supset$ NG	NG	15	0
(2b-s)	Po $\supset$ GN	GN	1	14

			Pr	Po
(22a)	SMAdj ⊃ Po	SMAdj	0	10
(22b-s)	AdjMS ⊃ Pr	AdjMS	13	1

			NG	GN
(23a)	PNCN ⊃ NG	PNCN	8	0
(23b-s)	CNPN ⊃ GN	CNPN	1	8

and there is one other statistical bilateral statement that Greenberg could have made, but did not:

		Pr	Po
AuxV ⊃ Pr	AuxV	9	1
VAux ⊃ Po	VAux	0	9

In each of these instances, Greenberg's implications amount to a prediction that just two language types exist [e.g., Pr & NG and Po & GN (2-s)]. Vennemann was probably influenced by these two-way correlations when proposing his NSP. But his overgeneralization of the two-way schema is not warranted by Greenberg's data, in which two-way typologies are a minority, even when one considers correlations with the two adposition orders (Pr and Po), rather than with the three basic verb positions. Compare the preceding co-occurrence quantities wih the following ones:

	Pr	Po
NA	12	7
AN	4	7

	Pr	Po
NRel	16	5
RelN	0	7
Both	0	1

	Pr	Po
ND	9	3
DN	7	11

	Pr	Po
NNum	4	4
NumN	12	9
Both	0	1

	Pr	Po
MVSV	16	8
SVMV	0	6

	Pr	Po
AdjAdv	7	1
AdvAdj	6	10
Both	2	0

In each case, either three or four language types are amply attested, not just two.

6. It is mathematically conceivable, as David Sankoff has pointed out to me, that verb position could still have a special status within Vennemann's NSP, given that his bilateral implications are statistical. For example, one could imagine VO being statistically correlated with Pr, and also with NG, without these latter necessarily being statistically correlated with one another. For example:

	VO	OV
Pr	5	1
Po	1	5

	VO	OV
NG	4	2
GN	2	4

	Pr	Po
NG	3	3
GN	3	3

Type			*Number*
VO	Pr	NG	3
VO	Pr	GN	2
VO	Po	NG	1

Type			Number
VO	Po	GN	0
OV	Pr	NG	0
OV	Pr	GN	1
OV	Po	NG	2
OV	Po	GN	3

However, both Vennemann's formulation of NSP and the linguistic facts rule out this mathematical possibility in this context. Vennemann's formulation of the NSP explicitly predicts consistent serializations for *all* operator–operand pairs, with greater than chance frequency. There is nothing in his NSP that allows for correlations between some operator–operand pairs and not others, or for reversible implications in some cases and nonreversible ones in others, etc. And empirically the correlations between non-verb-position word orders such as Pr and NG are typically as good (or bad) as those involving verb position. The Appendix II figures for the hypothetical co-occurrences reveal that the adposition and genitive co-occurrence figures are actually slightly better than those involving verb position:

	VO	OV
Pr	58	5
Po	20	59

	VO	OV
NG	55	11
GN	23	53

	Pr	Po
NG	57	9
GN	7	70

Type			Number
VO	Pr	NG	53
VO	Pr	GN	5
VO	Po	NG	2
VO	Po	GN	18
OV	Pr	NG	4
OV	Pr	GN	1
OV	Po	NG	7
OV	Po	GN	52

It is acceptable, therefore, for Vennemann to use various verb positions (OV or VO) as "typological indicators" or labels standing for whole language types (cf. Chapter 3). But it does not then follow that verb position has a special logical status synchronically and diachronically. And there is nothing, either in the theory or the data, that warrants this special status.

7. See Allwood, Andersson, and Dahl (1977:Chapter 8) for a good introduction to the function–argument relation within the context of a categorial grammar and an intensional logic.

8. The correspondence between Vennemann's operator–operand theory and the *X*-bar theory is not exact. For example, auxiliaries are specifiers of verb phrases within the *X*-bar theory, but are operands (i.e., heads) in Vennemann's theory. Nonetheless, the *X*-bar theory expresses Vennemann's category constancy insight far more closely than do the function–argument structures of a categorial grammar. See Section 4.6 for a discussion of the cross-language predictions of the *X*-bar theory.

9. These figures become even worse when we adopt the redefined operator–operand theory of Vennemann's more recent work (Section 2.5) and treat subjects as operators on their verbs as operands, for SVO languages now become inconsistent, having the subject on the left and the object on the right of the verb. As a result, for Appendix II, only Type 1 (19 languages) and Type 23 (28 languages) are consistent with Vennemann's predictions. That is, only 47 out of 142 languages, or 33.1%, are consistent with the NSP. Of the 95 inconsistent languages, 57 are inconsistent with respect to one out of five operator–operand orders, and 38 with respect to two. Hence, 57 languages have an inconsistency rate of 20%, and 38 an inconsistency rate of 40%.

10. 1–10% inconsistency: Burmese (9 OV properties/1 VO property), Hebrew (1 OV/9 VO), Hindi (10 OV/1 VO), Malay (1 OV/9 VO), Thai (1 OV/9 VO), Welsh (1 OV/9 VO), Zapotec (1 OV/10 VO).

11–20% inconsistency: Berber (1 OV/8 VO), Masai (1 OV/8 VO), Quechua (8 OV/2 VO).

21–30% inconsistency: Basque (8 OV/3 VO), Chibcha (8 OV/3 VO), Italian (3 OV/8 VO), Maori (2 OV/7 VO), Songhai (2 OV/7 VO).

31–40% inconsistency: Finnish (6 OV/4 VO), Greek (4 OV/7 VO), Maya (4 OV/6 VO), Nubian (6 OV/3 VO), Serbian (4 OV/7 VO).

41–50% inconsistency: Guarani (5 OV/5 VO), Loritja (4 OV/4 VO), Norwegian (5 OV/6 VO).

11. Mallinson and Blake (1981) have argued that such figures do still provide support for Vennemann's predictions:

> The significance of [such] figures . . . becomes apparent if we consider that if . . . only half the VO languages exhibited NG, half the OV languages GN, and so on, then the chances of a language having a particular basic word order plus [a given] set of five [word order] features . . . would be 1 in 32 (there are 64 possible types if all languages can be categorized as *X* or *not X* for each parameter) [p. 379].

As the NSP-predicted co-occurrences each account for considerably more than the random proportions in these samples, this is regarded as strong confirming evidence for Vennemann's theory.

It seems to me that it is not. We shall be arguing in Section 3.1.1 that there is a very large discrepancy between the mathematically possible and the actually attested number of word order types, and that we must attempt to define this balance as precisely as possible, and to predict relative language frequencies. Vennemann's NSP performs neither of these tasks. It merely elevates two word order types to preferential status. These two types are indeed relatively more frequent than others, and have many more exemplifying languages than mathematical probabilities alone would assign to them. But the fact remains that NSP is making word order co-occurrence predictions which have too many exceptions; that there are many "exceptional" attested language types that NSP fails to distinguish in a principled way from the large number of mathematically possible but totally unattested types; and that there are interesting frequency differences between the attested language types about which NSP says nothing. In short, we need to do better, and I will argue that the kind of extension of Greenberg's and Vennemann's ideas to be proposed in this book does do better.

Mallinson and Blake make it appear as if Vennemann's NSP has more numerical support than is actually the case, by providing a set of calculations rather different from our own. Our own methodology consists in calculating the proportion of languages that have consistent orderings for all operator–operand pairs, relative to those that do not. And for languages that have at least one inconsistency we then measure the ratio of consistent to inconsistent operator–operand orders. Mallinson and Blake calculate the proportion of languages that are consistent with NSP's predictions for *each individual operator–operand order* in relation to VO or OV respectively. For example, NSP predicts the co-occurrence of VO with Pr + NP, and of OV with NP + Po. The proportion of Greenberg's 30-language sample that conforms to this by having either one or the other of these pairs is 27/30, or 90%. If this figure had been 50%, the distribution would have been random, since an equal number of languages would have had the unpredicted pairs as well as the predicted pairs.

The 90% figure is well above 50%. And quite generally the pursuit of this method seems to give better quantitative support for NSP.

I have two objections to this method of testing Vennemann's NSP: There are still too many exceptions; and it rests on a rather questionable interpretation of the NSP itself.

Consider the first point. Mallinson and Blake rely heavily on Greenberg's 30-language sample. But the evidence of Appendix II plus my Expanded Sample suggests that the 30-language sample often gives misleadingly high correlations in favor of Mallinson and Blake's interpretation of the NSP. I have extensive data for the following six sets of predictions:

Prediction 1: VO & Pr and OV & Po

30-language sample:	27/30	= 90%
Appendix II:	117/142	= 82.4%
Expanded Sample:	298/336	= 88.7%

Prediction 2: VO & NA and OV & AN

30-language sample:	20/30	= 66.7%
Appendix II:	81/142	= 57%
Expanded Sample:	209/336	= 62.2%

Prediction 3: VO & NG and OV & GN

30-language sample:	26/30	= 86.7%
Appendix II:	108/142	= 76.1%
Expanded Sample:	277/336	= 82.4%

Prediction 4: VO & NRel and OV & RelN

30-language sample:	26/28	= 92.9%
Expanded Sample:	96/124	= 77.4%

Prediction 5: VO & ND and OV & DN

30-language sample:	19/30	= 63.3%
Expanded sample:	100/153	= 65.4%

Prediction 6: VO & NNum and OV & NumN

30-language sample:	13/30	= 43.3%
Expanded Sample:	69/136	= 50.7%

It will be apparent that the success rate for Predictions 2, 5, and 6 is not good—the figures here are dangerously close to the random distribution of 50%. And for Predictions 1, 3, and 4, the larger samples give less good correlations than the 30-language sample. Mallinson & Blake's method of calculation therefore provides better results for NSP, but there are still many exceptions. But, second, how legitimate is this interpretation of NSP? Not very, I would argue. Vennemann's NSP is intended as a collapsed set of implicational universals, as these were proposed in Greenberg (1966) (cf. Section 2.3.3). These implications state that if a language has some word order *P*, then it also has word order *Q*. We saw in Section 2.1 that one and the same *P* order guaranteed several other *Q* orders, and that many of these *Q*s were in turn antecedent or consequent word orders in further implicational universals. Vennemann noticed a more general regularity in all these co-occurrences, and reduced all the implications to a single statement. In effect, he generalized Greenberg's many 'if *P* then *Q*' universals by proposing a single universal in which the *Q* property is a conjunction of all those word orders whose operator–operand serialization is the same as that of the antecedent *P* property (VO or OV). If we now measure NSP by quantifying the co-occurrence of VO/OV with each word order taken singly, we are effectively treating Vennemann's theory as if it were no different from Greenberg's implications in which *P* and *Q* are both (predominantly) single word orders. And we are undoing the whole force of Vennemann's innovation.

Vennemann is claiming that if a given language has, for example, VO, then *all* the operator–operand orders will serialize in a consistent way *in that language.* If they do, the language is consistent; if they do not, it is inconsistent to the relevant degree. Mallinson and Blake's calculations are therefore more appropriate for Greenberg-type universals, defined on word order pairs. At the very least, they would appear to assume a weakening of NSP's predictions, and even these weakened predictions have more exceptions than the 30-language sample would lead us to believe.

12. Vennemann's analysis, in which *Mary* is an argument of *screams* as function, agrees with that of Keenan and Faltz (1979), and is at variance with that of Montague, who treats *Mary* as a function of category s/(s/n) (cf. Vennemann 1981).

13. Surprisingly, Vennemann (1981) argues as if the modified theory is the theory he has held all along, and he criticizes critics of the earlier theory for failing to appreciate that the NSP was an ideal typology, and not a universal or theory. But to the extent that Vennemann was proposing "ideal types" in his earlier work, these ideal types were actually defined by a theory comprising Greenberg-type statistical universals (Section 2.3.3). And no definition of an ideal typology, separate from a theory plus universals, was proposed, as it is in Vennemann (1981).

Vennemann (1981) writes:

> Since typologies of languages are not theories, they cannot be either true or false but have to be evaluated by different criteria . . . e.g. 'useful', 'adequate', 'revealing'.
>
> The error of confusing typologies with theories is committed in Hawkins (1980a). Hawkins refers to the ideal word order typology . . . and . . . goes on to present some figures from Greenberg 1966 which show that quite a number of languages are not ideal according to this typology. . . . Hawkins is free to believe to have shown all kinds of defects of the ideal typology under discussion. E.g. that it does not do the kinds of things Hawkins expects a typology to do, viz. that it "makes no predictions concerning the relative sizes of . . . attested co-occurrence types" (Hawkins 1980a:200), and that it should be replaced by a different one. But believing to have falsified it is committing a logical error: Ideal typologies are not the type of objects that can be falsified [p. 15].

In Hawkins (1980a), I was explicitly citing and criticizing Vennemann's (1972, 1974a, 1974b, 1975) statistical universals and theory. I was arguing that his theory was false as it stood, since there were too many counterexamples and theoretical problems. The criticisms I made were legitimate objections to an explicit "theory of basic word order" and to a set of reformulated Greenberg-type statistical universals. In their stead I proposed two types of reformulated word order universals, defining all and only the attested word order co-occurrences (implicational universals), and their relative frequencies (the distributional universal).

If there was any confusion between typologies on the one hand, and theories and universals on the other, therefore, the confusion would appear to have originated with Vennemann himself, as the relevant distinctions were not drawn in his earlier work. Furthermore, implicational universals define different language types, and to this extent link up with typology (see Section 2.6.2). But my "predictions concerning the relative sizes of . . . attested co-occurrence types" would in any case have nothing to do with language typologies, as the types are already defined, and only the size of their membership is at issue.

3 : *Implicational Universals in Greenberg's Data and the Expanded Sample*

In this chapter we shall provide a set of reformulated implicational universals for much of Greenberg's word order data. We begin, in Section 3.1, with a discussion of the general properties of adequate implicational universals of word order. In Section 3.2 we define implicational universals for the data of Appendix II (Table 2); and in Section 3.3 we do the same for word order properties in the 30-language sample (Table 1). In both sections additional data from the Expanded Sample in Chapter 8 are also taken into account. In Section 3.4 some principles are proposed explaining why the implicational universals are the way they are, that is, why they define all and only the co-occurrences which they do. In Section 3.5 we discuss the notion "word order type" in the light of our reformulated universals. And Section 3.6 discusses the relationship between constituency and word order universals.

3.1 General Properties of Adequate Implicational Universals

The implicational universals to be proposed in this chapter have the following properties: they are almost all NONSTATISTICAL (I.E., EXCEPTIONLESS) RATHER THAN STATISTICAL, relative to the data base; they are all UNILATERAL (if *P* then *Q*) RATHER THAN BILATERAL (if *P* then *Q* and vice versa, as in Vennemann's NSP); and a significant number are MULTITERMED RATHER THAN BITERMED (i.e., defined in terms of at least three rather than just two properties).

The need for unilateral and multitermed statements was illustrated in the last chapter. Unilateral implications define three-way typologies, whereas bilateral implications define two-way typologies, and we saw, and will continue to see, ample evidence for the former, and relatively little for the latter. And multitermed statements are on many occasions able to capture regularities of co-occurrence that bitermed statements cannot, by, in effect, raising the antecedent of the implication from one property to two. The co-occurrence of a third can then often be predicted in a straightforward manner (see Section 2.2.2).

The one general property that is still in need of theoretical justification is the nonstatistical rather than statistical status of implicational universals. We have seen that most of Greenberg's universals are nonstatistical, whereas all of Vennemann's (1972, 1974a, 1974b, 1975) universals are stated as statistical tendencies only. The position to be taken here is that such statistical tendencies are theoretically undesirable. Where they have been proposed I hope to show that there are alternative implicational universals which are exceptionless and which define all and only the attested co-occurrences. We will occasionally be forced to use statistical implicational statements for descriptive convenience, but we shall do so only when the number of exceptions is very small.

3.1.1 THE NEED FOR NONSTATISTICAL RATHER THAN STATISTICAL IMPLICATIONAL STATEMENTS

There are several general theoretical considerations that support the regular use of nonstatistical rather than statistical implicational statements in the attempt to define co-occurring and non-co-occurring word orders.

In particular, the available data samples reveal that numerous mathematically possible word order co-occurrences are not attested in any known language. Statistical 'if *P* then *Q*' statements are unable to predict that any word order co-occurrence is totally nonoccurring, as they explicitly allow the offending **P* & −*Q* co-occurrence to exist, albeit as an infrequent type. The case for the regular use of nonstatistical implicational statements therefore stands or falls according to whether there is, or is not, a productive discrepancy between the mathematically possible and the actually attested word order co-occurrences.

The existence of such a discrepancy is easy to demonstrate. It can be seen in current samples. It can also be confidently predicted to hold for much larger samples of languages and word order properties.

Consider just the word orders exemplifying the operator–operand orderings listed in the discussion of Vennemann's theory (Section 2.3). There are 17 in all. If we add indirect object + verb, oblique NP + verb, and also subject + verb (Section 2.5.1), we have a total of 20 word order pairs, each of which can be serialized with the operator either before or after the operand. As these orders are for the most part logically independent of one another, we have some 2^{20}, or over a million possible co-occurrences; and these 20 do not begin to exhaust all the definable word orders of a language.[1]

Now, assuming (with Ruhlen 1976:1) that the number of currently existing languages is in the region of 4000–8000, even if each of them were to have a different co-occurrence array from every other (i.e., different with respect to at least one word order), the total number of attested co-occurrence types could not exceed 8000, which would represent just .76% of the mathematical possibilities for 20 varying word orders. And if (cf. Note 1) the number of possible co-occurrence types is more like many hundreds of millions, the actually attested co-occurrences could be no more than a tiny fraction of 1% of these.

There is therefore a trivial sense in which a huge discrepancy must exist between the mathematical possibilities and the actually attested co-occurrences—there are not enough languages to go around.

Given that this is so, an important question is raised. Any theory of language must attempt to define the notion "possible human language," and it must do so by projecting the set of actually attested languages onto sets of possible versus impossible languages. But when, as in the present instance, the mathematical combinatorial possibilities are so huge, the attested ones can be only a small fraction of these. So how can we be sure that today's languages are not just a limited set of 8000 word order co-occurrences, with so-called co-occurrence regularities merely a mathematical artifact? Can we with any confidence rule out some word order co-occurrences as impossible, rather than just contingently absent? And are the actual co-occurrences sufficient to make the projection onto possible co-occurrences?

The answer is that we cannot define possible versus impossible human languages with absolute certainty, either in this or in most other areas of universal grammar. But, having said that, there are several considerations which suggest that we can be FAIRLY confident that today's languages provide a data base of sufficient size for extracting the universals of word order variation.

First, the attested languages cluster with striking frequency around small common sets of co-occurrences. Second, clear linguistic patterns emerge distinguishing the attested from the unattested co-occurrences (Section 3.4). And third, there is a very regular and principled decline in the quantities of languages which have the various attested co-occurrences (Chapter 4).

The first consideration indicates that unattested co-occurrences are not just the result of limited language numbers: For the fewer the language quantities, and the greater the mathematical co-occurrence possibilities, the less is the likelihood that languages will share co-occurrence arrays—yet time and time again we find languages exemplifying shared word order pairs, triples, quadruples, etc. For example, consider the 30-language sample (Table 1). In Section 2.4.4 we tested Vennemann's NSP against this sample, using 11 operator–operand word orders. If we add subject + verb there are $2^{12} = 4096$ mathematically possible combinations of these word orders, at most 30 of which could be attested. I calculate that as many as 18 of these languages (=60%) exemplify just 5 of the 4096 co-occurrences (=.12%)[2]; that is, 60% of this random sample clusters around .12% of the word order possibilities. This would be a remarkable coincidence, were it not for the existence of clear linguistic regularities in this area. Appendix II (Table 2) is also revealing. There, 88 languages (Types 1, 9, 23, and 24) occupy just 4 of the 24 possible co-occurrences; that is, 62% of the languages of this sample cluster around 16.67% of the co-occurrences. This discrepancy is impressive, but it is not so great as in the 30-language sample, because the word order properties are much fewer and the languages more numerous. Appendix II is also interesting in that 8 (actually 9)[3] of the 24 co-occurrences are completely unattested.

It should therefore be clear that there is a large discrepancy between the mathematically possible and the actually attested co-occurrences in the area of word order. Very many more of the mathematically possible co-occurrences are *un*attested than attested, both because the mathematical possibilities are enormous, and because there are linguistic regularities which constrain languages in the selections they make, regularities which we shall be defining in this chapter and the next. But in order to state, and ultimately explain, these regularities, we must first define the relatively small number of attested co-occurrences precisely. And this can only be done by the regular use of stronger, exceptionless implicational statements, rather than weaker statistical ones. These latter will always allow the offending **P* & −*Q* co-occurrences to exist, even when no **P* & −*Q* languages have been found. If such languages should subsequently turn up in a larger sample, our universals must be reformulated accordingly, or abandoned. But at each stage in the research process, it is only good methodology to define the balance between attested and nonattested co-occurrences as accurately and simply as possible, and this is our first reason for preferring nonstatistical implicational universals.

Second, where Greenberg uses statistical implications (see Sections 2.1, 2.4.1), he does so in order to make what are in essence distributional statements (Section 2.2.3), distinguishing very frequent co-occurrences such as VSO & NA, from less frequent ones, VSO & AN. But we argue in Section 4.3.3 that implicational statements of this kind are not the appropriate device with which to capture regularities of language distribution. Hence, if distributional generalizations are more adequately captured in another way, this particular motivation for statistical implications disappears.

Third, notice that nonstatistical implicational statements are also used productively in other areas of universal grammar. Consider, for example, Keenan and Comrie's (1977) implicational universals of relativization. Their hierarchy constraints are NOT statistical approximations of the form 'if a primary relativization strategy operates on oblique NPs, then with greater than chance frequency it operates on indirect and direct objects as well', or 'identical relativization strategies in a language will in general operate on a continuous segment of the Accessibility Hierarchy'. They are nonstatistical claims which account for all and only the co-occurring relativization possibilities in the languages of Keenan and Comrie's sample. Exceptions are clearly recognizable and would lead to a reformulation of their claims (and have in fact already done so: compare the 1972 and 1977 versions of their paper). The data of this chapter suggest that there is every reason for extending the rigor of Keenan and Comrie's relativization implications to suitably reformulated universals of word order. In both cases, currently available data samples indicate that some co-occurrences of linguistic phenomena are attested whereas a great many are not.

3.2 Implicational Universals for Appendix II (and the Expanded Sample)

The adjective and genitive data in Appendix II discussed in Section 2.4.4 point to the following regularity within the exceptions to Vennemann's (1972, 1974a, 1974b, 1975) NSP: If the genitive departs from the operator–operand serialization of verb and object, then so does the adjective; but the adjective may depart from this serialization without the genitive doing so. It seems, therefore, that we need to set up implicational co-occurrence statements defined on specific operator–operand constructions, in order, in effect, to predict which will depart first from Vennemann's NSP ordering. The result is universal statements more akin to Greenberg's earlier formulations than to Vennemann's reformulation.

We saw in Section 2.4.2 that unilateral 'if *P* then *Q*' statements (where *P* and *Q* are individual operator–operand constructions, e.g., NA and NG respectively) permit three language types: *P* & *Q*, −*P* & *Q* and −*P* & *Q*;

and disallow *P & Q. By contrast, Vennemann's (1972, 1974a, 1974b, 1975) NSP consists of a set of bilateral implications of the form 'if P then Q, and if Q then P', the result of which is to permit only two language types: P & Q and $-P$ & $-Q$ (e.g., NA & NG and AN & GN).

The data of Appendix II (Table 2) are compatible with various unilateral implications mentioning specific operator–operand constructions, which we shall now enumerate.

3.2.1 IMPLICATIONAL UNIVERSAL (I) SOV ⊃ (AN ⊃ GN)

Consider SOV languages. The adjective and genitive co-occurrences permit the following implication:

If the adjective precedes the noun, then the genitive precedes the noun, i.e., AN ⊃ GN.

SOV languages	(P & Q)	AN & GN:	Types 19 and 23
	($-P$ & Q)	NA & GN:	Type 24
	($-P$ & $-Q$)	NA & NG:	Types 17 and 21
	(*P & Q)	*AN & NG:	No examples (potentially Types 18 and 22)

Our first implicational universal is, therefore:

(I) If a language has SOV word order, then if the adjective precedes the noun, the genitive precedes the noun; i.e., SOV ⊃ (AN ⊃ GN).

This implication holds also for the Expanded Sample of Chapter 8: Exactly the same co-occurrences are attested with SOV, and there are still no examples of *SOV & AN & NG (Types 18 and 22). However, the discovery of OV languages that are not subject initial, such as Hixkaryana (Derbyshire 1977, 1979; Derbyshire and Pullum 1979; Pullum 1981), suggests that a more general formulation of (I) is in order. Derbyshire (1979:40–45) assigns to Hixkaryana a basic word order of OVS & Po & NA & GN, that is, Type 24 with OVS in place of SOV. Hixkaryana is clearly an OV type in the Lehmann—Vennemann sense, in that it has OV, Po, and GN orders. It also has a noun modifier co-occurrence, NA & GN, which is very productive in SOV languages, and which is ruled out in VSO (VOS and V-initial) languages.[4] Pending further study of the cross-categorial word order co-occurrences within other OVS languages, we can convert (I) into the more general (I′):

(I′) If a language has OV word order, then if the adjective precedes the noun, the genitive precedes the noun; i.e., OV ⊃ (AN ⊃ GN).

3.2.2 IMPLICATIONAL UNIVERSAL (II) VSO $\supset$ (NA $\supset$ NG)

VSO languages exhibit the exact mirror-image pattern:

If the adjective follows the noun, then the genitive follows the noun, i.e., NA $\supset$ NG.

VSO languages	(P & Q)	NA & NG:	Type 1
	($-P$ & Q)	AN & NG:	Type 2
	($-P$ & $-Q$)	AN & GN:	Types 3 and 7
	(*P & $-Q$)	*NA & GN:	No examples (potentially Types 4 and 8)

Our second implicational universal is, therefore:

(II) If a language has VSO word order, then if the adjective follows the noun, the genitive follows the noun; i.e., VSO $\supset$ (NA $\supset$ NG).

This implication also holds for the Expanded Sample of Chapter 8, in which the same co-occurrences are attested with VSO and there are still no examples of *VSO & NA & GN (Types 4 and 8).

It is not possible to collapse VSO and SVO into the more general antecedent, VO, thereby matching (I′), because all four noun modifier co-occurrences are found in SVO languages. In particular, SVO & NA & GN is attested in Types 12 and 16. However, the Expanded Sample does suggest that a generalization is being missed in (II). In addition to languages with VSO, the Expanded Sample contains languages with basic VOS (most from Keenan 1978b), and languages which are best classified as V-initial on account of the frequency of both VSO and VOS (e.g., Samoan; see Chapter 1, Note 1). These languages all have either a Type 1 (Pr & NA & NG) or a Type 2 (Pr & AN & NG) co-occurrence:

Type 1: Baure (VOS), Coeur d'Alene (VOS), Fijian (V-initial), Gilbertese (VOS), Malagasay (VOS), Samoan (V-initial), Toba Batak (VOS), Tongan (V-initial)

Type 2: Classical Mayan (VOS), Otomi (VOS), Squamish (V-initial), Tzeltal (VOS)

A further VOS language discussed by Keenan (1978b), Ineseño Chumash, straddles both types by having "doubling" on the adjective: VOS & Pr & NA/AN & GN (see Sections 1.5.1, 3.3.8).

The regularity uniting all these languages is that the verb is first in the sentence with S and O following: In the great majority, S precedes O; in some, O precedes S; and in just a handful, both orders occur with more or less equal frequency. This suggests that we generalize the verb-first classification to include all these languages, and define the noun modifier co-occurrences using (II′) rather than (II):

(II′) If a language has verb-first order, then if the adjective follows the noun, the genitive follows the noun; i.e., V-1 ⊃ (NA ⊃ NG).

The label "Verb-first" (V-1) will be used to designate this total class, with "Verb-initial" reserved for that subclass which has no basic relative order of subject and object. The three subclasses of V-1 are therefore VSO, VOS, and V-initial.

3.2.3 IMPLICATIONAL UNIVERSAL (III) PREP ⊃ (NA ⊃ NG)

The property Prep seems to have the same conditioning effect on the co-occurrence of adjective and genitive orders as does VSO(/V-first).

Prep languages:	(P & Q)	NA & NG: Types 1 and 9 and 17
	($-P$ & Q)	AN & NG: Types 2 and 10
	($-P$ & $-Q$)	AN & GN: Types 3 and 11 and 19

The co-occurrence *NA & GN (*P & $-Q$) does not occur together with Prep in both VSO and SOV languages:

*NA & GN: No examples of Types 4 and 20

However, there is one example in Appendix II of an SVO language in which Prep co-occurs with *NA & GN: Arapesh, Type 12. Bearing in mind this counterexample, we have the following (statistical) universal:

(III) If a language has Prep word order, then if the adjective follows the noun, the genitive follows the noun; i.e., Prep ⊃ (NA ⊃ NG).

Implicational Universal (III) generates interesting predictions in conjunction with Implications (I) and (II). Implication (I), SOV ⊃ (AN ⊃ GN), permits an SOV language to have AN & GN, NA & GN, or NA & NG. The first and third of these co-occurrences, but not the second, overlap with the permitted co-occurrences of the mirror-image implication NA ⊃ NG within Universal (III):

Implication (I)	*Implication (III)*
AN & GN	AN & GN
NA & GN	*NA & GN
NA & NG	NA & NG
*AN & NG	AN & NG

It follows that if a language has both SOV and Prep, then it can have neither of the starred co-occurrences (Types 18 and 20). This is what we find. The only two attested SOV & Prep co-occurrences are Types 17 and 19, which have NA & NG and AN & GN respectively.

Both Universals (II) and (III) define the same noun modifier co-occurrences (NA ⊃ NG), and so do not further restrict the possibilities for a language with both VSO and Prep.

The Expanded Sample exhibits exactly the same noun modifier co-occurrences with prepositions as Appendix II. There are no counterexamples to (III) in prepositional languages with V-first or SOV word order (i.e., Types 4 and 20). But there are now four SVO languages with the co-occurrence *Pr & NA & GN (Kaliai-Kove, Arapesh, Gitua, Karen), which confirms the statistical nature of (III). A nonstatistical version of (III) is, therefore:

(III′) If a language has Prep and any verb position other than SVO, then if the adjective follows the noun, the genitive follows the noun; i.e., Prep & −SVO ⊃ (NA ⊃ NG).

3.2.4 IMPLICATIONAL UNIVERSAL (IV) POSTP ⊃ (AN ⊃ GN)

The property Postp has the same conditioning effect on the co-occurrence of adjective and genitive orders as does SOV.

Postp languages:	(*P* & *Q*)	AN & GN: Types 7 and 15 and 23
	(−*P* & *Q*)	NA & GN: Types 16 and 24
	(−*P* & −*Q*)	NA & NG: Type 21

The co-occurrence *AN & NG (**P* & −*Q*) does not occur together with Postp in both VSO and SOV languages:

*AN & NG: No examples of Types 6 and 22

But, again, Greenberg's Appendix II shows there to be a limited number of counterexamples with *Po & AN & NG in SVO languages: Rutulian and other Daghestan languages, Type 14. The Appendix II data would lead us to set up the following statistical universal, therefore:

(IV) If a language has Postp word order, and if the adjective precedes the noun, then the genitive precedes the noun; Postp ⊃ (AN ⊃ GN).

In fact, the SVO Daghestan languages of the Caucasus should be classified as Type 15 (SVO & Po & AN & GN) rather than Type 14 (Maner Thorpe, personal communication; cf. Chapter 2, Note 2), which then removes the exceptions to (IV), making it nonstatistical. This change is reflected in the Expanded Sample, in which the nonpermitted co-occurrences (Types 6, 14, and 22) are all unattested.

Universal (IV) defines the same noun modifier co-occurrences as Universal (I), and so does not further restrict the range of possibilities in a language with both SOV and Postp. The collective predictions of Universals (II) VSO ⊃ (NA ⊃ NG) and (IV) are, however:

Implication (II)	*Implication (IV)*
NA & NG	NA & NG
AN & NG	*AN & NG
AN & GN	AN & GN
*NA & GN	NA & GN

If a language has both VSO and Postp, therefore, it cannot have either of the starred co-occurrences (Types 6 and 8). It is significant that the one attested VSO & Postp type (Type 7) has one of the two permitted orders, AN & GN.[5]

The Expanded Sample exhibits the same noun modifier co-occurrences with postpositions as Appendix II. There are no counterexamples to (IV) (i.e., no examples of Types 6, 14, and 22). Notice that the three noun modifier co-occurrences permitted by (IV) (AN & GN; NA & GN; NA & NG) are all found in SOV & Po languages (Types 23, 24, and 20), and we would predict that all three could occur in SVO & Po languages (Types 15, 16, and 13), with just two in VSO & Po languages (Types 5 and 7) because of the opposing implication (II). In fact, SVO & Po types 15 and 16 and VSO & Po type 7 are attested, but the predicted SVO & Po type 13 and VSO & Po type 5 are missing. The possible absence of 5 and 13 in a sample of this size will be accounted for by the distributional principle of Chapter 4 (Section 4.3.4).

3.2.5 SUMMARY OF THE IMPLICATIONAL UNIVERSALS FOR APPENDIX II (AND THE EXPANDED SAMPLE)

The four implicational universals derived from Appendix II are (with the excluded co-occurrence types in parentheses):

(I)	SOV ⊃ (AN ⊃ GN)	(18, 22)
(II)	VSO ⊃ (NA ⊃ NG)	(4, 8)
(III)	Prep ⊃ (NA ⊃ NG)	(4, 12, 20) statistical
(IV)	Postp ⊃ (AN ⊃ GN)	(6, 14, 22)

Alternative versions of these, compatible with both Appendix II and the Expanded Sample, and all of them exceptionless, are:

(I′)	OV ⊃ (AN ⊃ GN)	(18, 22)
(II′)	V-1 ⊃ (NA ⊃ NG)	(4, 8)
(III′)	Prep & −SVO ⊃ (NA ⊃ NG)	(4, 20)

In addition, (IV) holds without exceptions in the Expanded Sample.

We have seen that these universals define attested versus nonattested word order co-occurrences. Operating in conjunction with one another they then predict whether whole co-occurrence types will be attested or not. A co-occurrence type will not be attested if any one of its word orders violates any one of these implications. There are 9 unattested co-occurrence types in Appendix II (including Type 14, for the reasons already given): Types 4, 5, 6, 8, 13, 14, 18, 20, and 22. Seven of these (Types 4, 6, 8, 14, 18, 20, and 22) are ruled out by the exceptionless implications (I), (II), (III′), and (IV). The 2 remaining unattested types (5 and 13) are logically possible (Section 3.2.4), but will be predicted by the distributional principle of Chapter 4 to be rare or nonoccurring in a sample this size. The 15 co-occurrences that are attested are all permitted by these universals. Implications (I), (II), (III′), and (IV) therefore allow for 17 co-occurrence types to exist —the 15 that do occur, plus Types 5 and 13. Formal proof of the predictions made by these implications, using truth tables to illustrate exactly which values of *P* and *Q* etc. are permitted to co-occur, is given in Hawkins (1978).

The Expanded Sample of Chapter 8 contains the same 15 attested co-occurrence types as Appendix II, and the 9 unattested types remain unattested, with V-first replacing VSO in the classification.

A final word on the formulation of these and subsequent implicational universals. For each implicational statement there will be an infinite number of logically equivalent formulations. In general, I adopt the following convention in selecting between these: Choose that implicational statement among logically equivalent ones whose antecedent and consequent properties explicitly mention those word orders that are found in the greatest number of languages. For example, (IV) Postp ⊃ (AN ⊃ GN) is logically equivalent to Postp ⊃ (NG ⊃ NA), yet the co-occurrence Po & AN & GN is found in very many more languages than Po & NA & NG, and so the former formulation is preferred.[6]

3.3 Implicational Universals for the 30-Language Sample and the Expanded Sample

Exceptionless implicational universals are also possible for the additional word order properties of the 30-language sample. We shall concentrate on the following: adposition order within the adposition phrase; noun modifier orders within the noun phrase (demonstrative determiner, numeral, adjective, genitive, and relative clause orders in relation to the head noun); and adjective modifier orders within the adjective phrase (adverbs and NP-standard of comparison relative to the adjective head).

The typological ambivalence of SVO reduces the interest and generality of verb-based predictions of co-occurrence (cf. Section 3.2.2; also Sections 2.2.4 and 2.4.6). We shall accordingly pursue the co-occurrence requirements of the more general typological indicators: prepositions and postpositions. These word orders make significant co-occurrence predictions both in Appendix II and in the 30-language sample. Because of the limited number of languages in this latter sample, less weight can be attached to the exceptionlessness of a universal. We shall therefore draw extensively on additional languages from the Expanded Sample (Chapter 8), in order to corroborate the universals proposed. The Expanded Sample was collected primarily as a supplement to Appendix II, with particular reference to the word orders of that sample. But additional information was compiled for many entries and will be used in this context.

3.3.1 IMPLICATIONAL UNIVERSAL (V) PREP ⊃ (NDEM ⊃ NA)

The data of Appendix II led to the implication NA ⊃ NG in prepositional languages; that is, Prep ⊃ (NA ⊃ NG) (=statistical)/Prep & −SVO ⊃ (NA ⊃ NG) (=nonstatistical). This implication could also have been established on the basis of the prepositional languages of the 30-language sample:

Prep languages:	NA & NG:	Berber, Fulani, Hebrew, Italian, Malay, Maori, Masai, Swahili, Thai, Welsh, Yoruba, Zapotec
	AN & NG:	Greek, Maya, Serbian
	AN & GN:	Norwegian
	*NA & GN:	No examples

The adjective is a more unstable operator than the genitive. It departs first from the serialization pattern defined by the adposition (AN & NG), and if the genitive is preposed, the adjective must be as well (AN & GN).

It appears that the demonstrative determiner is in turn more unstable than the adjective in prepositional languages. It may be preposed while the adjective is still postposed (DemN & NA), and if the adjective is preposed, the demonstrative must be as well (DemN & AN). The following implication therefore holds:

> If the demonstrative determiner follows the noun, then the adjective follows the noun; i.e., NDem ⊃ NA.

Prepositional languages exhibit the following co-occurrences (in this and all other subsections of 3.3, the languages of Greenberg's 30-language sample will be listed first, preceded by "/", with the languages of the

Expanded Sample following — ordering is alphabetic within each sample):

Prep languages:	NDem & NA:	Berber, Fulani, Hebrew, Malay, Swahili, Thai, Welsh, Yoruba, Zapotec/ Aghem, Arosi, Bahasa Indonesian, Dyola, Easter Island, Gilbertese, Haya, Ikwere, Indonesian, Irish, Jacaltec, Kaliai-Kove, Karen, Khasi, Khmer, Luangiua, Macassarese, Marshallese, Mokilese, Niuean, Rotuman, Sundanese, Takuu, Thai, Toba Batak, Tongan, Ulithian, Vietnamese
	DemN & NA:	Italian, Maori, Masai/ Baure, Douala, French, Iraqi Arabic, Portugese, Spanish, Tunen, Xhosa
	DemN & AN:	Greek, Maya, Norwegian, Serbian/ Amharic, Bukidnon, Czech, Danish, Dutch, German, Hiligaynon, Icelandic, Kiriwinan, Maung, Old Persian, Otomi, Russian, Slovenian, Swedish
	*NDem & AN:	No examples

Our fifth implicational universal is:

(V) If a language has Prep word order, then if the demonstrative determiner follows the noun, the adjective follows the noun; i.e., Prep ⊃ (NDem ⊃ NA).

3.3.2 IMPLICATIONAL UNIVERSAL (VI) PREP ⊃ (NNUM ⊃ NA)

Numerals (i.e., quantifiers) pattern like the demonstrative determiner in relation to the adjective in prepositional languages:

If the numeral follows the noun, then the adjective follows the noun; i.e., NNum ⊃ NA.

Prep languages:	NNum & NA:	Fulani, Masai, Swahili, Yoruba/ Aghem, Crau, Douala, Dyola, Haya, Igbo, Ikwere, Kaliai-Kove, Karen, Khmer, Malagasay, Marshallese, Mokilese, Niuean, Ogbah, Rotuman, Takuu, Tongan, Tunen

NumN & NA:	Berber, Hebrew, Italian, Malay, Maori, Thai, Welsh, Zapotec/ Bahasa Indonesian, Baure, Easter Island, Fijian, French, Gilbertese, Indonesian, Iraqi Arabic, Irish, Jacaltec, Macassarese, Sre, Sundanese, Syrian Arabic, Thai, Toba Batak, Trukese, Ulithian, Vietnamese
NumN & AN:	Greek, Maya, Norwegian, Serbian/ Amharic, Czech, Danish, Dutch, German, Hiligaynon, Kampangan, Kiriwinan, Maung, Old Persian, Russian, Slovenian, Swedish, Tzeltal
*NNum & AN:	No examples

Our sixth implicational universal is:

(VI) If a language has Prep word order, then if the numeral follows the noun, the adjective follows the noun; i.e., Prep ⊃ (NNum ⊃ NA).

3.3.3 TWO FURTHER IMPLICATIONAL UNIVERSALS BY TRANSITIVITY

Given universals (III), (V), and (VI),

(III) Prep ⊃ (NA ⊃ NG) (=statistical)
(V) Prep ⊃ (NDem ⊃ NA)
(VI) Prep ⊃ (NNum ⊃ NA)

two more implicational statements can be derived by transitivity:

(VII) Prep ⊃ (NDem ⊃ NG)
(VIII) Prep ⊃ (NNum ⊃ NG)

Because of two counterexamples to each of (VII) and (VIII), both in SVO languages, these implicational universals must be considered statistical. Nonstatistical versions hold for all languages with verb positions other than SVO. In the interests of economy, the supporting languages will not be listed here in the main text.[7]

3.3.4 IMPLICATIONAL UNIVERSAL (IX) PREP $\supset$ (NG $\supset$ NREL)

The genitive is in turn a more unstable operator than the relative clause in prepositional languages. Although there is a very strong tendency for prepositional languages to have both postposed genitives and relative clauses, the genitive does depart first from the adposition serialization (GN & NRel), and if the relative clause is preposed, the genitive must be as well (GN & RelN):

> If the genitive follows the noun, then the relative clause follows the noun; i.e., NG $\supset$ NRel.

Prep languages:	NG & NRel:	Berber, Fulani, Greek, Hebrew, Italian, Malay, Maori, Masai, Maya, Serbian, Swahili, Thai, Welsh, Yoruba, Zapotec/ Aghem, Albanian, Arosi, Bahasa Indonesian, Bandem, Baure, Bikol, Bukidnon, Cebuano, Classical Mayan, Czech, Douala, Dyola, Easter Island, Fijian, French, Ge'ez, Gilbertese, Hausa, Hawaiian, Haya, Hiligaynon, Icelandic, Indonesian, Ineseño Chumash, Iraqi Arabic, Irish, Jacaltec, Kampangan, Khmer, Luangiua, Macassarese, Malagasay, Marshallese, Niuean, Otomi, Pangasinan, Persian (Tajik), Persian (Tehran), Portugese, Rotuman, Rumanian, Russian, Samoan, Scots Gaelic, Spanish, Sre, Sundanese, Syrian Arabic, Tagabili, Tagalog, Takuu, Thai, Toba Batak, Tongan, Tunen, Ulithian, Vietnamese, Xhosa, Zulu
	GN & NRel:	Norwegian/ Danish, Kaliai-Kove, Karen, Kiriwinan, Lithuanian, Maung, Nahuatl, Old Persian, Swedish
	GN & RelN:	/ Amharic
	*NG & RelN:	No examples

Our ninth implicational universal is:

(IX) If a language has Prep word order, then if the genitive follows the noun, the relative clause follows the noun; i.e., Prep ⊃ (NG ⊃ NRel).

3.3.5 THREE FURTHER IMPLICATIONAL UNIVERSALS BY TRANSITIVITY

Given Universals (III), (V), (VI), and (IX),

(III) Prep ⊃ (NA ⊃ NG) (=statistical)
(V) Prep ⊃ (NDem ⊃ NA)
(VI) Prep ⊃ (NNum ⊃ NA)
(IX) Prep ⊃ (NG ⊃ NRel)

three further implicational statements can be derived by transitivity:

(X) Prep ⊃ (NA ⊃ NRel)
(XI) Prep ⊃ (NDem ⊃ NRel)
(XII) Prep ⊃ (NNum ⊃ NRel)

These universals are all exceptionless, relative to my data.[8]

3.3.6 IMPLICATIONAL UNIVERSAL (XIII) PREP ⊃ (−SOV ⊃ NRel)

The four noun modifiers—demonstratives, numerals, adjectives, and genitives—are found postposed or preposed in prepositional languages. But only one prepositional language has preposed relative clauses: Amharic.[9] This language is also one of the relatively small number of prepositional languages with SOV. Hence, all prepositional languages with non-SOV have postnominal relatives, whereas those with SOV have either pre- or postnominal relatives. This justifies the following implicational universal:

(XIII) If a language has Prep word order, then if the verb position is not SOV, the relative clause follows the noun; i.e., Prep ⊃ (−SOV ⊃ NRel).

Universal (XIII) defines three noun-modifier co-occurrences in prepositional languages:

Prep languages:	−SOV & NRel:	All VSO and SVO languages
	SOV & NRel:	E.g., Tunen and Bandem
	SOV & RelN:	Amharic
	*−SOV & RelN:	No examples

3.3.7 THE PREPOSITIONAL NOUN MODIFIER HIERARCHY

Our major noun modifier implicational universals with Prep as ultimate antecedent, (III), (V), (VI), and (IX):

(III) Prep ⊃ (NA ⊃ NG) (=statistical)
(V) Prep ⊃ (NDem ⊃ NA)
(VI) Prep ⊃ (NNum ⊃ NA)
(IX) Prep ⊃ (NG ⊃ NRel)

can be more economically collapsed into the following single implication, which defines a Prepositional Noun Modifier Hierarchy (PrNMH):

(XIV) Prep ⊃ ((NDem ∨ NNum ⊃ NA) & (NA ⊃ NG) & (NG ⊃ NRel))

In effect, this hierarchy defines the relative instability of noun modifiers in maintaining the operator–operand serialization of the adposition phrase. The demonstrative and numeral are more unstable than the adjective, the adjective is more unstable than the genitive, and the genitive is more unstable than the relative clause. Derivatively, the demonstrative and numeral are more unstable than both the genitive and the relative clause, and the adjective is more unstable than the relative clause.

The PrNMH permits the following co-occurrences:

Prepositional Noun Modifier Hierarchy

1.	Prep & NDem & NNum & NA & NG & NRel						0 modifiers preposed: N_1
2a.	Prep	DemN	NNum	NA	NG	NRel	1 modifier preposed: N_2
2b.	Prep	NDem	NumN	NA	NG	NRel	
3.	Prep	DemN	NumN	NA	NG	NRel	2 modifiers preposed: N_3
4.	Prep	DemN	NumN	AN	NG	NRel	3 modifiers preposed: N_4
5.	Prep	DemN	NumN	AN	GN	NRel	4 modifiers preposed: N_5
6.	Prep	DemN	NumN	AN	GN	RelN	5 modifiers preposed: N_6

Out of the $2^5 = 32$ mathematically possible co-occurrences of these five noun modifiers, just 7 are claimed to be possible on the basis of the attested co-occurrences in Greenberg's and my own data. This hierarchy asserts that the preposing of noun modifiers in prepositional modifiers follows a fixed and predictable pattern: first the demonstrative or numeral; then both; then the adjective; then the genitive; and finally the relative clause. And as these modifiers are progressively preposed, the position of the noun within the noun phrase moves further to the right: second position (N_2); third position (N_3); fourth position (N_4); etc.

3.3.8 DOUBLING AND THE PRNMH

The PrNMH of Section 3.3.7 was set up using basic or unique operator–operand orders within the noun phrase in prepositional languages. But we observed in Section 1.5.1 that some noun modifiers in various languages exhibit variant orders, or doubling. One interesting feature of noun modifier doubling in relation to the PrNMH is that it most often involves adjacent subtypes. French, with its DemN & NumN & AN/NA & NG & NRel co-occurrence, combines Subtypes 3 and 4 (DemN & NumN & NA & NG & NRel and DemN & NumN & AN & NG & NRel, respectively). English, with DemN & NumN & AN & GN/NG & NRel, combines Subtypes 4 and 5. And German, with DemN & NumN & AN & GN/NG & RelN/NRel, combines Subtypes 4, 5, and 6.

It is thought provoking to reflect on the causes of such adjacency. These doubling languages are combining all and only the word orders of two whole subtypes in combination; that is, all and only the word orders that occur as unique operator–operand orders in two or more prepositional languages of the relevant subtypes. It transpires that the only way in which co-occurrences involving doubling can match all and only the word orders of a plurality of subtypes in combination is if these subtypes are adjacent on the hierarchy.

For example, imagine the following language type, with doubling on the genitive: DemN & NumN & NA & GN/NG & NRel. This co-occurrence contains all the word orders of Subtype 3 (DemN & NumN & NA & NG & NRel), plus the GN order of Subtypes 5 and 6. However, it does not combine Subtype 3 with 5 or 6: Subtype 5 has AN where Subtype 3 has NA; and Subtype 6 has AN & RelN where Subtype 3 has NA & NRel. Hence, the co-occurrence DemN & NumN & NA & GN/NG & NRel corresponds to no two unique order subtypes in combination. And this will always occur when the potentially available subtypes for some doubling co-occurrence are nonadjacent (e.g., 3 & 5, 3 & 6), rather than adjacent (2 & 3, 3 & 4, etc.).

A consequence of this adjacency of doubling subtypes is, in turn, that doublets occur at the transition points between preposed and postposed modifiers on the hierarchy: All the operators to the left of the doubling operator on the PrNMH in French, English, and German are preposed, and all those to the right are postposed. Thus, in the adjacent subtypes 3 and 4 (DemN & NumN & AN/NA & NG & NRel) the adjective is the transition point between the preposed demonstrative and numeral on the one hand, and the postposed genitive and relative clause on the other. In the adjacent subtypes 4 and 5 (DemN & NumN & AN & GN/NG & NRel) the genitive is the transition point between the preposed demonstrative, numeral, and adjective, and the postposed relative clause, and so on.

Such adjacency in doubling is a natural diachronic reflex of the Doubling Acquisition Hypothesis (DAH) of Chapter 5, which claims that the historical acquisition of doublets in a language is predictable from the implicational universals defined on basic word orders across languages. For example, if a Subtype 4 language (DemN & NumN & AN & NG & NRel) is going to acquire a doublet on one operator order, it is predicted to be the adjective or genitive, rather than the demonstrative, numeral, or relative clause. If it introduces RelN at the same time that it has NG, it will be innovating a co-occurrence at variance with Universal (IX) Prep ⊃ (NG ⊃ NRel). And if it introduces NDem or NNum at the same time that it has AN, it will be innovating co-occurrences at variance with (V) Prep ⊃ (NDem ⊃ NA) and (VI) Prep ⊃ (NNum ⊃ NA). But by innovating NA alongside AN, or GN alongside NG, no universal is being offended. A DemN & NumN & AN/NA & NG & NRel co-occurrence is compatible with all universals, as is DemN & NumN & AN & GN/NG & NRel (cf. Section 3.3.7). Thus, by having doubling along adjacent and continuous subtypes of the PrNHM, the innovated minority word orders are most compatible with the implicational universals for basic word orders (see Chapter 5).

However, although adjacency in doubling for languages in a synchronic sample is in general expected, it is not strictly a NECESSARY consequence of the DAH, on account of an important caveat in DAH's predictions (see Chapter 5, Note 1). The hypothesis makes predictions for the relative timing of the ACQUISITION of word orders in diachrony, but not for their LOSS. It is claimed that various idiosyncratic and language-particular factors can retard the loss of some word order, whereas acquisition is deeply determined by the typological state of a language at some particular stage, in conjunction with language universals. It is therefore logically possible for languages in a synchronic sample to have doublets that do not exemplify adjacent subtypes of the PrNHM. One example would appear to be Welsh, which combines Subtypes 2b (NDem & NumN & NA & NG & NRel) with some AN doublets, even though Prep ⊃ (AN ⊃ DemN).

Some interesting consequences of such nonadjacent doubling for historical reconstruction follow from this account: namely, such word order co-occurrences can arise only through the reduction in productivity of some earlier more productive word order, and not through a relatively recent process of acquisition. In these cases it is possible to infer which word order doublet is the historical relic, and this can shed light on the earlier typological state of the language (cf. the reconstruction of doubling innovations) [RDI] (in Section 7.4).

I have not undertaken an in-depth study of the proportion of doubling languages which occupy adjacent subtypes of the PrNMH compared to those which do not. But impressionistically the majority do. This preponderance is diachronically natural by the DAH, as the minority doubling structures then obey all the implications which hold for basic word orders synchronically, and which are required to hold diachronically for incoming minority word orders as well. And the extent to which a language can retard the loss of some earlier minority word order which is at variance with the implications for the corresponding basic word orders is, it seems, limited. In all cases of doubling there are, of course, strict synchronic predictions regarding which of two doublets is basic. For example, if there is doubling on the genitive in a language with exclusive NA order, then NG rather than GN must be basic [on account of (III) Prep $\supset$ (NA $\supset$ NG)].

I have the following examples in my data of doubling along adjacent subtypes of PrNMH:

1 + 2a:	Malagasay, Ogbah
1 + 2b:	Hebrew, Malay, Thai
1 + 2a + 2b:	Samoan
2a + 3:	Iraqi Arabic
3 + 4:	French, Ineseño Chumash, Italian, Pangasinan
2a + 3 + 4:	Portugese, Spanish
3 + 4 + 5:	Old Persian
4 + 5:	Danish, Dutch, English, Slovenian, Swedish
4 + 5 + 6:	German

There are some linguists who would argue that the existence of variant word orders in some languages undermines the whole attempt to set up word order universals. We have already argued against this assumption in Section 1.5.1. The approach adopted here is to first set up exceptionless implicational universals for the clear cases; that is, cases where a language has only one order for some operator – operand pairs, or where basicness is not an issue (e.g., German postnominal relative clauses). Doubling can then be shown to be a natural process of linguistic change, in the gradual shift from one word order to another. By setting up precise synchronic universals for the clear cases, we can then make equally precise predictions for the acquisition of minority doublets (cf. DAH), and for the further development of these into more frequent and eventually basic or exclusive orders (cf. the Frequency Increase Hypothesis). The apparent disorder posed by word order variants is thereby subjected to precise analysis by separating clear from less clear cases, and synchronic from diachronic predictions.

3.3.9 IMPLICATIONAL UNIVERSAL (XV) POSTP ⊃ (DEMN ⊃ GN)

We now consider the universals that hold for postpositional languages. In Section 3.2.4 we saw evidence from Appendix II for an exceptionless universal, (IV) Postp ⊃ (AN ⊃ GN), matching (III) Prep ⊃ (NA ⊃ NG). In both cases, the adjective is more unstable than the genitive. It can depart from the adposition serialization before the genitive, and if the genitive departs, the adjective must as well.

This mirror-image pattern between prepositional and postpositional languages extends to universals involving demonstrative determiner and numeral in relation to the genitive. The demonstrative can be postposed while the genitive is still preposed (NDem & GN). The following implication therefore holds for postpositional languages:

> If the demonstrative determiner precedes the noun, then the genitive precedes the noun; i.e., DemN ⊃ GN.

Because postpositional languages are predominantly prespecifying (i.e., operator before operand), it is more perspicuous to reformulate these noun modifier implications using preposed word orders—in this way the implication explicitly mentions the most common noun modifier orders in postpositional languages, and it is easier to see which noun modifier departs first from the serialization of the adposition (see Section 3.2.5 and Note 6).

Postpositional languages exhibit the following co-occurrences (as in previous subsections, the languages of Greenberg's 30-language sample are given first, with the languages of the Expanded Sample following):

Postp languages:	DemN & GN:	Burmese, Burushaski, Chibcha, Finnish, Guarani, Hindi, Japanese, Kannada, Nubian, Quechua, Turkish/ Adyge, Ainu, Bengali, Brahui, Evenki, Fore, Hua, Hungarian, Ijo, Izon, Kabardian, Kokama, Laz, Modern Armenian, Motu, numerous Mongol languages, numerous N.E. Caucasian languages, Piro, Punjabi, Ryukyuan, Svan, Tamil, Ubykh, Usarufa, Warao, Wedauan, Yaqui
	NDem & GN:	Basque, Loritja, Songhai/ Biloxi, Daga, Diegueño, Gugáda, Havasupai, Lisu, Mojave, Paipai, Selepet,

		Siroi, Twi, Walapai, Waskia, Yuma, Zarma-Songhai
	NDem & NG:	No examples
	*DemN & NG:	No examples

There are no examples of the permitted co-occurrence NDem & NG in my data. Its absence has a distributional cause (see Chapter 4), and reflects the still relatively small number of postpositional languages on which I have relevant data. Thus NDem & NG is predicted to be the least frequent of the three permitted co-occurrences by far.

Our fifteenth universal is:

(XV) If a language has Postp word order, then if the demonstrative precedes the noun, the genitive precedes the noun; i.e., Postp ⊃ (DemN ⊃ GN).

3.3.10 IMPLICATIONAL UNIVERSAL (XVI) POSTP ⊃ (NUMN ⊃ GN)

Numerals pattern just like the demonstrative determiner in postpositional languages:

If the numeral precedes the noun, then the genitive precedes the noun; i.e., NumN ⊃ GN.

Postpositional languages exhibit the following co-occurrences:

Postp languages:	NumN & GN:	Basque, Burmese, Burushaski, Finnish, Hindi, Japanese, Kannada, Quechua, Turkish/ Ainu, Bengali, Fore, Hua, Hixkaryana, Hungarian, Ijo, Izon, Kokama, Laz, Manchu, numerous Mongol languages, numerous N.E. Caucasian languages, Piro, Punjabi, Ryukyuan, Svan, Ubykh, Usarufa, Waskia, Yaqui
	NNum & GN:	Chibcha, Loritja, Nubian, Songhai/ Adyge, Assiniboine, Biloxi, Diegueño, Gugada, Havasupai, Kabardian, Lisu, Mojave, Paipai, Selepet, Walapai, Warao, Yuma, Zarma-Songhai
	NNum & NG:	No examples
	*NumN & NG:	No examples

Again, there are no examples of the third permitted co-occurrence, NNum & NG, for distributional reasons.

Our sixteenth implicational universal is, therefore:

(XVI) If a language has Postp word order, then if the numeral precedes the noun, the genitive precedes the noun; i.e., Postp ⊃ (NumN ⊃ GN).

3.3.11 IMPLICATIONAL UNIVERSAL (V′) NDEM ⊃ NA

The relative instability of demonstratives and numerals compared to adjectives in prepositional languages [cf. (V) Prep ⊃ (NDem ⊃ NA) and (VI) Prep ⊃ (NNum ⊃ NA)] does not appear to extend to postpositional languages. Consider demonstratives. Instead of the expected mirror-image implication, Postp ⊃ (DemN ⊃ AN), we find that postpositional languages obey the same implicational regularity as prepositional languages: NDem ⊃ NA. And because of the opposite serialization of the adposition, it is now the adjective that is more unstable. It can be postposed while the demonstrative is still preposed (Po & NA & DemN), and if the demonstrative is postposed, the adjective must be as well (Po & NA & NDem); that is,

If the adjective precedes the noun, then the demonstrative determiner precedes the noun; i.e., AN ⊃ DemN (equivalently: NDem ⊃ NA).

Postp languages:

AN & DemN: Burushaski, Finnish, Hindi, Japanese, Kannada, Quechua, Turkish/ Ainu, Bengali, Brahui, Evenki, Fore, Hua, Hungarian, Ijo, Izon, Manchu, Modern Armenian, numerous Mongol languages, numerous N.E. Caucasian languages, Piro, Punjabi, Ryukyuan, Svan, Tamil, Usarufa, Yaqui

NA & DemN: Burmese, Chibcha, Guarani, Nubian/ Adyge, Kabardian, Kokama, Motu, Ubykh, Warao, Wedauan

NA & NDem: Basque, Loritja, Songhai/ Biloxi, Daga, Diegueño, Gugada, Havasupai, Lisu, Maranungku, Mojave, Paipai, Selepet, Twi, Walapai, Waskia, Yuma

*AN & NDem: No examples

We can therefore generalize Implicational Universal (V) to cover both postpositional and prepositional languages, in an exceptionless manner:

(V′) If a language has noun before demonstrative, then it has noun before adjective; i.e., NDem ⊃ NA (equivalently: AN ⊃ DemN).

3.3.12 IMPLICATIONAL UNIVERSAL (VI′) NNUM ⊃ NA

Numerals and adjectives in postpositional languages pattern just like demonstratives and adjectives and are compatible with the following implication:

If the adjective precedes the noun, then the numeral precedes the noun; i.e., AN ⊃ NumN (equivalently: NNum ⊃ NA).

Postp languages:	AN & NumN:	Burushaski, Finnish, Hindi, Japanese, Kannada, Quechua, Turkish/ Ainu, Bengali, Fore, Hua, Hungarian, Ijo, Izon, Laz, Manchu, numerous Mongol languages, numerous N.E. Caucasian languages, Piro, Punjabi, Ryukyuan, Svan, Usarufa, Yaqui
	NA & NumN:	Basque, Burmese/ Hixkaryana, Kokama, Ubykh
	NA & NNum:	Chibcha, Loritja, Nubian, Songhai/ Adyge, Assiniboine, Biloxi, Diegueño, Gugada, Havasupai, Kabardian, Lisu, Mojave, Paipai, Selepet, Tsang, Walapai, Warao, Waskia, Yuma, Zarma-Songhai
	*AN & NNum:	No examples

We can therefore generalize Universal (VI) Prep ⊃ (NNum ⊃ NA) to cover both postpositional and prepositional languages, exceptionlessly:

(VI′) If a language has noun before numeral, then it has noun before adjective; i.e., NNum ⊃ NA (equivalently: AN ⊃ NumN).

3.3.13 IMPLICATIONAL UNIVERSAL (IX′) NG ⊃ NREL

Genitive and relative clause co-occurrences in prepositional languages were compatible with Universal (IX) Prep ⊃ (NG ⊃ NRel). As with the NDem ⊃ NA and NNum ⊃ NA implications of the previous subsections, the implication NG ⊃ NRel holds also for postpositional languages. The relative clause is therefore a more unstable operator in these languages than the genitive. It can be postposed while the genitive is still preposed (Po & GN & NRel), and if the genitive is postposed, the relative clause must be as well; that is,

If the relative clause precedes the noun, then the genitive precedes the noun; i.e., RelN ⊃ GN (equivalently: NG ⊃ NRel).

Postp languages:	RelN & GN:	Basque, Burmese, Burushaski, Chibcha, Japanese, Kannada, Turkish/ Ainu, Fore, Hua, Manchu, numerous Mongol languages, Motu, numerous N.E. Caucasian languages, Ryukyuan, Tsang
	NRel & GN:	Finnish, Guarani, Hindi, Quechua, Songhai/ Adyge, Bengali, Brahui, Daga, Diegueño, Ewe, Gruzin, Hungarian, Kokama, Modern Armenian, Mojave, Piro, Selepet, Svan, Tocharian, Twi, Wara, Wedauan, West Greenlandic Eskimo, Yaqui, Zarma-Songhai
	NRel & NG:	/ Galla, Sumerian, Walbiri
	*RelN & NG:	No examples

We can therefore generalize Universal (IX) to cover both language types exceptionlessly, as follows:

(IX′) If a language has noun before genitive, then it has noun before relative clause; i.e., NG ⊃ NRel (equivalently: RelN ⊃ GN).

3.3.14 IMPLICATIONAL UNIVERSAL (XI′) NDEM ⊃ NREL

Postpositional languages also obey a similar co-occurrence regularity to prepositional languages with respect to demonstratives and relative clauses [recall (XI) Prep ⊃ (NDem ⊃ NRel)]. And because of the opposite serialization of the adposition, it is now the relative clause that is more unstable than the demonstrative.

Postpositional languages exhibit the following co-occurrences:

Postp languages:	RelN & DemN:	Burmese, Burushaski, Chibcha, Japanese, Kannada, Turkish/ Ainu, Brahui, Fore, Hua, Man-

		chu, numerous Mongol languages, Motu, numerous N.E. Caucasian languages, Ryukyuan, Tsang
	NRel & DemN:	Finnish, Guarani, Hindi, Quechua/ Adyge, Bengali, Gruzin, Hungarian, Kokama, Modern Armenian, Piro, Wedauan, Yaqui
	NRel & NDem:	Songhai/ Daga, Diegueño, Mojave, Selepet, Twi, Zarma-Songhai
	*RelN & NDem:	Basque/

These co-occurrences are compatible with:

> If the relative clause precedes the noun, then the demonstrative determiner precedes the noun; i.e., RelN ⊃ DemN (which is logically equivalent to NDem ⊃ NRel).

Notice that there is one exceptional language with the forbidden co-occurrence RelN & NDem, Basque. Because of this language, the implication RelN ⊃ DemN must be classified as statistical. Alternatively, we could simply assert that all four co-occurrences are possible in postpositional languages; that is, Postp ⊃ ((RelN ∨ NRel) & (DemN ∨ NDem)). But as all postpositional languages except Basque obey the same implication as all prepositional languages, I prefer, pending any further counterexamples, to generalize Implicational Universal (XI) to cover postpositional languages as well, as follows:

> (XI′) If a language has noun before demonstrative, then it has noun before relative clause; i.e., NDem ⊃ NRel (equivalently: RelN ⊃ DemN). (statistical)

3.3.15 IMPLICATIONAL UNIVERSAL (XII′) NNUM ⊃ NREL

Numerals pattern just like demonstratives in postpositional languages:

> If the relative clause precedes the noun, then the numeral precedes the noun; i.e., RelN ⊃ NumN (equivalently: NNum ⊃ NRel).

Postp languages:	RelN & NumN:	Basque, Burmese, Burushaski, Japanese, Kannada, Turkish/ Ainu, Fore, Hua, Manchu, nu-

merous Mongol languages, numerous N.E. Caucasian languages, Ryukyuan

NRel & NumN: Finnish, Hindi, Quechua/ Bengali, Brahui, Gruzin, Hungarian, Kokama, Piro, Svan, Yaqui

NRel & NNum: Songhai/ Adyge, Diegueño, Mojave, Selepet, Zarma-Songhai

*RelN & NNum: Chibcha/ Tsang

Again, the relative clause is the more unstable operator. And again, there is just one exception with *RelN & NNum in the 30-language sample, Chibcha, and one also in the Expanded Sample. Rather than allowing for all four noun modifier possibilities [i.e., Postp ⊃ ((RelN ∨ NRel) & (NumN ∨ NNum))], I prefer to generalize Implicational Universal (XII) Prep ⊃ (NNum ⊃ NRel) to cover postpositional languages as well:

(XII′) If a language has noun before numeral, then it has noun before relative clause; i.e., NNum ⊃ NRel (equivalently: RelN ⊃ NumN). (statistical)

3.3.16 IMPLICATIONAL UNIVERSAL (XVII) POSTP ⊃ ((AN ∨ NA) & (RELN ∨ NREL))

Adjective and relative clause co-occurrences in prepositional languages were compatible with Universal (X) Prep ⊃ (NA ⊃ NRel). In postpositional languages no such implication is possible, as all four co-occurrences are productively attested:

Postp languages:

AN & RelN: Japanese, Kannada, Turkish/ Ainu, Fore, Hua, Manchu, numerous Mongol languages, numerous N.E. Caucasian languages, Ryukyuan

NA & RelN: Basque, Burmese, Chibcha, Guarani/ Motu, Tsang

NA & NRel: Songhai/ Adyge, Diegueño, Ewe, Galla, Kokama, Mojave, Selepet, Sumerian, Twi, Walbiri, Wara, Wedauan, Zarma-Songhai

AN & NRel: Burushaski, Finnish, Hindi, Quechua/ Bengali, Brahui, Gruzin, Hungarian, Modern Armenian, Piro, Svan, Yaqui

The result is the following (non-)universal:

(XVII) If a language has Postp word order, then it has either noun before adjective or adjective before noun, and either relative clause before noun or noun before relative clause; i.e., Postp ⊃ ((AN ∨ NA) & (RelN ∨ NRel)).

3.3.17 THE POSTPOSITIONAL NOUN MODIFIER HIERARCHY

The noun modifier implications of relevance to postpositional languages are:

(IV) Postp ⊃ (AN ⊃ GN)
(XV) Postp ⊃ (DemN ⊃ GN)
(XVI) Postp ⊃ (NumN ⊃ GN)

(V′) NDem ⊃ NA
(VI′) NNum ⊃ NA
(IX′) NG ⊃ NRel

(XI′) NDem ⊃ NRel (statistical)
(XII′) NNum ⊃ NRel (statistical)

(XVII) Postp ⊃ ((AN ∨ NA) & (RelN ∨ NRel))

These can all be collapsed into the following Postpositional Noun Modifier Hierarchy (PoNMH):

(XVIII) Postp ⊃ ((AN ∨ RelN ⊃ DemN & NumN) & (DemN ∨ NumN ⊃ GN))

The PoNMH defines the following permissible co-occurrences:

Postpositional Noun Modifier Hierarchy

1.	Postp & AN & RelN & DemN & NumN & GN						0 modifiers postposed:	N_6
2a.	Postp	NA	RelN	DemN	NumN	GN	1 modifier postposed:	N_5
2b.	Postp	AN	NRel	DemN	NumN	GN		
3.	Postp	NA	NRel	DemN	NumN	GN	2 modifiers postposed:	N_4
4a.	Postp	NA	NRel	NDem	NumN	GN	3 modifiers postposed:	N_3
4b.	Postp	NA	NRel	DemN	NNum	GN		
5.	Postp	NA	NRel	NDem	NNum	GN	4 modifiers postposed:	N_2
6.	Postp	NA	NRel	NDem	NNum	NG	5 modifiers postposed:	N_1

Just 8 of the $2^5 = 32$ mathematically possible co-occurrences are claimed to be possible in postpositional languages. Of these 8 co-occurrences, 3 overlap with those permitted in prepositional languages (Subtypes 1, 2b, and 6 of the PoNMH correspond to Subtypes 6, 5, and 1 of the PrNMH respectively). The other 5 offend at least one of the noun modifier implications for prepositional languages [e.g., Prep ⊃ (NA ⊃ NG)]. As the noun modifiers are progressively postposed in the PoNMH, the noun moves correspondingly forward in the noun phrase.

3.3.18 DOUBLING AND THE PONMH

As in prepositional languages (Section 3.3.8), doubling in postpositional languages frequently involves adjacent subtypes of the PoNMH. I have the following examples in my data of adjacent doubling:

1 + 2a: Burmese, Piro
1 + 2b: Bengali, Evenki, Finnish, Hindi, Quechua, Tamil
2b + 3: Kokama
3 + 4b: Adyge, Guarani

3.3.19 IMPLICATIONAL UNIVERSAL (XIX) PREP ⊃ (ADJADV ⊃ AMS)

We propose now two universals involving the adjective phrase. The data come exclusively from Greenberg's 30-language sample, and are not as extensive as I would like. Nonetheless, a pattern emerges in prepositional and postpositional languages which is reminiscent of Universals (III) Prep ⊃ (NA ⊃ NG) and (IV) Postp ⊃ (AN ⊃ GN). Just as the adjective is a more unstable operator than the NP-dominating genitive within the noun phrase, so the adverb is more unstable than the NP-dominating standard of comparison within the adjective phrase. That is, the ordering which Vennemann's NSP would predict for the adjective phrase in a prepositional language is the adjective (as head of phrase, or operand) before both adverb and standard of comparison. This ordering is frequently occurring, but one also finds the adverb preposed while the standard of comparison is still postposed, giving, for example, English *deliciously tasty* (AdvAdj) and *bigger than you* (AdjMS). This suggests the implication:

> If the adverb follows the adjective within the adjective phrase, then the standard of comparison follows the adjective; i.e., AdjAdv ⊃ AMS.

Prep languages:	AdjAdv & AMS:	Fulani, Hebrew, Malay, Swahili, Thai, Zapotec
	AdvAdj & AMS:	Greek, Italian, Norwegian, Serbian
	AdvAdj & SMA:	No examples
	*AdjAdv & SMA:	No examples

I would attribute the absence of the AdvAdj & SMA co-occurrence to distributional factors. The two attested co-occurrences show clearly that the adverb is the more unstable operator, even though we cannot show that the preposing of the standard of comparison requires that the adverb must be preposed as well. Pending more data, I propose:

(XIX) If a language has Prep word order, then if the adverb follows the adjective within the adjective phrase, the standard of comparison follows the adjective; i.e., Prep ⊃ (AdjAdv ⊃ AMS).

3.3.20 IMPLICATIONAL UNIVERSAL (XX) POSTP ⊃ (ADVADJ ⊃ SMA)

Postpositional languages are compatible with the mirror-image implication:

If the adverb precedes the adjective within the adjective phrase, then the standard of comparison precedes the adjective; i.e., AdvAdj ⊃ SMA.

Postp languages:	AdvAdj & SMA:	Basque, Burmese, Burushaski, Chibcha, Hindi, Japanese, Kannada, Turkish
	AdjAdv & SMA:	Guarani
	AdjAdv & AMS:	No examples
	*AdvAdj & AMS:	No examples

The adverb can be postposed while the standard of comparison is still preposed (AdjAdv & SMA), although we do not have enough data to show that the postposing of the standard of comparison necessitates the postposing of the adverb. The same relative stability pattern does emerge as in (XIX), however. The third permitted co-occurrence (AdjAdv & AMS) is predicted to be the least frequent of the three in Section 4.3.3.

Our twentieth universal is:

(XX) If a language has Postp word order, then if the adverb precedes the adjective within the adjective phrase, the standard of comparison precedes the adjective; i.e., Postp ⊃ (AdvAdj ⊃ SMA).

3.4 Explaining the Implicational Universals

The purpose of this section is to propose some generalizations that bring us closer to an explanation of the two noun modifier hierarchies of Section 3.3.

The noun modifier co-occurrences of our data clearly obey strict regularities: The majority of our universals are exceptionless; and the distributional differences between the attested co-occurrence types will be shown in the next chapter to be subject to further correct predictions. What requires immediate explanation is why these implications should be allowing and disallowing the respective co-occurrences that they do, and why prepositional and postpositional languages should differ in some respects, yet agree in others.

3.4.1 AN INITIAL EXPLANATION

3.4.1.1 Heaviness

Consider first the PrNMH:

(XIV) Prep ⊃ ((NDem ∨ NNum ⊃ NA) & (NA ⊃ NG) & (NG ⊃ NRel))

The component implications of this hierarchy—(III) Prep ⊃ (NA ⊃ NG), etc. (Section 3.3.7)—all have the logical form $P \supset (Q \supset R)$, where P, Q, and R are consistently serialized operator–operand structures in Vennemann's (NSP) sense; P represents prepositions; and Q and R are word orders with one and the same operand (noun). These formulations permit languages with P to co-occur with the following values of Q and R:

$P \mathbin{\&} Q \mathbin{\&} R$
$P \mathbin{\&} -Q \mathbin{\&} R$
$P \mathbin{\&} -Q \mathbin{\&} -R$
$*P \mathbin{\&} Q \mathbin{\&} -R$

The property P does not impose its own serialization pattern on Q and R necessarily. It defines possible and impossible co-occurrences. Both the operators upon the noun may be consistent with the serialization of P, or they may both be inconsistent with it. But, if just one of these operators departs from P's serialization, it is always Q (e.g., the adjective) and not R (the genitive).

There is a simple pattern to these departures from the serialization of the preposition: First the demonstrative and/or numeral are preposed; then the adjective; then the genitive; and finally the relative clause (recall Section 3.3.7). And as these preposings occur, there is a corresponding decline in language frequencies (cf. Chapter 4).

Intuitively, prepositional languages are placing "lighter" constituents to the left of the head, and "heavier" ones to the right. Demonstrative and numeral determiners are typically morphologically shorter than descriptive adjectives. The adjective, which consists of a single descriptive predicate, is morphologically and syntactically shorter than the genitive, which consists of a whole NP or PP, in conjunction often with a genitive marker. And the NP/PP structure of the genitive is morphologically and syntactically shorter than the relative clause, which comprises a whole S, including a verb, its NP and PP arguments, sentential complements, etc.

More precisely, I propose the following Heaviness Hierarchy:

HEAVINESS HIERARCHY (HH)

$$\text{Rel} \geqslant \text{Gen} \geqslant \text{Adj} \geqslant \begin{Bmatrix}\text{Dem}\\ \text{Num}\end{Bmatrix}$$

where "⩾" means 'greater than, or equal to, in heaviness'.

Relative heaviness is a composite notion defined in terms of (at least) the following four factors:

1. *Length and quantity of morphemes:* The morphological structure of descriptive adjectives typically comprises syllabically longer morphemes and more compounding of bound and free morphemes than that of demonstrative determiners; and in both of these respects descriptive adjectives are either greater than or equal to numerals.
2. *Quantity of words:* Relative clauses typically contain more words than genitives; genitives typically contain more than single-word adjectives and determiners.
3. *Syntactic depth of branching nodes:* The number of branching nodes is typically greater in a relative S than in a genitive NP/PP; the number is also typically greater in a genitive construction than in single-word descriptive adjectives and determiners.
4. *Inclusion of dominated constituents:* A relative S may dominate a genitive NP/PP, and vice versa (i.e., a relative S may contain a genitive NP/PP, and a genitive may contain a relative S); Rel and Gen may both dominate adjectives and demonstrative/numeral determiners, though not vice versa; and Adj and Dem/Num cannot dominate one another; hence, given a constituent *A* on the left of the HH, and a constituent *B* to its right, the ability of *A* to dominate *B* is greater than, or equal to, that of *B* to dominate *A*.

For one constituent to be considered "heavier" than another, one or more of these factors must be capable of imposing an ordering between them.

We now incorporate HH into a Heaviness Serialization Principle, as follows:

HEAVINESS SERIALIZATION PRINCIPLE (HSP)

$$\text{Rel} \geqslant_{R} \text{Gen} \geqslant_{R} \text{Adj} \geqslant_{R} \begin{Bmatrix}\text{Dem}\\ \text{Num}\end{Bmatrix}$$

where "$\geqslant_R$" means 'exhibits more or equal rightward positioning relative to the head noun across languages'. That is, heavier noun modifiers occur to the right.

It will be apparent that prepositional languages are systematically positioning their lighter noun modifiers to the left, and their heavier ones to the right. In effect, all the implications of PrNMH follow from HSP.

The HSP would appear to be just part of a much more general universal regularity involving heavy constituents. Consider Greenberg's (1966) Universal (25)—If the pronominal object follows the verb, so does the nominal object. This allows for languages with V + ProO & V + NomO (e.g., English: *I see her* & *I see the woman*); ProO + V & V + NomO (e.g., French); and ProO + V & NomO + V (e.g., Japanese); but not *V + ProO & NomO + V. The excluded co-occurrence is precisely the one in which the shorter and lighter pronominal object follows the verb, while the heavier nominal object precedes. Where there is a mixed order, the lighter pronominal object must precede (French: *je la vois* 'I see her' & *je vois la femme* 'I see the woman').

The rightward preference for heavy constituents can also be seen in rules such as English Complex/Heavy NP Shift (*Joe gave to Berta a book that was about the skinning of cats in Alberta between 1898 and 1901;* see Ross 1967, Kimball 1973, Postal 1974). And it is evident in the frequent clause-final position of sentential complements across languages, documented in Grosu and Thompson (1977) and Dryer (1980) (see Section 3.4.2.1).

The different orderings of adjectives and adjective phrase modifiers in English (*the yellow book / the book yellow with age;* see C. Smith 1961) are also in accordance with our "heaviness to the right" principle, and they suggest some interesting possible extensions of the HSP, along two dimensions. First, it should be possible to supplement the HSP with further categories; for example, adjective phrases may in general exhibit more or equal rightward positioning compared to single adjectives across languages. Second, where the categories of the HSP are divisible into subcategories at least some of which occur on opposite sides of the head (i.e., there is noun modifier doubling for these categories), the orderings should be in accordance with the "heaviness to the right" principle, where differences in heaviness exist (remember that we are still considering prepositional languages only, for reasons to be discussed in Section 3.4.1.2).

Different subtypes of relative clauses provide the most obvious data with which to test this doubling prediction, and the evidence of Modern German and Ancient Greek suggest that it may be correct. The prenominal relative clauses of German are limited with regard to the number and nature of modifiers of the verb, embedding possibilities, and positions relativized on, in a way that postnominal relatives are not (cf. Weber 1971). The result is heavier postnominal than prenominal relatives according to the grammatical criteria listed here (quantity of words, syntactic depth of branching nodes, etc.). A similar situation obtains for pre- and postposed relatives in Ancient Greek (Albert Rijksbaron, personal communication and 1981). Finnish (which is postpositional) also has a more restricted prenominal strategy compared with its postnominal relative clauses (Karlsson 1972).

3.4.1.2 Mobility

Despite the apparent generality of the HSP, it cannot be the only principle operating in this area. If it were, prepositional and postpositional languages would always pattern alike. Instead, they agree with respect to some implications, and disagree with respect to others. Recall the PoNMH:

(XVIII) Postp ⊃ ((AN ∨ RelN ⊃ DemN & NumN) & (DemN ∨ NumN ⊃ GN))

Postpositional languages include mirror-image co-occurrences to prepositional languages in those cases where the genitive is the ultimate consequent property:

(III)	Prep	⊃ (NA ⊃ NG)	permits Prep & *A*N & N*G*
(VII)	Prep	⊃ (NDem ⊃ NG)	permits Prep & *Dem*N & N*G*
(VIII)	Prep	⊃ (NNum ⊃ NG)	permits Prep & *Num*N & N*G*
(IV)	Postp	⊃ (AN ⊃ GN)	permits Postp & N*A* & *G*N
(XV)	Postp	⊃ (DemN ⊃ GN)	permits Postp & N*Dem* & *G*N
(XVI)	Postp	⊃ (NumN ⊃ GN)	permits Postp & N*Num* & *G*N

All these co-occurrences with Postp are at variance with the HSP: The lighter constituent occurs to the right, and the heavier one to the left. For adjective and relative clause co-occurrences, prepositional languages obey Universal (X), which permits three co-occurrences in accordance with the HSP, whereas all four co-occurrences are possible in postpositional languages, including Postp & N*A* & *Rel*N (e.g., Basque), which is at variance with the HSP:

(X) Prep ⊃ (NA ⊃ NRel)
(XVII) Postp ⊃ ((AN ∨ NA) & (RelN ∨ NRel))

Universals (XI′) and (XII′) are nonstatistical for prepositional languages, but statistical for postpositional languages:

(XI′) NDem ⊃ NRel permits *Dem*R & N*Rel*, not *N*Dem* & *Rel*N
(XII′) NNum ⊃ NRel permits *Num*N & N*Rel*, not *N*Num* & *Rel*N

that is, postpositional languages exhibit a small number of *NDem & RelN co-occurrences at variance with the HSP, etc. And the two language types agree only with respect to Universals (V′), (VI′), and (IX′):

(V′) NDem ⊃ NA permits *Dem*N & N*A*, not *N*Dem* & *A*N
(VI′) NNum ⊃ NA permits *Num*N & N*A*, not *N*Num* & *A*N
(IX′) NG ⊃ NRel permits *G*N & N*Rel*, not *N*G* & *Rel*N

that is, demonstrative and numeral determiners always obey the HSP in conjunction with the adjective, and the genitive always obeys it in conjunction with the relative clause.

Evidently, the HSP can be disobeyed on some occasions, but only in postpositional languages, and only with some noun modifier co-occurrences.

We can account for all of these similarities and differences if we assume the following Mobility Principle:

Mobility Principle (MP)

$$\begin{Bmatrix} \text{Adj} \\ \text{Dem} \\ \text{Num} \end{Bmatrix} \geqslant_{M} \begin{Bmatrix} \text{Rel} \\ \text{Gen} \end{Bmatrix}$$

where "$\geqslant_M$" means 'exhibits greater or equal mobility away from the adposition + NP serialization'.

The MP claims that Adj, Dem, and Num are more mobile than Gen and Rel and can move around their heads more easily, producing a serialization which is opposite to that of the adposition in relation to its modifiers (e.g., AN & Pr + NP, NA & NP + Po, etc.). In Section 3.4.2.2 we shall consider what the relevant generalization might be which distinguishes more from less mobile constituents. In the interim, let us simply regard the MP as an organizing principle and pursue its predictions.

Consider first prepositional languages. Consistent noun modifiers in prepositional languages are postposed (in accordance with both Vennemann's NSP and the evidence of language quantities; see Chapter 4). Both the HSP and the MP make predictions for the relative order in which modifiers become preposed, and it transpires that these predictions overlap completely: The HSP predicts that Dem/Num preposes before Adj, Adj before Gen, and Gen before Rel; and the MP predicts Adj, Dem, and Num before Rel and Gen.[10] Hence, no contrary predictions are made by the two principles (though the HSP is more fine tuned), and both serve to explain PrNMH.

Not so for postpositional languages. Consistent noun modifiers in postpositional languages are preposed (according to Vennemann's NSP), and the two sets of predictions do not always overlap. Where two constituents are equally mobile, relative ordering predictions will, of course, be made exclusively by the HSP: Thus, Dem & Adj, and Num & Adj co-occurrences are dictated entirely by heaviness in all languages [cf. (V′), (VI′)], as are Gen & Rel co-occurrences [cf. (IX′)]. But the more mobile constituents by MP are also lighter than their less mobile counterparts, and when noun modifiers become postposed in postpositional languages, some contrary predictions will be made. In general, an ordering predicted by the MP predominates over one predicted by the HSP. More precisely, the following interaction principle determines the relationship between the HSP and the MP:

Mobility and Heaviness Interaction Principle (MHIP)

The Mobility Principle (MP) and the Heaviness Serialization Principle (HSP) interact in the following way: For some word order co-occurrences the two principles make the same predictions (e.g., Pr & AN & NRel); for other word order co-occurrences the HSP makes predictions with respect to which the MP is neutral (e.g., HSP predicts DemN & NA, where MP makes no prediction); on yet other occasions the two principles are in conflict. The conflicts arise only in postpositional languages, and where such conflicting predictions are made for two noun modifier orderings, they are resolved as follows:

The larger the heaviness difference between the two modifiers on the Heaviness Hierarchy (HH), the greater or equal the ability of HSP to override MP's contrary predictions; but HSP will override MP only when the heavier noun modifier is the relative clause.

We can calculate the difference in heaviness between two modifiers as follows: Two adjacent modifiers on the Heaviness Hierarchy will be considered to have a heaviness difference of 1; two modifiers separated by one intervening modifier will have a heaviness difference of 2; and two modifiers separated by two intervening modifiers a heaviness difference of 3.

The resolution of conflicting predictions in postpositional languages can be set out as follows:

Heaviness Difference	Co-occurrence	Outcome
3	Dem & Rel	HSP almost invariably overrides MP: The co-occurrence Po & NDem & RelN predicted by MP is only occasionally attested; the mirror-image Po & DemN & NRel predicted by HSP is productively attested [cf. (statistical) Universal (XI′), Section 3.3.14).
3	Num & Rel	HSP almost invariably overrides MP: The co-occurrence Po & NNum & RelN predicted by MP is only occasionally attested; the mirror-image Po & NumN & NRel predicted by HSP is productively attested [cf. (statistical) Universal (XII′), Section 3.3.15].
2	Adj & Rel	HSP sometimes overrides MP: The co-occurrence Po & NA & RelN predicted by MP occurs productively, as does the mirror-image Po & AN & NRel predicted by HSP [cf. Universal (XVII), Section 3.3.16].
2	Dem & Gen	HSP never overrides MP: The co-occurrence Po & ND & GN predicted by MP occurs productively; the mirror-image Po & DemN & NG predicted by HSP is nonoccurring [cf. Universal (XV), Section 3.3.9].
2	Num & Gen	HSP never overrides MP: The co-occurrence Po & NNum & GN predicted by MP occurs productively; the mirror-image Po & NumN & NG predicted by HSP is nonoccurring [cf. Universal (XVI), Section 3.3.10].
1	Adj & Gen	HSP never overrides MP: The co-occurrence Po & NA & GN predicted by MP occurs productively; the mirror-image Po & AN & NG predicted by HSP is nonoccurring [cf. Universal (IV), Section 3.2.4].

These results are completely in accordance with the MHIP. They make clear how MP is the stronger of the two principles: In half of the six cases of conflict HSP never overrides MP (i.e., in all those co-occurrences which do not involve a relative clause), and there is never an occasion on which HSP completely overrides MP.

Summarizing, we see that there are two principles that force noun modifiers to the right of their heads—heaviness and mobility—and two that force noun modifiers to the left—lightness and mobility. But as the more mobile constituents are simultaneously lighter than their less mobile counterparts, lightness alone effectively determines movement to the left in prepositional languages (which have predominantly N + Modifier orders), whereas both principles operate to effect movements to the right in postpositional languages (which have predominantly Modifier + N orders), and this produces the apparent discrepancy between these two language types. Prepositional languages consistently place lighter modifiers to the left and heavier ones to the right, whereas postpositional languages have some heavier constituents to the right with lighter ones to the left, and conversely some lighter constituents to the right with heavier ones to the left, in accordance with the MHIP.

This difference between prepositional and postpositional languages can be seen particularly clearly by comparing, finally, the actual quantities of languages with preposed and postposed noun modifiers in each of the two types. The quantities from the Expanded Sample are set out in Table 4.

The majority of prepositional languages have N + Modifier orders, but the proportion with preposed modifiers increases as the heaviness of the modifier decreases: RelN is found in only .9% of prepositional languages, GN in 11.9%, AN in 31.5%, and DemN and NumN in 49.4% and 65.7% respectively. These results are completely in accordance with the HSP. In addition, the extent of the difference between AN, DemN, and NumN on the one hand, and RelN and GN on the other, might be explained on the basis of the fact that the former are *both* lighter and more mobile than the latter.

The majority of postpositional languages have Modifier + N orders, but the figures are slightly more difficult to interpret because of the conflicts between MP and HSP. Nonetheless, where there are no such conflicts, the effects of HSP are clearly visible: The heavier NRel (38.6%) exceeds NG (5.9%), and the heavier NA (42.0%) exceeds NNum (30%) and NDem (24.1%). Moreover, the figure for NG is so low because the

TABLE 4 : Expanded Sample Quantities for Noun Modifier Orders in Prepositional and Postpositional Languages

		Prep Languages		
increase ↓	RelN	.9%	(1/106)	(NRel = 99.1%)
	GN	11.9%	(19/160)	(NG = 88.1%)
	AN	31.5%	(51/162)	(NA = 68.5%)
	DemN	49.4%	(39/79)	(NDem = 50.6%)
	NumN	65.7%	(44/77)	(NNum = 34.3%)
		Postp Languages		
increase ↑	NRel	38.6%	(22/57)	(RelN = 61.4%)
	NG	5.9%	(11/188)	(GN = 94.1%)
increase ↑	NA	42.0%	(79/188)	(AN = 58.0%)
	NNum	30.0%	(21/70)	(NumN = 70%)
	NDem	24.1%	(19/79)	(DemN = 75.9%)

Note: The first parenthesis gives the proportion of languages in the Expanded Sample which have the word order in question (cf. Chapter 8 and Language Index). The second parenthesis gives the percentage of languages with the opposite word order to that listed.

genitive is less mobile than the adjective, numeral, and demonstrative, and less heavy than the relative clause.

The quantities of preposed and postposed noun modifiers are therefore a function of both heaviness and mobility, operating in conjunction with the basic noun modifier ordering (see Section 3.4.1.3). By dividing the languages of the world into Prep and Postp classes we can see these organizing principles quite clearly.

3.4.1.3 Modifier–Head

The third factor, in addition to heaviness and mobility, which contributes to the explanation of the word order co-occurrences of this chapter is the modifier–head relation (see Sections 2.4.3, 2.6.1). As the MP is formulated, it assumes a modifier–head theory whereby an adjective and a noun stand in the same (modifier–head) relation to one another within the NP, as do an NP and an adposition within the adposition phrase. The MP defines the relative mobility with which noun modifiers can depart from a modifier–head serialization that is consistent with that of the adposition phrase. But the MP could not be stated as such unless we assumed that there was a modifier–head generalization linking Adj and N, and NP and Adp, in the first place. If, for example, Adp were to be regarded as modifier and NP as head, while N remains the head of the noun phrase, then the relative mobility of modifiers of the noun would be exactly the opposite of that defined by our current MP. A co-occurrence such as Pr + NP & AN & NRel would lead us to say that the relative clause was the more mobile noun modifier, as it has departed first from the modifier before head serialization of the prepositional phrase.

It would be quite possible to formulate the MP in this way, and redefine relative mobility between the respective noun modifiers. But there is both theoretical and empirical support for the modifier–head theory that we are assuming. At a theoretical level, the modifier–head theory represents a significant generalization based on the defining criterion of category constancy (Sections 2.4.3, 2.6.1). And, empirically, we saw in Table 4 that the majority of prepositional languages have postposed noun modifiers (if we aggregate the percentages for all five postposed modifiers we get an average of 68.1%), and a majority of postpositional languages have preposed noun modifiers (71.9% on average). These majority patterns support the generalizations underlying our current modifier–head theory (cf. Section 2.6.1). More generally, we will adduce frequency data in Chapter 4 which support a head of phrase generalization uniting all our putative head of phrase categories: noun (within NP), verb (within VP), adposition (within AdpP), and adjective (within AdjP). It will be shown that the more that these heads occupy a similar position relative to their respective modifiers, the more languages there are. Such quantitative differences support the reality of our current modifier–head theory, and so provide further justification for assuming this theory in the formulation of the MP.

3.4.2 GOING BEYOND THE INITIAL EXPLANATION

3.4.2.1 Heaviness

I would argue that there is ultimately a psycholinguistic explanation for the Heaviness Serialization Principle, involving language processing. Numerous psycholinguists (e.g., Clark & Clark 1977; Fodor, Bever, & Garrett 1974; Moore 1972) have argued that an early stage in the processing of sentences involves identification of the major arguments of the verb, especially recognition of SV(O) constituents. For example, Moore (1972) ran experiments in which people were asked to make grammaticality judgments under time pressure. His results suggest that the processing of relations between the verb and its arguments takes place before the processing of relations internal to each argument, that is, before the processing of modifiers within the subject and object NPs. When a strict subcategorization or selectional restriction violation involved head noun and verb (e.g., *Sensible* ***ideas distrust*** *public officials*), as opposed to modifier and head noun (e.g., *Factory foremen appreciate* ***eager tools***), subjects were significantly faster in recognizing the violation. We can conclude from this that the head nouns of subject and object NPs are identified early, as these are crucial for recognizing subject and object within the canonical SVO structure, and any modifiers of the head are processed later.

Let us now combine this finding about the relative earliness of head recognition with some fairly traditional psycholinguistic thinking about processing (à la Fodor, Bever, & Garrett 1974). Speech is processed from left to right. As every left-to-right constituent of an NP is processed, therefore, comprehension decisions must be made which will presumably include a yes/no decision on head status. Assume, with Moore, that this head recognition decision precedes decisions about the precise integration of any modifiers into the syntax and semantics of the NP. If the head is initial, the yes/no head decision can be accomplished immediately with a positive result, a choice between head and nonhead no longer needs to be made for any subsequent postnominal constituents, and these latter can then be integrated into the NP syntax and semantics directly as modifiers. But if there are modifiers to the left of the head, there will be two interlinked additions to the processing load. Head recognition is first of all delayed. As a result, the yes/no decision task on head status has to be applied to each constituent until the head is reached, and the overall number of decision tasks to be taken in NP processing therefore increases. And second, a modifier to the left of its head must be held in short-term memory until the head has been processed, whereupon it can be integrated into the syntax and semantics of the NP. The longer a preposed modifier (in constituents and morphemes), or the more preposed modifiers there are, the greater will be the head recognition delay, the overall number of decision tasks, and the burden on short-term memory. Hence, all things being equal, the earlier the head appears within the NP, the better from the point of view of processing load. And for this reason, heavier modifiers are placed after the head, rather than before it, in the HSP.

Prenominal relative clauses will delay recognition of the head the most—hence their position on the HSP. They serialize most readily to the right. Antinucci *et al.* (1979) point to additional perceptual problems posed by prenominal relatives. For example, they provide more opportunity for misanalyzing subordinate as main clauses, in structures such as:

(1) a. $[N_s\ V]\ N_s\ N_o\ V$
 b. $N_s\ [N_o\ V]\ N_o\ V$

Examples of (1a) and (1b) from Japanese are respectively:

(2) a. *Inu-ga kande-iru kodoma-ga neko-o nadete-iru.*
 dog-nom biting-is child-nom cat-acc patting-is
 'The child whom the dog is biting is patting the cat.'

 b. *Inu-ga ringo-o tabete-iru kodomo-o kande-iru.*
 dog-nom apple-acc eating-is child-acc biting-is
 'The dog is biting the child who is eating the apple.'

Antinucci *et al.* argue that although verb marking or nominal case marking in such languages will prevent actual ambiguity in most instances, the on-line processing of clauses such as (a) and (b) will involve adopting first one recognition hypothesis (in favor of main clause status for the NPs preceding the first verb, $[N_s\ V]$ in (a) and $N_s\ [N_o\ V]$ in (b)), and then rejecting it (in favor of subordinate clause status), to a much greater extent than with postnominal relatives.[11]

More generally, I would argue that all the rankings on the HSP are explained by the processing preference for the head noun to occur early in the noun phrase. The relative clause ordering preference is just one instance of a more general phenomenon. The full effects of the HSP are not always so obvious because the HSP interacts with two other principles in subtle ways. But once we factor out these other predictions, we see the empirical consequences of the HSP, and hence the effects of the putative processing principle for which we have argued.

These effects can be seen clearly in those cases where the MP is neutral to the HSP's predictions. Recall Universals (V′), (VI′), and (IX′):

(V′)	NDem ⊃ NA	permits *Dem*N & N*A*, not	*N*Dem* & *A*N
(VI′)	NNum ⊃ NA	permits *Num*N & N*A*, not	*N*Num* & *A*N
(IX′)	NG ⊃ NRel	permits *G*N & N*Rel*, not	*N*G* & *Rel*N

The possible and impossible noun-medial co-occurrences in all languages are here predicted by the HSP alone. Language frequency data support this pattern. We would expect that the lighter modifier in each pair (Dem and Adj etc.) will be found before the head in more languages than the heavier modifier. This is confirmed in each case. The following figures are derived from Table 4 by aggregating the percentages for prepositional and postpositional languages (in order to control for uneven numbers of languages across the two types for some modifiers):

DemN = 63%	(NDem = 37%)	NumN = 68%	(NNum = 32%)	NG = 47%	(GN = 53%)
AN = 45%	(NA = 55%)	AN = 45%	(NA = 55%)	NRel = 69%	(RelN = 31%)

There is a roughly 20% difference for each pair, with Dem and Num preferring leftward position over Adj, and Rel preferring rightward position over Gen. Since each pair comprises modifiers that are adjacent on the Heaviness Hierarchy, a 20% difference in frequency across all languages is a good result.

The extreme nature of the processing difficulty caused by prenominal relatives can explain the interaction between the HSP and the MP in those cases where they are in conflict (cf. the MHIP, Section 3.4.1.2). Conflicts arise only in postpositional languages, and the HSP can override contrary MP predictions only if the postposed modifier is a relative clause. Thus, the co-occurrence Po & DemN & NRel predicted by the HSP is productively occurring; the co-occurrence Po & NDem & RelN predicted by the MP is only occasionally attested. As relative clauses are the most perceptually problematic structures when they are in prenominal position, it makes sense that they should be the noun modifiers which assert themselves the most in overriding conflicting predictions by the MP.

There is a final set of figures which supports the reality of the HSP and its proposed explanation. As far as the Modifier-Head theory is concerned, ordering modifiers before heads is neither better nor worse than ordering heads before modifiers. Hence, if this were the only determinant of word order we should expect a random distribution of the world's languages among the two types, with roughly half being modifier + head, and half head + modifier. The MP should merely reinforce this pattern. The frequent preposing of the more mobile modifiers in head + modifier languages will be matched by the postposing of these same mobile modifiers in modifier + head languages. The effects of greater mobility will cancel each other out across the two language types, and the net result of both principles should be a roughly 50–50 distribution for all modifier + head and head + modifier pairs across languages. This expectation is confirmed for the major typological indicator word orders outside the noun phrase. Consider verb and object. The ratio of VO to OV languages in my Expanded Sample is 48% to 52%, that is, almost exactly equal. For Pr + NP and NP + Po the ratio is 44% to 56%. There is a slight skewing here, but this may just be my particular sample (Greenberg's 30-Language Sample has 53% Pr + NP and 47% NP + Po).

By contrast, the distribution of prenominal and postnominal modifiers is far from even in many cases. We have seen that numerals and demonstrative determiners precede the head in 68% and 63% of all languages respectively, and relative clauses follow the head in 69% of all languages. These figures reveal a 2-to-1 skewing. Only for the intermediate modifiers on the Heaviness Hierarchy is the aggregated distribution roughly 50–50: NGen = 47% and GenN = 53%; and NA = 55% and AN = 45%.

The HSP predicts this leftward–rightward asymmetry. Light modifiers prefer a leftward positioning, heavy modifiers a rightward positioning. Intermediate modifiers have, we suggest, neither sufficient heaviness nor sufficient lightness to counter the equal distribution predicted by the other principles.

The HSP is an asymmetrical word order principle, therefore, which interacts with other principles in subtle ways, but whose effects are clearly visible once these other predictions are factored out. We have argued that a psycholinguistic principle underlies it, involving ease of processing: There is a preference for shorter modifiers in prenominal position and heavier ones in postnominal position, since the recognition of the head is then faster and easier, and the burden on short-term memory is less. The importance, and earliness, of head recognition is in turn a consequence of the importance, and earliness, of argument–predicate recognition. The comprehension of a sentence first requires recognition of what the arguments and predicates are, and of which arguments go with which predicates. And head recognition is simply an important heuristic for argument recognition, and hence for argument–predicate matching. We see our

Heaviness Hierarchy, therefore, as a consequence of the following general principles of processing:

1. An (early) argument–predicate recognition strategy
2. The left-to-right seriality of speech
3. General psycholinguistic processes involving comprehension decisions and short-term memory

These independently motivated considerations, operating in conjunction with one another, explain the rankings of the HSP. Derivatively they explain: the possible and impossible co-occurrences of noun modifier orders for which the MP makes no contrary predictions; the relative quantities of languages having prenominal and postnominal orders for these modifiers; the resolution of conflicts with the MP; and the 2-to-1 skewing in the distribution of the lightest and the heaviest modifiers, contra the predictions of other principles.

This is not the context in which to mount a defense of general psycholinguistic mechanisms. Instead, our explanation can be strengthened by showing how another set of cross-language data can be convincingly explained in terms of heaviness and the argument–predicate recognition problem. Grosu and Thompson (1977) and Dryer (1980) establish a universal hierarchy governing the position of clausal complements of the verb (i.e., structures like *that Harry is a fool* in *John believes that Harry is a fool*). Such clauses occur in final position within their S in English, and this is by far the most frequent position across the language of the world, even in many languages whose basic order is subject–object–verb, which should give an order in which the complement precedes the verb. Considerably less frequent, but well attested, is the clausal complement in S-initial position (*that Harry is a fool John believes*), and least frequent of all is medial position (*John that Harry is a fool believes*). Grosu and Thompson (1977) offer a processing account of this cross-language distribution. Clausal complements are heavy subordinate constitutents of a sentence (in a way that is quite consistent with our heaviness criteria in Section 3.4.1.1), and they argue that the heavier such a constituent, the greater is the load on temporary memory as it is processed. The position of a heavy subordinate constituent within the matrix S then has consequences for the relative ease with which the argument–predicate relations of the matrix S can be recognized, and the heavy constitutent correctly integrated into the matrix. A heavy medial complement is worst because it interrupts the left-to-right processing of the matrix, maximizing the argument–predicate recognition problem, and rendering most acute the temporary memory load posed by the heavy constituent. A heavy initial complement is better because, although it delays the left-to-right processing of the main clause, it does not necessarily interrupt it, and argument–predicate relations can be more clearly recognized. And a final heavy complement is best of all, because it occurs at a point where the matrix argument–predicate relations have already been established.

Problems involving argument–predicate recognition are probably also what underlie the Complex/Heavy NP Shift examples of English. The potential confusion in the interpretation of *Joe gave a book that was about the skinning of cats in Alberta between 1898 and 1901 to Berta* results from the (in this case ultimately unsuccessful) attempt to assign *to Berta* to the relative S modifying *book* rather than to the matrix S as an argument of *gave.* The confusion is resolved in *Joe gave to Berta a book that was about the skinning of cats in Alberta between 1898 and 1901* where the correct argument–predicate relations are clarified by the surface adjacency of *gave* and *to Berta,* in conjunction with Kimball's (1973) parsing principle of Right Association: Terminal symbols optimally associate to the lowest nonterminal node.

It should be pointed out that these processing explanations for the ordering of heavy constitutents are given in terms of language comprehension rather than language production. But as both Elinor Ochs and Pim Levelt have pointed out to me (personal communication), it is more likely that the ultimate explanation resides in relative *production* difficulties rather than in comprehension (just how generous can we assume that speakers are in accommodating their hearer's comprehension difficulties?). As so much less is known about production than comprehension, I have expressed my explanation in terms of the latter. But I assume that processing difficulties involving argument–predicate recognition and short-term memory in comprehension will have numerous parallels with difficulties involving production, whose precise nature awaits discovery, and that we can use comprehension data in the meantime as an index of relative processing ease in general.

Let us comment finally on the general form of the explanation that we are proposing here. Our appeal to processing considerations is in the spirit of, for example, Grosu and Thompson (1977), and goes beyond the role that has traditionally been assigned to this aspect of language performance, in several respects. Both in the linguistic literature (e.g., Chomsky 1965:Chapter 1) and in the psycholinguistic literature (Fodor, Bever, & Garrett 1974), processing considerations are normally invoked in discussions of acceptability differences in performance. Rules of the grammar which are otherwise productive may lead to unacceptability when they result in, for example, self-embedding structures such as *The woman the man the boy saw kissed left* or *That that two plus two equals four surprised Jack bothered Mary.* Processing factors are thereby seen primarily as a filter on the competence grammar, though a few more ambitious examples of processing explanations for the existence and nature of the rules of grammar themselves can be found in Bever (1970, 1974), involving rule differences in main and subordinate clauses.

It seems to me eminently reasonable that ease of processing should be one of the causal factors explaining why languages employ the rules and structures that they do, a sentiment that is shared by Gazdar (1981):

> The sentences of a natural language can be parsed. We do it all the time. Furthermore, we do it very fast. . . . The ready parsability of natural languages is a property that has been almost entirely ignored by linguists until very recently (see Fodor 1978). And yet it is a property that stands in need of explanation: there are many mathematically conceivable classes of languages that can be shown to be unparsable for all practical purposes [p. 62].

To say that natural languages are parsable, whereas many mathematically conceivable classes of language are unparsable, is to claim that natural languages have certain properties which make them parsable, and that failure to exhibit these would make them unparsable, and hence unusable and impossible. And I regard the classical self-embedding examples as merely the tip of an iceberg full of cases where the parser constrains the grammar. In addition to these examples, there will be lots of strings of morphemes from every language which are unparsable and for which no rule of grammar can be motivated to generate them as grammatical in the first place. A parsing constraint on transformational rules, for example, may be the mirror-image prohibition of Chomsky (1972): No language appears to transform strings like *John put his car into the garage* into their pure mirror-image *garage the into car his put John.* It has also been proposed that the boundedness of rightward-moving transformations is explainable in terms of processing (Fodor 1979). Constraints on scrambled word orders across languages are also likely candidates for ungrammaticality through unparsability. For example, English has no rule that takes the definite article out of an NP and positions it elsewhere (giving, e.g., **soprano has the sung exquisitely* or **soprano has sung exquisitely the*), and it might be argued that there is a processing explanation for such prohibitions: Such a rule would break up the NP constituent, would invite confusion over which noun in a sentence the definite article was to be matched with, etc.

To develop a theory of unparsability one will need to examine both possible and impossible rules across languages, as well as limitations on the productivity of rules, and one will need to consider the cross-linguistic evidence in conjunction with the results of psycholinguistic experimentation (cf. Hawkins 1982b). And the first respect in which our heaviness explanation goes beyond most traditional discussions of processing in linguistics, therefore, is in its appeal to processing as an explanation for the rules of the grammar themselves (PS-rules for S-complements, rightward-moving T-rules for heavy clauses, etc).

Second, our HSP assumes that processing difficulty is a gradient notion: Some structures and rule types are more difficult to process than others. At the extreme end of this gradient, the difficulty will be so great that the relevant structures will be nonoccurring across all languages (cf. the mirror-image structures, the boundedness of rightward movements, and the determiner shift examples given earlier). But otherwise the degree of processing difficulty will be reflected in the relative quantities of languages with the structures in question (cf. the clausal complement hierarchy: final position more frequent than initial position more frequent than medial position), and in the frequency with which a processing consideration can either assert itself in the absence of contrary predictions, or can override an independently motivated grammatical principle. The literature hitherto, which is based largely on English, has assumed that cases of processing difficulty are in general of the absolute kind: A particular sentence type either is or is not usable in performance. But an examination of other languages reveals that some of the most discussed examples are better regarded as explanations for the relative infrequency of certain structures, rather than for their total absence. Self-embedding relative clauses do occur quite grammatically in some languages, though not, to my knowledge, as frequently as the basic phrase-structure rules of certain languages would lead one to expect. For example, the German sentence *Der Bauer, der die Kuh, die schlechte Milch gab, schlachtete, ist mein Freund* ('the farmer who the cow which bad milk gave slaughtered is my friend', i.e., 'The farmer who killed the cow which gave bad milk is my friend') is judged fully grammatical by native speakers. And left-branching structures are less frequent across the languages of the world than right-branching ones (see Yngve 1960): A lot of languages that we would expect to have left-branching relative clauses have right-branching ones (cf. HSP and MHIP); a lot of languages that we would expect to have preverbal, left-branching clausal complements have postverbal right-branching complements (see Grosu & Thompson 1977, Dryer 1980); that is, a lot of languages that we would expect to have left-branching structures have right-branching ones, but the converse fails.

As processing difficulty can explain some limitations on cross-linguistic rules of grammar, and as the notion of processing difficulty is intrinsically gradient, it follows that the number of languages which tolerate the difficulty in question should vary with the degree of difficulty involved, the number being 0 in the most extreme cases. Hence, where language frequencies are to be explained in processing terms (and they are not all to be explained in this way; see Sections 4.3.1, 4.6, and the introductory section of Chapter 6), there will be a correlation with the degree of processing difficulty involved, all things being equal.

All things will often not be equal, however. As in the case of the HSP, there may be contrary or overlapping principles, and care must be taken to control for these before deriving conclusions for the degree of processing difficulty involved.

Comparison of the German self-embedded relative clause with self-embeddings in English highlights a third respect in which traditional discussions of performance limitations should be looked at more critically. English sentences like *The farmer who the cow which the boy liked killed is my friend* are commonly regarded as grammatical but unacceptable. The German self-embedded relative given earlier, however, is fully grammatical, acceptable, processable, etc. And it is therefore unmotivated to say that these self-embeddings are grammatical in both English and German. Native speaker responses are as different in the two languages as they are for the pair *Ich weiß, daß du den Jungen gesehen hast* / **I know that you the boy seen have.* The German sentence is clearly grammatical, its closest English equivalent is not. For this and other reasons (see Hawkins 1982b) I regard English self-embeddings as simply ungrammatical, and I reject the validity of the acceptability–grammaticality distinction. Its only theoretical support is that acceptability is a performance limitation. No one would dispute this, but it does not follow that the relevant sentences should be regarded as grammatical. I would say instead that these and many other strings of English morphemes are ***ungrammatical for performance reasons,*** but that this is a matter of explanation rather than description. Descriptively, all the relevant sentences are ungrammatical, and admit of the same degrees of ungrammaticality as sentences with other causes of ungrammaticality.[12]

Finally, our explanation for HSP differs from the standard Chomskyan explanation for language universals, given in terms of innateness (see Section 1.3.1). We are arguing that psycholinguistic principles involving language use (i.e., processing difficulty, memory, complexity, etc.) constitute a part of the explanation for attested versus nonattested, and frequent versus infrequent, word order co-occurrences across languages. We consider it likely that these processing principles will generalize to other cognitive domains as well (cf. Swinney & Smith 1982). But, even if they remain unique to language, the cause of explanation will involve language performance, rather than some aspect of the internal organization of the grammar (see further Hawkins 1982b).

3.4.2.2 Mobility

I see two interrelated causal factors underlying the Mobility Principle: one syntactic, the other historical.

Syntactically, notice that the more mobile constituents (Adj, Dem, and Num) are (*a*) nonbranching constituents dominating single terminal elements; and (*b*) "nonphrasal" nodes in the sense of Emonds (1976), that is, nodes that do not dominate NP by virtue of applying base (PS-)rules. The less mobile constituents (Gen and Rel), on the other hand, are (*a*) constituents that can branch, dominating a plurality of terminal and nonterminal elements; and (*b*) "phrasal nodes" (NP, PP, and S), that is, nodes that can dominate NP by virtue of applying base rules. As a result, the more mobile constituents clearly involve that much less syntactic structure, whereas the less mobile constituents involve greater complexity of syntactic structure. But why should this added complexity make a constituent less mobile, that is, less capable of departing from the basic modifier–head serialization typified by the adposition phrase?

The answer is to be found in language history. Word orders change through time (see Chapters 5, 6, and 7). There is scarcely a language family that does not show at least some evidence of word order change among its daughters. And there are many language families (e.g., Indo-European) that reveal extensive word order changes in the relatively recent past. Now, wherever we can observe such word order changes in process (as in the extensive historical records for Indo-European), they are gradual. A language does not shift overnight from AdjN to NAdj, or from NRel to RelN, etc. There are numerous intervening stages in the transition from one word order to another, in the form of doubling, frequency increase, increased grammaticalization, etc. Thus the stage from NAdj to AdjN will always proceed via a doubling stage, NAdj > NAdj/AdjN > AdjN, during which both orders exist, with the new order gaining gradually in frequency and grammaticalization until it perhaps ousts the older order completely. Numerous examples are discussed in Chapter 5. One particularly revealing example from the point of view of the gradualness of change involves the emergence of RelN structures in Early New High German (Section 5.3.5), structures such as *der die schöne Frau liebende Mann* ('the the beautiful woman loving man', i.e., 'the man who loves the beautiful woman'). This structure gained gradually in frequency in the sixteenth and seventeenth centuries, at the expense of corresponding postnominal relatives. And as it did so, the relevant grammatical processes became increasingly productive. Prior to the sixteenth century, German had only lexically compound prenominal attributes corresponding to the English *heart-breaking, time-saving* type. But then the lexical compounding rule gave way to a prenominal relative transformation permitting an increasing number of constituents to be preposed before the participial verb: initially just adverbs, then full NPs, etc. (see König 1971:39 for the relevant transformation in Modern German; Weber 1971 for detailed documentation of the historical developments, with frequency counts; and also Chapter 5, Note 14).

The MP is in part a consequence of such gradualness in word order change. I would argue that if a language is going to reorder any of its noun modifiers, it will reorder the single-constituent, nonphrasal nodes, before the more complex nodes. There are two reasons for this. First of all, the single constituents, Adj, Dem, and Num, are included in the set of categories that Rel (S) and Gen (NP) can dominate. If Rel and Gen change order, then any dominated categories necessarily change order as well. The prior reordering of these latter is therefore a natural prerequisite for an order change involving a more inclusive, dominating category. But, second, single-constituent, nonphrasal nodes can be reordered with less drastic restructuring of the NP than by first shifting the more complex phrasal nodes. There may be no formal grammatical correlate of this ease of reordering, in terms of the generative PS-rules involved. It is just as easy to convert the rule NP → S NP into NP → NP S as it is to convert NP → Det N into NP → N Det, with subsequent rewriting rules taking care of the constituents dominated by S and Det respectively, as Dick Hudson has pointed out to me (personal communication). But in terms of the resulting surface structures, the former rule change has the effect of reordering many more surface constituents than the latter. Thus, just as the gradualness of word order change is evident in reorderings involving one and the same modifier, so I would argue that it can be seen also in reorderings involving different modifiers of one and the same head. If a language is going to reorder one modifier before another, gradualness predicts that it will effect a small change in surface structure before it effects a larger and more inclusive change. Once the smaller surface reorderings have been accomplished (involving Adj, Dem, and Num), the larger and more inclusive rearrangements in terms of Gen and Rel can be brought about. Hence, the greater mobility of the former, and the lesser mobility of the latter.

Notice now an interesting general consequence of this explanation for the MP. We are, in effect, claiming that constraints on diachrony are an important part of the explanation for synchronic universals. Specifically, one reason why languages exhibit some synchronic co-occurrences of phenomena, but not others, has to do with possible and impossible forms of language change, leading to the current language states that we observe in our samples. Languages can only change in certain ways, and not others, in accordance with gradualness. Thus, a Po & AN & GN language that is moving toward modifier postposing has to move its Adj before or simultaneously with its Gen, in accordance with the MP—it cannot first shift Gen, producing Po & AN & NG. This type of historical explanation is a more ambitious one than is normally proposed. Historical explanations for synchrony are often invoked in the context of exceptions to synchronic regularities (e.g., strong verbs in English), or in the context of frozen morphology (cf. Givón 1971), but not as in this present case, where historical considerations are claimed to explain current productive syntactic rules throughout the grammars of the world's languages.[13]

We pointed out in Section 3.4.1.2 that the more mobile constituents by MP were simultaneously lighter constituents on the HSP, and hence that noun modifier movements to the left in prepositional languages were effectively dictated by the HSP alone, whereas movements to the right were dictated by both heaviness and mobility. We have argued (Section 3.4.2.1) that heaviness has a processing explanation, whereas mobility is a grammatically based phenomenon which interacts with the gradualness of language change. Within the NP, the more mobile constituents are nonbranching and nonphrasal. It now remains to be seen how adequate this characterization of mobility is, by looking at many more modifiers in more types of phrases. I shall conclude this subsection by considering some more relevant data.

We would predict that possessive adjectives (*my, his,* etc.) would pattern like Adj, Dem, and Num, rather than like Gen and Rel, where they are nonbranching and nonphrasal, as they typically are. It appears that this is indeed what happens. Possessive adjectives are more mobile than both genitives and relative clauses. As far as I know, they are also typically less heavy than descriptive adjectives, so we might expect them to pattern more like Dem and Num. This is what we find. The following universal is compatible with my Expanded Sample data, and mirrors (V′) NDem ⊃ NA and (VI′) NNum ⊃ NA:

(XXI) If the possessive adjective follows the noun, then the descriptive adjective follows the noun; i.e., NPoss ⊃ NA (equivalently: AN ⊃ PossN).

Prep languages

NPoss & NA: Aghem, Arosi, Bahasa Indonesian, Dyola, Fulani, Haya, Hebrew, Indonesian, Iraqi Arabic, Luangiua, Macassarese, Malagasay, Malay, Marshallese, Niuean, Sundanese, Swahili, Syrian Arabic, Thai, Vietnamese, Xhosa

PossN & NA: Douala, Easter Island, Fijian, French, Irish, Jacaltec, Kaliai-Kove, Samoan, Tongan, Tunen

PossN & AN: Amharic, Classical Mayan, Czech, Danish, Dutch, German, Hiligaynon, Maung, Otomi, Russian, Slovenian, Swedish, Tzeltal

*NPoss & AN: No examples predicted

Postp languages

AN & PossN: Ainu, Brahui, Finnish, Hindi, Ijo, Korean, Manchu, Mongol languages, Piro, Ryukyuan, Usarufa, Yaqui

NA & PossN: Kokama, Mojave, Twi, Warrau, Waskia, Zarma-Songhai, Zuni

NA & NPoss: Assiniboine, Maranungku

*AN & NPoss: No examples

There are, however, two exceptional languages, Bukidnon and Kampangan, with Pr & VSO & NPoss & AN, so Universal (XXI) must be classified as statistical.

We can incorporate (XXI) into the PrNMH as follows:

(XIV′) Prep ⊃ ((NDem ∨ NNum ∨ NPoss ⊃ NA) & (NA ⊃ NG) & (NG ⊃ NRel))

It will be clear from (XIV′) that the possessive adjective can depart from the Pr + NP serialization before the descriptive adjective (cf. Pr & PossN & NA languages)—on account of heaviness; and that both can depart from the adposition serialization before the genitive and relative clause (cf. Pr & PossN & AN & NG & NRel languages)—on account of both heaviness and mobility.

In order to incorporate (XXI) into the PoNMH (Section 3.3.17), we must consider possessive adjectives in relation to genitive full NPs and relative clauses. Mirroring (XV) Postp ⊃ (DemN ⊃ GN) and (XVI) Postp ⊃ (NumN ⊃ GN), we have (XXII), in which the possessive adjective is more mobile than the genitive full NP and departs from the NP + Po serialization first:

(XXII) If a language has Postp word order, then if the possessive adjective precedes the noun, the genitive precedes the noun; i.e., Postp ⊃ (PossN ⊃ GN).

Postp languages

PossN & GN: Ainu, Fore, Brahui, Finnish, Hindi, Ijo, Japanese, Korean, Manchu, Mojave, Mongol languages, Piro, Ryukyuan, Twi, Usarufa, Warrau, Waskia, Yaqui, Zarma-Songhai, Zuni

NPoss & GN: Assiniboine, Gugada, Maranungku

NPoss & NG: No examples

*PossN & NG: No examples

Possessive adjectives also behave just like demonstratives and numerals in co-occurrence with relative clauses in postpositional languages—though in all these cases the co-occurrences are determined more by heaviness (on account of the MHIP; Section 3.4.1.2). Universal (XXIII) mirrors (XI′) NDem ⊃ NRel and (XII′) NNum ⊃ NRel exactly:

(XXIII) If the possessive adjective follows the noun, then the relative clause follows the noun; i.e., NPoss ⊃ NRel (equivalently: RelN ⊃ PossN).

Data for prepositional languages are unnecessary. For postpositional languages we have:

Postp languages

RelN & PossN:	Ainu, Fore, Japanese, Korean, Manchu, Mongol languages, Ryukyuan
NRel & PossN:	Brahui, Kokama, Mojave, Piro, Twi, Warrau, Yaqui, Zarma, Songhai
NRel & NPoss:	No examples
*RelN & NPoss:	No examples

The expanded PoNMH thus reads as follows:

(XVIII′) Postp ⊃ ((AN ∨ RelN ⊃ DemN & NumN & PossN) & (DemN ∨ NumN ∨ PossN ⊃ GN))

Our prediction that possessive adjectives should pattern like Dem, Num, and Adj with regard to mobility is therefore confirmed. The additional prediction that it should be more similar to Dem and Num with respect to both mobility and heaviness is also confirmed.

We predict also that nonbranching and nonphrasal adverbial modifiers of adjectives within the adjective phrase (e.g., *deliciously tasty* in English should be more mobile than the PP or NP modifiers of adjectives within the adjective phrase in comparative constructions (e.g., *bigger than Harry*). This also appears to hold (see Sections 3.3.19 and 3.3.20 for the relevant universals). Thus, English, a prepositional language, gives us precisely AdvAdj, in which the adverb is to the left of the adjective head, but AdjPP, with the PP to the right, in accordance with the adposition + NP serialization. Conversely, Guarani, a postpositional language, exhibits the mirror-image AdjAdv ('tasty deliciously') & PPAdj ('Harry than big'), with the more mobile adverb to the right of the head, and the PP to the left, matching postpositions.

At the sentence level, adverbs also appear to be more mobile than NPs and PPs. Thus, in verb-first languages, adverbs can regularly precede the verb (Greenberg 1966:79), whereas NPs and PPs follow; and, in nonrigid

SOV languages, adverbs generally follow the verb, whereas many or all of the NPs and PPs precede.

The behavior of adverbs is very suggestive in this context. We have already pointed out (Section 3.4.1.1) that heaviness is operative in accounting for the positioning of pronominal and full NPs relative to the verb, for the positioning of clausal complements, and for the existence of rules such as Complex/Heavy NP Shift. But the adverb distribution now provides clear evidence for a second, more grammatically sensitive, word order principle, operating at the sentence level, and matching mobility within the NP. Both heaviness and mobility would therefore appear to be contributory determinants of word order variation in both the NP and the S.

There is additional data that needs to be accounted for at the sentence level, which may be attributable to mobility, but which may involve a third principle altogether. Movements to the right of the verb in SOV languages appear to reflect different degrees of semantic proximity or bonding (D. Smith 1978, Tomlin 1977) between the verb and its arguments. Thus, there are numerous nonrigid SOV language in which all oblique constituents follow V, and just the direct object precedes (e.g., Bambara and Kapelle; see Givón 1975). When only some oblique constituents follow the verb and others precede, it is the more loosely bound and nonstrictly subcategorized constituents which follow, and the more tightly bound and strictly subcategorized constituents which precede. The more loosely bound constituents are precisely those which can function as "afterthoughts" (Hyman 1975) in SOV languages. The following German example is not atypical. Bierwisch (1963:51) points out that in a sentence like *Du hast die Maschine vor einigen Tagen in den Schrank gestellt* ('you have the machine a few days ago in the cupboard put'), the strictly subcategorized *in den Schrank* ('in the cupboard') cannot be postposed after the verb (**Du hast die Maschine vor einigen Tagen gestellt in den Schrank*), whereas the nonstrictly subcategorized time adverbial *vor einigen Tagen* ('a few days ago') can be (*Du hast die Maschine in den Schrank gestellt vor einigen Tagen*). Whether this rightward serialization possibility for less bound constituents can be subsumed under a more general mobility principle, or whether (as is more likely) it represents a separate interacting principle altogether, must await further research.

3.4.2.3 Overview

Commenting on some of the implicational universals presented in this chapter (namely, (I)–(IV); cf. Hawkins 1980a), N. Smith (1981) writes:

> . . . multi-valued implicational statements can be devised *ad hoc* for . . . new complexities, but the strong impression remains that no counter-example to

> any of these universals would be a very great surprise; in brief, anything seems to be possible. If Hawkins' implicational universals turn out NOT to be *ad hoc* manipulations, it is worth emphasizing that, being absolute, they could reasonably be taken to be part of the defining characteristics of language in a way which Greenberg's, being probabilistic, could not. This would overcome one of the problems of Greenberg's system, namely how to construe the 'universals' as something the speakers of languages could properly have knowledge of [pp. 42–43].

It should be clear from this chapter that it is not the case that "anything seems to be possible." Our Universals (I)–(IV) were originally formulated on the basis of Appendix II, and they all make the same simple claim: Noun–adjective order, when it is parallel to adposition type or verb position, determines noun–genitive order. This admits a small number of exceptions of Type 12 and 14. Upon greatly enlarging and correcting the sample (cf. Chapter 8), *no* new complexities have arisen to invalidate this claim: Exceptions to Type 12 remain, but 14 is no longer a problem. And my reformulations of (I) and (II) [cf. (I′) and (II′)] do not constitute any real revision: They are just stronger versions of the same claims applied to a wider class of languages. This stability of the claims is precisely what would not happen if anything were possible. Further, the patterns defined by the additional implications given in Section 3.3 are also not what we would expect if we were merely making ad hoc descriptions of random co-occurrences, but are instead a set of strong constraints showing a good deal of parallelism and symmetry, reflecting the high degree of structure in the data. This structure can be seen in our two hierarchies, the PrNMH and the PoNMH, which are consistent with our three organizing principles: the Heaviness Serialization Principle, the Mobility Principle, and the Mobility and Heaviness Interaction Principle.

As for the explanation of these organizing principles and the word order hierarchies which they define, we have argued that they are the consequence of an interaction of processing, structural (grammatical), and historical principles. Smith conceives of universals in the narrow Chomskyan sense, as formal and substantive properties which speakers of each language in some sense know (Section 1.3.1). But the variation-defining universals of the type we have illustrated here are explainable by considerations going beyond any such innate grammatical knowledge (as discussed in Sections 1.3.2 and 1.3.3), and reflect constraints on language processing, and constraints on the rate at which languages can change while preserving communicability between speakers, etc. (see Hawkins 1982b for a more general discussion of the explanation of language universals). The existence of a productive discrepancy between the mathematically possible and the actually attested word order co-occurrences (Section 3.1.1), coupled with the discovery of general causes underlying this discrepancy therefore makes it clear that there ARE good reasons why our implicational universals define the range of word order co-occurrences that they do, and so removes Smith's charge of ad hoc manipulations.

Smith's comments highlight one important point about implicational universals, however. Now that we have proposed higher order explanatory principles, our implicational statements are technically superfluous. The implications of the noun modifier hierarchies are direct consequences of our principles, and do not need to be stated in the atomistic way in which we have presented them.

Nonetheless, we shall continue to employ individual implicational statements for the following reasons: Each of them still needs to be tested against further data, both diachronic and synchronic, and it is convenient to have a specific statement for each subarea of word order data.

3.5 On the Notion "Word Order Type"

We have seen that the notion of a word order type no longer means uniform serialization for all operator–operand categories. It means, instead, that the languages in question conform to a restricted set of co-occurrence possibilities permitted by our implicational universals, each of which contains a shared common property, such as prepositions, functioning as the "typological indicator."

As a result, the notion of a language type becomes more abstract, in two respects. First, a type has been defined hitherto in terms of a set of co-occurring properties, all of which are claimed to occur in the languages of the type, with more than chance frequency at least, and for which the typological indicators are VO and OV respectively. We have argued that the proposed correlations with VO and OV do not hold to a satisfactory degree (Section 2.4.4). The reason is a fundamental one: A typological indicator does not define a set of properties each of which is present in each language of the type; it defines a restricted number of families of co-occurring properties, for example, the co-occurrences of the PrNMH. Hence, you cannot check correlations between Prep and individual properties (Pr & NA, Pr & NG, etc.) when setting up types: There will be too many exceptions to each such correlation. But you CAN establish exceptionless combinatorial patterns of adjective and genitive order, etc., which correlate with the typological indicator. These combinatorial patterns effectively define several subtypes of the type in question, but these subtypes are highly constrained and considerably less numerous than the mathematical possibilities would allow. And by explicitly setting up subtypes in this way, we are able to discover descriptive patterns and explanations for the combinatorial restrictions that would go undetected if the co-occurrences of prepositional and postpositional languages were all thrown together.

Second, a word order type must have certain families of word order combinations that are unique to it, if it is to have generality. Our objection to many verb positions as typological indicators has been precisely that there are no other word orders or word order combinations that correlate exclusively with them (cf., e.g., VOS languages, Section 3.2.2). However, there is no reason to expect that ALL the correlating word order combinations should be unique to each type: Some may overlap with other types. For example, languages with exclusively preposed and exclusively postposed noun modifiers may co-occur with either Prep or Postp, and hence these word order combinations are shared by the PrNMH and the PoNMH. This provides a second respect in which our revised notion of a word order type differs from its predecessors, and becomes correspondingly further removed from a simple one-to-one correlation between typological properties.

More precisely, let us define a word order type as the set-theoretic union of sets of co-occurring word orders (e.g., the subtypes of the PrNMH), whose members are predictable by our implicational universals, and each of which contains at least one shared common property, such as prepositions, functioning as the typological indicator(s). Typological indicators are therefore those word orders in the intersection of the relevant sets, whose union constitutes the type.

The major typological indicators in our approach are Prep, Postp, V-1, and SOV (possibly OV). It is significant that these word orders are predominantly "operand-peripheral": The verb occurs leftmost or rightmost in the sentence; and the adposition is either leftmost or rightmost within the adposition phrase. These operand-peripheral orders seem to exert strong co-occurrence requirements outside their own categories. By contrast, we have seen that SVO, in which the operand is not peripheral in the sentence, is not a reliable typological indicator: There are scarcely any other word orders or combinations which correlate with SVO at all, let alone uniquely, and attempts to generalize SVO to VO in order to gain such uniqueness merely destroy the generality of the correlations that can be made on the basis of the other VO word orders (Sections 2.2.4, 2.4.6).

This typological ambivalence of SVO languages makes verb position a less productive and less useful indicator of language type than has hitherto been thought. If we say, as Greenberg did, that verb position is the major typological indicator, we define into existence types such as VSO, SVO, and SOV, one of which has no unique type characteristics. Nor do VOS,

V-initial, and OVS languages, the other attested basic verb positions, appear to have unique type characteristics. And although we can collapse these basic verb positions into V-1 and OV, and define some co-occurrence predictions on these more general categories (Sections 3.2.1, 3.2.2), the ambivalence of SVO, the second most frequent verb position, destroys the generality of a verb-based typology. Much better type indicators are Prep and Postp. These word orders make genuine co-occurrence predictions for all the languages of Greenberg's sample. We therefore propose that there exist two major word order types: prepositional and postpositional languages. Both exert co-occurrence requirements on numerous noun phrase and adjective phrase co-occurrences, but only distributional preferences, as we shall see, in favor of the various verb positions.

Finally, the more abstract approach to typology that we have derived from our word order data merits serious testing in other grammatical domains: Are language types in general better described as families of subtypes, that is, as subsets of property combinations with typological indicators in their intersection? (Pursuing this possibility for many other grammatical properties apart from word order (and for other grammatical correlations with word order) may result in the same kinds of benefits that we have derived from the study of word order alone: More precise typologies; and the discovery of more cross-language generalizations, suggesting more, and more sophisticated, explanations for the parameters on language variation.

3.6 Constituency and Word Order Universals

So far we have proposed two noun modifier hierarchies (PrNMH and PoNMH); three organizing statements which constitute an initial explanation for these hierarchies (HSP, MP, and MHIP); and some further explanations for these organizing statements in terms of processing, grammatical (syntactic), and historical principles.

But the word orders we have been seeking explanations for have been limited in one respect: They involve sequences of just two categories, one modifier and its head (NG, NRel, Pr + NP, etc.). And we have been pursuing essentially two questions: Given a plurality of such modifiers for one and the same head category (the noun), each modifier being considered singly in conjunction with the head, which modifiers precede the head, and which follow, in the languages of our sample? And how does the pre- or postposing of modifiers within one category (the noun phrase) relate to or depend on that of another (the adposition phrase)?

What, then, about noun phrases that contain more than one modifier at the same time (e.g., both Dem and Adj—*that nice man*)? What relative orderings of these categories occur, and what kinds of cross-categorial generalizations obtain for these longer sequences? We have already broached these questions in connection with the verb and its two modifiers, subject and object. The constraints on sequencing for these three categories were scarcely considerable. All of VSO, VOS, V-initial (i.e., both VSO and VOS), SVO, OVS, SOV, and even OSV are currently claimed to exist (see Sections 2.1, 2.2.4), although there are significant differences in frequency (Section 4.3.1). And though some cross-categorial generalizations can be linked to the relative position of V, S, and O (see Sections 3.2.1, 3.2.2), not all relative positions of these three elements yield cross-categorial generalizations (Sections 2.2.4, 2.4.6).

It appears, however, that there are significant universal constraints on sequencing within the noun phrase. I have not made a systematic survey of the languages in my sample in this respect, but I do have some relevant data with which to supplement and amend an important sequencing universal for noun modifiers proposed by Greenberg. Here I will present the universal in question (Section 3.6.1), and will discuss some theoretical attempts to explain such sequencings in terms of (syntactically and/or semantically motivated) constituent structure (Section 3.6.2). I will argue that constituency does have a (not entirely problem-free) role to play in this area, and that this role is independent of (though it interacts with) the modifier–head principles of the last section (heaviness and mobility). Finally, we consider the fact of language variation in relation to constituent structure (Section 3.6.3). Our discussion will be brief. I do not have a lot of universal sequencing data, and the current state of the art on constituent structure is a textbook example of theoretical disagreement. As a result, discussions of the relationship between constituency and word order must be viewed somewhat critically.

3.6.1 A SEQUENCING UNIVERSAL FOR NOUN PHRASES

Consider Greenberg's (1966:87) Universal (20):

(20) When any or all of the items (demonstrative, numeral and descriptive adjective) precede the noun, they are always found in that order. If they follow, the order is either the same or its exact opposite.

In other words, the English sequencing *these five large houses* is typical of languages in which all three modifiers precede the head noun. Where one or more modifiers follow, Greenberg tells us (p. 87), the favorite order is actually the mirror-image one, in which the same relative adjacency of modifiers to the head is preserved, as in *houses large five these.*

The universal sequencing data that I have support the first part of this universal (20a), and they confirm the preference for mirror-image orderings among postposed modifiers. But they suggest, first, that the disjunction in the second part, (20b), will have to be abandoned. They enable us, second, to restrict a number of options left open by the "any or all of the items" clause, and third, to remove a certain ambiguity in the formulation itself. We will take these points in reverse order, and then propose a revision of (20).

The pronoun *they* occurs twice in (20), and on both occasions its reference admits of an unfortunate ambiguity. The first *they* ("when any or all of the items . . . precede the noun, *they* are always found. . . . ") does not refer literally to any or all of the modifiers, but only to that subset which precedes the noun. That is, Greenberg is not claiming that the relative order Dem – Num – Adj obtains throughout the noun phrase just in case at least one modifier precedes the head. This cannot be what is intended because (20b) admits mirror-image orderings for postposed modifiers, and so permits sequences like Dem – N – Adj – Num, contradicting Dem – Num – Adj, even though Dem precedes the head. Since (20a) is formulated as an exceptionless universal, Greenberg evidently intended the sequencing Dem – Num – Adj to hold only for those modifiers which actually are in prenominal position. The intended interpretation of the second *they* ("if *they* follow, the order is. . . ."), it turns out from a close reading of page 87, is 'if any or all the items . . . follow . . .', and the disjunctive sequencing prediction must again be relativized, this time to the subset of modifiers that occur in postnominal position, in order not to contradict (20a). The mirror-image preference therefore holds for this subset only.

The "any or all" clause allows for a number of sequencing options that do not occur. For example, where two modifiers precede the head, Universal (20a) is compatible with all of the following:

Dem – Num – N – Adj
Dem – Adj – N – Num
Num – Adj – N – Dem

In each case the relative ordering of Dem – Num – Adj is preserved in prenominal position, and any or all of these items are permitted to precede. Yet only the first possibility is attested in my data (cf. French *ces trois étudiants intelligents* 'these three students intelligent'; i.e., Dem – Num – N – Adj). Indeed, only the first possibility is consistent with implicational universals (V′) NDem ⊃ NA and (VI′) NNum ⊃ NA, which do not allow a postnominal demonstrative or numeral to co-occur with a prenominal adjective. As far as I can tell, the following are all and only the occurring sequences of these four categories (exemplifying languages are placed alongside the attested sequences; for postposed modifiers, only the preferred ordering is listed, other possibilities are discussed in what follows):

(3) (A) *3 modifiers on the left / 0 on the right*[14]

	Dem – Num – Adj – N	Chinese (Mandarin), English, Finnish, Hindi, Hungarian, Maung

(B) *2 modifiers on the left / 1 on the right*

(i)	Dem – Num – N – Adj	French, Italian
(ii)	* Dem – Adj – N – Num	No examples
(iii)	* Num – Adj – N – Dem	No examples

(C) *1 modifier on the left / 2 on the right*

(i)	Dem – N – Adj – Num	Kabardian, Warao
(ii)	Num – N – Adj – Dem	Basque, Easter Island, Indonesian, Jacaltec, Maori, Vietnamese, Welsh
(iii)	* Adj – N – Num – Dem	No examples

(D) *0 modifiers on the left / 3 on the right*

	N – Adj – Num – Dem	Selepet, Yoruba

The starred sequences are those which are compatible with Greenberg's universal (20) yet ruled out by Universals (V′) and (VI′). If Greenberg's (20) is allowed to operate in conjunction with (V′) and (VI′), therefore, it will make exactly the right predictions for preposed noun modifiers, and the "any or all" clause will be limited in just the right ways.

The situation with postposed noun modifiers is much more complicated. In addition to the preferred mirror-image orderings, Greenberg mentions that postposed modifiers can occur in the same relative order as preposed modifiers, citing (p. 87) the example of Kikuyu with N – Dem – Num – Adj. But N – Adj – Num – Dem and the reverse N – Dem – Num – Adj are not the only possibilities. Aghem, for instance, has the obligatory order N – Adj – Dem – Num (cf. Hyman 1979:27), that is, a mixed order with Dem and Num in the Kikuyu order, and Adj in the preferred mirror-image position adjacent to the noun. And Noni (see Hyman 1981:31) has the Kikuyu order N – Dem – Num – Adj, as well as N – Dem – Adj – Num, in which Adj and Num are reversed relative to the Kikuyu order. These examples suggest that the disjunction of Greenberg's universal (20b) must be abandoned.

We can now revise Greenberg's (20) as follows:

(20′) When any or all of the modifiers (demonstrative, numeral, and descriptive adjective) precede the noun, they (i.e., those that do precede) are always found in that order. For those that follow, no

> predictions are made, though the most frequent order is the mirror-image of the order for preceding modifiers. In no case does the adjective precede the head when the demonstrative or numeral follow.

Notice that the last sentence of (20′) in effect incorporates Universals (V′) NDem ⊃ NA and (VI′) NNum ⊃ NA into Greenberg's sequencing universal. Technically, this is superfluous. In a more formalized universal grammar, in which different components interact to predict all and only the attested language types, such repetition will be unnecessary. Universals (V′) and (VI′) are accounted for by the HSP, which is logically independent of any sequencing statement. The HSP and the MP may limit the class of permissible sequences, but they make no predictions for the relative order of modifiers to one another. And sequencing universals, as we shall see, are essentially compatible with any modifier preceding or following the head. But if the preposing or postposing of noun modifiers is explained by a combination of heaviness and mobility, what are these independent linguistic generalizations that explain the relative sequencing of a plurality of modifiers?

3.6.2 THE ORIGINS OF SEQUENCING: CONSTITUENCY AND ADJACENCY

Constituent structure can impose numerous constraints on sequencing. Consider the English noun phrase *the king of England from England,* as discussed by Jackendoff (1977:59). Jackendoff proposes the following tree, within the context of his version of the X-bar theory (which we shall be discussing more fully in Section 4.6.2):

(4)

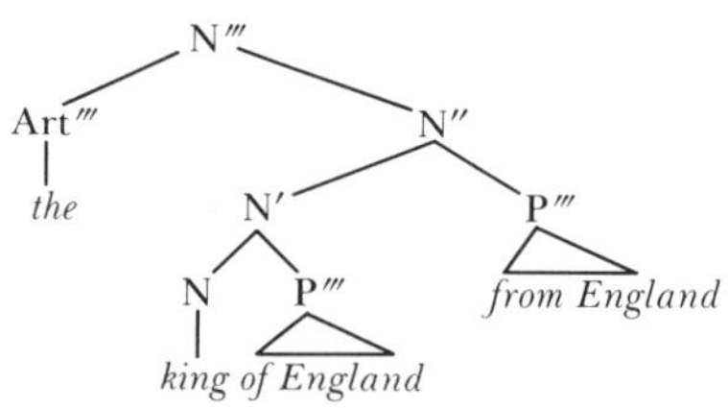

And he remarks that the two PPs (cf. P‴) can occur in only one of two possible orders: *the king of England from England,* not **the king from England of England.* This ordering provides some of the motivation for his proposed constituent structure. But it does so only in conjunction with a major assumption which has been almost universally held within generative grammar since its inception: the assumption of the adjacency of daughter constituents (i.e., that daughter constituents cannot be discontinuous from one another, separated by a constituent or constituents dominated by a different higher node). The adjacency assumption explains the ungrammaticality of **the king from England of England*, since the only tree structure it could have, given the independently motivated constituency of (4), would be (5), with crossed branches resulting from the discontinuity of *king* and *of England.*

(5)

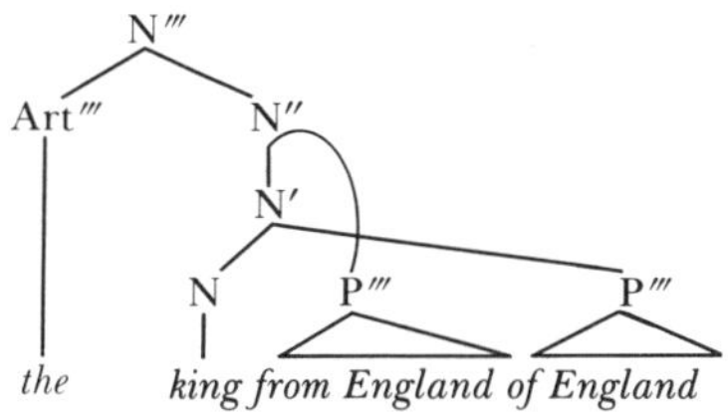

Similar reasoning underlies Jackendoff's (1977:63) argument that appositive relative clauses are daughters of N ‴ and restrictive relatives daughters of N″, which then results in restrictive relatives being closer to the head, given the adjacency assumption: *the man that bought the strawberries, who was dangerous* versus **the man, who was dangerous, that bought the strawberries.*

The tree that Jackendoff gives (p. 127) for the noun phrase type *these five large houses,* discussed here in Section 3.6.1, is:

(6)

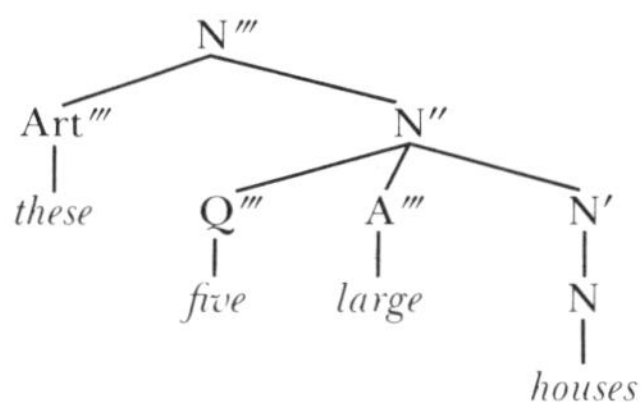

The relative proximity of *five large* to the head, and the relative distance of *these,* is determined by constituency plus adjacency (crossed branches would be required otherwise), whereas the relative order of *five* and *large* is simply fixed by the PS-rule rewriting N″ (p. 105). Grammatical theories that posit exclusively binary branching structures (such as categorial grammar, see Keenan's 1979 function–argument structures, Vennemann 1976, Ades & Steedman 1982, and many others) would use the relative ordering facts as motivation for a deeper branching structure as in (7).

(7)

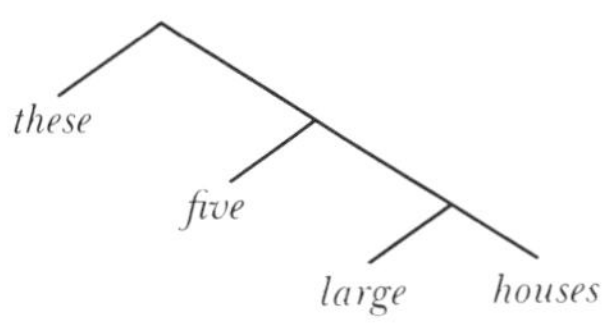

They might seek further justification for such a tree in the cross-language variation documented in (3), and in the preferred relative orderings for postposed modifiers. All of the relative orderings listed in (3) are consistent with a constituency such as (7), in conjunction with an adjacency assumption outlawing crossed branches:

(8)

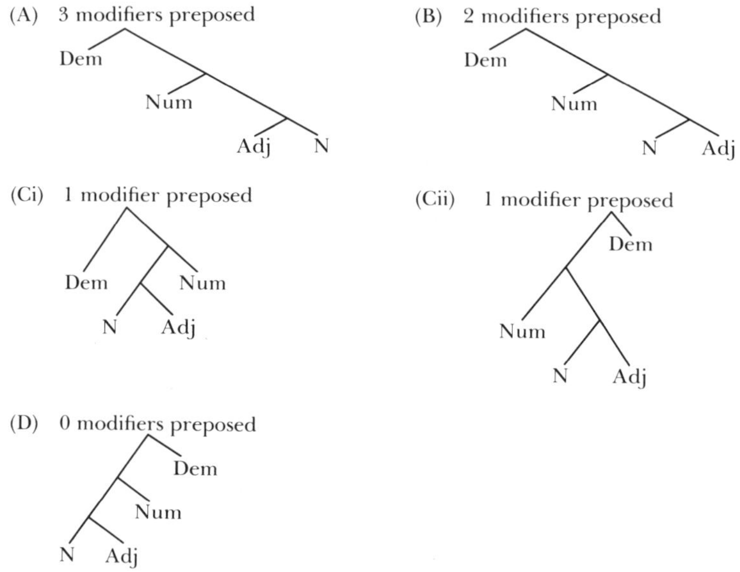

Constituency and adjacency are also consistent, of course, with unattested sequences such as (3Bii) *Dem – Adj – N – Num:

(9)

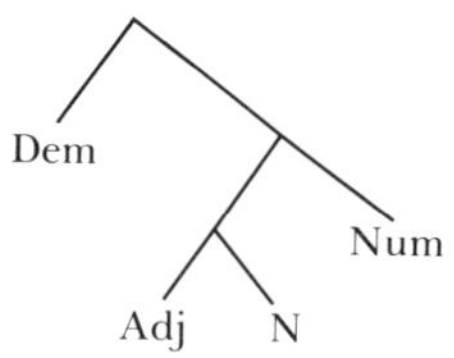

but we have already argued that there are independent considerations, involving heaviness, which rule these cases out.

To attempt to explain sequencing variation in terms of constituency and adjacency, however, is only as convincing as the proposed constituent structures are independently motivated. It is no use saying that a constituent structure such as (7) explains word order sequencing, if the only evidence for that constituent structure is the word order itself. Transformational grammarians have been particularly concerned with the need to motivate constituent structure, by both syntactic and semantic means.

The most crucial tests have involved rule sensitivity; that is, syntactic rules can be found which move, delete, or substitute particular constituents, such as NP or VP, and these rules can then serve as diagnostics for the constituents in question in given sentences. Rules of semantic interpretation involving, for example, anaphoric pronouns, can also provide evidence for consistuency, on account of the relevance of the constituent-command relation to coreference versus noncoreference (cf. Reinhart 1981). Semantic generalizations may further corroborate independent syntactic tests of constituency, as when Jackendoff (1977) argues that his three bar levels—in trees such as (4)–(6)—have a semantic counterpart: Complements of X′ are functional arguments, those of X″ are restrictive modifiers, and those of X‴ appositive modifiers. And word order itself can provide an additional argument for constituent structure (in conjunction with adjacency).

Unfortunately, there is considerable disagreement between theories. Even within generative grammar, it is not certain precisely what the constituents are to which various syntactic processes are sensitive; there is disagreement over the number of bar levels within X-bar theory (cf. Chomsky 1970 versus Jackendoff 1977); and so on. And across theories, different weight is attached to syntactic or to semantic criteria. Within categorial grammar, for example, semantic criteria (plus word order) are used to motivate constituent structure, whereas the typical transformational tests involving rule sensitivity (so meticulously exemplified in, e.g., Jackendoff 1977) are generally ignored. And, conversely, whatever semantic motivation underlies the binary branching structures of categorial grammars is not considered within generative grammar, as the modifier–head theory which underlies generative PS-rules is irreconcilable with the function–argument relation of categorial grammars (Sections 2.4.3, 2.6.1). This indeterminacy about constituent structure weakens considerably the claim that constituency does in fact explain word order sequencing.

Nor is the adjacency assumption on completely firm ground. The axiom of "no crossed branches" is not shared by all syntactic theories, as McCawley (1982a) points out, and he provides some compelling arguments for discontinuous constituents in several surface structures of English (involving parentheticals, extraposed relatives, Right Node Raising, Heavy NP Shift, and Particle Shift), and in scrambling structures in Latin.

The extent to which constituency can be invoked to explain word order sequencing must therefore be qualified. Where one or more firmly established independent criteria for constituency do exist, as in the case, say, of Jackendoff's (4) (*the king of England from England*); and where this constituent structure is compatible with some word order sequences and not others, assuming adjacency; and where there are no good reasons for doubting what may be the reasonable assumption of "adjacency in the unmarked case"—then constituency may be said to explain word order sequencing. But where independent arguments for constituency are not given, and the proposed constituent structures are derived crucially from the word order itself, then clearly no explanation for word order is available.

There is a real danger, particularly in the primarily semantically inspired work of categorial grammar, that constituent structures are being proposed on the basis of little more than an a priori assumption about binary branching structure, in conjunction with surface word order. And linguistic generalizations may be being subsumed under the notion of constituency which are really quite independent. For example, I can see no syntactic justification for the binary branching condition, either in surface structure or in deep structure. More radically still, it is quite conceivable that deep and surface structures are considerably "flatter" than has hitherto been thought within generative grammar. For example, Hale (1978, 1982) and Chomsky (1981) introduce a distinction between configurational languages, such as English, and nonconfigurational languages, such as Japanese. They argue that a Japanese sentence consisting of a subject, direct object, indirect object, oblique constituent, and verb would have a flat structure, as in (10), and that numerous independent properties of Japanese conspire to motivate this lack of internal constituency, properties that distinguish Japanese from a configurational language like English which has a VP (and possibly further constituent groupings with VP):

(10)

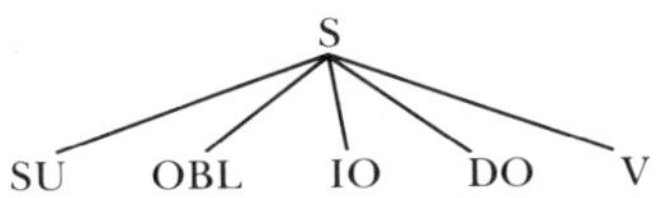

A categorial grammar tree would be (11):

(11)

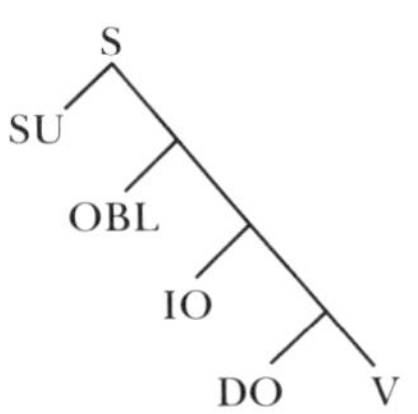

One might seek to justify a structure like (11) by arguing (with D. Smith

1978) that SU–OBL–IO–DO–V is the preferred and unmarked sequencing for Japanese, and that there is a hierarchy of "semantic bonding" between the different arguments and the verb. But, clearly, whatever syntactic evidence there is for (10) is evidence against (11) as a syntactic structure. And constituency is not the only means available in the grammar for capturing unmarked word order sequencing, or semantic cohesion. Unmarked word orders can result from the combination of an initial word order specification plus later rules of permutation. And semantically, standard predicate logic operates with a flat constituent structure for these four-place predicates, as in (10). The semantic bonding intuition may then result from independent factors such as the obligatory versus optional presence of some argument in the lexical entry, or from the real-world interpretation of the predicate in question. Keenan's (1979) attempt to motivate the function–argument assignments within his form of categorial grammar on the grounds that function categories may vary in their interpretations with their arguments (compare, e.g., *the boy ran, the water ran, the stocking ran*) might be explained differently by appealing to the referential nature of his argument categories (NPs and Ns)—they pick out objects, and the kinds of objects they select (boys, water, stockings, etc.) will determine how the accompanying descriptive predicate or function categories are understood. Objects can (in general) exist independently of the descriptive actions and states that are predicated of them, and their interpretation will remain constant across real-world interpretations to a greater extent than that of function categories. But if referentiality is what underlies the varying interpretations to which Keenan draws attention, then his function–argument distinction overlaps with the nonreferential–referential distinction, and it would be the latter and not the former which actually explains the semantic variation in question. The referential–nonreferential distinction could then coexist with a quite different set of function–argument assignments, and with quite different assumptions about constituency.

The point here is that constituency is the locus of considerable theoretical disagreement, both because it is not clear exactly which linguistic properties are to be subsumed under it and because different weight is attached to different criteria. Where numerous independent arguments conspire to motivate given constituent structures, then clear word order predictions are made, in conjunction with adjacency. But otherwise there is a danger that the true syntactic and semantic generalizations which explain sequencing are being missed, and that constituency is being offered as an explanation, when the evidence for the constituent structures in question is either not compelling or includes the very word order facts that constituency is supposed to be explaining.

3.6.3 CONSTITUENCY, ADJACENCY, AND LANGUAGE VARIATION

The example of Japanese in Section 3.6.2 raises the issue of language variation in the context of constituency and adjacency. Let us assume that some of the disagreements we have just discussed can be resolved, and that constituency can emerge as a stronger explanation for word order sequencing than it is at present. What, then, will be the ways in which we might expect languages to differ from one another?

Three major sources of variation present themselves:

1. Languages may vary within the constraints permitted by constituency and adjacency.
2. Languages may vary by having different constituent structures.
3. Languages may vary in the extent to which adjacency holds.

The first possibility was illustrated in (8). Constituency and adjacency impose an upper limit on sequencing within the noun phrase, assuming a common constituency across languages. However, the existence of variant orders among postposed modifiers within the noun phrase (N – Adj – Num – Dem as well as N – Dem – Num – Adj, N – Adj – Dem – Num; see Section 3.6.1) reveals that the languages in question either have different constituent structures or no adjacency of daughters (or conceivably both). I shall not speculate here on what the constituent structures of Kikuyu or Aghem, etc., are.

The possibility of languages having different constituent structures is what underlies the distinction between configurational and nonconfigurational languages. This possibility has also received a lot of attention in the debate over the VP node in VSO and SOV languages (see Schwartz 1972). Without going into details here, notice only that the general claim of different constituencies across languages may be relativized by positing a constituent structure difference in surface structure only, rather than throughout a derivation. Hale's nonconfigurationality analysis for Japanese holds throughout the syntactic derivation. But one might argue that a flat VSO structure, for example, is derived from an underlying tree containing a VP constituent (see Emonds 1980, Anderson & Chung 1977). These latter analyses of VSO languages are motivated by arguing that certain rules (such as Topicalization) apply to a VP constituent, even though there is no evidence of such a constituent in surface structure, assuming adjacency. The result is, then, a weakening of the claim that languages have different constituent structures, since at more underlying levels there is similarity.

Finally, languages may vary with regard to adjacency. Again, nonadjacency may be assumed for certain strings throughout a derivation, or in surface structure only (see McCawley 1982a). And the number and nature of discontinuous structures may vary from language to language.

Language variation along these three dimensions will in turn result in further variation. For example, languages with flat verb-final structures, as in (10), typically have rich case-marking systems, and permit considerable word order freedom, or scrambling (see Keenan 1978, Thompson 1978). One might hypothesize that case marking in nonconfigurational languages serves to indicate the syntactic grouping and grammatical functions which constituency and adjacency define in configurational languages. Word order permutations would then be possible among sister constituents in flat structures whose grammatical functions are clearly encoded morphologically. And a loss in case marking (as in the history of English) can be expected to result in richer constituency and tighter adjacency (the VP node, SVO order, the reduction in word order freedom, etc.; see Hawkins, 1984).

Notes

1. $2^{20} = 1{,}048{,}576$ possible co-occurrences. Additional word orders that could be reckoned in to the calculations are, for example, possessive adjective + noun (e.g., *my dog*); adjective phrases as opposed to simple adjectives (cf. *the boy green with envy* versus *the green leaf*); infinitival versus finite sentence complements of the verb (some languages, such as German, have potentially different orderings for these two types of sentence complements relative to the governing verb); various modifiers of the adposition phrase (e.g., *right* in *right near the park*). If just these five extra operator–operand word orders are added in, the possible word order co-occurrences are over 30 million: $2^{25} = 33{,}554{,}432$. If one then considers in addition the relative sequencing of operators to one another (see, e.g., Greenberg's universal (20) and Section 3.6), the mathematical possibilities soar to many hundreds of millions at least.

2. Four languages have Vennemann's OV properties across the board: Burushaski, Japanese, Kannada, and Turkish.

Three languages have all Vennemann's VO properties except for SV: Fulani, Swahili, and Yoruba.

Six languages have all VO properties except for NumN: Berber, Hebrew, Malay, Thai, Welsh, and Zapotec.

Two languages have OV properties except for NA, NNum, and MVSV: Chibcha and Nubian.

Three languages have VO properties except for AN, DN, NumN, and AdvAdj: Greek, Maya, and Serbian.

The remaining twelve languages of the 30-language sample each exemplify a different co-occurrence type.

3. Type 14 should also be unattested (see Chapter 2, Note 2).

4. Hixkaryana is clearly GN, but adjective phrases as such do not occur (Derbyshire, 1979:42). However, adjective-like modifiers of the noun, including particles (p. 84), clearly follow the noun: *kamaro ymo* 'jaguar augmentative', i.e., 'the big bad jaguar'; *toto heno kom* 'person now-dead collective', i.e., 'the people now dead'. And Derbyshire writes: "Preposed modifiers are infrequent in noun phrases, being restricted to numerals and the nominal form *anaro* 'another' [p. 44]."

5. According to the distributional universal of Chapter 4, the co-occurrences Postp & VSO and Prep & SOV are both predicted to be very rare, but not impossible. The smaller number of Postp & VSO compared to Prep & SOV simply reflects the much smaller number of VSO languages compared to SOV. A predictably rare co-occurrence will therefore be that much less frequent in VSO than in SOV languages (see also Chapter 2, Note 2).

6. The motivation for this formulation principle is a practical one: It makes it easier to check whether languages are, or are not, consistent with the implicational universals. If a large number of languages have the properties that are explicitly mentioned in the universal (e.g., Po & AN & GN), their adherence to its predictions is straightforwardly confirmed. But, if only a small number of languages have the explicitly mentioned properties (e.g., Po & NA & NG), the majority of languages must be checked by first computing the appropriate negative values for antecedent and consequent. And as a result, the evaluation of consistency or inconsistency is more cumbersome for many more languages.

7. The supporting languages for (VII) Prep ⊃ (NDem ⊃ NG) are:

Prep languages

NDem & NG:	Berber, Fulani, Hebrew, Malay, Swahili, Thai, Welsh, Yoruba, Zapotec/ Aghem, Arosi, Bahasa Indonesian, Bikol, Dyola, Easter Island, Ekpeye, Fijian, Gilbertese, Haya, Ikwere, Indonesian, Irish, Jacaltec, Kaliai-Kove, Khasi, Khmer, Luangiua, Macassarese, Marshallese, Mokilese, Niuean, Rotuman, Sundanese, Tagalog, Takuu, Thai, Toba Batak, Tongan, Ulithian, Vietnamese
DemN & NG:	Greek, Italian, Maori, Masai, Maya, Serbian/ Baure, Bukidnon, Czech, Douala, Dutch, French, Hiligaynon, Icelandic, Ineseño Chumash, Otomi, Pangasinan, Portugese, Russian, Spanish, Tunen, Xhosa
DemN & GN:	Norwegian/ Amharic, Danish, Kiriwinan, Maung, Old Persian, Swedish, Tiwi
*NDem & GN:	No examples predicted

There are two languages in the Expanded Sample that do have the co-occurrence *Pr & NDem & GN: Kaliai-Kove and Karen. But as with the exceptions to Universal (III), they are both SVO.

Our seventh implicational universal is, therefore, more precisely:

(VII) If a language has Prep word order, then if the demonstrative determiner follows the noun, the genitive follows the noun; i.e., Prep ⊃ (NDem ⊃ NG). (statistical)

(VII′) If a language has Prep and any verb position other than SVO, then if the demonstrative determiner follows the noun, the genitive follows the noun; i.e., Prep & −SVO ⊃ (NDem ⊃ NG).

The supporting languages for (VIII) Prep ⊃ (NNum ⊃ NG) are:

Prep languages

NNum & NG:	Fulani, Masai, Swahili, Yoruba/ Aghem, Chrau, Douala, Dyola, Ekpeye, Haya, Igbo, Ikwere, Khmer, Malagasay, Marshallese, Mokilese, Niuean, Ogbah, Rotuman, Takuu, Tongan, Tunen
NumN & NG:	Berber, Greek, Hebrew, Italian, Malay, Maori, Maya, Serbian, Thai, Welsh, Zapotec/ Bahasa Indonesian, Baure, Bikol, Chorti, Czech,

Dutch, Easter Island, Fijian, French, Gilbertese, Hiligaynon, Indonesian, Ineseño Chumash, Iraqi Arabic, Irish, Jacaltec, Kampangan, Macassarese, Pangasinan, Russian, Sre, Sundanese, Syrian Arabic, Tagalog, Thai, Toba Batak, Tzeltal, Ulithian, Vietnamese

NumN & GN: Norwegian/ Amharic, Danish, Maung, Old Persian, Swedish, Tiwi

*NNum & GN: No examples predicted

Exactly the same three co-occurrences are predicted. The only difference is that numerals precede the noun more frequently than demonstrative determiners. Again, there are two exceptional languages in the Expanded Sample with *Pr & NNum & GN (& SVO): Kaliai-Kove and Karen.

We have, therefore, our eighth implicational universal:

(VIII) If a language has Prep word order, then if the numeral follows the noun, the genitive follows the noun; i.e., Prep ⊃ (NNum ⊃ NG). (statistical)

(VIII′) If a language has Prep word order and any verb position other than SVO, then if the numeral follows the noun, the genitive follows the noun; i.e., Prep & −SVO ⊃ (NNum ⊃ NG).

8. The supporting languages for (X) Prep ⊃ (NA ⊃ NRel) are:

Prep languages

NA & NRel: Berber, Fulani, Hebrew, Italian, Malay, Maori, Masai, Swahili, Thai, Welsh, Yoruba, Zapotec/ Aghem, Albanian, Arosi, Bahasa Indonesian, Bandem, Baure, Douala, Dyola, Easter Island, Fijian, French, Ge'ez, Gilbertese, Hawaiian, Haya, Indonesian, Iraqi Arabic, Irish, Jacaltec, Kaliai-Kove, Karen, Khmer, Luangiua, Macassarese, Malagasay, Marshallese, Niuean, Persian (Tajik), Persian (Tehran), Portugese, Rotuman, Rumanian, Samoan, Scots Gaelic, Spanish, Sre, Sundanese, Syrian Arabic, Tahitian, Takuu, Thai, Toba Batak, Tongan, Trukese, Tunen, Ulithian, Vietnamese, Xhosa, Zulu

AN & NRel: Greek, Maya, Norwegian, Serbian/ Bukidnon, Cebuano, Classical Mayan, Czech, Danish, Dutch, German, Hausa, Hiligaynon, Icelandic, Kampangan, Kiriwinan, Lithuanian, Maung, Nahuatl, Old Persian, Otomi, Pangasinan, Russian, Slovenian, Swedish, Tagabili, Tzeltal

AN & RelN: / Amharic

*NA & RelN: No examples

For (XI) Prep ⊃ (NDem ⊃ NRel) we have:

Prep languages

NDem & NRel: Berber, Fulani, Hebrew, Malay, Swahili, Thai, Welsh, Yoruba, Zapotec/ Aghem, Arosi, Bahasa Indonesian, Bikol, Easter Island, Fijian, Gilbertese, Haya, Indonesian, Irish, Jacaltec, Kaliai-Kove, Karen, Khmer, Luangiua, Macassarese, Marshallese, Niuean, Rotuman, Sundanese, Takuu, Tagalog, Thai, Toba Batak, Tongan, Ulithian, Vietnamese

DemN & NRel: Greek, Italian, Maori, Masai, Maya, Norwegian, Serbian/ Baure, Bukidnon, Czech, Danish, Douala, Dutch, French, German, Hiligaynon, Icelandic, Ineseño Chumash, Kiriwinan, Maung, Old Persian, Otomi, Pangasinan, Portugese, Russian, Slovenian, Spanish, Swedish, Tunen, Xhosa

DemN & RelN: / Amharic

*NDem & RelN: No examples

And for (XII) Prep ⊃ (NNum ⊃ NRel):

Prep languages

NNum & NRel: Fulani, Masai, Swahili, Yoruba/ Aghem, Chrau, Douala, Dyola, Haya, Kaliai-Kove, Karen, Khmer, Malagasay, Marshallese, Niuean, Rotuman, Takuu, Tongan, Tunen

NumN & NRel: Berber, Greek, Hebrew, Italian, Malay, Maori, Maya, Norwegian, Serbian, Thai, Welsh, Zapotec/ Bahasa Indonesian, Baure, Bikol, Czech, Danish, Dutch, Easter Island, Fijian, French, German, Gilbertese, Hiligaynon, Indonesian, Ineseño Chumash, Iraqi Arabic, Irish, Jacaltec, Kampangan, Macassarese, Old Persian, Pangasinan, Russian, Slovenian, Sre, Sundanese, Swedish, Syrian Arabic, Tagalog, Thai, Toba Batak, Trukese, Tzeltal, Ulithian, Vietnamese

NumN & RelN: / Amharic

*NNum & RelN: No examples

9. It is interesting in this regard that Amharic, according to Little (1977), is moving historically toward postpositions and away from prepositions, and already has a significant number of postpositions.

10. More precisely, each of these hierarchies predicts that a constituent *A* will prepose before *or simultaneously with* a constituent *B*, wherever an ordering is defined between *A* and *B*.

11. Kuno (1974) has also discussed the position of relative clauses from the point of view of processing load. His account differs from that which we have offered in the main text. He sets out to explain the fact that VSO languages invariably have postnominal relative clauses, whereas strict SOV languages such as Japanese tend to have prenominal relatives. He attributes this distribution to the avoidance of center embedding, which is perceptually difficult. Thus, VSO languages with postnominal relatives have much less center embedding than they would with prenominal relatives:

VSO with prenominal relative clauses

(i) *Died (loved Mary) boy.* (center embedding)
(ii) *Hated (loved Mary) boy Jane.* (center embedding)
(iii) *Hated Jane (loved Mary) boy.* (center embedding)

VSO with postnominal relative clauses

(i) *Died boy (loved Mary).*
(ii) *Hated boy (loved Mary) Jane.* (center embedding)
(iii) *Hated Jane boy (loved Mary).*

while SOV languages with prenominal relatives have much less center embedding than they do with their postnominal counterparts:

SOV with prenominal relative clauses

(i) *(Mary loved) boy died.*
(ii) *(Mary loved) boy Jane hated.*
(iii) *Jane (Mary loved) boy hated.* (center embedding)

SOV with postnominal relative clauses

(i) *Boy (Mary loved) died.* (center embedding)
(ii) *Boy (Mary loved) Jane hated.* (center embedding)
(iii) *Jane boy (Mary loved) hated.* (center embedding)

Kuno's theory therefore makes different predictions for SOV languages than our own. And whereas our theory attaches importance to a combination of head recognition delay, number of decision tasks, short-term memory burden, and misanalysis of clause boundaries, Kuno pins everything on center embedding and its associated processing difficulties.

There are three problems for Kuno's theory which lead us to reject it in favor of the account we have offered here. First, the empirical prediction that SOV languages should have prenominal relatives is false: Only 30 out of 54 SOV languages in the Expanded Sample do so (55.6%). In our terms, the processing pressure in favor of *postnominal* relatives in all languages is sufficient to counterbalance the typological pressure in favor of modifier before head in SOV languages, resulting in what appears to be a random distribution but is really a stand-off between conflicting forces. Second, Kuno's theory predicts that SVO languages should have roughly equal numbers of prenominal and postnominal relative clauses: Prenominal relatives will produce center embedding on the object but not on the subject; postnominal relatives will produce center embedding on the subject but not on the object. In fact, all but four SVO languages in the Expanded Sample have postnominal relatives, as in VSO languages. Once again, the preference for postnominal relatives is asserting itself, in contrast to Kuno's predictions, and only when independent typological counterprinciples are operative is this preference overcome. Languages that serialize modifiers before heads contain such a counterprinciple, and my impressionistic evidence suggests that the more rigidly they serialize modifiers before heads in general, the more they resist the relative clause ordering preference (to produce Japanese-type languages). Finally, it should be pointed out that the type of center embedding which is involved in relative clause modifiers of a noun is very different from that which is found in clausal (i.e., S) complements. Grosu and Thompson (1977) and Dryer (1980) have discussed in some detail the processing difficulties that are caused by clause-internal complements, and which lead to a clear cross-linguistic aversion to center embedding in favor of clause-initial and especially clause-final position for such Ss (cf. discussion in the main text, Section 3.4.2.1). But relative clauses are different: They are semantic and syntactic modifiers of a main clause argument, and their interpretation is therefore anchored to this main clause element in a way that is typically not the case with clausal complements, and this presumably lessens the processing difficulties involved. At any rate, the empirical evidence does not support Kuno's theory, and this leads us to reject his account of the processing difficulties involved.

12. If acceptability really were distinct from grammaticality, then in addition to the putative cases of unacceptable but grammatical sentences, we should expect to find examples of the converse: acceptable but ungrammatical sentences. I have yet to see any convincing cases of this kind. Their absence supports my contention that the acceptability–grammaticality distinction is motivated only by the awareness that there are different explanatory causes of ungrammaticality (those with a processing explanation, and those without).

13. There is another use that has been made of diachrony in the explanation of synchronic universals: Attempts have been made to set up diachronic links between the properties that are correlated in implicational universals (see Mallinson & Blake 1981: Chapter 6 for a summary). For example, a head noun before genitive construction (*the back of the hut*) may shift diachronically into a prepositional phrase (*back of the hut*), whereas a genitive before head would become a postpositional phrase. Such considerations are then invoked to explain the word order correlations themselves.

However, although such diachronic drifts do undoubtedly occur, and although they can explain some diachronic developments in numerous individual languages, they are not sufficient to explain the synchronic universals. First, the synchronic universals for which we have seen evidence are no longer the simple one-to-one correlations that such diachronic links presuppose. For example, there are numerous exceptions to the NGen & Pr + NP and GenN & NP + Po correlations. And, more generally, we have seen the need for multitermed and unilateral implicational statements, in order to capture cross-language word order patterns. Diachronic links would appear to be unable to explain the attested and unattested language types that such implications define. Second, even with a set of synchronic one-to-one correlations of a statistical nature (e.g., the NSP), the number of word order pairs for which diachronic links are plausible is very limited, compared with the total number of correlations that such theories define. Diachronic links are only plausible for those word order pairs which are sufficiently closely related semantically that the one structure can merge gradually into the other, which is a small number. Third, it is not clear how well supported these diachronic drifts are: For how many languages have they been attested or reconstructed?

Overall, therefore, this kind of diachronic explanation for synchronic universals lacks generality. By contrast, the gradualness of language change is a more solidly attested, and general, diachronic universal, and it is this that we claim constitutes the historical contribution to the explanation of word order universals, in conjunction with synchronic syntactic regularities (branching/nonbranching constituents, phrasal/nonphrasal nodes).

14. In an important paper, Whitman (1981) argues that the adjective may on some occasions precede demonstrative and numeral when all three precede the noun and the language is verb final: namely, when the adjective has a nonrestrictive as opposed to a restrictive interpretation. His analysis receives additional plausibility from the fact that prenominal relative clauses in verb-final languages also seem to receive a nonrestrictive as opposed to a restrictive interpretation depending on whether they precede or follow their determiner respectively. Greenberg's Universal (20) therefore holds for adjectives with restrictive interpretations only.

4 : *A Distributional Universal in Greenberg's Data and the Expanded Sample*

Having set up implicational universals distinguishing attested from nonattested word order co-occurrences in Greenberg's data and the Expanded Sample, we can now show that the numerical distribution of languages across the attested types is principled. Underlying the relative sizes of the word order co-occurrence types there emerges a distributional generalization which I shall call the principle of Cross-Category Harmony (CCH). After a presentation of the basic insight (Section 4.1), CCH will be defined and tested against data from Greenberg's Appendix II (Section 4.2). After some general remarks about CCH (Section 4.3), the principle will be further tested using the Expanded Sample (Section 4.4), and Greenberg's 30-language sample (Section 4.5). Issues of explanation are discussed in Section 4.6.

4.1 Cross-Category Harmony (CCH)

4.1.1 THE BASIC INSIGHT

The primary purpose of CCH is to predict the relative quantities of languages that have the implicationally permitted word order co-occurrence sets. These quantities vary considerably, as can be seen by comparing the attested types in Greenberg's Appendix II.

Contrary to Vennemann's NSP, the majority of languages do not serialize all their operators on a consistent side of their operands (all on the left, or all on the right). We saw in Section 2.4.4 that only 48% of

Greenberg's Appendix II languages, and 23% of the 30-language sample, had cross-categorial word orders in accordance with NSP. Even within one and the same phrasal category, languages regularly have mixed preposing and postposing of operators on the operand head. For example, most languages are like English in having some operators on the noun to the left and some to the right within the noun phrase (23 of the languages in Greenberg's 30-language sample—i.e., 77%—have both preposed and postposed noun modifiers); the majority of languages have some operators on the verb to the right and some to the left (18 languages in the 30-language sample—i.e., 60%—are either SVO or nonrigid SOV and hence have both preposed and postposed modifiers of the verb).

In a nutshell, CCH asserts instead that there is a quantifiable preference for the ratio of preposed to postposed operators within one phrasal category (i.e., NP, VP/S, AdjP, AdpP) to generalize to the others. Whatever position the operand of one phrasal category occupies in relation to all its operators will preferably be matched by the position of the operand in each of the other phrasal categories. And the more the word order co-occurrence sets of languages depart from this "ideal" harmonic ordering, the fewer exemplifying languages there are.

The "ideal" that CCH defines is therefore different from that of Vennemann's NSP. And CCH, but not NSP, makes an explicit quantitative prediction to the effect that the more a language type departs from the most harmonic ordering, the fewer exemplifying languages there will be. If we recast NSP slightly, so that it too can make predictions for relative language frequencies, we will see that NSP's predictions are consistently less successful than those of CCH. Whereas NSP is founded on the intuition of "all operators to the left, or all to the right," CCH builds on the notion of an ordering balance across phrasal categories, regardless of whether all operators occur on the left, or most occur on the left and some on the right, some on the left and most on the right, etc.

Consider as a preliminary illustration the quantities of languages exemplifying the various co-occurrences of noun position within NP, and verb position within S, as shown in Table 5. Rigid verb-final languages are generally noun final within the NP (5 out of 6 languages are N_3 in Table 5), whereas nonrigid verb-final languages (which have at least one operator on the verb regularly following the verb) are generally not noun final: They regularly (in 4 out of 5 cases in Table 5) have the adjective operator following the noun, matching the operator(s) after the verb. With VSO and SVO we notice correspondingly that the more leftward position of the verb in VSO languages is matched by a more leftward position of the noun within the NP. Thus, 100% of VSO languages in Table 5 are noun first,

TABLE 5 : Co-occurrences of Noun Position within NP and Verb Position within S in the 30-Language Sample

6 SOVr languages	5 SOVnr languages	13 SVO languages	6 VSO languages	
SOVr & N_3 5	SOVnr & N_3 1	SVO & N_3 2	VSO & N_3 0	8 N_3 languages
SOVr & N_2 1	SOVnr & N_2 4	SVO & N_2 5	VSO & N_2 0	10 N_2 languages
SOVr & N_1 0	SOVnr & N_1 0	SVO & N_1 6	VSO & N_1 6	12 N_1 languages

Note: SOVr = rigid SOV; SOVnr = nonrigid SOV; N_1 = noun-first (N before A and G); N_2 = noun-second (or -medial; N between the two); N_3 = noun-third (or -final; N after both).

whereas only 6 out of 13 SVO languages have this co-occurrence, with the remaining 7 preferring at least one operator before the noun.

Appendix II and the Expanded Sample corroborate this pattern. Universals (I) SOV ⊃ (AN ⊃ GN) and (IV) Postp ⊃ (AN ⊃ GN) permit the following co-occurrence possibilities (Appendix II language quantities listed first, Expanded Sample quantities given in parentheses):

23. SOV & Po & AN & GN	28 languages (96)	*decline* ↓
24. SOV & Po & NA & GN	24 languages (55)	
21. SOV & Po & NA & NG	7 languages (11)	

Universals (II) VSO ⊃ (NA ⊃ NG) and (III) Prep ⊃ (NA ⊃ NG) permit the following:

1. VSO & Pr & NA & NG	19 languages (38)	*decline* ↓
2. VSO & Pr & AN & NG	5 languages (13)	
3. VSO & Pr & AN & GN	1 language (1)	

Prepositional languages with SVO pattern just like VSO & Pr languages:

9. SVO & Pr & NA & NG	21 languages (56)	*decline* ↓
10. SVO & Pr & AN & NG	8 languages (17)	
11. SVO & Pr & AN & GN	3 languages (7)	

If the operators on the verb and on the adposition are all preposed (SOV & Po), then the most favored languages are those in which the operators on the noun are all preposed as well (AN & GN), the next favored languages have only one noun operator postposed (NA & GN), and the least favored have two postposed (NA & NG). And, if the operators on the verb and adposition are predominantly postposed (VSO/SVO), then the most favored languages are those with both operators on the noun postposed (NA & NG), the next favored have only one noun operator preposed (AN & NG), and the least favored have both preposed (AN & GN).

Evidently, there are quantifiable preferences for the position of the noun in relation to its operators to mirror the position of the verb and the adposition in relation to their operators. And as the order of these operands across the respective phrasal categories comes into increasing conflict, the number of exemplifying languages decreases.

4.1.2 A METHODOLOGICAL PRELIMINARY

So far we have a rough initial hypothesis, and preliminary motivation for a distributional principle of Cross-Category Harmony. Before we define this principle more precisely, notice that the quantitative data from Appendix II (Section 4.1.1) consider the noun in conjunction with both verb and adposition orders. But this kind of quantification gives us no means of knowing whether it is verb position alone, adposition order alone, or some combination of the two which results in fewer languages as a consequence of the conflict with noun position. In order to tease this out, we must first consider operand orders pairwise, noun with verb (as in Table 5), noun with adposition, and verb with adposition, before considering all three together.

4.1.3 SUBJECTS AS OPERATORS ON VERBS

The distributional facts considered in Section 4.1.1 support the inclusion of subject and verb in the operator–operand relation, as in Vennemann's redefinition (Section 2.5.1). Preposed noun modifiers (adjectives and genitives) do not occur in VSO languages in the data of Table 5, whereas they are productive in SVO languages. And in Appendix II (Table 2) preposed noun modifiers are significantly less frequent in VSO than in SVO languages (7 out of 26 VSO languages, or 27%, have either adjective or genitive or both preposed, compared to 31 out of 52 SVO languages, or 60%). In addition, prepositions do not occur as productively in SVO languages as they do in VSO languages (one-third of SVO languages are postpositional, whereas hardly any VSO languages are; see Tables 2 and 3). If subjects are operators, then their preposing before the verb produces an operator-before-operand ordering which is harmonic with preposed noun modifiers and postpositions. Thus, SVO languages would have one solid operator-before-verb ordering, even though the other operators on the verb are all generally postposed. And the resulting predominance of prepositions and postposed noun modifiers in SVO languages (21 out of 52 SVO languages, or 40%, have both adjective and genitive postposed; 22 languages, or 42%, have one preposed and one postposed; and only 9, or 17%, have both preposed) then reflects the majority serialization relative to the verb: operand before operator. But VSO (and VOS and V-initial) languages have no basic operator before the verb, and the preposing of operators before noun and adposition conflicts with the basic verb position, and is therefore correspondingly rarer.

This reanalysis of subjects, for which the distributional data provide support, now results in an interesting generalization. Greenberg (1966) proposed two types of SOV languages: rigid and nonrigid. In the former, exemplified by Japanese, the verb is rigidly final in the clause, whereas in the latter, exemplified by Basque, at least one operator on the verb typically follows the verb as the basic order. The VSO–SVO distinction can now be seen to mirror the rigid–nonrigid SOV dichotomy. As we have seen, VSO languages have basic verb-first order, whereas SVO languages have one operator on the verb before the verb.

In fact, there seems to be a continuum from verb-first order at one end to rigid verb-final order at the other. Languages with the following basic verb positions are attested:

(i)	V S DO IO OBL ADV}	VSO
(ii)	S V DO IO OBL ADV}	SVO
(iii)	S DO V IO OBL ADV	
(iv)	S IO DO V OBL ADV	SOV nonrigid
(v)	S OBL IO DO V ADV	
(vi)	S ADV OBL IO DO V}	SOV rigid

Types (i) and (ii) are VSO and SVO languages respectively. Some languages of Type (iii) are discussed by, for example, Givón (1975). Types (iii), (iv), and (v) represent different degrees of nonrigid verb-finality, whereas Type (vi) languages are rigidly verb final.

4.1.4 OPERATOR–OPERAND = MODIFIER–HEAD

Though I accept Vennemann's redefinition of the subject–verb relation (Section 2.5.1), I do not accept his abandonment of category constancy as a defining criterion for operator versus operand status. As I argue in Sections 2.4.3 and 2.6.1, I regard the essential insight which underlies his operator–operand distinction to be that of the modifier–head relation, with category constancy preserved between the head and the higher node immediately dominating head and modifier(s), as in the X-bar theory or Emonds's (1976) theory of phrase structure. And I shall continue throughout this book to regard operators simply as (attribute or complement) modifiers on their respective operands as heads of phrase.

4.2 Defining and Testing Cross-Category Harmony Using Greenberg's Appendix II

I shall begin my justification of CCH by playing what is probably my weakest card: Appendix II. The number of operators considered in this sample is small (two on the verb, two on the noun, and one on the adposition). This limits the number of relative frequency predictions that can be made. It also poses more serious disadvantages. The principle of CCH predicates its frequency predictions on the notion of a cross-categorial balance, holding for all the operators on each operand within the phrasal categories. It is expected that the ratio of operator preposing to postposing within one phrasal category will generalize to the others, and that there will be a progressive decrease in language numbers as this ratio is distorted. If only two operators on some operand category are considered, therefore, we must assume that these are typical for all the relevant operators, and that their position relative to their operand establishes a valid paradigm for cross-categorial generalization.

Thus, for Appendix II we must assume that subject and object orders are typical of all operator orders relative to the verb. But this assumption requires qualification. An SVO language has all its operators on the verb (DO, IO, etc.) after the verb, except for the subject. It differs from VSO, therefore, in only one operator–operand ordering. In contrast, SOV languages may be either rigid or nonrigid (Section 4.1.3). Those that are extremely nonrigid and have only subject and object preceding the verb will also differ from SVO languages in just one operator–operand ordering (that of the direct object). But all other SOV languages (the great majority) will differ from SVO over more than one operator–operand ordering. As a result, SVO is more similar to VSO than to SOV, and the cross-categorial generalizations can be expected to mirror the greater similarity between SVO and VSO, precisely because of the shared ordering of operators on the verb which are missing from the sample. And SVO, which is verb medial in this sample of properties, is not in fact representative of a language type in which half of all operators precede and half follow the verb.

The adjective operator on nouns presents similar problems within the noun phrase. We saw in the PrNMH (Section 3.3.7) that a prepositional language with preposed adjective and postposed genitive—that is, noun medial within this sample (AN & NG, Subtype 4)—must have other preposed noun modifiers as well. But the Appendix II noun-medial co-occurrence for postpositional languages (NA & GN; see PoNMH, Section 3.3.17) may be indicative of a language type in which all noun modifiers precede the noun but for the adjective, or conversely, in which all noun modifiers follow the noun but for the genitive. In other words, the sample co-occurrence Po & NA & GN is compatible with a wide range of operator preposing and postposing patterns, in contrast to the Pr & AN & NG co-occurrence, which typifies a noun-medial co-occurrence much more faithfully (see further Section 4.2.1).

A further confounding factor in the quantitative analysis of Greenberg's Appendix II, and indeed in all the other samples to be considered in this chapter, is the existence of other, interacting frequency principles. Keenan's (1979) "Subjects Front" is one such. This principle will lead us to expect VSO languages to be quantitatively less numerous than SVO languages, on grounds that are independent of CCH. And this will then have consequences for CCH's cross-categorial predictions for word order quantities in the languages of these types (see further Section 4.3.1).

Despite these difficulties, the number of languages in Appendix II makes it an important sample for any word order frequency predictions. And it is significant that the principle of CCH can nonetheless be extracted from it. Appendix II does enable us to discover why CCH gives significantly better predictions than NSP, even when NSP is explicitly reformulated so as to make relative frequency predictions.

4.2.1 CROSS-CATEGORIAL WORD ORDER CO-OCCURRENCE QUANTITIES

We begin by dividing the word orders of Appendix II into pairs of operand orders—noun and adposition orders, verb and adposition orders, and noun and verb orders—in accordance with the methodological preliminary of Section 4.1.2. These are set out in Table 6, with the quantities of exemplifying languages placed at the intersection of the relevant row and column. Thus, there are 44 Pr & N_1 languages in Appendix II, 14 Pr & N_2 languages, and so on. As in Table 5, we are collapsing AN & NG and NA & GN into a single category, N_2 (or noun medial within this sample), as the noun is on each occasion the second daughter constituent of the noun phrase. When we consider possible explanations for CCH (Section 4.6), we will need to take account of such differences. But for the moment I wish to justify CCH only in terms of the actual numbers of operators preceding or following each operand, regardless of their category status.

More generally, I wish to make no more theoretical assumptions at this stage than are absolutely necessary and to remain as theory neutral as possible. (The distinction between operators and operands is the only major theoretical assumption upon which our presentation of CCH will rest.) When we have a convincing descriptive principle, stated with the

TABLE 6 : Appendix II Cross-Category Word Order Pairs

A. Noun–adposition orders

63 Pr languages	79 Po languages	
44	7	51 N_1 languages
14	37	51 N_2 languages
5	35	40 N_3 languages

B. Verb–adposition orders

63 Pr languages	79 Po languages	
25	1	26 V_1 languages
33	19	52 V_2 languages
5	59	64 V_3 languages

C. Noun–verb orders

26 V_1 languages	52 V_2 languages	64 V_3 languages	
19	21	11	51 N_1 languages
5	22	24	51 N_2 languages
2	9	29	40 N_3 languages

Note: N_1 = noun-first (N before A and G); N_2 = noun-second (N between the two); N_3 = noun-final (N after both). V_1 = VSO; V_2 = SVO; V_3 = SOV.

minimum number of assumptions, we can ask how different theories could try to explain these differences in language frequency, and we can hopefully convince the proponents of each that there is something fundamental to be explained, irrespective of the assumptions of any one approach.

Before we define and test CCH explicitly, notice some of the patterns in Table 6 which lend support to the CCH intuition of a cross-categorial balance, with a decline in language frequencies as this balance becomes distorted. Consider (A). Prepositional languages have their (unique) NP operator to the right of the adposition. The preferred noun order co-occurrence is N_1, that is, NA & NG (44 languages), with both operators on the noun also on the right. All the operators on the noun in this sample (2 only) thereby match all the operators on the adposition (1 only). Less preferred is Pr & N_2, that is, AN & NG (14 languages), with one noun operator to the left and one to the right of the noun. This relative infrequency can be attributed to the fact that the pre- and postposing of operators on the noun in Pr & N_2 finds no parallel in the uniquely postposed operators on the adposition. Least preferred is Pr & N_3, that is, AN & GN (5 languages), because, we hypothesize, all the operators on the noun now precede, whereas all the operators on the adposition follow. The cross-categorial imbalance is therefore at its greatest.

Conversely, we expect that the preferred co-occurrence with postpositions will be N_3 (AN & GN), with N_2 (NA & GN) less preferred and N_1 (NA & NG) least preferred. In fact, Po & N_3 and Po & N_2 are more or less the same (35 and 37 languages respectively), but both are significantly more frequent than Po & N_1 (7 languages). The relatively high figure for Po & N_2 is a consequence of the fact that the co-occurrence NA & GN is shared by many postpositional languages of numerous subtypes on the PoNMH (Section 3.3.17; Subtypes 2a, 3, 4a, 4b, and 5). By contrast, a Po & AN & GN language will be either Subtype 1 or 2b only, and a Pr & N_2 (AN & NG) language corresponds uniquely to Subtype 4 on the PrNHM (Section 3.3.7). Thus Po & N_3 is indeed the preferred co-occurrence in postpositional languages. But the Po & N_2 combination is compatible with numerous subtypes of postpositional languages, each of which is less frequent than Po & N_3, but which collectively give a language total which is about the same as that of the preferred co-occurrence.

In (B) the decline in frequencies from Po & V_3 (59 languages) to Po & V_2 (19) to Po & V_1 (1) is completely in accordance with CCH: The more the operators on the verb (subject and object) become postposed, the greater the imbalance with the exclusively preposed operators on the adposition. In prepositional languages, both Pr & V_1 (25 languages) and Pr & V_2 (33) are significantly more frequent than Pr & V_3 (5), as predicted, but Pr & V_1 is not more frequent than Pr & V_2, contrary to CCH's predictions. This will be explained (Section 4.3.1) as a consequence of the much smaller number of V_1 languages compared to V_2 (26 to 52). Within the class of V_1 languages, prepositions occupy a much larger slice of the available languages (25 of out 26, i.e., 96%) than they do in V_2 languages (33 out of 52, i.e., 63%), in accordance with CCH's predictions. But the actual number of V_1 languages is small, for independent reasons.

In some previous publications in which I introduced the notion of Cross-Category Harmony (Hawkins 1980a, 1982a) I made all my calculations in terms of percentages, primarily in order to factor out the effects of such independent principles, and of unrepresentative word order samples. By using percentages, Pr & V_1 can be shown to be (relatively) more frequent than Pr & V_2. But in the present more detailed and comprehensive study I prefer to make conflicting frequency predictions explicit, to discuss the extent to which given samples of operators are or are not representative of their phrasal categories as a whole, and to explain the (relatively few) exceptions to CCH in terms of these countertendencies. As a result, we shall now be able to motivate CCH using raw numbers, which is more convincing.

For (C) we predict (correctly) that V_1 should be most frequent in conjunction with N_1 (19 languages), less frequent with N_2 (5), and least frequent with N_3 (2), as the operators on the noun gradually precede their operand, so becoming disharmonic with the postposing of operators on the verb. Conversely, V_3 & N_3 should be most frequent (29 languages), V_3

& N_2 less so (24), and V_3 & N_1 less still (11). This also holds. For V_2, the ideal noun match-up should be N_2, and V_2 & N_1 and V_2 & N_3 should each be less frequent, as the mixed preposing and postposing of operators in V_2 fails to carry over to the noun phrase. In fact, V_2 & N_2 (22 languages) exceeds V_2 & N_3 (9) convincingly, and (just) exceeds V_2 & N_1 (21).

There are many other predictions which CCH makes for the data of Table 6. Before we test these (Tables 8–12), we define the principle itself.

4.2.2 THE PRINCIPLE OF CROSS-CATEGORY HARMONY

We have so far been comparing two word order co-occurrence pairs, W and W', where W comprises word order pair A & B, and W' comprises A' & B'. (For example, W = Po & SOV [A & B], and W' = Po & SVO [A' & B']; hence, $A = A'$ and $B \neq B'$). All four word orders—A, A', B, and B'—can be regarded as ordered sets of grammatical categories satisfying the following conditions. Sets A and A' have the same categories as members: one operand, a, and at least one operator upon a (to be designated by lower case letters late in the alphabet, x, y, z, etc.). And Sets B and B' have the same categories as members: one operand, b, where $b \neq a$, and at least one operator upon b (similarly designated by late lower case letters). The ordering of operand to operators differs either between A and A', or between B and B', or, as we shall see, between both.

The illustrative example that has been given can be set out as follows:

Co-occurrence pair W = Po & SOV (A & B)
Co-occurrence pair W' = Po & SVO (A' & B')

A: $\langle x, a\rangle$ i.e., NP + adposition (x = NP, a = Adp)
A': $\langle x, a\rangle$ i.e., NP + adposition (x = NP, a = Adp)
B: $\langle y, z, b\rangle$ i.e., S + O + V (y = S, z = O, b = V)
B': $\langle y, b, z\rangle$ i.e., S + V + O (y = S, b = V, z = O)

Between Sets A $\langle x, a\rangle$ and B $\langle y, z, b\rangle$ there is greater cross-category harmony than between A' $\langle x, a\rangle$ and B' $\langle y, b, z\rangle$, given that operands a and b are both rightmost in A & B, whereas in A' & B' the rightmost position of a is not matched by b. Thus $\langle x, a\rangle$ and $\langle y, b, z\rangle$ deviate by one position, and $\langle x, a\rangle$ and $\langle b, y, z\rangle$ (=VSO) would deviate by two.

Similarly, consider the following paired sets:[1]

A: $\langle w, x, a\rangle$ i.e., N_3 (w = G, x = A, a = N)
A': $\langle w, a, x\rangle$ i.e., N_2 (w = G, a = N, x = A)
B: $\langle y, z, b\rangle$ i.e., V_3 (y = S, z = O, b = V)
B': $\langle y, z, b\rangle$ i.e., V_3 (y = S, z = O, b = V)

Sets A $\langle w, x, a\rangle$ and B $\langle y, z, b\rangle$ are maximally harmonic, as their respective operands are both rightmost. Sets A' $\langle w, a, x\rangle$ and B' $\langle y, z, b\rangle$ differ by one operand position; $\langle a, w, x\rangle$ (N_1) and $\langle y, z, b\rangle$ (V_3) would differ by two. Similarly, $\langle w, a, x\rangle$ (N_2) is most harmonic with $\langle y, b, z\rangle$ (V_2). And $\langle w, x, a\rangle$ (N_3) would differ from $\langle y, b, z\rangle$ (V_2) by one operand ordering, as would $\langle a, x, w\rangle$ (N_1). The set $\langle b, y, z\rangle$ (V_1) would also differ from $\langle w, a, x\rangle$ (N_2) by one operand ordering, as would $\langle y, z, b\rangle$ (V_3).

Notice that the number of operators is not always the same for each operand in our calculations. In the present sample of properties, we are considering two operators on the verb, two on the noun, but only one on the adposition. Thus, even though $\langle x, a\rangle$ (NP + Po) is similar to $\langle y, b, z\rangle$ (e.g., SVO) in that one operator precedes the operand in both cases, yet there is also one postposed operator in $\langle y, b, z\rangle$ but not in $\langle x, a\rangle$, and hence operand b is not rightmost relative to the total number of operators in its set. We therefore consider $\langle x, a\rangle$ to be most harmonic with $\langle y, z, b\rangle$, as all operators, regardless of their different number, precede their respective operands, less harmonic with $\langle y, b, z\rangle$ and least harmonic with $\langle b, y, z\rangle$. In so doing, we are measuring the comparative position of the operand relative to however many operators there are in each member of the word order co-occurrence pair.

We can now quantify the cross-category harmony of a word order co-occurrence pair precisely in the following way. Calculate the number of operator–operand ordering deviations (if any) made by the verb or the noun from the nearest ordering or orderings with no deviations, that is, from the nearest maximally harmonic ordering(s) for that pair. Then, the fewer the number of deviations, the greater is the cross-category harmony of the co-occurrence pair. Thus, Po & V_3 exhibit 0 deviations, Po & V_2 exhibit 1 deviation, and Po & V_1 exhibit 2. For verb–noun pairs, V_2 & N_2 and V_1 & N_1 exhibit 0 deviations. In contrast, V_2 & N_1 exhibits 1 deviation from the preferred verb-medial/noun-medial (V_2 & N_2) or verb-first/noun-first (V_1 & N_1) match-up. And V_3 & N_1 exhibits 2 deviations from the preferred V_3 & N_3 or V_1 & N_1.[2] The higher these deviation quantities, the less is the cross-category harmony of the respective word order pair.

Where the number of operators is identical across a co-occurrence pair, the calculation of CCH is most straightforward (for any number of operators). Comparison between a one-operator set and a two-operator set (or more generally between a one-operator and an *n*-operator set) is also straightforward. Some interpretation of similarity must be imposed, however, when comparing sets of unequal numbers of operators greater than one; for example, a two-operator set $\langle a, x, w\rangle$ with a three-operator set $\langle b, y, z, j\rangle$. In this example, I would, as before, consider orders $\langle b, y, z,$

$j\rangle$, $\langle y, b, z, j\rangle$, $\langle y, z, b, j\rangle$, and $\langle y, z, j, b\rangle$ progressively disharmonic with $\langle a, x, w\rangle$ on account of the increased preposing of operators on b. Similarly for the comparison of any co-occurrence pair in which a or b are operand peripheral (i.e., rightmost or leftmost). The only problem lies in the interpretation of co-occurrence pair $\langle x, a, w\rangle$ and $\langle y, b, z, j\rangle$ compared to $\langle x, a, w\rangle$ and $\langle y, z, b, j\rangle$. I would consider these pairs equally harmonic, as there is no principled reason for considering either nonperipheral position of b more harmonic with the medial position of a.

The general prediction that we are making is that whichever co-occurrence pair, W or W', has more cross-category harmony (i.e., fewer ordering deviations between A & B or between A' & B'), will be attested in a greater number of languages. The illustrative examples of CCH's predictions discussed in Section 4.2.1 were limited, both in number and in kind. We shall ultimately broaden these predictions in three major ways.

First, the A & B (W) and A' & B' (W') pairs selected (Pr & N_1 and Pr & N_2, etc.) were all such that the relative ordering of operator(s) to operand differed either between A and A' or between B and B', but not between both. In Pr & N_1 and Pr & N_2, one operator–operand ordering, Pr + NP, is identical, and only one is different across the two co-occurrence pairs. But we will also make predictions for co-occurrence pairs in which neither A and A' nor B and B' have identical operator–operand orderings. For example, Pr & N_1 (A & B) has greater CCH than Po & N_2 (A' & B'). Letting a stand for adposition, and b for noun, Pr & N_1 languages combine Set A $\langle a, x\rangle$ with Set B $\langle b, y, z\rangle$, while Po & N_2 languages combine word order Set A' $\langle x, a\rangle$ with Set B' $\langle y, b, z\rangle$. Sets A $\langle a, x\rangle$ and B $\langle b, y, z\rangle$ are perfectly harmonic, and exhibit 0 deviations, as operands a and b are leftmost in both sets. But the medial position of b in B' $\langle y, b, z\rangle$ is one position at odds with the rightmost position of a in A' $\langle x, a\rangle$.

Similarly, Pr & N_2 is more harmonic than Po & N_1, and exhibits fewer deviations. The medial position of the noun $\langle y, b, z\rangle$ (N_2) is only one position removed from the leftmost position of the adposition $\langle a, x\rangle$ (Pr), whereas the initial position of the noun $\langle b, y, z\rangle$ (N_1) is two positions removed from the rightmost position of the adposition $\langle x, a\rangle$ (Po). But a co-occurrence such as Po & N_3 ($\langle x, a\rangle$ and $\langle y, z, b\rangle$) is not more harmonic than Pr & N_1 ($\langle a, x\rangle$ and $\langle b, z, y\rangle$), as the harmonic rightmost position of the operands in the former case is matched by the equally harmonic leftmost position of the operands in the latter. The measurement of CCH thus generalizes naturally to cases where all four sets—A, B, A', and B'—differ in their operator–operand orderings for identical categories.

A second and more ambitious extension will involve abandoning the requirement that A & B (W) and A' & B' (W) actually share identical categories. That is, all our word order co-occurrence pairs so far have included exactly the same operators and operands, differently ordered, for example, Pr & N_1 (*W*) and Pr & N_2 (*W′*), or Pr & N_1 (*W*) and Po & N_2 (*W′*). We shall subsequently make predictions (Section 4.2.5) for word order co-occurrence pairs that do not necessarily share the same categories. For example, Pr & VSO (*W*) will be predicted to be more frequent than VSO & N_2 (*W′*), Pr & VSO (*W*) more frequent than SOV & N_2 (*W′*). The "shared category word order pairs" are a proper subset of the total class of word order pairs for which CCH makes predictions. Before considering the total class, we shall define and test CCH predictions for shared category word order pairs only.

Third, we shall eventually consider not just pairs of co-occurring word orders but whole language types (see, e.g., Section 4.2.7).

4.2.3 DEFINING CCH PREDICTIONS FOR SHARED CATEGORY WORD ORDER PAIRS

GIVEN: Two word order co-occurrence pairs, *W* and *W′*, satisfying the following conditions:

1. *W* consists of word order co-occurrence pair *A* & *B*, and *W′* consists of *A′* & *B′*.
2. *A*, *A′*, *B*, and *B′* are all ordered sets of grammatical categories (but see Note 1).
3. Sets *A* and *A′* have the same categories as members: one operand, *a*, and at least one operator upon *a*. Sets *B* and *B′* have the same categories as members: one operand, *b*, where $b \neq a$, and at least one operator upon *b*.
4. The relative orderings of operand to operator(s) differ either between *A* and *A′*, or between *B* and *B′*, or between both, and are subject to the co-occurrence predictions of implicational universals.

THEN: The relative cross-category harmony of *W* and *W′* is determined as follows:

1. Calculate the number of operator–operand deviations from the nearest operand ordering(s) with no deviations for each pair (see Note 2).
2. The fewer the number of deviations, the greater is the cross-category harmony of co-occurrence pair *W* (*A* & *B*) or *W′* (*A′* & *B′*).

PREDICTION: Whichever co-occurrence pair, *W* or *W′*, has more CCH (if any), the greater will be the number of Type *W* or Type *W′* languages.

The relation 'greater CCH than' is transitive If co-occurrence pair *W* has more CCH than *W′*, and *W′* has more CCH than *W″*, then *W* has more

CCH than *W″*. As a result, if Pr & N_1 (0 CCH deviations) is predicted to exceed Pr & N_2 (1 deviation), and Pr & N_2 is predicted to exceed Pr & N_3 (2 deviations), the greater size of Pr & N_1 compared to Pr & N_3 follows by transitivity, and is not a "basic" prediction of CCH. We can distinguish, therefore, between basic predictions and total predictions, where the latter include the former plus additional predictions following by transitivity.

When we calculate the results of CCH's predictions, we shall be more interested in the total predictions, as they turn out to provide a more accurate reflection of the CCH intuition, and its success or failure. The following hypothetical example shows why this is so. Imagine that we have five language types, A, B, C, D, and E, each comprising two word order pairs, each type having 0, 1, 2, 3, and 4 CCH deviations respectively, and with attested language numbers as shown in Table 7. Cross-Category Harmony predicts that the 0-deviation languages will exceed those with 1 deviation, the 1-deviation languages those with 2 deviations, and so on, and makes some $(2 \times 2) + (2 \times 2) + (2 \times 2) + (2 \times 2) = 16$ basic predictions. In general, the decline in language numbers follows CCH's predictions very closely, but there are two exceptions: Language type 1a (0 deviations) with 30 languages does not exceed Language types 3 and 4 (1 deviation) with 40 and 36 exemplifications respectively. Hence, Table 7 scores 14 out of 16 basic predictions correct. Imagine now that in place of Language type 1a we have Language type 1b, also with 0 deviations, but with just 2 exemplifications. This would be a catastrophic result for CCH, as it effectively places Language type 1b in the same numerical ballpark as Types 9 and 10 with 4 CCH deviations and 3 and 1 exemplifications respectively. But when we calculate basic predictions only, the effect of substituting 1b for 1a gives exactly the same results as before: Type 1b has fewer exemplifications than Types 3 and 4, though all other basic predictions hold, and hence the final score is again 14/16.

Compare this result with that for the total predictions. Each language type is now predicted to have more exemplifying languages than every other with less CCH, making $(2 \times 8) + (2 \times 6) + (2 \times 4) + (2 \times 2) = 40$ total predictions. When Language type 1a is selected in Table 7, there are just the same two exceptions as before, and the final score is 38/40 correct. But Type 1b has a lower number of exemplifications than every language type except for Type 10. As a result, there are now seven exceptions to CCH's total predictions, and the final score is 33/40 correct. Hence, by using total predictions we can capture the fact that Language type 1b provides a disastrous result for CCH, in a way that we cannot using basic predictions. The total predictions reflect the intuition that a language type with a given CCH deviation is expected to have more exemplifications than *every* other language type with higher deviations. Of course, if all basic predictions are

TABLE 7 : Hypothetical Example Contrasting Basic and Total Predictions of CCH

	Language type	CCH deviations	Languages (N)
A	1a	0	30 (1b = 2)
	2	0	50
B	3	1	40
	4	1	36
C	5	2	25
	6	2	20
D	7	3	10
	8	3	7
E	9	4	3
	10	4	1

Basic predictions: Each language type with 0 CCH deviations is predicted to have more exemplifying languages than each type with 1 CCH deviation, each type with 1 CCH deviation is predicted to exceed each with 2, each with 2 to exceed each with 3, and each with 3 to exceed each with 4: (2 × 2) + (2 × 2) + (2 × 2) + (2 × 2) = 16 basic predictions.

Total predictions: Each language type with 0 CCH deviations is predicted to have more exemplifying languages than every type with 1, 2, 3, and 4 deviations; each type with 1 deviation is predicted to exceed every type with 2, 3, and 4 deviations; each type with 2 to exceed every type with 3 and 4 deviations; and each type with 3 to exceed each type with 4: (2 × 8) + (2 × 6) + (2 × 4) + (2 × 2) = 40 total predictions.

Results: Basic predictions
With Language 1a: 14/16 correct
With Language 1b: 14/16 correct
Results: Total predictions
With Language 1a: 38/40 correct
With Language 1b: 33/40 correct

correct, all total predictions will necessarily be correct as well. But if any one of the basic predictions is incorrect, it becomes important to test all the predictions by transitivity in order to see if, and to what extent, they hold. As we are explicitly going to allow for some limited exceptions to CCH, because of counterprinciples and unrepresentative word order samples, total predictions become all the more appropriate, in order not to camouflage bad results of the 1b kind. We shall regularly give the results of both basic and total predictions.

4.2.4 TESTING CCH ON SHARED CATEGORY WORD ORDER PAIRS

Tables 8, 9, and 10 present CCH's predictions for the relative quantities of languages with the shared category word order pairs of Appendix II

TABLE 8 : Adposition and Noun Predictions of CCH

Co-occurrence pair	CCH deviations	Languages in Appendix II
Pr & N_1	0	44
Po & N_3	0	35
Pr & N_2	1	14
Po & N_2	1	37
Pr & N_3	2	5
Po & N_1	2	7

Predictions: Each word order co-occurrence pair with 0 CCH deviations is predicted to have more exemplifying languages than every pair with 1 and 2 deviations: $2 \times (2 + 2) = 8$ predictions. Each co-occurrence pair with 1 CCH deviation is predicted to have more exemplifying languages than each pair with 2 deviations: $2 \times 2 = 4$ predictions. Total predictions = 12.

Results: Out of 12 predictions, 11 are correct (91.7%) (7 out of 8 basic predictions are correct, i.e., 87.5%). The one exception is: Po & N_3 (0 deviations) does not exceed Po & N_2 (1 deviation). In addition:

Average number of languages for each pair with 0 CCH deviations = 39.5
Average number of languages for each pair with 1 CCH deviation = 25.5
Average number of languages for each pair with 2 CCH deviations = 6

TABLE 9 : Adposition and Verb Predictions of CCH

Co-occurrence pair	CCH deviations	Languages in Appendix II
Pr & V_1	0	25
Po & V_3	0	59
Pr & V_2	1	33
Po & V_2	1	19
Pr & V_3	2	5
Po & V_1	2	1

Predictions: Each word order co-occurrence pair with 0 CCH deviations is predicted to have more exemplifying languages than every pair with 1 and 2 deviations: $2 \times (2 + 2) = 8$ predictions. Each co-occurrence pair with 1 CCH deviation is predicted to have more exemplifying languages than each pair with 2 deviations: $2 \times 2 = 4$ predictions. Total predictions = 12.

Results: Out of 12 predictions, 11 are correct (91.7%) (7 out of 8 basic predictions are correct, i.e., 87.5%). The one exception is: Pr & V_1 (0 deviations) does not exceed Pr & V_2 (1 deviation). In addition:

Average number of languages for each pair with 0 CCH deviations = 42
Average number of languages for each pair with 1 CCH deviation = 26
Average number of languages for each pair with 2 CCH deviations = 3

TABLE 10 : Verb and Noun Predictions of CCH

Co-occurrence pair	CCH deviations	Languages in Appendix II
V_1 & N_1	0	19
V_2 & N_2	0	22
V_3 & N_3	0	29
V_1 & N_2	1	5
V_2 & N_1	1	21
V_2 & N_3	1	9
V_3 & N_2	1	24
V_1 & N_3	2	2
V_3 & N_1	2	11

Predictions: Each word order co-occurrence pair with 0 CCH deviations is predicted to have more exemplifying languages than every pair with 1 and 2 deviations: $3 \times (4 + 2) = 18$ predictions. Each co-occurrence pair with 1 CCH deviation is predicted to have more exemplifying languages than each pair with 2 deviations: $4 \times 2 = 8$ predictions. Total predictions = 26.

Results: Out of 26 predictions, 21 are correct (80.8%) (15 out of 20 basic predictions are correct, i.e., 75%). The exceptions are:

V_1 & N_1 (0 deviations) does not exceed V_2 & N_1 and V_3 & N_2 (both 1 deviation).

V_2 & N_2 (0 deviations) does not exceed V_3 & N_2 (1 deviation).

V_1 & N_2 and V_2 & N_3 (both 1 deviation) do not exceed V_3 & N_1 (2 deviations).

In addition:

Average number of languages for each pair with 0 CCH deviations = 23.3
Average number of languages for each pair with 1 CCH deviation = 14.8
Average number of languages for each pair with 2 CCH deviations = 6.5

(cf.Table 6). Table 8 gives the adposition and noun predictions, Table 9 the adposition and verb predictions, and Table 10 the verb and noun predictions.

In each table we predict that a word order co-occurrence pair with 0 CCH deviations will have more exemplifying languages than a pair with 1 and 2 deviations, and a pair with 1 deviation will have more exemplifications than a pair with 2. In both Tables 8 and 9, 11 out of 12 total predictions are correct; in Table 10, 21 out of 26 total predictions are correct.

These results are good, but not perfect. The exceptions are explainable, however, either on account of general counterprinciples, or on account of the unrepresentative nature of certain sample word orders, as discussed in Section 4.2.1.

In Table 8, Po & N_3 (0 deviations) does not exceed Po & N_2 (1 deviation), because the latter co-occurrence (Po & NA & GN) is compatible with many more subtypes of postpositional languages (Section 3.3.17) than Po & N_3, and although each of the Po & N_2 subtypes is less frequent than Po & N_3, they give collectively a language total which just slightly exceeds that of the preferred co-occurrence.

In Table 9, Pr & V_1 (0 deviations) does not exceed Pr & V_2 (1 deviation), because the number of V_1 languages is half the number of V_2, for independent reasons (Section 4.3.1), even though the proportion of prepositions within the former far exceeds that in the latter.

The five exceptions in Table 10 are explainable in a similar manner. Thus, V_1 & N_1 (0 deviations) does not exceed V_2 & N_1 and V_3 & N_2 (both 1 deviation) because the number of V_1 languages (26) is much less than V_2 (52) and V_3 (64). In addition, the V_3 & N_2 co-occurrence is especially high (24 languages), because the great majority of V_3 languages (92%) have postpositions, and the Po & N_2 co-occurrence is, as we have seen, compatible with many more language subtypes and language numbers than other co-occurrences. This explains also why V_2 & N_2 (0 deviations) does not exceed V_3 & N_2. The majority of V_2 languages (63%) are prepositional, and Pr & N_2 (Pr & AN & NG) is compatible with just one prepositional language subtype (Section 3.3.7), one that is not even very harmonic with prepositions as there are numerous other preposed noun modifiers. The actual number of V_2 languages is also slightly less than V_3. For all these reasons, V_2 & N_2 does not exceed V_3 & N_2.

Finally, V_1 & N_2 (1 deviation) does not exceed V_3 & N_1 (2 deviations), in part because of the size of V_1 compared to V_3. But also V_1 is an extreme operand-peripheral order, occurring almost exclusively with prepositions, and V_1 is very disharmonic with the additional noun modifier preposing entailed by Pr & N_2 (Pr & AN & NG). But V_3 is compatible with all types of SOV, from extreme nonrigid (i.e., only S and O before V) to extreme rigid (see Section 4.1.3), and many V_3 languages (the nonrigid ones) will be more harmonic with N_1 than V_1 is with N_2. A similar consideration may explain the last exception: V_2 & N_3 (1 deviation) does not exceed V_3 & N_1 (2 deviations). The majority of V_2 languages are prepositional, and the N_3 co-occurrence with Prep (AN & GN) is indicative of extreme noun modifier preposing (Section 3.3.7), at variance with V_2 almost as much as it would be with V_1. Hence the slightly greater number of V_3 & N_1 languages.

4.2.5 DEFINING CCH PREDICTIONS FOR ALL APPENDIX II WORD ORDER PAIRS

In the last section we tested only shared category word order pairs. We might try now to be more ambitious. It is within the spirit of our CCH intuition that greater CCH between any word order co-occurrence pairs should be matched by more languages. For example, we predict that the frequency with which Po and SOV will combine, relative to the other combinatorial possibilities for these same operators and operands (Po & SVO, Pr & SOV, Pr & SVO, etc.), will exceed the frequency with which SVO and N_3 combine, relative to the other combinatorial possibilities for these shared sets of operators and operands (VSO & N_3, SVO & N_1, SOV & N_2, etc.).

We define these more general predictions as follows:

GIVEN: Two word order co-occurrence pairs, *W* and *W′*, satisfying the following conditions:

1. *W* consists of word order co-occurrence pair *A* & *B*, or *B* & *C*, or *A* & *C*; *W′* consists either of *A′* & *B′*, or *B′* & *C′*, or *A′* & *C′*.
2. *A*, *A′*, *B*, *B′*, *C*, and *C′* are all ordered sets of grammatical categories (but see Note 1).
3. Sets *A* and *A′* have the same categories as members: one operand, *a*, and at least one operator upon *a*. Sets *B* and *B′* have the same categories as members: one operand, *b*, where $b \neq a$, and at least one operator upon *b*. Sets *C* and *C′* have the same categories as members: one operand, *c*, where $c \neq b$ or *a*, and at least one operator upon *c*.
4. The relative orderings of operand to operator(s), and the selection of categories for each word order co-occurrence pair, are free, subject only to the co-occurrence predictions of implicational universals.

THEN: The relative cross-category harmony of *W* and *W′* is determined as follows:

1. Calculate the number of operator–operand deviations from the nearest operand ordering(s) with no deviations for each pair (see Note 2).
2. The fewer the number of deviations, the greater is the cross-category harmony of co-occurrence pair *W* or *W′*.

PREDICTION: Whichever word order co-occurrence pair, *W* or *W′*, has more CCH (if any), the greater will be the number of type *W* or type *W′* languages.

4.2.6 TESTING CCH ON ALL WORD ORDER PAIRS

The results of these more general predictions are set out in Table 11. Out of 146 predictions 134 are correct (91.8%); in addition, the average numbers of languages with 0, 1, and 2 deviations are 33.3, 20.3, and 5.2 respectively, which is fully in accordance with our principle. The exceptions are attributable to the kinds of considerations discussed in Sections 4.2.1 and 4.2.4. Given that the great majority of these predictions (96 out of 146) are defined on word order co-occurrence pairs that do not even

TABLE 11 : CCH Predictions for All Appendix II Word Order Pairs

Co-occurrence pair	CCH deviations	Languages in Appendix II
Pr & N_1	0	44
Po & N_3	0	35
Pr & V_1	0	25
Po & V_3	0	59
V_1 & N_1	0	19
V_2 & N_2	0	22
V_3 & N_3	0	29
Pr & N_2	1	14
Po & N_2	1	37
Pr & V_2	1	33
Po & V_2	1	19
V_1 & N_2	1	5
V_2 & N_1	1	21
V_2 & N_3	1	9
V_3 & N_2	1	24
Pr & N_3	2	5
Po & N_1	2	7
Pr & V_3	2	5
Po & V_1	2	1
V_1 & N_3	2	2
V_3 & N_1	2	11

Predictions: Each word order co-occurrence pair with 0 CCH deviations is predicted to have more exemplifying languages than every pair with 1 and 2 deviations: $7 \times (8 + 6) = 98$ predictions. Each co-occurrence pair with 1 CCH deviation is predicted to have more exemplifying languages than each pair with 2 deviations: $8 \times 6 = 48$ predictions. Total predictions = 146.

Results: Out of 146 predictions, 134 are correct (91.8%) (92 out of 104 basic predictions are correct, i.e., 88.5%). In addition:

Average number of languages for each pair with 0 CCH deviations = 33.3
Average number of languages for each pair with 1 CCH deviation = 20.3
Average number of languages for each pair with 2 CCH deviations = 5.2

share the same categories in their constituent word orders, this result is surprisingly good, and attests to the reality behind these CCH deviation figures and their impact on word order co-occurrence frequencies.

4.2.7 PREDICTING THE RELATIVE SIZES OF WHOLE LANGUAGE TYPES

So far we have been dealing only with pairs of word orders, making predictions for the relative numbers of languages exhibiting one co-occurrence pair rather than another. But every language consists of many such pairs. For example, the language type SOV & Postp & N_3 can be analyzed into three overlapping word order pairs: SOV & Po, Po & N_3, and SOV &

N_3. We might expect, therefore, that the relative frequency with which languages will select these three pairs in combination will reflect the overall CCH of all three together. In this instance all three word order pairs are maximally harmonic. But consider the language type SOV & Prep & N_1, which is analyzable into SOV & Pr, Pr & N_1, and SOV & N_1. Although Prep & N_1 are maximally harmonic (0 deviations), SOV & Prep and SOV & N_1 are maximally disharmonic (2 deviations each). Similarly, SVO & Prep & N_3 is analyzable into the pairs SVO & Pr, Pr & N_3, and SVO & N_3. In SVO & Pr the verb is one operand position removed from the preferred leftmost position (VSO), in Prep & N_3 the noun is two operand positions removed from the preferred N_1, and in SVO & N_3 there is one operand deviation from the preferred verb-medial – noun-medial or verb-final – noun-final match-up.

We can quantify this overall CCH by first dividing each co-occurrence type into its three constituent word order pairs. For each pair we then calculate the number of operator – operand ordering deviations (if any) made by the verb or the noun from the nearest ordering or orderings with no deviations. By totaling the number of deviations for all three word order pairs, we quantify the CCH of a whole language type; the fewer the total number of deviations, the greater the CCH, and the more languages of that type there are predicted to be.

In the examples we have just considered, the co-occurrence type SOV & Postp & N_3 would have a total of 0 deviations, and SOV & Prep & N_1 and SVO & Prep & N_3 would have a total of 4 deviations each. The co-occurrence SVO & Postp & N_2 exemplifies a type with a total of 2 deviations: SVO & N_2 are maximally harmonic, while SVO & Po and Po & N_2 exhibit 1 deviation each.

Notice that in totaling up CCH deviations for a whole language type we count each word order pair equally. It is, of course, conceivable that some pairs, and even some individual operands, contribute to the prediction of language frequencies to a greater or lesser extent than others. However, it is much simpler to assume that each constituent word order pair of a whole language type counts equally, and we will see that this assumption does give surprisingly good results (Section 4.2.9). As I am not aware of any compelling theoretical reasons for abandoning it, the assumption will remain.

4.2.8 DEFINING CCH PREDICTIONS FOR WHOLE LANGUAGE TYPES

GIVEN: Two language types, T and T', satisfying the following conditions:

1. T consists of co-occurring word orders A & B & C; T' consists of A' & B' & C'.

2. *A, A′, B, B′, C,* and *C′* are all ordered sets of grammatical categories (but see Note 1).
3. Sets *A* and *A′* have the same categories as members: one operand, *a*, and at least one operator upon *a*. Sets *B* and *B′* have the same categories as members: one operand, *b*, where $b \neq a$, and at least one operator upon *b*. Sets *C* and *C′* have the same categories as members: one operand, *c*, where $c \neq b$ or *a*, and at least one operator upon *c*.
4. The relative orderings of operand to operator(s) differ between at least one of *A* and *A′*, *B* and *B′*, and *C* and *C′*, and are subject to the co-occurrence predictions of implicational universals.

THEN: The cross-category harmony of *T* and *T′* is determined as follows:

1. Divide *T* and *T′* into their respective constituent word order pairs: *A* & *B*, *B* & *C*, *A* & *C* for *T*; *A′* & *B′*, *B′* & *C′*, *A′* & *C′* for *T′*.
2. Calculate the number of operator–operand deviations from the nearest operand ordering(s) with no deviations for each pair (see Note 2).
3. Total the number of deviations for the word order pairs of *T* and *T′* respectively.
4. The fewer the total number of deviations, the greater is the cross-category harmony of *T* (*A* & *B* & *C*) or *T′* (*A′* & *B′* & *C′*).

PREDICTIONS: Whichever language type, *T* or *T′*, has more CCH (if any), the greater will be the number of type *T* or *T′* languages.

4.2.9 TESTING CCH ON WHOLE LANGUAGE TYPES

Table 12 presents CCH's predictions for whole language types.[3] A total of 92 predictions are made, of which there are just 4 exceptions. Three of these can be attributed to the lower number of V_1 languages. The final case, in which Po & V_2 & N_3 (2 deviations) does not exceed Po & V_3 & N_1 (4 deviations), is a genuine counterexample. The overall success rate—95.7%—is very high, however. And the decline in average numbers for 0, 2, and 4 CCH deviations is also very much in accordance with the CCH intuition (23.5, 13, and 1.7 languages, respectively).

4.3 Some General Remarks about Cross-Category Harmony

We have so far illustrated the need for Cross-Category Harmony on the basis of a language sample that is restricted in the number of word orders that it contains. Even so, we achieved a 95% success rate in Table 12.

TABLE 12 : CCH Predictions for Whole Language Types in Appendix II

Language type		Total number of CCH deviations	Languages in Appendix II
(1)	Pr & V_1 & N_1	0	19
(23)	Po & V_3 & N_3	0	28
(2 + 4)	Pr & V_1 & N_2	2	5
(9)	Pr & V_2 & N_1	2	21
(10 + 12)	Pr & V_2 & N_2	2	9
(22 + 24)	Po & V_3 & N_2	2	24
(15)	Po & V_2 & N_3	2	6
(14 + 16)	Po & V_2 & N_2	2	13
(3)	Pr & V_1 & N_3	4	1
(17)	Pr & V_3 & N_1	4	4
(11)	Pr & V_2 & N_3	4	3
(18 + 20)	Pr & V_3 & N_2	4	0
(19)	Pr & V_3 & N_3	4	1
(21)	Po & V_3 & N_1	4	7
(7)	Po & V_1 & N_3	4	1
(13)	Po & V_2 & N_1	4	0
(6 + 8)	Po & V_1 & N_2	4	0
(5)	Po & V_1 & N_1	4	0

Predictions: Each language type with 0 CCH deviations is predicted to have more exemplifying languages than every type with 2 and 4 deviations: $2 \times (6 + 10) = 32$ predictions. Each language type with 3 CCH deviations is predicted to have more exemplifying languages than each type with 4 deviations: $6 \times 10 = 60$. Total predictions = 92.

Results: Out of 92 predictions, 88 are correct (95.7%) (68 out of 72 basic predictions are correct, i.e., 94.4%). The exceptions are:

Pr & V_1 & N_1 (0 deviations) does not exceed either Pr & V_2 & N_1 or Po & V_3 & N_2 (both 2 deviations).

Both Pr & V_1 & N_2 and Po & V_2 & N_3 (both 2 deviations) do not exceed Po & V_3 & N_1 (4 deviations).

In addition:

Average number of languages for each type with 0 CCH deviations = 23.5
Average number of languages for each type with 2 CCH deviations = 13
Average number of languages for each type with 4 CCH deviations = 1.7

Before we test CCH against further word orders, we shall justify our claim that some of the exceptions encountered so far are independently explainable (Section 4.3.1). We shall contrast CCH with Vennemann's NSP, and show exactly where the differences between them lie (Section 4.3.2). We then compare CCH with Greenberg's statistical implications, which also effectively define frequency differences between language types (Section 4.3.3). And we shall conclude by arguing the need for a two-tier approach to cross-categorial word order universals, which first defines all and only the attested language types, and then predicts frequency differences between the attested types only. Implicational and distributional universals will be argued to be descriptively and explanatorily independent of onė another (Section 4.3.4).

4.3.1 A COUNTERPRINCIPLE TO CCH: SUBJECTS FRONT

There exist counterprinciples that operate upon some word orders but not others, in such a way as to affect the number of exemplifying languages. In Chapter 3, we saw that there were independent reasons (involving heaviness) for NRel languages to greatly exceed RelN in number. In this chapter, we have come to suspect that an independent principle involving VSO languages is distorting the independently motivated quantitative predictions of CCH. This independent principle turns out to be Keenan's (1979) "Subjects Front" (SF).

The number of OV languages in the globe is roughly the same as the number of VO (i.e., VSO, VOS, V-initial, and SVO; see Section 3.2.2) languages: 51.8% to 48.2% in the Expanded Sample. I do not know the exact proportion of rigid to nonrigid OV languages, but the 30-language sample suggests that it is on the order of 55–45% in favor of rigid OV. Within the class of VO languages, however, the number of verb-first languages (VSO, VOS, V-initial) is significantly smaller than that of SVO languages: almost exactly one to two in each of Appendix II, the Expanded Sample, and the 30-language sample. The class of V_1 languages is therefore considerably smaller than the class of SOV languages, and noticeably smaller, too, than the class of rigid SOV languages (over half of the 52% of the world's OV languages are putatively rigid; one-third of the 48% of the world's VO languages are putatively V_1). As a result, the CCH preferred co-occurrence Pr & V_1 & N_1 has many fewer attested languages than the equally preferred Po & V_3 & N_3, and, I estimate, noticeably fewer also than the co-occurrence Po & rigid V_3 & N_3. Yet both the verb-first and the verb-final co-occurrence are maximally harmonic. And we even find the co-occurrence Pr & V_2 & N_1 (2 deviations) having more exemplifications than the more harmonic Pr & V_1 & N_1.

The explanation for this skewing is to be found in Keenan's (1979) Subjects Front (SF) Principle. In a consistently postspecifying VO language (cf. Vennemann 1976, 1977, 1981), the subject should follow not only the verb but the other arguments of the verb as well (as it should also according to Keenan's 1979 function–argument serialization principle, Section 2.4.3), to give VOXS, the exact mirror image of SXOV. Evidence for an independent principle fronting subjects (probably on account of their topical nature; see Keenan 1976b) comes from the following distribution: VOS languages in which the subject does occur normally in clause-final position (VOXS) are extremely rare (e.g., Malagasay); VOS languages in which the subject follows the object, but precedes other arguments of the verb (i.e., VOS*X*; e.g., Toba Batak, Gilbertese, and Otomi) are slightly more frequent; VSO languages are considerably more frequent; and SVO languages most frequent of all.

increase ↓		
	VO*X*S	(Malagasay)
	VOS*X*	(Toba Batak, Gilbertese, Otomi)
	VSO*X*	(12.2% of the Expanded Sample)
	SVO*X*	(32.4% of the Expanded Sample)

Thus, the most numerous VO languages obey SF in its entirety (SVO), and there are progressively fewer VO languages the less that SF is implemented. But OV languages are independently predicted by Vennemann's and Keenan's function–argument assignments to have the subject before the verb, and before all the other arguments of the verb as well, so the subject is already at the front, and the progressive implementation of SF cannot produce the variability in subject positions that it does for VO languages.

As a result, an independent principle involving subject position conflicts not only with Vennemann's and Keenan's logical structures, but also with some of the preferences defined by CCH. The co-occurrence Pr & V_2 & N_1 will be more preferred than Pr & V_1 & N_1 by SF, less preferred by CCH.

4.3.2 COMPARISON WITH VENNEMANN'S NSP

Both CCH and Vennemann's NSP are founded upon a similar division of categories into operators and operands. Yet they differ in several ways. Two major differences were summarized in Section 4.1.1. First, the "ideal" that each defines is different: NSP is founded on the intuition that all operators occur on the left of their respective operands, or all on the right, with greater than chance frequency; CCH builds on the notion of an ordering balance across phrasal categories, regardless of where these operators are positioned relative to their operands. Second, CCH, but not NSP, makes a precise quantitative prediction to the effect that the more a language type departs from the "ideal" harmonic ordering, the fewer exemplifying languages there will be.

We have also seen a third difference. The NSP consists of a set of (bilateral) implicational statements defining occurring and nonoccurring word orders, with more than chance frequency. In contrast, CCH does not consist of a set of implicational statements. It predicts quantitative differences among word order co-occurrence types whose well-formedness is already defined by independently needed implicational statements.

Thus, CCH is a distributional principle which is supplementary to, and which operates upon the output of, a set of implicational universals, but which does not of itself define possible language types. This third difference is still in need of theoretical justification, and we shall say more about it in Section 4.3.4.

Recall that the NSP as formulated by Vennemann is both too strong and too weak (Section 2.4.4):

$$\{\text{Operator}\{\text{Operand}\}\} \rightarrow \begin{cases} [\text{Operator } [\text{Operand}]] & \text{in OV languages} \\ [[\text{Operand}] \text{ Operator}] & \text{in VO languages} \end{cases}$$
$$\text{with greater than chance frequency}$$

There are too many exceptions: Only 48% of Appendix II co-occurrences and 23% of the 30-language sample are fully consistent (the success rate for Appendix II is only 33% if the subject is counted as an operator; see Sections 2.5, 4.1.3, and Chapter 2, Note 9). And there are too many totally unattested language types which are not being successfully distinguished from those which are attested.

Let us try to improve the NSP by formulating it as an explicitly distributional principle: We might expect that the more a language type is consistent with NSP, the more exemplifying languages there will be. Technically, this does not follow from Vennemann's formulation: The majority principle could be true at the same time that the quantitative decline in language numbers required by this reinterpretation was false. Nonetheless, it is sufficiently in the spirit of Vennemann's principle that it should be explicitly defined, compared with CCH, and tested.

We are going to need to quantify different degrees of consistency with NSP, in terms of which relative quantity predictions can be made. The only legitimate way of doing this, without making further assumptions, is to add up the number of operator–operand deviations from the majority serialization for some word order co-occurrence pair or whole language type. For example, there are five operator–operand pairs in the word orders of Appendix II: subject + verb, object + verb, NP + adposition, adjective + noun, and genitive + noun. In a type such as Po & V_3 & N_3, all five are consistent: hence 0 deviations. In Pr & V_1 & N_2, four are consistently postposed, and one operator on N is preposed: hence 1 deviation. In Po & V_1 & N_3 three are preposed, and two (both operators on the verb) are postposed. The three preposed operator–operand orders are in the majority: hence 2 deviations.

By proceeding in this manner, we can assign a 0-, 1-, or 2-deviation total to all the co-occurrences of Appendix II, and we can then compare the quantitative predictions that these three degrees of NSP-consistency make with the three degrees of harmony defined by CCH for the same sample (0, 2, and 4 CCH deviations respectively).

We first redefine NSP in the manner indicated, so that it makes predictions for whole language types (compare the corresponding formulation of CCH in Section 4.2.8). We will call this revised NSP, "NSP′," in order not to confuse it with Vennemann's original formulation.

The Revised Natural Serialization Principle (NSP′)

Given: Two language types, *T* and *T′*, satisfying the following conditions:

1. *T* and *T′* contain the same set of operator–operand pairs.
2. The relative ordering of operand to operator differs for at least one of these pairs between *T* and *T′*.

THEN: The NSP-consistency of *T* and *T′* is determined as follows:

1. Calculate the number of operator–operand deviations from the majority (or consistent) serialization for each type.
2. The fewer the total number of deviations, the greater is the NSP-consistency of *T* or *T′*.

PREDICTION: Whichever language type, *T* or *T′*, has more NSP-consistency, the greater will be the number of type *T* or *T′* languages.

In Table 13 we explicitly contrast CCH and NSP′ with respect to the Appendix II data. The overall impression is at first quite similar: The rankings defined by CCH and NSP′ differ only for four language types. Yet these four have a significant impact on the results. There are only 4 exceptions to CCH's predictions, as opposed to 20 to those of NSP′. The success rate for CCH is 95.7% for total predictions, and 94.4% for basic predictions. For NSP′, the success rate is only 78.3% for total predictions, and 72.2% for basic predictions. (The distinction between basic and total predictions in the case of NSP′ is the same as for CCH: Basic predictions are made between adjacent deviation classes only—0-deviation language types exceed 1-deviation types, 1-deviation types exceed 2, etc.—and do not include predictions that follow by transitivity—0-deviation types exceed 2-deviation types; cf. Section 4.2.3.) The scores of CCH are therefore appreciably higher for both total and basic predictions.

What is it about CCH's ranking that gives better results? A comparison of the definitions of CCH (Section 4.2.8) and NSP′ with Table 13 reveals the source of the problem. Most of the exceptions to NSP′ are caused by assigning an intermediate ranking to (19) Pr & V_3 & N_3 and (5) Po & V_1 & N_1 (both with 1 NSP deviation and 4 CCH deviations), which have 1 and 0 attested languages respectively. The operator–operand ordering in the adposition phrase conflicts with the otherwise fully consistent serializations in the verb phrase and noun phrase, and so there is just 1 NSP deviation in both cases. But according to CCH, these language types are

TABLE 13 : Comparing CCH and NSP′ Predictions for Whole Language Types in Appendix II

	Language type	CCH deviations	NSP deviations	Languages in Appendix II
(1)	Pr & V_1 & N_1	0	0	19
(23)	Po & V_3 & N_3	0	0	28
(2 + 4)	Pr & V_1 & N_2	2	1	5
(9)	Pr & V_2 & N_1	2	1	21
(10 + 12)	Pr & V_2 & N_2	2	2	9
(22 + 24)	Po & V_3 & N_2	2	1	24
(15)	Po & V_2 & N_3	2	1	6
(14 + 16)	Po & V_2 & N_2	2	2	13
(3)	Pr & V_1 & N_3	4	2	1
(17)	Pr & V_3 & N_1	4	2	4
(11)	Pr & V_2 & N_3	4	2	3
(18 + 20)	Pr & V_3 & N_2	4	2	0
(19)	Pr & V_3 & N_3	4	1	1
(21)	Po & V_3 & N_1	4	2	7
(7)	Po & V_1 & N_3	4	2	1
(13)	Po & V_2 & N_1	4	2	0
(6 + 8)	Po & V_1 & N_2	4	2	0
(5)	Po & V_1 & N_1	4	1	0

Predictions

CCH: See Table 12: Total predictions = 92.

NSP′: Each language type with 0 NSP deviations is predicted to have more exemplifying languages than every type with 1 and 2 deviations: 2 × (6 + 10) = 32 predictions. Each language type with 1 NSP deviation is predicted to have more exemplifying languages than each type with 2 deviations: 6 × 10 = 60 predictions. Total predictions = 92.

Results

CCH: See Table 12: Out of 92 predictions, 88 are correct (95.7%). (Out of 72 basic predictions 68 are correct, i.e., 94.4%.)

NSP′: Out of 92 predictions, 72 are correct (78.3%). (Out of 72 basic predictions 52 are correct, i.e., 72.2%.)

among the most disharmonic that there are: Both verb position and noun position are 2 operand positions removed from the adposition order within the adposition phrase. What this means is that we cannot just add up the number of operator–operand constructions in a language type, assign to each an equal value, and make predictions for language quantities as a function of the proportion of the operator–operand pairs that are consistently ordered. The adposition order counts for more than one operator–operand deviation in these calculations: It represents a whole phrasal category, with equal value to each of the other phrasal categories (NP and VP/S). The more the ratio of operator preposing or postposing in the verb phrase and the noun phrase departs from the operator–operand serialization in the adposition phrase, the fewer languages there are. More generally, the greater any pre- and postposing imbalance across phrasal categories, the fewer languages there are. This intuition is recognized by CCH, which calculates the degree of ordering similarity between one phrasal category and every other phrasal category, considering them pairwise, and makes its predictions irrespective of the number of operators that there happen to be within a given phrasal category in a given language sample. But NSP′ counts all operator–operand constructions equally; it expects them all to serialize in the same order (in the most consistent case); and it fails to capture the intuition of a cross-categorial ordering balance between phrasal categories (AdpP, NP, and VP/S) regardless of pre- or postposing.

We shall see even more striking examples of this difference between CCH and NSP′ when we consider language samples with more operators within the phrasal categories. Compare the following illustrative examples of contrary predictions for word order types in which there are three operators on both the verb and the noun (see Section 4.5):

Po & V_4 & N_4	0 CCH deviations	0 NSP deviations
Po & V_4 & N_3	2 CCH deviations	1 NSP deviation
Po & V_3 & N_3	2 CCH deviations	2 NSP deviations
Pr & V_1 & N_3	4 CCH deviations	2 NSP deviations
Pr & V_3 & N_3	4 CCH deviations	3 NSP deviations
Pr & V_4 & N_4	6 CCH deviations	1 NSP deviations
Po & V_2 & N_1	6 CCH deviations	2 NSP deviations
Pr & V_4 & N_1	6 CCH deviations	3 NSP deviations

The success rate of CCH will consistently be significantly higher.

4.3.3 COMPARISON WITH GREENBERG'S STATISTICAL IMPLICATIONS

We must also consider CCH in relation to Greenberg's statistical implications (Section 2.1). Some of the statistical universals which he proposes to cover the data of Appendix II are:

> In languages with prepositions, the genitive almost always follows the governing noun [Greenberg's universal (2a-s)].
>
> In languages with postpositions, the genitive almost always precedes the governing noun [Greenberg's universal (2b-s)].
>
> With overwhelmingly more than chance frequency, languages with dominant order VSO have the adjective after the noun [Greenberg's universal (17-s)].

Exceptional *P & $-Q$ languages exist for all these statements, in the form of *Prep & GN languages, *Postp & NG languages, and *VSO & AN languages respectively. Now although these co-occurrences are all attested, they are extremely disharmonic according to CCH. Thus *Prep & GN languages co-occur only with AN and not with NA [recall Implication (III) Prep ⊃ (NA ⊃ NG), logically equivalent to Prep ⊃ (GN ⊃ AN)]; Prep & GN & AN is symbolized as Pr & N_3 in our notation for Appendix II. Similarly, *Postp & NG languages co-occur only with NA and not with AN [recall Implication (IV) Postp ⊃ (AN ⊃ GN), logically equivalent to Postp ⊃ (NG ⊃ NA)]; Postp & NG & NA is symbolized as Po & N_1. Both Pr & N_3 and Po & N_1 are maximally disharmonic. The co-occurrence *VSO & AN is compatible with both VSO & AN & GN (i.e., VSO & N_3) and with VSO & AN & NG (i.e., VSO & N_2) by Implication (II) VSO ⊃ (NA ⊃ NG). These co-occurrences are less frequent than VSO & NA & NG (i.e., VSO & N_1).

Notice, therefore, how Greenberg's statistical implications differ in an important respect from his nonstatistical implications. The latter are defined in terms of two word orders, P and Q, and rule out all co-occurrences of *P & $-Q$. But his statistical statements are not defining attested versus nonattested co-occurrences. They are, in effect, distinguishing between harmonic (and frequent) P & Q co-occurrences (e.g., Prep & N_1), and disharmonic (and infrequent) *P & $-Q$ co-occurrences (e.g., Prep & N_3). As a result, they constitute an alternative method for defining language frequencies.

In Section 3.1.1, we observed that the overuse of statistical statements by Greenberg and especially Vennemann was unfortunate, as it resulted in a failure to distinguish in a precise way between attested and completely unattested word order co-occurrences. Notice now in this context that statistical implications cannot adequately capture distributional regularities either. For, if we were to attempt to capture all distributional facts using them, we would need to set up a separate implicational statement for each (frequent) P & Q versus (infrequent) *P & $-Q$ pair; that is, we would need a separate implicational statement for each of the output predictions of CCH, thereby missing the overall regularity.

Worse yet, statistical implications could only be set up for values of P & Q that had a very high frequency of occurrence where *P & $-Q$ had a very low frequency of occurrence. This is because the number of *P & $-Q$ exceptions that any implicational statement can tolerate is limited. One cannot claim that the presence of one linguistic property, P, guarantees the co-occurrence of another (which is what an if P then Q statement asserts) if there are many languages with P that do not have Q. Hence the only distributional facts that statistical statements could potentially define are those involving very high versus very low frequencies. But the data of Appendix II reveal many fine distinctions between large-, medium-, and small-sized language groups, distinctions that CCH can show to be principled.

By reserving implicational statements for the task of distinguishing attested from nonattested co-occurrences, we can therefore formulate just one supplementary distributional regularity which avoids many unnecessary statistical implications, and which captures generalizations that these latter are intrinsically unable to state.

4.3.4 THE INDEPENDENCE OF IMPLICATIONAL AND DISTRIBUTIONAL UNIVERSALS

Unlike Greenberg and Vennemann, we are proposing a two-tier approach to the description of word order universals: We first define all and only the attested word orders, using implicational statements; we then predict relative frequencies among all the attested language types, using a single and very general distributional universal. I have tried to argue that this approach produces better results at a descriptive level. We shall subsequently see that this difference corresponds to two major types of explanation for language universals. Underlying some language universals there are absolute causes, which predict that certain linguistic features constitute a possible language type, and others an impossible language type. But the explanation for other universals involves intrinsically gradient causes: A certain language type can be more or less preferred along a continuum defined by the explanatory gradient. The result is that the more preferred languages are more frequent than the less preferred ones. CCH is one example of such a preference continuum (see further Section 4.6, and also Section 3.4.2.1 and the introductory section of Chapter 6). In contrast, HSP and MP are absolute causes (see Chapter 3), although their interaction has a certain gradient effect in postpositional languages (see MHIP, Section 3.4.1.2).

Quite apart from these differences in explanation, the need for two types of universals in the area of word order is justified on purely descriptive grounds.

First, there are two types of facts: There is the large discrepancy between attested and unattested word order types (Section 3.1.1), and there are significant and regular frequency differences among the attested types.

Second, it might be argued that the unattested word orders are simply those which would be predicted to be least frequent by CCH (i.e., languages with extreme disharmony), which are nonoccurring in samples of the size we have been considering. If this argument were to go through, our two types of facts could be reduced to just one: CCH. But the evidence before me suggests that this reduction cannot be made. The unattested word orders do not in general correspond to those which are least harmonic by CCH, or even to those with low CCH. And, conversely, the most disharmonic word orders may be unattested, but equally may not be.

Consider the following examples of unattested word order types whose absence cannot be explained by CCH. In the Expanded Sample (see Section 4.4) the co-occurrence Po & V_3 & N_2 (2 CCH deviations) has 55 exemplifying languages where N_2 stands for NA & GN, but 0 exemplifying languages where N_2 stands for AN & NG. The explanation is to be found in Universal (IV) Postp $\supset$ (AN $\supset$ GN), which forbids *Po & AN & NG co-occurrences. Yet both Po & NA & GN and *Po & AN & NG are identical from the point of view of CCH: They both have sufficient cross-category harmony to be amply attested. Clearly, CCH cannot explain the total absence of the latter. The same moral emerges even more clearly from richer word order samples than Appendix II. In Section 4.5.1 we shall see, for example, that the co-occurrence Pr & V_2 & N_2 (with 2 CCH deviations) has higher CCH than Pr & V_2 & N_3 (4 deviations) and Pr & V_2 & N_4 (6 deviations), with N being considered relative to Adj, Gen, and Rel. The language frequencies decline accordingly. But the only N_2 order permitted by our prepositional implications is AN & NG & NRel. The implicationally excluded N_2 orders—*NA & GN & NRel and *NA & NG & RelN—are therefore unattested, despite their relatively high CCH. It is clear that unattested (and implicationally excluded) word order types may exhibit varying degrees of harmony or disharmony, and any appeal to CCH to explain the absence of all unattested types is doomed.

This does not rule out, however, that some disharmonic word order types may be unattested in samples of a given size, and perhaps even in all currently spoken languages. I would attribute the absence of exemplifying languages for both (13) Po & V_2 & N_1 and (5) Po & V_1 & N_1 (both with 4 CCH deviations; see Table 12) to distributional reasons, in fact. All the constituent word order pairs in these types are independently attested [e.g., Po & SVO, SVO & NA & NG, Po & NA & NG for (13)], and permitted by implicational laws, and for this reason extreme disharmony is plausibly the cause of their absence. But even here this argument is weakened by the existence of numerous language types with 4 CCH deviations in Table 12 which are attested. So why are (13) and (5) not? The answer may lie in the fact that the NA & NG co-occurrence in postpositional languages is indicative of extreme postposing of noun modifiers, making Po & N_1 extremely disharmonic, and this, combined with the extreme disharmony of Po & V_1 and Po & V_2 (both of which are more disharmonic than the opposite Pr & V_3, because of the rigid/nonrigid SOV distinction; see Section 4.1.3), may explain why Po & V_2/V_1 & N_1 have fewer attestations than their opposite number (19) Pr & V_3 & N_3 (4 deviations) with 1.

But in general the attempt to set up an equation between unattested language types and low CCH fails in both directions.

Third, the independence of implicational and distributional universals is supported by the very form of the universals for which we have found independent motivation. Implicational universals, as we have formulated them, make no predictions for frequency (except when they are statistical —and even these are an unsatisfactory way of defining language frequencies; cf. Section 4.3.3). And CCH predicts relative language frequencies, and does not even refer to individual categories such as Adj and Gen, on the basis of which many unattested types could be excluded. The only occasion on which a language type is predicted to be nonoccurring in some sample is if some other language type with more harmony has 0 or 1 exemplifying languages.

Finally, the Expanded Sample, to which we now turn, corroborates our assumption of the independence of implicational and distributional universals, for the implicationally excluded co-occurrences of Appendix II are still absent in the Expanded Sample, while the relative frequencies of attested language types remain similar, with higher actual language totals on account of the greater number of languages in the sample.

4.4 Testing Cross-Category Harmony Using the Expanded Sample

We shall now test CCH on the Expanded Sample. The results are very similar to those for Appendix II, though slightly better. In the interests of space we shall not test the word order pairs, but will go straight to CCH's predictions for whole language types (see Section 4.2.8). Table 14 presents these, and compares CCH once again with NSP′. From the table we see that whereas CCH scores 97.8% total predictions correct, and 97.2% basic predictions correct, NSP′ scores 81.5% for total predictions, and 76.4% for basic predictions. Once again, CCH's success rate is appreciably higher than that of NSP′.

There are just two exceptions to CCH in Table 14: Pr & V_1 & N_1 (0 CCH deviations) with 38 languages does not exceed Pr & V_2 & N_1 and Po & V_3 & N_2 (both 2 deviations), with 56 and 55 exemplifications respectively. The higher figure for Pr & V_2 & N_1 is understandable in terms of "Subjects Front" (Section 4.3.1): In the Expanded Sample, V_2 (SVO)

TABLE 14 : CCH and NSP′ Predictions for Whole Language Types in the Expanded Sample

Language type		CCH deviations	NSP deviations	Languages in Expanded Sample
(1)	Pr & V_1 & N_1	0	0	38
(23)	Po & V_3 & N_3	0	0	96
(2 + 4)	Pr & V_1 & N_2	2	1	13
(9)	Pr & V_2 & N_1	2	1	56
(10 + 12)	Pr & V_2 & N_2	2	2	21
(22 + 24)	Po & V_3 & N_2	2	1	55
(15)	Po & V_2 & N_3	2	1	12
(14 + 16)	Po & V_2 & N_2	2	2	13
(3)	Pr & V_1 & N_3	4	2	1
(17)	Pr & V_3 & N_1	4	2	10
(11)	Pr & V_2 & N_3	4	2	7
(18 + 20)	Pr & V_3 & N_2	4	2	0
(19)	Pr & V_3 & N_3	4	1	2
(21)	Po & V_3 & N_1	4	2	11
(7)	Po & V_1 & N_3	4	2	1
(13)	Po & V_2 & N_1	4	2	0
(6 + 8)	Po & V_1 & N_2	4	2	0
(5)	Po & V_1 & N_1	4	1	0

Predictions

CCH: Each language type with 0 CCH deviations is predicted to have more exemplifying languages than every type with 2 and 4 deviations: 2 × (6 + 10) = 32 predictions, etc.; see Table 12. Total predictions = 92.

NSP′: Each language type with 0 NSP deviations is predicted to have more exemplifying languages than every type with 1 and 2 deviations: 2 × (6 + 10) = 32 predictions, etc.; see Table 13. Total predictions = 92.

Results

CCH: Out of 92 predictions, 90 are correct (97.8%). (Out of 72 basic predictions, 70 are correct, i.e., 97.2%.) The exceptions are: Pr & V_1 & N_1 (0 CCH deviations) does not exceed Pr & V_2 & N_1 and Po & V_3 & N_2 (both with 2 deviations).

NSP′: Out of 92 predictions, 75 are correct (81.5%). (Out of 72 basic predictions, 55 are correct, i.e., 76.4%.)

languages exceed V_1 (verb-first) by a ratio of two to one (109 versus 53). The higher figure for Po & V_3 & N_2 results from the selection of subject and object as the representative operators on the verb in this language sample. Subject and object are the first and second operators to prepose respectively as the verb moves to the right in the clause (cf. the verb-position continuum in Section 4.1.3). Hence this selection of operators can differentiate between rigid and nonrigid verb-first languages.

But in V_3 (SOV) languages, it is the oblique constituents (OBL, IO, etc.; see Section 4.1.3) which postpose first as the verb moves to the left in the clause, and hence V_3 does not capture the distinction between rigid and nonrigid verb-finality, and so represents more language types, and more actual languages, than each of V_1 and V_2. In fact, as V_1 and V_2 are both VO, and V_3 is OV, and as the class of VO languages is roughly equal to that of OV languages across the globe, we find the following pattern: The number of V_1 languages is approximately half that of V_2 (on account of SF), and approximately one-third that of V_3 (53 compared to 174 languages in the Expanded Sample), as V_1 and V_2 together are approximately equal to V_3.

Now within the class of V_1 languages, the co-occurrence Pr & N_1 is by far the most preferred (38 languages, compared with a total of 15 for all the other co-occurrences with V_1). But the actual number of V_1 languages is sufficiently small that even this CCH-preferred co-occurrence does not have more exemplifying languages than less CCH-preferred co-occurrences with more populous verb-position types.

4.5 Testing Cross-Category Harmony Using Greenberg's 30-Language Sample

4.5.1 NOUN IN RELATION TO ADJ, GEN, AND REL

The 30-language sample enables us to test more detailed predictions using more operators on the verb and the noun. In the first set of predictions, I shall consider the position of the noun in relation to three operators—Adj, Gen, and Rel; the position of the verb in relation to three—subject, object, and an arbitrary oblique constituent (*X*); and the position of the adposition in relation to one operator—the NP. The following abbreviations will be used:

V_1 = verb first in the sentence (VSO*X*)
V_2 = verb second (SVO*X*)
V_3 = verb third (SOV*X*)
V_4 = verb final (S*X*OV)
(Here V_3 and V_4 correspond to Greenberg's nonrigid and rigid SOV respectively.)
N_1 = noun initial within the NP (relative to Adj, Gen, and Rel)
N_2 = noun second (one modifier precedes, two follow)
N_3 = noun third (two modifiers precede, one follows)
N_4 = noun final (all three modifiers precede)

Which noun modifiers precede and which follow in N_2 and N_3 orders will depend on whether the language is prepositional or postpositional. If it is prepositional, it will obey the implications of the Prepositional Noun Modifier Hierarchy (Section 3.3.7), which result in the following co-occurrence possibilities, ignoring demonstrative and numeral:

Prep &	NAdj &	NGen	NRel	$= N_1$
Prep	AdjN	NGen	NRel	$= N_2$
Prep	AdjN	GenN	NRel	$= N_3$
Prep	AdjN	GenN	RelN	$= N_4$

If the language is postpositional, it will follow the implications of the Postpositional Noun Modifier Hierarchy (Section 3.3.17), which permit all and only the following co-occurrences:

Postp &	AdjN &	RelN &	GenN	$= N_4$
Postp	NAdj	RelN	GenN	$= N_3$
Postp	AdjN	NRel	GenN	$= N_3$
Postp	NAdj	NRel	GenN	$= N_2$
Postp	NAdj	NRel	NGen	$= N_1$

Table 15 presents the relevant data for 28 languages from the 30-language sample.[4] Tables 16–18 present CCH's predictions for shared category word order pairs (cf. the definition in Section 4.2.3), in the manner of Tables 8–10 for Appendix II. In the interests of space, we will not present the predictions for all word order pairs in this sample (in the manner of Table 11 for Appendix II),[5] but will go straight to CCH's most important predictions: those for whole language types, presented in Table 19 (see the definition in Section 4.2.8, and also Table 12 for the Appendix II data). Because a significant number of word order pairs and types have no exemplifications in this much more limited sample, we are going to have to alter CCH's predictions as follows: whichever co-occurrence pair or language type has more CCH (if any), the greater *or equal* will be the relevant numbers of languages. A similar qualification is made for NSP′, whose predictions are also considered in these tables.

The results are surprisingly good, especially for so small a sample. The selection of just 30 out of 4000–8000 current languages runs enormous risks of choosing unrepresentative language quantities. For this reason I shall not even try to offer explanations for the exceptions, although it will be readily clear that many of them are indeed attributable to the same kinds of considerations that we adduced for Appendix II and the Expanded Sample.

As shown by Tables 16–19, CCH scores 96% or 97% total predictions correct for the shared category word order pairs (with basic predictions between 92% and 95%) and 98% for the whole language types (97% for basic predictions). The NSP′ scores are consistently lower: between 75%

TABLE 15 : Language Quantities in the 30-Language Sample (N Relative to Adj, Gen, and Rel)

Prepositional languages

N_1: Berber (V_1), Hebrew (V_1), Welsh (V_1, Maori (V_1), Masai (V_1), Zapotec (V_1), Fulani (V_2), Italian (V_2), Malay (V_2), Swahili (V_2), Thai (V_2), Yoruba (V_2) = 12
N_2: Greek (V_2), Maya (V_2), Serbian (V_2) = 3
N_3: Norwegian (V_2) = 1
N_4: ∅

Postpositional languages

N_4: Burushaski (V_4), Japanese (V_4), Kannada (V_4), Turkish (V_4) = 4
N_3: Burmese (V_4), Hindi (V_4), Basque (V_3), Chibcha (V_3), Quechua (V_3), Finnish (V_2) = 6
N_2: Guarani (V_2), Songhai (V_2) = 2
N_1: ∅

16 Pr languages	12 Po languages	
12	0	12 N_1 languages
3	2	5 N_2 languages
1	6	7 N_3 languages
0	4	4 N_4 languages

16 Pr languages	12 Po languages	
6	0	6 V_1 languages
10	3	13 V_2 languages
0	3	3 V_3 languages
0	6	6 V_4 languages

6 V_1 languages	13 V_2 languages	3 V_3 languages	6 V_4 languages	
6	6	0	0	12 N_1 languages
0	5	0	0	5 N_2 languages
0	2	3	2	7 N_3 languages
0	0	0	4	4 N_4 languages

and 86% for shared category word order pairs (basic predictions between 69% and 81%); and 86% for whole language types (basic predictions 84%).

Clearly, these figures provide further confirmation for the insight underlying CCH, to the effect that relative language frequencies are predictable on the basis of the cross-categorial ordering balance holding between phrasal categories.

4.5.2 NOUN IN RELATION TO ADJ, GEN, AND DEM/NUM

In Section 3.3 we defined implicational universals for demonstrative and numeral, in addition to adjective, genitive, and relative clause. This gives a total of five noun modifiers whose relative position to the noun we can test vis-à-vis verb and adposition orders. However, as there are only three operators on the verb in Section 4.5.1, it will greatly simplify the calculation of relative cross-category harmony if we keep the number of verb and noun modifiers the same (Section 4.2.2). In the last section we added the relative clause to the adjective and genitive modifiers of Appendix II. In this section we shall replace the relative clause first with the

TABLE 16 : Adposition and Noun Predictions (30-Language Sample: Adj, Gen, and Rel)

Co-occurrence pair	CCH deviations	NSP deviations	Languages (*N*)
Pr & N_1	0	0	12
Po & N_4	0	0	4
Pr & N_2	1	1	3
Po & N_3	1	1	6
Pr & N_3	2	2	1
Po & N_2	2	2	2
Pr & N_4	3	1	0
Po & N_1	3	1	0

Predictions

CCH: The number of exemplifying languages for each word order co-occurrence pair with 0 CCH deviations is predicted to exceed or equal the number for every pair with 1, 2, and 3 deviations: $2 \times (2 + 2 + 2) = 12$ predictions. The number of exemplifying languages for each co-occurrence pair with 1 CCH deviation is predicted to exceed or equal the number for every pair with 2 and 3 deviations: $2 \times (2 + 2) = 8$ predictions. The number of exemplifying languages for each co-occurrence pair with 2 CCH deviations is predicted to exceed or equal the number for each pair with 3 deviations: $2 \times 2 = 4$ predictions. Total predictions = 24.

NSP′: The number of exemplifying languages for each word order co-occurrence pair with 0 NSP deviations is predicted to exceed or equal the number for every pair with 1 and 2 deviations: $2 \times (4 + 2) = 12$ predictions. The number of exemplifying languages for each co-occurrence pair with 1 NSP deviation is predicted to exceed or equal the number for each pair with 2 deviations: $4 \times 2 = 8$ predictions. Total predictions = 20.

Results

CCH: Out of 24 predictions 23 are correct (95.8%). (Out of 12 basic predictions 11 are correct, i.e., 91.7%.) The one exception is: Po & N_4 (0 deviations) does not exceed or equal Po & N_3 (1 deviation).

NSP′: Out of 20 predictions 15 are correct (75%). (Out of 16 basic predictions 11 are correct, i.e., 68.8%.)

demonstrative, and then with the numeral, keeping adjective and genitive constant. In this way we will always have three modifiers on the noun.

The permissible co-occurrences sanctioned by PrNMH (Section 3.3.7) for demonstratives and numerals respectively are

Prep &	NDem &	NAdj &	NGen	$= N_1$
Prep	DemN	NAdj	NGen	$= N_2$
Prep	DemN	AdjN	NGen	$= N_3$
Prep	DemN	AdjN	GenN	$= N_4$

Prep &	NNum &	NAdj &	NGen	$= N_1$
Prep	NumN	NAdj	NGen	$= N_2$
Prep	NumN	AdjN	NGen	$= N_3$
Prep	NumN	AdjN	GenN	$= N_4$

TABLE 17 : Adposition and Verb Predictions (30-Language Sample: Adj, Gen, and Rel)

Co-occurrence pair	CCH deviations	NSP deviations	Languages (*N*)
Pr & V_1	0	0	6
Po & V_4	0	0	6
Pr & V_2	1	1	10
Po & V_3	1	1	3
Pr & V_3	2	2	0
Po & V_2	2	2	3
Pr & V_4	3	1	0
Po & V_1	3	1	0

Predictions

CCH: The number of exemplifying languages for each word order co-occurrence pair with 0 CCH deviations is predicted to exceed or equal the number for every pair with 1, 2, and 3 deviations: $2 \times (2 + 2 + 2) = 12$ predictions; etc. (cf. Table 16). Total predictions = 24.

NSP′: The number of exemplifying languages for each word order co-occurrence pair with 0 NSP deviations is predicted to exceed or equal the number for every pair with 1 and 2 deviations: $2 \times (4 + 2) = 12$ predictions; etc. (cf. Table 16). Total predictions = 20.

Results

CCH: Out of 24 predictions 23 are correct (95.8%). (Out of 12 basic predictions 11 are correct, i.e., 91.7%.) The one exception is: Pr & V_1 (0 deviations) does not exceed or equal Pr & V_2 (1 deviation).

NSP′: Out of 20 predictions 17 are correct (85%). (Out of 16 basic predictions 13 are correct, i.e., 81.3%.)

and the co-occurrences permitted by PoNMH (Section 3.3.17) are

Postp & AdjN & DemN & GenN = N_4
Postp NAdj DemN GenN = N_3
Postp NAdj NDem GenN = N_2
Postp NAdj NDem NGen = N_1

Postp & AdjN & NumN & GenN = N_4
Postp NAdj NumN GenN = N_3
Postp NAdj NNum GenN = N_2
Postp NAdj NNum NGen = N_1

The values of V_1, V_2, etc., in this section will remain as in Section 4.5.1.

Table 20 presents the data for the noun in relation to Dem, Adj, and Gen. As we have already tested the predictions both for word order pairs and for whole language types for one set of values for N_1, N_2, etc., we shall save space by testing, in Table 21, only the predictions for whole language types. The language types will be exactly the same as those shown in Table 19. The results of Table 21 are not quite as good as those of Table 19, but they still offer strong confirmation for CCH: In Table 21, 96% of CCH's

TABLE 18 : Verb and Noun Predictions (30-Language Sample: Adj Gen, and Rel)

Co-occurrence pair	CCH deviations	NSP deviations	Languages (*N*)
V_1 & N_1	0	0	6
V_2 & N_2	0	2	5
V_3 & N_3	0	2	3
V_4 & N_4	0	0	4
V_1 & N_2	1	1	0
V_2 & N_1	1	1	6
V_2 & N_3	1	3	2
V_3 & N_2	1	3	0
V_3 & N_4	1	1	0
V_4 & N_3	1	1	2
V_1 & N_3	2	2	0
V_2 & N_4	2	2	0
V_3 & N_1	2	2	0
V_4 & N_2	2	2	0
V_1 & N_4	3	3	0
V_4 & N_1	3	3	0

Predictions

CCH: The number of exemplifying languages for each word order co-occurrence pair with 0 CCH deviations is predicted to exceed or equal the number for every pair with 1, 2, and 3 deviations: $4 \times (6 + 4 + 2) = 48$ predictions; etc. Total predictions = 92.

NSP′: The number of exemplifying languages for each word order co-occurrence pair with 0 NSP deviations is predicted to exceed or equal the number for every pair with 1, 2, and 3 deviations: $2 \times (4 + 6 + 4) = 28$ predictions; etc. Total predictions = 92.

Results

CCH: Out of 92 predictions 89 are correct (96.7%). (Out of 56 basic predictions 53 are correct, i.e., 94.6%.) The three exceptions are: V_2 & N_2, V_3 & N_3, and V_4 & N_4 (all 0 deviations) do not exceed or equal V_2 & N_1 (1 deviation).

NSP′: Out of 92 predictions 79 are correct (85.9%). (Out of 56 basic predictions 45 are correct, i.e., 80.4%.)

total predictions are correct, compared to 98% in Table 19 (basic predictions score 93% in Table 21 compared to 97% in Table 19). Table 21 also confirms the superiority of CCH to NSP′ (NSP′ scores 81% total predictions correct, 77% basic predictions).

Table 22 presents the data for the noun in relation to Num, Adj, and Gen,[6] and Table 23 the results of CCH's predictions. In Table 23, CCH's success rate is almost exactly the same as in Table 21 (96% for total predictions, 94% for basic predictions). The results for NSP′ are slightly better in Table 23: Total predictions score 83% (compared to 81% for Table 21), and basic predictions score 80% (compared with 77% for Table 21).

TABLE 19 : Predictions for Whole Language Types (30-Language Sample: Adj, Gen and Rel)

Language type	CCH deviations	NSP deviations	Languages (*N*)
Pr & V_1 & N_1	0	0	6
Po & V_4 & N_4	0	0	4
Pr & V_1 & N_2	2	1	0
Pr & V_2 & N_1	2	1	6
Pr & V_2 & N_2	2	2	3
Po & V_4 & N_3	2	1	2
Po & V_3 & N_4	2	1	0
Po & V_3 & N_3	2	2	3
Pr & V_1 & N_3	4	2	0
Pr & V_2 & N_3	4	3	1
Pr & V_3 & N_1	4	2	0
Pr & V_3 & N_2	4	3	0
Pr & V_3 & N_3	4	3	0
Po & V_4 & N_2	4	2	0
Po & V_3 & N_2	4	3	0
Po & V_2 & N_4	4	2	0
Po & V_2 & N_3	4	3	1
Po & V_2 & N_2	4	3	2
Pr & V_1 & N_4	6	3	0
Pr & V_2 & N_4	6	3	0
Pr & V_3 & N_4	6	2	0
Pr & V_4 & N_1	6	3	0
Pr & V_4 & N_2	6	3	0
Pr & V_4 & N_3	6	2	0
Pr & V_4 & N_4	6	1	0
Po & V_4 & N_1	6	3	0
Po & V_3 & N_1	6	3	0
Po & V_2 & N_1	6	2	0
Po & V_1 & N_4	6	3	0
Po & V_1 & N_3	6	3	0
Po & V_1 & N_2	6	2	0
Po & V_1 & N_1	6	1	0

Predictions

CCH: The number of exemplifying languages for each language type with 0 CCH deviations is predicted to exceed or equal the number for every type with 2, 4, and 6 deviations: $2 \times (6 + 10 + 14) = 60$ predictions; etc. Total predictions = 344.

NSP′: The number of exemplifying languages for each language type with 0 NSP deviations is predicted to exceed or equal the number for every type with 1, 2, and 3 deviations: $2 \times (6 + 10 + 14) = 60$ predictions; etc. Total predictions = 344.

Results

CCH: Out of 344 predictions 337 are correct (98%). (Out of 212 basic predictions 205 are correct, i.e., 96.7%.) The exceptions are: Po & V_4 & N_4 (0 deviations) does not exceed or equal Pr & V_2 & N_1 (2 deviations); Pr & V_1 & N_2 and Po & V_3 & N_4 (both 2 deviations) do not exceed or equal Pr & V_2 & N_3 and Po & V_2 & N_3 and Po & V_2 & N_2 (all 4 deviations).

NSP′: Out of 344 predictions 297 are correct (86.3%). (Out of 212 basic predictions 177 are correct, i.e., 83.5%.)

TABLE 20 : Language Quantities in the 30-Language Sample (N Relative to Dem, Adj, and Gen)

Prepositional languages

N_1: Berber (V_1), Hebrew (V_1), Welsh (V_1), Zapotec (V_1), Fulani (V_2), Malay (V_2), Swahili (V_2), Thai (V_2), Yoruba (V_2) = 9
N_2: Maori (V_1), Masai (V_1), Italian (V_2) = 3
N_3: Greek (V_2), Maya (V_2), Serbian (V_2) = 3
N_4: Norwegian (V_2) = 1

Postpositional languages

N_4: Burushaski (V_4), Hindi (V_4), Japanese (V_4), Kannada (V_4), Turkish (V_4), Quechua (V_3), Finnish (V_2) = 7
N_3: Burmese (V_4), Chibcha (V_3), Nubian (V_3), Guarani (V_2) = 4
N_2: Basque (V_3), Loritja (V_3), Songhai (V_2) = 3
N_1: ∅

16 Pr languages	14 Po languages	
9	0	9 N_1 languages
3	3	6 N_2 languages
3	4	7 N_3 languages
1	7	8 N_4 languages

16 Pr languages	14 Po languages	
6	0	6 V_1 languages
10	3	13 V_2 languages
0	5	5 V_3 languages
0	6	6 V_4 languages

6 V_1 languages	13 V_2 languages	5 V_3 languages	6 V_4 languages	
4	5	0	0	9 N_1 languages
2	2	2	0	6 N_2 languages
0	4	2	1	7 N_3 languages
0	2	1	5	8 N_4 languages

4.5.3 NOUN IN RELATION TO ADJ AND GEN; ADJ IN RELATION TO ADV AND STANDARD OF COMPARISON

Our most ambitious predictions of all will now be tested by incorporating the adjective phrase into the analysis. Implicational Universals (XIX) and (XX) (Sections 3.3.19, 3.3.20) defined permissible co-occurrences of adverb and standard of comparison operators withn the adjective phrase in prepositional and postpositional languages respectively. As we have two modifiers on the adjective, we shall employ two on the noun (Adj and Gen), and two on the verb (S and O) as well.

Table 24 lists the 19 languages for which Greenberg gives data on both Adv and NP-standard within the adjective phrase. And Table 25 presents both CCH and NSP′ predictions for whole language types. There are now 54 language types in all. For the purpose of calculating CCH, each co-occurrence type is divisible into six constituent word order pairs, rather than the three of previous analyses. For example, a type such as Pr & V_2 & N_1 & A_1 is divisible into the following pairs: Pr & V_2; Pr & N_1; Pr & A_1; V_2 & N_1; V_2 & A_1; and N_1 & A_1. By totaling the number of deviations for all

TABLE 21 : Predictions for Whole Language Types (30-Language Sample: Dem, Adj, and Gen)

Language type	CCH deviations	NSP deviations	Languages (N)
Pr & V_1 & N_1	0	0	4
Po & V_4 & N_4	0	0	5
Pr & V_1 & N_2	2	1	2
Pr & V_2 & N_1	2	1	5
Pr & V_2 & N_2	2	2	1
Po & V_4 & N_3	2	1	1
Po & V_3 & N_4	2	1	1
Po & V_3 & N_3	2	2	2
Pr & V_1 & N_3	4	2	0
Pr & V_2 & N_3	4	3	3
Pr & V_3 & N_1	4	2	0
Pr & V_3 & N_2	4	3	0
Pr & V_3 & N_3	4	3	0
Po & V_4 & N_2	4	2	0
Po & V_3 & N_2	4	3	2
Po & V_2 & N_4	4	2	1
Po & V_2 & N_3	4	3	1
Po & V_2 & N_2	4	3	1
Pr & V_1 & N_4	6	3	0
Pr & V_2 & N_4	6	3	1
Pr & V_3 & N_4	6	2	0
Pr & V_4 & N_1	6	3	0
Pr & V_4 & N_2	6	3	0
Pr & V_4 & N_3	6	2	0
Pr & V_4 & N_4	6	1	0
Po & V_4 & N_1	6	3	0
Po & V_3 & N_1	6	3	0
Po & V_2 & N_1	6	2	0
Po & V_1 & N_4	6	3	0
Po & V_1 & N_3	6	3	0
Po & V_1 & N_2	6	2	0
Po & V_1 & N_1	6	1	0

Predictions

CCH: The number of exemplifying languages for each language type with 0 CCH deviations is predicted to exceed or equal the number for every type with 2, 4, and 6 deviations: $2 \times (6 + 10 + 14) = 60$ predictions; etc. Total predictions = 344.

NSP′: The number of exemplifying languages for each language type with 0 NSP deviations is predicted to exceed or equal the number for every type with 1, 2, and 3 deviations: $2 \times (6 + 10 + 14) = 60$ predictions; etc. Total predictions = 344.

Results

CCH: Out of 344 predictions 330 are correct (95.9%). (Out of 212 basic predictions 198 are correct, i.e., 93.4%.)

NSP′: Out of 344 predictions 280 are correct (81.4%). (Out of 212 basic predictions 163 are correct, i.e., 76.9%.)

TABLE 22 : Language Quantities in the 30-Language Sample (N Relative to Num, Adj, and Gen)

Prepositional languages

N_1: Masai (V_1), Fulani (V_2), Swahili (V_2), Yoruba (V_2) = 4
N_2: Berber (V_1), Hebrew (V_2), Welsh (V_1), Maori (V_1), Zapotec (V_1), Italian (V_2), Malay (V_2), Thai (V_2) = 8
N_3: Greek (V_2), Maya (V_2), Serbian (V_2) = 3
N_4: Norwegian (V_2) = 1

Postpositional languages

N_4: Burushaski (V_4), Hindi (V_4), Japanese (V_4), Kannada (V_4), Turkish (V_4), Quechua (V_3), Finnish (V_2) = 7
N_3: Burmese (V_4), Basque (V_3) = 2
N_2: Chibcha (V_3), Loritja (V_3), Nubian (V_3), Songhai (V_2) = 4
N_1: ∅

16 Pr languages	13 Po languages	
4	0	4 N_1 languages
8	4	12 N_2 languages
3	2	5 N_3 languages
1	7	8 N_4 languages

16 Pr languages	13 Po languages	
6	0	6 V_1 languages
10	2	12 V_2 languages
0	5	5 V_3 languages
0	6	6 V_4 languages

6 V_1 languages	12 V_2 languages	5 V_3 languages	5 V_4 languages	
1	3	0	0	4 N_1 languages
5	4	3	0	12 N_2 languages
0	3	1	1	5 N_3 languages
0	2	1	5	8 N_4 languages

six word order pairs, we calculate the relative cross-category harmony. In this case, the total is 3: Pr & V_2, V_2 & N_1, and V_2 & A_1 are each one operand position removed from the preferred orderings, while the other three pairs are maximally harmonic. More generally, the deviation totals are either 0, 3, 4, 6, 7, or 8. The calculation of NSP-deviations proceeds as usual: There are seven operator–operand pairs (two on the verb, two on the noun, two on the adjective, and one on the adposition), and either 0, 1, 2, or 3 deviation totals.

As in Sections 4.5.1 and 4.5.2, fewer CCH- and NSP-deviation totals (i.e., greater CCH and more NSP-consistency) are predicted to be matched by a greater or equal number of languages.

A total of 1128 predictions are made by CCH, of which 1117 are correct (99%). The NSP′ makes fewer predictions, 924, and of these 852 are correct (92.2%). Once again, CCH scores higher than NSP′. However, the interest of these results is much reduced on account of the very limited number of languages in the sample. What is significant from the point of view of CCH is that all but 1 of the 19 languages cluster uniquely around the 0 and 3 deviation types. Had these languages been spread evenly across all deviation types, and in particular had they clustered round the 6-, 7-, and 8-deviation types, there would have been a considerable

TABLE 23 : Predictions for Whole Language Types (30-Language Sample: Num, Adj, and Gen)

Language type	CCH deviations	NSP deviations	Languages (*N*)
Pr & V_1 & N_1	0	0	1
Po & V_4 & N_4	0	0	5
Pr & V_1 & N_2	2	1	5
Pr & V_2 & N_1	2	1	3
Pr & V_2 & N_2	2	2	3
Po & V_4 & N_3	2	1	1
Po & V_3 & N_4	2	1	1
Po & V_3 & N_3	2	2	1
Pr & V_1 & N_3	4	2	0
Pr & V_2 & N_3	4	3	3
Pr & V_3 & N_1	4	2	0
Pr & V_3 & N_2	4	3	0
Pr & V_3 & N_3	4	3	0
Po & V_4 & N_2	4	2	0
Po & V_3 & N_2	4	3	3
Po & V_2 & N_4	4	2	1
Po & V_2 & N_3	4	3	0
Po & V_2 & N_2	4	3	1
Pr & V_1 & N_4	6	3	0
Pr & V_2 & N_4	6	3	1
Pr & V_3 & N_4	6	2	0
Pr & V_4 & N_1	6	3	0
Pr & V_4 & N_2	6	3	0
Pr & V_4 & N_3	6	2	0
Pr & V_4 & N_4	6	1	0
Po & V_4 & N_1	6	3	0
Po & V_3 & N_1	6	3	0
Po & V_2 & N_1	6	2	0
Po & V_1 & N_4	6	3	0
Po & V_1 & N_3	6	3	0
Po & V_1 & N_2	6	2	0
Po & V_1 & N_1	6	1	0

Predictions

CCH: The number of exemplifying languages for each language type with 0 CCH deviations is predicted to exceed or equal the number for every type with 2, 4, and 6 deviations: 2 × (6 + 10 + 14) = 60 predictions; etc. Total predictions = 344.

NSP′: The number of exemplifying languages for each language type with 0 NSP deviations is predicted to exceed or equal the number for every type with 1, 2, and 3 deviations: 2 × (6 + 10 + 14) = 60 predictions; etc. Total predictions = 344.

Results

CCH: Out of 344 predictions 330 are correct (95.9%). (Out of 212 basic predictions 200 are correct, i.e., 94.3%.)

NSP′: Out of 344 predictions 287 are correct (83.4%). (Out of 212 basic predictions 170 are correct, i.e., 80.2%.)

TABLE 24 : Quantities for the 30-Language Sample (N Relative to Adj and Gen; Adj Relative to Adv and Standard of Comparison)

Prepositional languages

V_1: Hebrew (N_1,A_1), Zapotec (N_1,A_1) = 2
V_2: Fulani (N_1,A_1), Malay (N_1,A_1), Swahili (N_1,A_1), Thai (N_1,A_1), Italian (N_1,A_1), Greek (N_2,A_2), Serbian (N_2,A_2), Norwegian (N_3,A_2) = 8
V_3: ∅

Postpositional languages

V_3: Burushaski (N_3,A_3), Hindi (N_3,A_3) Japanese (N_3,A_3), Kannada (N_3,A_3), Turkish (N_3,A_3), Basque (N_2,A_3), Burmese (N_2,A_3), Chibcha (N_2,A_3) = 8
V_2: Guarani (N_2,A_2) = 1
V_1: ∅

Note: Number of languages with $V_1 = 2$; with $V_2 = 9$; with $V_3 = 8$. Number with Pr = 10; with Po = 9. Number with $N_1 = 7$; with $N_2 = 6$; with $N_3 = 6$. Number with $A_1 = 6$; with $A_2 = 5$; with $A_3 = 8$.

TABLE 25 : Predictions for 30-Language Sample Word Order Types of Table 24

Language type	CCH deviations	NSP deviations	Number of languages
Pr & V_1 & N_1 & A_1	0	0	2
Po & V_3 & N_3 & A_3	0	0	5
Pr & V_1 & N_1 & A_2	3	1	1
Pr & V_1 & N_2 & A_1	3	1	0
Pr & V_2 & N_1 & A_1	3	1	4
Pr & V_2 & N_2 & A_2	3	3	2
Po & V_2 & N_2 & A_2	3	3	1
Po & V_2 & N_3 & A_3	3	1	0
Po & V_3 & N_2 & A_3	3	1	3
Po & V_3 & N_3 & A_2	3	1	0
Pr & V_1 & N_2 & A_2	4	2	0
Pr & V_2 & N_1 & A_2	4	2	0
Pr & V_2 & N_2 & A_1	4	2	0
Po & V_2 & N_2 & A_3	4	2	0
Po & V_2 & N_3 & A_2	4	2	0
Po & V_3 & N_2 & A_2	4	2	0
Pr & V_1 & N_1 & A_3	6	2	0
Pr & V_1 & N_3 & A_1	6	2	0
Pr & V_2 & N_2 & A_3	6	3	0
Pr & V_2 & N_3 & A_2	6	3	1
Pr & V_3 & N_1 & A_1	6	2	0
Pr & V_3 & N_2 & A_2	6	3	0
Pr & V_3 & N_3 & A_3	6	1	0
Po & V_1 & N_1 & A_1	6	1	0
Po & V_1 & N_2 & A_2	6	3	0
Po & V_1 & N_3 & A_3	6	2	0
Po & V_2 & N_1 & A_2	6	3	0
Po & V_2 & N_2 & A_1	6	3	0
Po & V_3 & N_1 & A_3	6	2	0
Po & V_3 & N_3 & A_1	6	2	0

(cont'd)

TABLE 25 : (Continued)

Language type	CCH deviations	NSP deviations	Number of languages
Pr & V_1 & N_2 & A_3	7	3	0
Pr & V_1 & N_3 & A_2	7	3	0
Pr & V_2 & N_1 & A_3	7	3	0
Pr & V_2 & N_3 & A_1	7	3	0
Pr & V_2 & N_3 & A_3	7	2	0
Pr & V_3 & N_1 & A_2	7	3	0
Pr & V_3 & N_2 & A_1	7	3	0
Pr & V_3 & N_2 & A_3	7	2	0
Pr & V_3 & N_3 & A_2	7	2	0
Po & V_1 & N_1 & A_2	7	2	0
Po & V_1 & N_2 & A_1	7	2	0
Po & V_1 & N_2 & A_3	7	3	0
Po & V_1 & N_3 & A_2	7	3	0
Po & V_2 & N_1 & A_1	7	2	0
Po & V_2 & N_1 & A_3	7	3	0
Po & V_2 & N_3 & A_1	7	3	0
Po & V_3 & N_1 & A_2	7	3	0
Po & V_3 & N_2 & A_1	7	3	0
Pr & V_1 & N_3 & A_3	8	3	0
Pr & V_2 & N_1 & A_3	8	3	0
Pr & V_3 & N_3 & A_1	8	3	0
Po & V_1 & N_1 & A_3	8	3	0
Po & V_1 & N_3 & A_1	8	3	0
Po & V_3 & N_1 & A_1	8	3	0

Predictions

CCH: The number of exemplifying languages for each language type with 0 CCH deviations is predicted to exceed or equal the number for every type with 3, 4, 6, 7, and 8 deviations: 2 × (8 + 6 + 14 + 18 + 6) = 104 predictions; etc. Total predictions = 1128.

NSP′: The number of exemplifying languages for each language type with 0 NSP deviations is predicted to exceed or equal the number for every type with 1, 2, and 3 deviations: 2 × (8 + 18 + 26) = 104 predictions; etc. Total predictions = 924.

Results

CCH: Out of 1128 predictions 1117 are correct (99%). (Out of 508 basic predictions 500 are correct, i.e., 98.4%.)

NSP′: Out of 924 predictions 852 are correct (92.2%). (Out of 628 basic predictions 572 are correct, i.e., 91%.)

number of exceptions to CCH. Instead, there are only 11 rather marginal counterexamples to the 1128 predictions.

4.6 Explaining the Distributional Universal

4.6.1 EXPLANATORY FACTORS UNDERLYING CCH

This chapter has tried to show that there is a principled regularity underlying the varying numbers of languages in Greenberg's data and the

Expanded Sample. In order to describe it, we have employed Vennemann's distinction between operator and operand categories, and we have adopted a numerical approach, quantifying numbers of operators to the left and to the right of their respective operands. Which operators occur to the left and which to the right is in large measure determined by implicational universals defining all and only the permitted co-occurrences. How many operators precede or follow in the varying quantities of languages is then subject to CCH. But we have not yet offered any explanation for our distributional universal. Why should languages strive for a harmonic balance in their cross-categorial operator–operand orderings? And why should there be such an uncannily regular decline in language quantities as CCH decreases?

As we stressed in Chapter 3 (when discussing our implicational universals), explanations for the universals of language are complex objects which must follow, and cannot precede, careful descriptive statements of increasing generality and coverage. There will quite likely be a variety of explanatory factors—syntactic, semantic, psycholinguistic, historical, etc.—each of which have to be identified and precisely defined, and each of which will have to be subjected to principles of interaction with every other.

I would suggest that the quantitative preferences that we have identified among the attested word order co-occurrences of our data point to the following three interrelated factors.

First, CCH points to the validity of the syntactic-semantic parallelism between the verb and its modifiers, the noun and its modifiers, the adposition and its modifiers, and the adjective and its modifiers. That is, CCH, like the implicational universals of Chapter 3 (see Section 3.4.1.3), supports, and reflects the reality of, the modifier–head theory (outlined in Sections 2.4.3 and 2.6.1). The crucial theoretical construct here is that of "head of phrase"—the more similar the cross-categorial positioning of the head, the more languages there are; and the less similar, the fewer are the languages. This distributional regularity supports a theory which can recognize the appropriate heads of phrase, and define them as such in a consistent and principled way.

Conversely, the function–argument principle (Sections 2.4.3 and 2.6.1) does not lend itself as readily to an explanation of these declining language frequencies. We have seen, for example, that prepositional languages become progressively less frequent, as more noun modifiers are preposed within the noun phrase (cf. the PrNMH, Section 3.3.7; and Tables 8 and 16). Ignoring the genitive ordering for the moment, this means, in function–argument terms, that prepositional languages become progressively less frequent as function categories increasingly precede their arguments within the noun phrase. But since functions precede arguments within the prepositional phrase, we are forced to say that these languages become progressively rarer, the more their grammars incorporate a linguistic generalization (function before argument serialization). This goes against all expectations. We would normally expect that the more a language incorporates a regularity like this, the more unmarked and frequent it will be. Of course, this raises once again the question of whether there ARE principled reasons for dissimilar orderings across the noun phrase and the prepositional phrase. If there are, then declining numbers will be expected to correlate with increasingly similar, rather than increasingly dissimilar, function–argument serializations. But in the absence of such reasons, the observed negative correlation between language numbers and linguistically significant generalizations must count against the attempt to predicate word order predictions on function–argument structures.

There is a related problem. If we use function–argument structures in this way, we will be forced to say that declining language numbers correlate with progressively SIMILAR function–argument orderings in some cases, but with increasingly DISSIMILAR orderings in others. For example, the most frequent co-occurrence of adposition and NP in relation to (transitive) verb and (direct object) NP is that in which functions precede arguments in both cases, that is, Pr+NP & V+NP and NP+Po and NP+V. Dissimilarity is marked by declining numbers here: Pr+NP & V+NP exceeds Pr+NP & NP+V by 136 to 12 languages in my Expanded Sample; and NP+Po & NP+V exceeds NP+Po & V+NP by 162 to 26 languages. Thus, as word orders across the adposition phrase and the verb phrase become progressively disharmonic and language numbers decline, we witness increasing dissimilarity in function–argument serialization. But across the adposition phrase and the noun phrase, the same declining language numbers correlate with increasing similarity in function–argument serialization. Thus, function–argument structures provide no uniform means of explaining language frequencies. Similarly, consider the genitive facts in prepositional languages. Keenan analyzes a NGen construction such as *father of John* as function (*father-of*) + argument (*John*), and the GenN *John's father* as argument (*John*) + function (*'s father*). As a result, NGen (function + argument) is indeed harmonic with Pr+NP (also function + argument), whereas the other head + modifier orders (NDem, NAdj, etc.) are disharmonic with prepositions (being argument + function). As we move down the subtypes of the PrNMH, therefore, we have to say that declining language numbers correspond to similar function–argument serializations in some cases, but dissimilar serializations in others. One and the same pair of phrasal categories here confirms the general point we are trying to make: A modifier–head theory can provide a uniform descriptive regularity for these declining language frequencies; a function–argument theory cannot.

The second factor to emerge from CCH is the existence of some form of analogy principle. The operator preposing and postposing balance within one category generalizes to another as a result both of the operator–operand generalization linking the two categories and of a natural tendency observable throughout language for like elements to be treated in a like manner. To the extent that the preposing/postposing balance of operators to operand within one category moves away from that of the other categories, the language becomes nonpreferred and infrequent, and is under increasing pressure to reintroduce a balance (see Sections 5.5.2, 6.1). Thus, the role of analogy as defined by CCH differs from its putative role in Vennemann's theory (Section 2.3). Analogy does not necessarily strive to create a uniform leftward or rightward serialization of operators, but instead to achieve a harmonic cross-categorial operator preposing/postposing balance.

The third factor for which I would argue in explaining CCH is grammatical complexity—more narrowly, syntactic complexity. This point is difficult to justify in the present state of syntactic theory, as detailed syntactic analyses of the appropriate languages are still in their infancy, and as so much of our general syntactic theory still derives from English. Nonetheless, the X-bar theory of generative grammar strikes me as the most promising step in this direction to date. This theory defines unmarked versus marked sets of cross-categorial phrase structure rules, and thereby assigns them preferred versus nonpreferred status. And in at least one version of the X-bar theory, Jackendoff (1977), it is quite transparent why languages with a more harmonic balance of operators to operands across the different categories should be preferred: because harmonic orderings permit the formulation of more, or more general, cross-categorial syntactic rules than disharmonic orderings. These latter preclude the collapsing of individual rules into more general cross-categorial rules, and as a result decreasing CCH is matched by increasing grammatical complexity.

Of these explanatory factors, grammatical complexity would appear to be the one with the most immediate explanatory potential. It would be a theoretically interesting result, and would make good sense, if decreasing quantities of languages could be shown to correlate with increasing grammatical complexity. As I consider the X-bar theory to offer the most hopeful basis for defining complexity, I shall devote the rest of this chapter to it, discussing it in the light of the universal word order properties of this book. Specifically, I shall consider X-bar in relation to CCH and its predictions (Sections 4.6.2, 4.6.3), and shall attempt to identify areas in which X-bar either is or is not an adequate universal theory (Section 4.6.4), and I will suggest some changes (Section 4.6.5).

4.6.2 THE X-BAR THEORY: JACKENDOFF (1977)

Both CCH and Vennemann's NSP are cross-categorial universals. Within generative grammar the pursuit of cross-categorial generalizations has resulted in the X-bar theory, first proposed by Chomsky (1970) and developed in the greatest detail to date in Jackendoff (1977). Generalizations which cut across noun phrases, verb phrases, adjective phrases, and prepositional phrases in the grammar of English are stated using PS-rules of the form (in their earliest formulation):

(1) a. $\overline{\overline{X}} \rightarrow (\text{Spec } \overline{X})\ \overline{X}$
    b. $\overline{X} \rightarrow X\ \text{Comp}$

where X stands for the head categories, N, V, Adj, and Prep; Comp for the complements of the head categories which enter into the strict subcategorization of the latter (cf. Chomsky 1965:Chapter 2), such as S, NP, PP, VP; and (Spec $\overline{X}$) for the various specifiers of these head categories and their complements (e.g., determiners and prenominal genitives for noun phrases, auxiliaries for verb phrases, qualifying and quantifying expressions for adjective phrases).

Jackendoff (1977) extends this schema by using three bar levels instead of two ($\overline{X}$ being rendered in his notation as X', a notation we shall use throughout the remainder of this book). Each level has its own complements. For example, within the noun phrase there exist complements of N' (e.g., the PP *of England* in the phrase *king of England,* or *for power* in *lust for power*), complements of N'' (e.g., restrictive relative clauses), and complements of N''' (e.g., appositive relative clauses). In addition, both X'' and X''' have their own specifiers. The three bar levels are justified by showing that rules of the grammar are regularly sensitive to, and most economically defined in terms of, for example, N', N'', or N'''.

This abstract cross-categorial approach to the PS-rules is motivated on the grounds that generalizations can be captured which would otherwise require separate rules and a complication of the grammar. At the level of the PS-rules such generalizations involve both immediate constituency and linear ordering. For example, the syntactic categories that can figure as immediately dominated complements at common bar levels across different categories are often similar, and where they are not similar a feature analysis captures whatever generalizations can be made. The linear ordering of specifiers, heads, and complements at each bar level also admits of cross-categorial generalizations, and this in turn defines the order of all specifiers relative to one another, and of all complements relative to one another, down the different bar levels. The constituency and relative ordering of the complements has a semantic counterpart. The complements of X′ are functional arguments, complements of X″ restrictive modifiers, and complements of X‴ appositive modifiers. Later transformational rules and constraints on rules are also formulated cross-categorially so as to apply to constituents with comparable domination and linear orderings across the different categories. See, for example, Halitsky's (1975) cross-categorial transformation extraposing sentential subject specifiers of V‴ and genitive (subject) specifiers of N‴, and Bresnan's (1976) cross-categorial reformulation of Ross's (1967) left-branch condition on transformations.

Sample trees generated by Jackendoff's PS-rules, including the categories mentioned in Greenberg's Appendix II, are given here for illustration. Examples of possible complements are listed under Comp, and sample specifiers are adjoined directly in leftmost position to their immediately dominating category. Specifiers are given in bar notation with the traditional description of the category in parentheses.

(2)

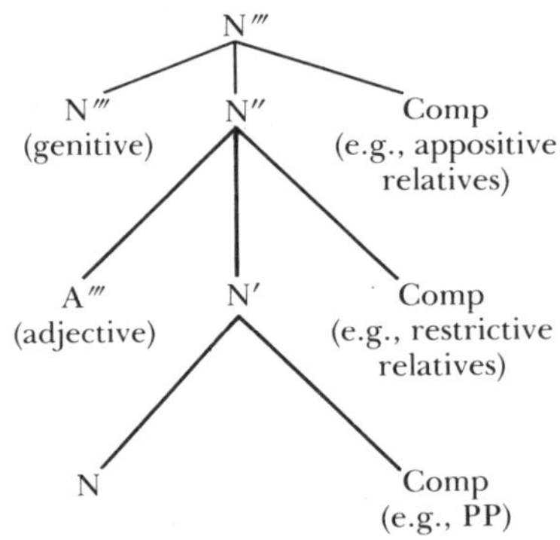

(3)

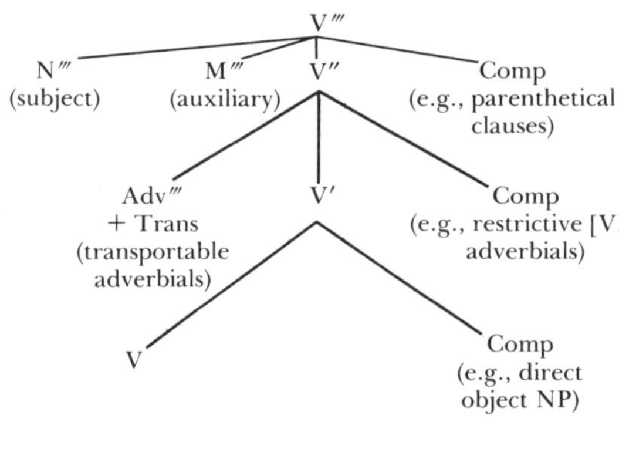

(4)

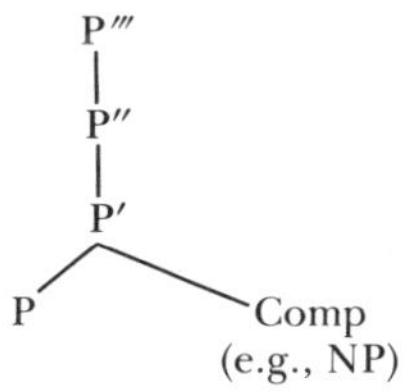

There are clear general similarities, although numerous differences in detail, between Jackendoff's X-bar theory and Vennemann's cross-categorial operator–operand theory. Both theories embody the distinction between a head category (Vennemann's operand, Jackendoff's X without a bar), and the modifiers of that head (Vennemann's operators, Jackendoff's specifiers and complements). However, the X-bar theory differs from Vennemann's NSP in one major respect: Rules (1a) and (1b) do not serialize all modifiers on the same side of the head. Specifiers and complements occur on opposite sides across all categories, and hence this theory offers a more hopeful basis for describing the majority of languages (Sections 4.1.1, 4.3.2).

But despite the specifier–complement distinction, word order disharmonies involving pre- and postposing of operators still create problems for Jackendoff, as they do for Vennemann. Jackendoff points out (1977:81–85) that any word order discrepancy among comparable daughters of X^n will preclude adequate cross-categorial PS-rule generalizations. For example, English permits a measure phrase as specifier to modify an N′ (*two parts steel* [NP–N′]), an A′ (*two miles long* [NP–A′]), and a P′ (*two miles down the road* [NP–P′]). Such measure phrases may also modify a V′, but this time they stand after the V′ (*he jumped into the air two times* [V′–NP]), as they do also in the alternative expression *down the road two miles* (P′–NP). The existence of measure phrases as specifier daughters of X″ is therefore a valid cross-categorial generalization. But the differences in specifier order across the categories preclude a satisfactory collapsing of the PS-rules rewriting N″, V″, A″, and P″ into a single rule rewriting X″. With the PS-rules as currently conceived, such collapsing presupposes cross-categorial parallelisms involving both immediate constituency and linear ordering.

Jackendoff also considers (p. 85) some potential problems from languages other than English, for example, OV languages with prepositions (NP–V & P–NP). Quoting Greenberg, he states that such languages are relatively rare. In fact, 5 of the 64 SOV languages in Appendix II have prepositions (7.81%). However, the opposite discrepancy, VO languages with postpositions (V–NP & NP–P) is not so rare. A total of 19 SVO languages (out of 52) and 1 VSO language (out of 26) have postpositions; in other words, 20 out of a total of 78 VO languages (25.64%). A total of

$5 + 20 = 25$ of the 142 languages in Appendix II (i.e., 17.61%) will therefore give rise to problems of complement ordering in the rewriting of X′.

There are even worse problems for the rewriting of X‴. Languages with SV (NP – V″) should be matched by GN (NP – N″). Yet a total of 31 SVO languages (out of 52) and 11 SOV languages (out of 64) have NG (NP – V″ & N″ – NP); that is, 42 out of 116 SV languages have NG (36.21%). There are also 2 VSO languages with GN (V″ – NP & NP – N″), (i.e., 7.69%). A total of $42 + 2 = 44$ out of 142 SV and VS languages (or 30.99%) will therefore give rise to problems of specifier ordering in achieving genuine X‴ generalizations.

The problem languages for the X-bar theory are more numerous than Jackendoff realizes. Evidently, the specifier – complement distinction is not sufficient to capture the various word order co-occurrences across languages. Faced with the existence of such problems, we might be tempted to lay the blame on current notations for failing to reveal the cross-categorial generalizations which are assumed to hold for all languages, including these. But Jackendoff offers no ready way of improving on them. In any case, there is a more reasonable, and in this context more promising, alternative solution. Let us accept, provisionally at least (see Sections 4.6.4, 4.6.5), Jackendoff's analysis of categories as shown in (2) – (4), together with the cross-categorial rule types, abbreviatory conventions, etc., that he proposes. When applying this model to the problem languages, we are simply forced to concede that where current theory and notation cannot readily collapse PS- or T-rules across different categories, such rules should not be collapsed. Hence, these languages permit the formulation of fewer or more complex cross-categorial rules in their grammars, and we might hypothesize, more generally, that languages will vary according to the degree of cross-categorial generalizations that their grammars incorporate. To the extent that there are discrepancies in the ordering of common constituents across X^n, the fewer or more complicated will be the cross-categorial rules.

By accepting that numerous grammars do not readily submit to rule collapsing (for at least some rules — in the present context primarily PS-rules), we are able to use Jackendoff's theory to define a parameter of syntactic variation across languages, and in particular to define a set of preferences for the different language types. Grammars with more cross-categorial generalizations will be simpler than, and hence preferred over, those with fewer. And such preferences can then be used to predict that languages with simpler grammars will be more numerous, that languages with more complex grammars will have an internal motive to move historically toward a more preferred type, and so on.

The quantitative predictions made by this interpretation of Jackendoff's theory turn out to be well supported by the data of Appendix II and the Expanded Sample. The model of (3) and (4) now predicts that an N‴ complement as immediate daughter of X′ should be preferably ordered on the same side of P and V, producing Pr + NP & VO and NP + Po & OV. These preferences lead to two clear empirical predictions: The preferred co-occurrences should collectively form a majority of the language sample; and each preferred co-occurrence should be relatively more frequent than each of the nonpreferred co-occurrences (i.e., the mixed word orders, such as Pr + NP & OV and NP + Po & VO). The data are set out in Table 26. A clear majority of the 142 languages in Appendix II, and of the 336 languages in the Expanded Sample, do indeed have the preferred co-occurrences, and all four of the relative frequency predictions hold.

In Table 27 we consider the prediction made by (2) and (3) that an N‴ specifier as immediate daughter of X‴ should be ordered on the same side of N″ and V″, producing GN & SV or NG & VS. These co-occurrences should collectively form a majority of the language sample. In addition, GN & SV and NG & VS should each be relatively more frequent than each of the mixed co-occurrences, NG & SV and GN & VS.

TABLE 26 : Predictions of Jackendoff's X-bar Theory: Adposition and Object

Predictions

An N‴ as immediate daughter of X′ should be ordered on the same side of P and V, producing Pr + NP & V + NP (VO) or NP + Po & NP + V (OV). These co-occurrences should form a (clear) majority of the language sample. And each preferred co-occurrence should be relatively more frequent than each of the mixed co-occurrences Pr + NP & NP + V (OV) and NP + Po & V + NP (VO) (four relative frequency predictions in all).

Appendix II language quantities: Total = 142

63 Pr + NP languages	79 NP + Po languages	
Pr & VO 58	Po & VO 20	78 VO languages
Pr & OV 5	Po & OV 59	64 OV languages

Expanded Sample language quantities: Total = 336

148 Pr + NP languages	188 NP + Po languages	
Pr & VO 136	Po & VO 26	162 VO languages
Pr & OV 12	Po & OV 162	174 OV languages

Results

Of the 142 languages in Appendix II, and the 336 languages in the Expanded Sample, a clear majority have the preferred orders Pr + NP & VO and NP + Po & OV: 117 in Appendix II (82.4%) and 298 in the Expanded Sample (88.7%). In addition, all four of the relative frequency predictions hold: Pr + NP & VO (58 and 136) and NP + Po & VO (59 and 162) each exceed Pr + NP & OV (5 and 12) and NP + Po & VO (20 and 26). Hence, all predictions are fulfilled.

TABLE 27 : Predictions of Jackendoff's X-bar Theory: Subject and Genitive

Predictions

An N‴ as immediate daughter of X‴ should be ordered on the same side of N″ and V″, producing GN & SV or NG & VS. These co-occurrences should form a (clear) majority of the language sample. And each preferred co-occurrence should be relatively more frequent than each of the mixed co-occurrences NG & SV and GN & VS (four relative frequency predictions in all).

Appendix II language quantities: Total = 142

76 GN languages	66 NG languages	
GN & SV 74	NG & SV 42	116 SV languages
GN & VS 2	NG & VS 24	26 VS languages

Expanded Sample language quantities: Total = 336

191 GN languages	145 NG languages	
GN & SV 189	NG & SV 94	283 SV languages
GN & VS 2	NG & VS 51	53 VS languages

Results

Of the 142 languages in Appendix II, and the 336 languages in the Expanded Sample, a majority have the preferred orders GN & SV and NG & VS: 98 in Appendix II (69%) and 240 (71.4%) in the Expanded Sample. In addition, three of the four relative frequency predictions hold: GN & SV (74 and 189) exceeds both NG & SV (42 and 94) and GN & VS (2 and 2); and NG & VS (24 and 51) exceeds GN & VS (2 and 2), but does not exceed NG & SV (42 and 94).

The majority prediction holds in Table 27, but there is one exceptional relative frequency prediction: The preferred NG & VS does not exceed NG & SV, though it does exceed GN & VS convincingly. But notice that within the class of VS languages, NG is the overwhelming preference, and the low overall total for NG & VS can therefore be attributed to the small number of VS languages, for which there are independent reasons (see Sections 4.3.1, 4.4).

When Jackendoff's theory is reinterpreted in the manner proposed, therefore, it makes good predictions for language frequencies. And the hitherto "exceptional" languages in his approach, instead of being prohibited, are now correctly predicted to be less frequent. But, similarly, the principle of CCH made correct predictions for the quantitative differences in Appendix II and the Expanded Sample (see Sections 4.2, 4.4), of which the preferences of Tables 26 and 27 are just a selection. So what is the relationship between CCH and the concept of cross-categorial simplicity which we have derived from Jackendoff's theory? Does each progressive distortion of the cross-categorial operator – operand ordering balance defined by CCH necessarily result in fewer collapsed cross-categorial syntactic rules throughout the grammars of the languages concerned? This would appear to be the case although the limited number of word order properties in Appendix II and the Expanded Sample makes an exact comparison difficult. The data of Tables 26 and 27 pick out single operator–operand pairs only (e.g., SV & GN) whereas CCH refers to a cross-categorial balance between all the operators of one operand and all the operators of another. Nonetheless, both CCH and Jackendoff's theory make correct predictions for language frequencies. And the two theories do seem in general to define the same preferences.

Languages that are verb initial (within V‴), noun initial (within N‴), and adposition initial (within P‴) will be optimally harmonic by CCH, and in terms of Jackendoff's theory their grammars will not preclude any cross-categorial PS- or T-rule collapsing on account of the discrepant left-to-right versus right-to-left ordering of comparable constituents relative to V, N, and P. But the more noun final the noun becomes within N‴, the more disharmonic the noun becomes by CCH, and the more exceptional the noun phrase becomes in relation to the other categories for the purpose of cross-categorial rules. For as the modifiers of the noun gradually precede the noun, this will progressively eliminate cross-categorial generalizations at the different bar levels. As the daughters of N‴ come to precede N″, those of N″ to precede N′, and those of N′ to precede N [cf. (2)], it becomes impossible to collapse the PS-rules rewriting N‴, N″, and N′ under more general X‴, X″, and X′ PS-rules respectively. Hence the more such discrepant word orders there are, the more X-bar generalizations are eliminated. And an analogous situation results when the verb becomes more verb final alongside noun-initial order. In addition, languages that are verb final, noun final, and postpositional would be maximally consistent in terms of both CCH and Jackendoff's theory, and would be compatible with progressively less CCH and less rule collapsing as either the noun or the verb (but not both) became progressively initial. And to the extent that the verb occupied a more medial position in the sentence, it would be desirable, according to both theories, to have the appropriate noun modifiers flanking the noun to right and left.

The prospects for exploiting Jackendoff's X-bar theory in defining grammatical complexity in a way that matches the predictions of CCH seem good, therefore. The mutual compatibility of word orders defined by CCH would appear to have direct consequences for the simplicity and number of cross-categorial rules that a language permits.

4.6.3 THE X-BAR THEORY: LIGHTFOOT'S (1979) HYPOTHESES

An alternative version of the X-bar theory is to be found in Lightfoot (1979). Lightfoot provides an explicit discussion of Chomsky's original

X-bar rules [cf. (1)] in terms of a theory of markedness, rendering them now as (1′), where the curly brackets indicate that the categories are unordered:

(1′) a. $X'' \rightarrow \{(\text{Spec } X')\ X'\}$
b. $X' \rightarrow \{X\ \text{Comp}\}$

These unordered rules are metagrammatical, that is, "part of the theory of grammar and not part of particular grammars (Lightfoot 1979:52)," and order is assigned by the particular grammar. For example, the grammar of English includes the ordered rules of (5), with specifiers on the left, and complements on the right of the head:

(5)
$$
\begin{aligned}
&S \rightarrow N''\ V'' \\
&N'' \rightarrow (\text{Spec } N')\ N' \\
&V'' \rightarrow (\text{Spec } V')\ V' \\
&P'' \rightarrow (\text{Spec } P')\ P' \\
&N' \rightarrow N \left(\begin{Bmatrix} P'' \\ S \end{Bmatrix}\right) \\
&V' \rightarrow V \left(\begin{Bmatrix} P'' \\ N'' \\ S \end{Bmatrix}\right) \\
&P' \rightarrow P \quad N''
\end{aligned}
$$

Examples of the relevant English phrase types are given in (6), with specifiers and complements indicated by bold face:

(6) (***the*** *dog*)$_{N''}$ (*the picture* ***of Mary***)$_{N''}$
(***has*** *gone*)$_{V''}$ (*lies* ***on the table***)$_{V''}$
(***right*** *to the kennel*)$_{P''}$ (*on* ***the table***)$_{P''}$

Metagrammatical principles such as (1′) may be either absolute or relative. If they are absolute, no language may deviate from them. If they are relative, a language that conforms to them will be highly valued whereas one that does not will be less highly valued and more marked. Languages with such marked grammars must be rare, and hence one of the "external domains" relative to which markedness theory can be tested involves language quantities (cf. Lightfoot 1979:77). Languages with marked grammars could not, for example, be more frequent than those with unmarked grammars.

A priori it is impossible to tell, Lightfoot asserts, whether (1′) is absolute or relative. But he argues that (1′) as it is formulated does embody some very clear predictions for all languages. It predicts that specifiers of all categories will either all precede or all follow the head, and hence that "all specifiers will be on the same side [p. 52]," which is hypothesized to be a relative rather than an absolute principle. It predicts also "on one interpretation of this notation . . . that in any given grammar, if the specifier precedes the head, the complement will follow it, and vice versa [p. 52]," and hence that "specifiers and complements must always be on opposite sides of the category head [p. 53]," which is hypothesized to be an absolute universal. The interpretation in question assumes that (Spec X′) and Comp must be adjacent to the head. Now, if one accepts these two hypotheses, there is another, which Lightfoot does not discuss explicitly, but which has to follow, namely, that all complements occur on the same side of the category head [just as in English, cf. (6)]. But if the first hypothesis is only relative, and some languages do not have all their specifiers on the same side, it follows from the second (putatively absolute) hypothesis that if any complement does not occur on the same side as (the majority of) other complements, it should still be ordered on the side opposite to its corresponding specifiers. That is, exceptions to the third hypothesis should result uniquely from the relative nature of the first.

We have, therefore, the following predictions for universal grammar:

(7) Hypothesis 1 (relative): All specifiers (of all categories) occur on the same side of the category head.
Hypothesis 2 (absolute): Specifiers and complements are always on opposite sides of the category head.
Hypothesis 3A (assuming 1 and 2): All complements (of all categories) occur on the same side of the category head.
Hypothesis 3B (assuming 2 only): The exceptional order of any complement, relative to other complements, should be predictable from the (opposite) order of the corresponding specifiers for the category in question.

Where the metagrammatical principle is absolute, no language can depart from the predicted word orders. Where it is relative we might make the same predictions that we did in the reinterpretation of Jackendoff's theory: The preferred word order co-occurrences must form collectively a majority of the language sample; and each preferred co-occurrence must be relatively more frequent than each of the nonpreferred co-occurrences.

We can use Greenberg's data and the Expanded Sample to test these hypotheses with respect to several specifiers and complements. Consider Hypothesis 1. For 19 languages, Greenberg gives data on the order of demonstrative determiner and head noun—that is, (Spec N′) and N—and on the order of inflected auxiliary and main verb—that is, (Spec V′) and V. The data and analysis are set out in Table 28. The prediction that these specifiers should occur on the same side holds for only 8 of the

TABLE 28 : Testing Lightfoot's Hypothesis 1: Demonstratives and Auxiliaries

Predictions

The specifiers of X′ should be ordered on the same side of N and V, producing NDem & VAux or DemN & AuxV co-occurrences. If Hypothesis 1 is absolute, no other co-occurrences are predicted. If it is relative, these co-occurrences should form a (clear) majority of the language sample. And each preferred co-occurrence should be relatively more frequent than each of the mixed specifier orders NDem & AuxV and DemN & VAux (four relative frequency predictions).

30-language sample quantities: Total = 19

4 NDem languages	15 DemN languages	
NDem & VAux 1	DemN & VAux 8	9 VAux languages
NDem & AuxV 3	DemN & AuxV 7	10 AuxV languages

Results

Of the 19 languages in the sample, only 8 (42.1%) have the predicted orders NDem & VAux (1 lg) or DemN & AuxV (7 languages); while 11 (57.9%) have the mixed orders NDem & AuxV (3 languages) or DemN & VAux (8 languages). In addition only one of the four relative frequency predictions holds: NDem & VAux (1) does not exceed either DemN & VAux (8) or NDem & AuxV (3), and DemN & AuxV (7) does not exceed DemN & VAux (8). Hypothesis 1 is therefore neither an absolute nor even a relative universal.

19 languages (42.1%). And in addition, only one of four relative frequency predictions holds (DemN & AuxV exceeds NDem & AuxV). Hypothesis 1 is therefore false, and represents neither an absolute nor a relative cross-categorial generalization about language.[7]

Three sets of predictions are made by Hypothesis 2 in relation to Greenberg's data and the Expanded Sample. First, there are 123 languages in the Expanded Sample for which we have data on the order of demonstrative determiner and head noun, (Spec N′) and N, and on the order of relative clause and noun, that is, N in relation to an S complement.

The data and analysis are set out in Table 29. The prediction that specifier and complement should occur on opposite sides holds only for 47 of the 123 languages (38.2%). And in addition, just two of the four relative frequency predictions hold. Hypothesis 2 is therefore false and represents neither an absolute nor a relative cross-categorial generalization about language.[8]

Second, if we follow the logic of Lightfoot's English examples in (6), and regard *of Mary* in (*the picture* ***of Mary***)$_{N''}$ as a genitive (P″) complement of the head noun *picture*, we can utilize Expanded Sample data on genitive–noun orders across languages as instances of noun complement constructions, whether this complement is a P″ (cf. German *das Haus von meinem Freund* 'the house of my friend') or an N″ (German *das Haus meines Freundes* 'the house my+Gen friend+Gen').[9]

TABLE 29 : Testing Lightfoot's Hypothesis 2: Demonstratives and Relatives

Predictions

Demonstrative specifiers of N′ should occur on the opposite side of N to relative clause (S) complements, producing DemN & NRel or NDem & RelN. If Hypothesis 2 is absolute, no other co-occurrences are predicted. If it is relative, these co-occurrences should form a (clear) majority of the language sample. And each preferred co-occurrence should be relatively more frequent than each of the co-occurrences in which specifier and complement occur on the same side, DemN & RelN and NDem & NRel (four relative frequency predictions).

Expanded Sample quantities: Total = 123

78 NDem languages	45 DemN languages	
DemN & NRel 46	NDem & NRel 44	90 NRel languages
DemN & RelN 32	NDem & RelN 1	33 RelN languages

Results

Of the 123 languages in the sample, only 47 (38.2%) have the predicted orders DemN & NRel (46 languages) or NDem & RelN (1 language); while 76 (61.8%) have the unpredicted orders DemN & RelN (32 languages) or NDem & NRel (44 languages). In addition, just two of the relative frequency predictions hold: DemN & NRel (46) exceeds DemN & RelN (32) and NDem & NRel (44) (just); but NDem & RelN (1) exceeds neither DemN & RelN (32) nor NDem & NRel (44). Hypothesis 2 is therefore neither an absolute nor a relative universal generalization.

The Expanded Sample contains 153 languages in which the predicted opposite order of demonstrative determiner and head noun, and genitive complement and head noun, can be tested. The data and analysis are set out in Table 30. Of these 153 languages, only 44 (28.8%) have the predicted orders. And in addition, none of the four relative frequency predictions holds. This further undermines Hypothesis 2.

Third, there are 19 languages for which Greenberg gives data on the order of inflected auxiliary in relation to main verb, (Spec V′) and V, and on the order of verb and direct object, that is, V in relation to an N″ complement. The data and analysis are set out in Table 31.

This time the results are very convincing. Of the 19 languages, 18 (94.7%) have the predicted opposite order of specifier and complement. In addition, all four relative frequency predictions hold. The one language which is an exception is Guarani. Based on these data alone, Hypothesis 2 could qualify as a relative, but not as an absolute, cross-categorial generalization about language.

Hypothesis 3A stipulates that the complements of X should be ordered on the same side. We can test this prediction using data from Appendix II and the Expanded Sample. It is predicted that the N″ complements of P and V and the genitive (N″ or P″) complements of N should be ordered on the same side in the majority of languages, producing Pr & VO & NG or Po & OV & GN co-occurrences. In addition, 12 relative frequency predic-

TABLE 30 : Testing Lightfoot's Hypothesis 2: Demonstratives and Genitives

Predictions

Demonstrative specifiers of N′ should occur on the opposite side of N to genitive (P″ or N″) complements, producing DemN & NGen or NDem & GenN. If Hypothesis 2 is absolute, no other co-occurrences are predicted. If it is relative, these co-occurrences should form a (clear) majority of the language sample. And each preferred co-occurrence should be relatively more frequent than each of the co-occurrences in which specifier and complement occur on the same side, DemN & GenN and NDem & NGen (four relative frequency predictions).

Expanded Sample quantities: Total = 153

96 NDem languages	57 DemN languages	
DemN & NGen 23	NDem & NGen 36	59 NGen languages
DemN & GenN 73	NDem & GenN 21	94 GenN languages

Results

Of the 153 languages in the sample, only 44 (28.8%) have the predicted orders, DemN & NGen (23 languages) or NDem & GenN (21 languages); while 109 (71.2%) have the unpredicted orders DemN & GenN (73 languages) or NDem & NGen (36 languages). In addition, none of the four relative frequency predictions holds: both DemN & NGen (23) and NDem & GenN (21) do not exceed either DemN & GenN (73) or NDem & NGen (36). Hypothesis 2 is therefore further disconfirmed.

tions are made between preferred and nonpreferred co-occurrence sets. The data and analysis are set out in Table 32. The results are convincing. Of the 142 languages in Appendix II, 105 (73.9%) have the predicted orders, while 275 of the 336 languages of the Expanded Sample (81.8%) have the predicted orders. And all 12 of the relative frequency predictions

TABLE 31 : Testing Lightfoot's Hypothesis 2: Auxiliaries and Objects

Predictions

Inflected auxiliary specifiers of V′ should occur on the opposite side of V to direct object (N″) complements, producing AuxV & VO or VAux & OV. If Hypothesis 2 is absolute, no other co-occurrences are predicted. If it is relative, these co-occurrences should form a (clear) majority of the language sample. And each preferred co-occurrence should be relatively more frequent than each of the co-occurrences in which specifier and complement occur on the same side, AuxV & OV and VAux & VO (four relative frequency predictions).

30-language sample quantities: Total = 19

10 AuxV languages	9 VAux languages	
AuxV & VO 10	VAux & VO 1	11 VO languages
AuxV & OV 0	VAux & OV 8	8 OV languages

Results

Of the 19 languages in the sample, 18 (94.7%) have the predicted orders AuxV & VO (10) or VAux & OV (8); while only 1 (5.2%) has one of the unpredicted orders. In addition, all four of the relative frequency predictions hold: AuxV & VO (10) and VAux & OV (8) each exceed AuxV & OV (0) and VAux & VO (1). Based on this evidence alone, therefore, Hypothesis 2 could qualify as a relative universal generalization.

TABLE 32 : Testing Lightfoot's Hypothesis 3A: Adposition, Object, and Genitive

Predictions

The complements of X should be ordered on the same side of P, V, and N, producing Pr & VO & NG or Po & OV & GN. If Hypothesis 3A is absolute, no other co-occurrence sets are predicted. If it is relative, these co-occurrences should form a (clear) majority of the language sample. And each preferred co-occurrence set should be more frequent than each co-occurrence set in which one complement order is at variance with the other two, as follows: Pr & VO & NG and Po & OV & GN each to exceed Pr & OV & NG, Pr & VO & GN, Pr & OV & GN, Po & VO & GN, Po & OV & NG, and Po & VO & NG (12 relative frequency predictions).

Appendix II language quantities: Total = 142

Pr & VO & NG:	53	Po & OV & GN:	52
Pr & OV & NG:	4	Po & VO & GN:	18
Pr & VO & GN:	5	Po & OV & NG:	7
Pr & OV & GN:	1	Po & VO & NG:	2

Expanded Sample language quantities: Total = 336

Pr & VO & NG:	124	Po & OV & GN:	151
Pr & OV & NG:	10	Po & VO & GN:	26
Pr & VO & GN:	12	Po & OV & NG:	11
Pr & OV & GN:	2	Po & VO & NG:	0

Results

Of the 142 languages in Appendix II, 105 (73.9%) have the predicted co-occurrence sets Pr & VO & NG (53 languages) and Po & OV & GN (52 languages); while 37 (26.1%) have mixed complement orders. For the Expanded Sample, 275 (81.8%) have the predicted co-occurrence sets, while 61 (18.2%) have the mixed orders. In addition, all 12 relative frequency predictions hold in both samples: Pr & VO & NG and Po & OV & GN each exceed each of the other co-occurrence sets. Hence, all predictions are fulfilled, and Hypothesis 3A can qualify as a relative universal generalization.

hold in both samples. Hypothesis 3A is therefore confirmed as a relative universal.

Table 33 uses data from the Expanded Sample in order to test relative clause order in addition to the three complements of Table 32. The predicted co-occurrences are Pr & VO & NG & NRel and Po & OV & GN & RelN. And this time there are 28 relative frequency predictions between preferred and nonpreferred co-occurrence sets. The results are again convincing. Of the 149 languages in the sample, 109 (73.2%) have the predicted orders, and all 28 relative frequency predictions hold. Hypothesis 3A would therefore appear to be further confirmed.

The Expanded Sample languages of Table 33 also enable us to test Hypothesis 3B in numerous cases. The exceptional complement orders in 40 of the 149 languages should be predictable from the opposite order of the corresponding specifiers for the category in question. Needless to say, they are not, because of the poor predictions of Hypothesis 2, which 3B assumes. Since Hypothesis 2 has already been amply illustrated, I shall say no more about 3B.

TABLE 33 : Testing Lightfoot's Hypothesis 3A: Adposition, Object, Genitive, and Relative Clause

Predictions

The complements of X should be ordered on the same side of P, V, and N, producing Pr & VO & NG & NRel or Po & OV & GN & RelN. If Hypothesis 3A is absolute, no other co-occurrence sets are predicted. If it is relative, these co-occurrences should form a (clear) majority of the language sample. And each preferred co-occurrence set should be more frequent than each co-occurrence set in which one or two complement orders are at variance with the others, as follows: Pr & VO & NG & NRel and Po & OV & GN & RelN each to exceed each of the other combinatorial possibilities (given in what follows) (28 relative frequency predictions).

Expanded Sample quantities: Total = 149

Pr & VO & NG & NRel:	78	Po & OV & GN & RelN:	31
Pr & OV & NG & NRel:	5	Po & VO & GN & RelN:	4
Pr & VO & GN & NRel:	8	Po & OV & NG & RelN:	0
Pr & OV & GN & NRel:	3	Po & VO & NG & RelN:	0
Pr & VO & NG & RelN:	0	Po & OV & GN & NRel:	9
Pr & OV & NG & RelN:	0	Po & VO & GN & NRel:	7
Pr & VO & GN & RelN:	0	Po & OV & NG & NRel:	3
Pr & OV & GN & RelN:	1	Po & VO & NG & NRel:	0

Results

Of the 149 languages in the sample, 109 (73.2%) have the predicted orders Pr & VO & NG & NRel (78) and Po & OV & GN & RelN (31); while 40 (26.8%) have mixed co-occurrences. In addition, all 28 relative frequency predictions hold: Pr & VO & NG & NRel and Po & OV & GN & RelN each exceed each of the other co-occurrence sets. Hence, all predictions are fulfilled.

Considering Lightfoot's hypotheses overall, we see that Hypothesis 3A is a convincing relative universal, as is Hypothesis 2 in relation to auxiliary specifiers. Hypothesis 1 and Hypothesis 2 in relation to demonstrative specifiers are false, however. In fact, what is interesting about the false predictions is that one of the co-occurrences always involves a demonstrative determiner. For all other categories, correct predictions are made by Hypothesis 2 and 3.

4.6.4 OVERVIEW OF CURRENT X-BAR THEORIES

The X-bar theories of the preceding subsections make sufficient correct predictions to be considered serious explanations for some cross-categorial word order universals. Given that the X-bar conventions were developed almost exclusively with English data, this is no mean achievement. In the interests of refining the explanatory adequacy of X-bar theories, this subsection will discuss some of the problems that these theories encounter in relation to our universal word order data, and will contrast their predictions with those that we have proposed in this chapter and the last. The chapter will then conclude with a proposal for a possible resolution of some of these problems.

Notice first that there are important differences between Jackendoff's X-bar theory and the Lightfoot version (which follows closely Chomsky's original proposals). From the point of view of word order, the crucial differences are:

> Jackendoff's X-bar theory predicts that the same categories (NP, measure phrase, etc.) at common bar levels across phrases serialize in the same direction; and the more this serialization regularity fails to hold the more complex the (PS-) rules of a particular grammar become.
>
> Lightfoot's X-bar theory predicts that all specifiers serialize in the same direction relative to their heads, and that all complements serialize in the same direction (opposite to that of specifiers); that is, there is an extensive collapsing of categories into macrocategories (specifier and complement), in terms of which the word order generalization "same ordering for same macrocategory" is made.

A major difference between these theories therefore involves the status of the macrocategories, specifier and complement, and the extent to which word order facts should be captured in terms of them, or rather in terms of identical (micro-) categories at common bar levels.

There is a related general difference between Jackendoff and Lightfoot, involving the notion of markedness. In Jackendoff's theory, markedness would appear to be equatable with the absence of cross-categorial generalizations in the grammar of a language. For Lightfoot, markedness results when a particular grammar does not conform to a general metagrammatical principle. But what I miss in Lightfoot's discussion is any explanation for why his metagrammatical principles are the way they are, and hence for why a particular grammar is any "better off" conforming with them rather than not. Phrase structure rules which do conform would appear to be no simpler than those which do not. In each case, the particular grammar defines the observed orders of specifiers and complements for the different categories, using exactly the same number and type of rules, whether all specifiers occur on the same side of their heads or not, etc. Within Jackendoff's theory, on the other hand, the degree of cross-categorial generalization incorporated in, say, the PS-rules of a grammar makes it transparent *why* one set of rules should be preferred over another (by being more general and simpler), and hence why particular grammars of one form should be more highly valued than those of another. But this generalization appears to be lost in Lightfoot's noncollapsed PS-rules of (5). In effect, therefore, we have two ways of defining markedness. Jackendoff's theory specifies general rule types, abbreviatory conventions, a general simplicity metric, etc.; and the different degrees of markedness or complexity can be related to, and shown to follow from, these very general stipulations of the theory. Lightfoot has the general theory define X-bar PS-rules, with which the specific rules of particular grammars then may or may not conform. But although the question "why should metagrammatical principles be the way they are and why should particular grammars conform?" may not in general be readily answerable, it is clear that we should prefer a theory and approach to markedness that *can* answer it to one that cannot.

The first problem that our word order data pose for X-bar theories affects those versions that attach importance to the specifier macrocategory (i.e., Lightfoot and Chomsky). Greenberg's data suggest that there is in fact no specifier generalization uniting Aux and Det: The predicted cross-categorial line-up does not occur (see Table 28). Nor does Det occur opposite the complements of N (see Tables 29 and 30). One therefore wonders whether the specifier generalization was inspired primarily by the word order facts of English, which do not generalize to the majority of languages. As the existence of other syntactic and semantic properties of specifiers also seems to be in doubt (cf. McCawley 1975, 1982b), the whole notion of a specifier category may be spurious. The complement macrocategory fares much better, however (Tables 32 and 33). This suggests that it may be possible to go beyond Jackendoff in generalizing interphrasal categories (setting up something along the lines of a complement macrocategory), but not as far as Lightfoot and Chomsky propose.

A second problem that we have encountered is particularly acute for Jackendoff's theory, but stems from an assumption that is shared by Lightfoot and Chomsky as well, namely, the assumption that the PS-rules define both linear ordering and constituency. This is not a necessary assumption. Constituency results automatically from rewrite rules with the kinds of formal properties that PS-rules (both context free and context sensitive) are defined to have, but linear ordering is optional. Now, for Lightfoot it does not matter whether linear order is defined by the PS-rules of particular grammars or not. As no attempt is made to capture cross-categorial generalizations using collapsed PS-rules within each particular grammar, the (basic) word order of a particular language *can* be simultaneously defined by the same set of rules that define constituency —but it does not have to be. Not so for Jackendoff's theory, in which collapsed cross-categorial PS-rules are proposed for each particular grammar. As he himself points out (see Section 4.6.2), this kind of collapsing presupposes cross-categorial parallelism involving both immediate constituency and linear ordering. If the linear ordering of identical microcategories at common bar levels across phrases is not the same (as in the example of measure phrases in English, NP + Po & VO languages, etc.), this actually prevents PS-rules from being set up which can perform the primary task of defining constituency. Jackendoff's theory cannot capture the cross-categorial constituency regularity that measure phrases are immediate daughters of X‴ in English, that NP is an immediate daughter of X′ in NP + Po & VO languages, etc. Notice, however, that if Jackendoff's PS-rules were unordered, all such cross-categorial constituency generalizations could be captured. And we have seen that there is nothing in Lightfoot's and Chomsky's X-bar rules that is irreconcilable with unordered PS-rules for particular grammars. Given that Jackendoff's theory is potentially more explanatory with regard to markedness, there might be advantages, therefore, in separating constituency-defining and serialization rules, in order to preserve the essentials of Jackendoff's approach. We shall return to this possibility in Section 4.6.5.

There is a third problem, which may be readily resolvable, but which is nonetheless a shortcoming of X-bar theories as they are currently formulated. Neither Jackendoff's nor Lightfoot's theory incorporates any correct absolute cross-categorial universals, distinguishing attested from nonattested language types. Yet we saw in Chapter 3 that there are numerous logically possible word order co-occurrences that are totally unattested, even in the Expanded Sample. Recall that the Prepositional Noun Modifier Hierarchy (Section 3.3.7) permits the following five co-occurrences:

1. Prep & NDem & NA & NG & NRel (e.g., Arabic, Thai)
2. Prep & DemN & NA & NG & NRel (e.g., Masai, Spanish)
3. Prep & DemN & AN & NG & NRel (e.g., Greek, Maya)
4. Prep & DemN & AN & GN & NRel (e.g., Swedish)
5. Prep & DemN & AN & GN & RelN (e.g., Amharic)

while ruling out the remaining 11 of the 16 mathematically possible co-occurrences:

6. *Prep & NDem & AN & NG & NRel
7. *Prep & NDem & NA & GN & NRel
8. *Prep & NDem & NA & NG & RelN
9. *Prep & NDem & AN & GN & NRel
10. *Prep & NDem & AN & NG & RelN
11. *Prep & NDem & NA & GN & RelN
12. *Prep & NDem & AN & GN & RelN
13. *Prep & DemN & NA & GN & NRel
14. *Prep & DemN & NA & GN & RelN
15. *Prep & DemN & NA & NG & RelN
16. *Prep & DemN & AN & NG & RelN

The PrNMH reveals a principled order in which postposed noun modifiers become preposed in prepositional languages: first the demonstrative determiner, then the adjective, then the genitive, and finally the relative clause. But these facts are not predicted by current X-bar theories. More generally, there is nothing in the theoretical apparatus of X-bar theories that suggests how these kinds of differences between attested and nonattested language types could be drawn.

Within the approach that I am advocating here, I would like to use X-bar insights for defining rule complexity and markedness, with predictions for relative language frequencies as a consequence. And I see the explanation for all and only the attested word orders as being quite independent, and attributable to the factors outlined in Chapter 3. Whether X-bar theorists would accept my explanations for all and only the attested language types is neither here nor there: Given the kinds of theories that they are proposing, they are going to have to accept SOME independent explanation for the co-occurrences of the PrNMH and PoNMH. And within the set of grammars so defined, X-bar theories may then be able to explain language distributions. But to the extent that X-bar theories define absolute universals, predicting attested and nonattested language types (and Lightfoot's theory does so explicitly), it must be said that such absolute universals are not adequate in relation to the kind of word order data that the PrNMH defines.

There is a fourth point that we can draw from our universal word order data of relevance to X-bar theory. It involves the notion of markedness, as used by Lightfoot (1979) and, more generally, by Chomsky (1981). The opposition marked – unmarked is a binary one. In Tables 28 – 33 we tested the derivative prediction that Lightfoot's unmarked word orders and PS-rules should be more frequent than marked word orders and rules. Thus, AuxV & VO is unmarked, VAux & VO marked; Pr & VO & NG is unmarked, Pr & OV & NG marked, etc. Now, if frequency data are indeed relevant to markedness, then there is one clear conclusion that can be drawn from this chapter: There are many degrees of preference between grammatical systems, not just the two that are suggested by the binary opposition marked – unmarked. That is, granting for the moment that the unmarked word orders of X-bar theory are very frequent (something that is not always the case, cf. Section 4.6.3, although in principle it could be), we need to set up principled gradations among the marked language types as well, in order to do full justice to the frequency facts and provide a principled explanation for them.

I suggest that it is more helpful to talk about different degrees of rule complexity in this context, rather than about markedness. We have argued that Jackendoff's theory will have more success in defining these different degrees, thereby providing language frequency predictions more in line with those of CCH. If we want to use the notion of markedness at all in this context, frequency data indicate that we should adopt a nonbinary approach, along the lines of Jackendoff's theory.

4.6.5 OUTLINE OF AN ALTERNATIVE X-BAR THEORY OF WORD ORDER

Despite the problems to which we drew attention in the last subsection, I have stressed the explanatory potential of the X-bar theory in this universal context, assuming that its predictions can be improved, and I would like to encourage X-bar theorists to take careful note of cross-language data for this reason. The theories we have considered provide important contributions to the question, Why should a grammar that incorporates word order disharmony (as defined by CCH) be any more complex or less highly valued than one that does not? In the present subsection, I shall give a brief outline of some modifications in X-bar theory which are compatible with our universal data.

I would make the following five proposals:

1. Separate serialization (i.e., word order) rules from constituency-defining rules, and so avoid losing constituency generalizations on account of word order.
2. Assume an X-bar system of PS-rules along the lines of Jackendoff's (1977) theory, though with unordered categories functioning as input to subsequent serialization rules.
3. Adopt the Jackendoff insight that identical categories at common bar levels across phrases serialize in the same direction in the preferred (or unmarked) case; that is, the serialization rules should be formulated cross-categorially, and they, rather than the PS-rules, should define word order preferences.
4. Adopt the further Jackendoff insight that the more a grammar departs from the unmarked word order regularity in (3), the more complex it is (and the fewer exemplifying languages there are predicted to be); that is, the locus of word complexity is now the serialization rules themselves, but the nature of this complexity remains essentially as before (and involves number of rules, generality of the categories to which they refer, etc.).
5. Adopt, where possible, the Lightfoot–Chomsky insight that microcategories can be collapsed into macrocategories for the purpose of serialization rules, thereby making these rules more general.

Let us illustrate how these proposals might be made to work. We can think of our serialization rules as rewrite rules, which take unordered categories as input, and assign an ordering as output. As these categories have been generated by Jackendoff-type X-bar PS-rules, we suggest that the serialization rules should be formulated so as to capture cross-categorial word order generalizations at each of Jackendoff's three bar levels. Each rule would therefore assign order to a head category plus at least one (specifier or complement) category. A simple example might be (8), for English:

(8) {NP – X} → X – NP

This rule serializes an NP sister of X (without a bar) to the right of X. It therefore serializes NP to the right of P, V, N, and A in the constituent structures of (9):

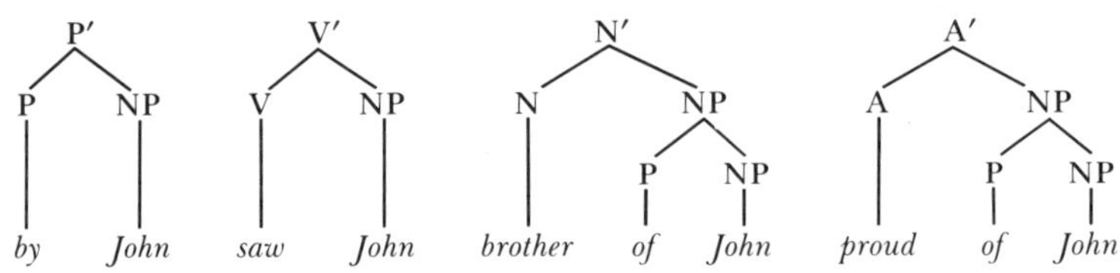

Rule (8) is a cross-categorial serialization rule. The cross-categorial formalism enables us to avoid stating four separate rules, all with the same serialization effect, as in (8′), and so makes explicit a linguistic generalization which these rules do not:

(8′) a. {NP – P} → P – NP
b. {NP – V} → V – NP
c. {NP – N} → N – NP
d. {NP – A} → A – NP

English is a simple and regular language with respect to the word orders of (9), and the simplicity of rule (8) reflects this. There is just one hitch, however. In addition to postnominal genitives (*brother of John*), English also has prenominal genitives, as in (10):

(10)

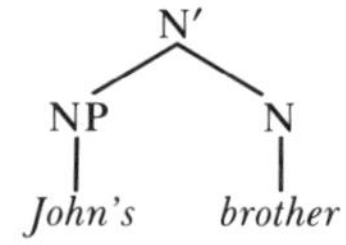

This irregularity produces a complication, for we must now introduce an additional rule serializing NP to the left of its head, just in case the head = N (and subject to numerous other conditions as well). Numerous formalisms and conventions suggest themselves, but we might simply describe the English data of (9) and (10) using the two rules of (11):

(11) a. {NP–X} → X–NP
b. {NP–N} → NP–N

As X stands for all head categories (including N), (11a) will produce postnominal genitives; (11b) produces prenominal genitives. The formalism will need to guarantee that the more specific rule, (11b), does not prevent (11a) from applying when X = N.

Imagine that English had only the prenominal genitive construction of (10) (i.e., no *brother of John* constructions). The following two rules would now be necessary:

(12) a. {NP–X} → X–NP where X = P, V, or A (or: X ≠ N)
b. {NP–N} → NP–N

Notice that (12) is slightly more complex than (11), as it contains more symbols, and an exception to the generality of X. Again, there are numerous possible alternative formalisms, but some kind of added complexity for (12) matches well the intuition that an English with exclusively preposed genitives would indeed be more complex (and a rarer language type), because the noun phrase would no longer have any sisters of N serialized in the same direction as the sisters of P, V, and A.

Consider now the problematic measure phrase data that Jackendoff drew attention to (see Section 4.6.2). Letting NP_m stand for "measure phrase" (as daughter of X″), English has the following word orders:

(13) a. NP_m–P′ *two miles down the road* P′–NP_m *down the road two miles*
b. V′–NP_m *(he) jumped into the air two times*
c. NP_m–N′ *two parts steel*
d. NP_m–A′ *two miles long*

A completely regular language would have all its measure phrases either to the left of X′ or to the right, with Rule (14) or (15) respectively:

(14) {NP_m–X′} → NP_m–X′

(15) {NP_m–X′} → X′–NP_m

Instead, the English data require the two rules of (16):

(16) a. {NP_m–X′} → NP_m–X′, where X′ = P′, N′, A′
b. {NP_m–X′} → X′–NP_m, where X′ = P′, V′

Clearly, this state of affairs is more complex than that of either (14) or (15).

Summarizing so far, it seems to be possible to capture the same rule complexity insight that we proposed for Jackendoff's theory, using instead an independent set of serialization rules. Where PS-rules could not be collapsed before, or could be more or less general, the same now holds for the serialization rules, precisely because these are also formulated cross-categorially. The gain is that we no longer lose the constituency generalizations that were lost before. We have seen two ways in which the relative complexity of PS-rules can be carried over to the serialization rules: First, a grammar that contains a single serialization rule such as (8), (14), or (15), ordering the same categories (e.g., NP-sister of X) in a uniform direction, is simpler than one that contains rules serializing categories to both right and left, as in (11), (12), and (16); second, the fewer the number of conditions on these rules, the simpler they would appear to be [compare (11) and (12)].

There is a third factor that contributes to the overall simplicity of the serialization rule system that we are proposing, one that involves the generality of the categories mentioned in these rules. Take the example of an extreme verb-final language, in which every single modifier precedes its respective head at each bar level. Such a language might require only one serialization rule, along the lines of (17):

(17) $\{C-X^n\} \rightarrow C-X^n$

where C stands for any category and X^n is a head category with any number of bars (including 0). In this example, the category X^n is more general than either X or X′, and C is more general than NP or NP_m. This greater generality, then, has consequences for the overall number of serialization rules that we need to set up for a given language, mentioning different categories at the different bar levels. In the present instance, no other rules are needed at all. Numerous rules intermediate in generality between (17) and the rules we have already considered suggest themselves. The rule of (17) may hold only when $X^{n\leq 1}$; that is, when all constituents precede their heads for all head categories with bar levels less than or equal to 1, while modifiers of X″ all follow, as in (18):

(18) a. $\{C-N^{n\leq 1}\} \rightarrow C-X^{n\leq 1}$
b. $\{C-X''\} \rightarrow X''-C$

or else, only prepositional phrase modifiers of V″ may follow:

(19) a. $\{C-X^n\} \rightarrow C-X^n$ where $X^n \neq V''$
b. $\{PP-V''\} \rightarrow V''-PP$

These suggestions are deliberately schematic. I offer them to professional X-bar theorists as an illustration of the kinds of rules and insights that emerge from our cross-language data. Descriptions of numerous languages in these terms will need to be made before their viability as predictors of language frequencies through rule complexity can be convincingly established. In the meantime, there is considerable support for our general hypothesis, viz, the more similar the ordering of common constituents across phrasal categories at the relevant bar levels, the simpler are the word order rules of the grammar; and the simpler these rules, the more exemplifying languages there are.

Notes

1. We are not strictly interested in this context in the relative order of the operators to one another, but only in the order of each single operator relative to its operand. Thus, it makes no difference for our distributional calculations whether –N stands for $\langle w, x, a \rangle$ or $\langle x, w, a \rangle$, as long as both w and x precede a. Our predictions relate to the number of operators that precede and the number that follow the operand, irrespective of the sequencing of the operators (cf. Section 3.6). We should, therefore, more accurately represent –N as a set of ordered subsets: $\{\langle w, a \rangle, \langle x, a \rangle\}$. Similarly, we make no distinction between VSO $\langle b, y, z \rangle$ and VOS $\langle b, z, y \rangle$ (for the purposes of CCH), and should more accurately collapse these as $\{\langle b, y \rangle, \langle b, z \rangle\}$. However, it will greatly improve readability if we do NOT complicate the formalism in this way. And we shall retain $\langle w, x, a \rangle$ as a shorthand for $\{\langle w, a \rangle, \langle x, a \rangle\}$, understanding thereby that the relative ordering defined holds only for each operator in relation to its operand, and not necessarily for each operator in relation to each other operator. I shall, nonetheless, attempt in these formulae to order the operators relative to one another in the way that most languages do in fact order them (e.g., VSO rather than VOS).

2. For the co-occurrence pairs that include an adposition order, the number of deviations has to be quantified by holding the adposition order constant, and varying the noun and verb positions, as both noun and verb have more than one operator in our sample. The adposition can occur only in two positions relative to its single (NP) operator, before or after. When comparing Pr & V_1, Pr & V_2, and Pr & V_3 we can say that the verb is 0, 1, and 2 operator positions respectively removed from the ideal Pr & V_1 match-up. Similarly, the noun is 0, 1, and 2 operator positions removed from the ideal in the progression Pr & N_1, Pr & N_2, and Pr & N_3. But, if we attempted to vary the adposition order to match the verb and noun, Pr & V_1 would be just one adposition operator position removed from Po & V_1, and Po & V_3 just one position removed from Pr & V_3. But how would we then measure Pr & V_2, Po & V_2, and also Pr & N_2 and Po & N_2? Though Pr & V_1 and Pr & N_1 are most harmonic, and Po & V_1 and Po & N_1 least harmonic, there is no way of assessing the intermediate CCH of the adposition with these verb-medial and noun-medial orders, on account of the unique operator on the adposition. Only on the basis of the verb and noun operators can we quantify the intermediate status of Pr & V_2 (between Pr & V_1 and Pr & V_3), and of Pr & N_2 (between Pr & N_1 and Pr & N_3). But for word order pairs which include both a noun and a verb, the number of deviations can be calculated by either varying the noun to match the verb, or by varying the verb to match the noun, giving two possible maximally harmonic orderings in each case.

3. Table 12 contains two language types, (6 + 8) Po & V_1 & N_2 and (18 + 20) Pr & V_3 & N_2, which can be argued to be unattested for reasons independent of their low CCH. We showed in Section 3.2.1 that SOV (V_3) cannot co-occur with AN & NG (N_2), and in Section 3.2.3 that Prep cannot co-occur with NA & GN (N_2). Hence, Pr & V_3 cannot co-occur with either realization of N_2. Similarly, VSO (V_1) cannot co-occur with NA & GN (N_2) (see Section 3.2.2), and Postp cannot co-occur with AN & NG (N_2) (see Section 3.2.4). So neither realization of N_2 in Po & V_1 & N_2 is possible. However, rather than exclude these language types from CCH's calculations, I have decided to include them, for the following reasons. It is quite conceivable that many other language types are either unattested or rare for independent reasons which have yet to be discovered, and as such language types are clearly not being excluded, it seems safer to exclude none, in principle. Second, given our present relative ignorance about the interaction of explanatory forces in the explanation of word order universals, it is better methodology to try and formulate and test whatever principles we are relatively certain about in the most general way that we can. It is not inconceivable, for example, that the total absence of Types 6, 8, 18, and 20 results from their low CCH, and not from conflicting implicational universals, as argued in Section 3.2. More generally, one might argue that all the implicationally excluded co-occurrences of Chapter 3 are simply those with low CCH, and that the two sets of principles (one predicting all and only the attested types, the other frequencies) are unnecessary. I shall be arguing against this possibility in Section 4.3.4, but subsequent research may prove me wrong. And, for this reason, I shall not doctor the language types upon which CCH's predictions are tested. Finally, even if we did exclude these types from Table 12, CCH's success rate would be almost the same: 94.7% instead of 95.7% for total predictions, and 93.3% instead of 94.4% for basic predictions.

4. For one language, Loritja, Greenberg gives no information on relative clause order. And for another, Nubian, both orders are found, with no indication given as to which (if any) is basic, and so it has been left out of Table 15.

5. It is in any case difficult to compare the predictions of NSP′ for all word order pairs because of the unequal number of operator–operand pairs in the different co-occurrence pairs. Thus, Pr & N_1 involves four operator–operand constructions (three operators on the noun, one on the adposition), whereas V_1 & N_1 involves six (three on both noun and verb). The maximum number of deviations in the former case is, therefore, 2 (e.g., Pr & N_2), and in the latter case 3 (e.g., V_2 & N_3), but this difference is an artifact of the different numbers of operator–operand pairs being considered, and there is no reason to suppose that the former should be any more preferred by NSP′ than the latter.

6. Guarani is listed as having both pre- and postposed numerals in Greenberg's 30-language sample, and so has been excluded from Table 22 on the grounds of undecidability.

7. Lightfoot's Hypothesis 1 does considerably better, however, for specifiers of one and the same category head. If we assume that both demonstrative determiners and numerals are specifiers, then Hypothesis 1 predicts that the majority of languages should have both to the left or both to the right of the noun. And each of these preferred co-occurrences should be relatively more frequent than each of the mixed specifier orders, DemN & NNum and NDem & NumN. The Expanded Sample quantities are as follows (total = 127):

47 NDem languages	80 DemN languages	
NDem & NNum 28	DemN & NNum 9	37 NNum languages
NDem & NumN 19	DemN & NumN 71	90 NumN languages

A total of 99 languages have the preferred orders (78%), NDem & NNum (28 languages) and DemN & NumN (71 languages). And all four relative frequency predictions hold.

8. The almost total absence of languages with NDem & RelN in Table 29 is, of course attributable to Universal (XI′) NDem ⊃ NRel (cf. 3.3.14), and is explainable in terms of the HSP, MP, and MHIP of Chapter 3. We might try to set up Lightfoot's hypotheses so that they interact with other universals of this sort, and explain the unexpected absence of NDem & RelN languages in this way. But we would then expect that the great majority of languages would gravitate toward Lightfoot's other preferred co-occurrence, DemN & NRel, which they clearly do not.

9. There is a certain indeterminacy about the status of genitives in X-bar theories. For Jackendoff (1977), the genitive is a specifier when it precedes the head (*Mary's picture*) and a complement when it follows (*the picture of Mary*). But clearly, this kind of indeterminacy about the membership of constituents in the categories of specifiers and complements makes vacuous any predictions about their respective orders, and also results in a less constrained grammar. The specifiers and complements of the theory must be defined in advance if any testable claims are to be made, along the lines of Lightfoot's hypotheses. I shall assume throughout this book that the genitives of Greenberg's sample are complements, for three reasons. First, they are either PP or NP constituents, and these along with S are the typical complement constituents in Lightfoot (1979, 1980). Second, the problem typified by English, in which there are both preposed and postposed genitives, is very rare across languages. Most languages have only one order, those that have both being disharmonic languages in which the position of the noun within the NP is considerably at variance with the adposition order and generally with the position of the verb as well (cf. Section 4.5). The genitive order in the majority of languages will therefore not be subject to such indeterminacy and the NP or PP modifier of N will occur in one clearly recognizable order only. Third, the noun–genitive constructions in other languages do typically translate the N–P″ constructions of English, which Lightfoot labels complements.

5 : *The Diachronic Predictions of Implicational Universals*

Chapters 5, 6, and 7 will discuss the synchronic universals of Chapters 2, 3, and 4 in relation to language change. We have already seen the relevance of historical considerations to the explanation of synchronic universals in two separate contexts in this book. In Vennemann's earlier theory (see Section 2.3), language history was invoked as an explanation for the existence of languages inconsistent with the Natural Serialization Principle. These languages were claimed to be in transition from one universal word order type to another. We are going to argue against the viability of this kind of historical argument, but its structure is interesting. Then, in Chapter 3 (Section 3.4.2.2), we argued that part of the explanation for the Mobility Principle was a historical one: The gradualness of language change was compatible with some grammatical restructurings taking place before others. And this resulted in certain grammatical categories being more mobile than others. We pointed out that such an appeal to historical considerations in the explanation of synchronic grammars was a more ambitious one than is normally made, as it is being claimed that general principles of language change contribute to the explanation of major grammatical regularities (as opposed to irregularities) in all languages (as opposed to just individual languages) (see also Chapter 3, Note 13).

The next three chapters are going to consider the obverse side of this synchronic – diachronic coin. Whether or not we grant the (partial) role of historical principles in explaining synchronic universals, what can synchronic universals do to help explain language change? Three questions will be of primary concern throughout our discussion. First, what predictions are made by synchronic universals for language change?

Second, what use can we make of such predictions in linguistic reconstruction? Third, why should a language change any of the word orders that it has at a given point of time? Specifically, what can synchronic universals contribute to a greater understanding of the why of word order change?

This chapter considers the predictions made by implicational universals for language change, and their potential role in explaining why word orders change. The next chapter does the same for distributional universals. And Chapter 7 discusses the use that can (and cannot) be made of both implicational and distributional universals in the method of historical reconstruction.

Within the present chapter, Section 5.1 enumerates the predictions made by implicational universals for the timing of changes relative to one another in a language's history. Some finer diachronic predictions—the Doubling Acquisition Hypothesis and the Frequency Increase Hypothesis—are formulated in Section 5.2. Section 5.3 uses detailed data taken from Indo-European (primarily Germanic) in order to test our diachronic predictions. Section 5.4 gives a summary and critique of an alternative theory of the role of synchronic universals in predicting and explaining change: the trigger-chain theory. And Section 5.5 (together with Chapter 6) presents an alternative framework for explaining word order change, which captures the basic insight of the trigger-chain theory (that synchronic universals can both predict and explain word order change), while avoiding its theoretical and empirical problems.

5.1 The Principle of Universal Consistency in History and Its Relative Timing Predictions

We have argued in Section 3.1.1 that there is a large discrepancy between the attested and nonattested word order co-occurrences across languages on current synchronic evidence, and we have formulated (Sections 3.2, 3.3) a restrictive set of implicational universals which operate in combination to define all and only the attested word order types. If we now assume a uniformitarianist principle (namely, that the laws of the present are also those of the past; see Lass 1980:53–57), we can use these synchronic implications to make predictions for the relative order and timing of changes in language history, that is, in the histories of all languages. If impossible word order co-occurrences in the present are also impossible in the past, this constrains the pathways of change (the ordering of certain changes relative to others) in the gradual transition from one historical stage to another.

We shall begin this chapter by exemplifying these synchronic predictions in simple and abstract form before we define more subtle predictions (Section 5.2) sensitive to doubling, which will be tested on data from Indo-European. The particular version of the uniformitarianist principle to be assumed here is the principle of Universal Consistency in History:

UNIVERSAL CONSISTENCY IN HISTORY (UCH): At each stage in their historical evolution, languages remain consistent with implicational universals derived from current synchronic evidence.

5.1.1 RELATIVE TIMING PREDICTIONS MADE BY UCH: EXAMPLE 1

Let us take an implicational universal 'if *P* then *Q*', and a language, *L*, which has neither of these properties ($-P$ & $-Q$) at some early stage in its history, but which is subsequently attested with both (P & Q). How did *L* effect the transition from $-P$ & $-Q$ to P & Q? There are three possibilities: It could have acquired *P* first, *Q* first, or both together, as in (1a)–(1c) respectively:

(1) a. $-P$ & $-Q >$ *P & $-Q > P$ & Q
b. $-P$ & $-Q > -P$ & $Q > P$ & Q
c. $-P$ & $-Q > P$ & Q

The UCH rules out (1a), but permits (1b) and (1c). Sequence (1a) would involve postulating an intermediate language type that violates all the current synchronic evidence, and for which there is therefore no independent support. That is, *wherever we have an implicational universal 'if P then Q' and a language with −P &−Q, the acquisition of P can occur either after that of Q or simultaneously with that of Q, but not before it,* in order to avoid a *P & $-Q$ co-occurrence. If *P* is acquired, this guarantees either the prior presence, or the simultaneous acquisition, of *Q*.

5.1.2 RELATIVE TIMING PREDICTIONS MADE BY UCH: EXAMPLE 2

Consider now a more complex, but still abstract, example. Let us take a hierarchy-defining implicational universal with the logical form of (2), defining all and only the permitted co-occurrence sets (or subtypes) of Type *P* languages in (2′); and a language, *L*, which is Subtype 5 in the earliest records and subsequently Subtype 1. How did *L* effect the transition?

(2) $P \supset ((Q \supset R) \& (R \supset S) \& (S \supset T))$

(2′) Subtype 1 $P \& Q \& R \& S \& T$
Subtype 2 $P -Q \quad R \quad S \quad T$
Subtype 3 $P -Q -R \quad S \quad T$
Subtype 4 $P -Q -R -S \quad T$
Subtype 5 $P -Q -R -S -T$

The transitivity of implication, operating in conjunction with UCH, makes some very constrained predictions for the relative timing of historical changes. For example, *L* may have moved stepwise up the hierarchy of (2′) changing one property at a time, $-T > T$, $-S > S$, etc. Or it may have acquired *S* and *T* simultaneously, then *R*, and finally *Q*. Or, it may have acquired *T*, then *R* and *S* simultaneously, and finally *Q*. As can be seen, there are several more possibilities, but UCH rules out innumerable scenarios. Thus, when *L* is Subtype 5 it cannot change $-R > R$ first, without previously acquiring *S* and *T*; if *L* moves from Subtype 5 to Subtype 4, it cannot then change $-Q > Q$ alone, etc. That is, *for each of the overlapping implications in (2), when an implying, antecedent property is acquired,* ***all*** *the implied, consequent, properties must either be already present in L or must be acquired simultaneously,* in order not to violate UCH.

5.1.3 DIACHRONIC PREDICTIONS AND UNIVERSAL GRAMMAR

Notice more generally that interesting diachronic predictions are made by the current synchronic facts in this area, whether or not one accepts my particular formulation of the synchronic universals. The very fact of a discrepancy between attested versus nonattested co-occurrences of phenomena on synchronic evidence enables us to predict the relative ordering of individual changes, by locating the acquired properties within the set(s) of co-occurrences in which they are attested across languages, and surveying the necessary accompanying properties (here word orders) within these sets.

Thus, if we accept such a discrepancy between attested and nonattested co-occurrence sets (as we must) and if we accept further that unattested co-occurrence sets cannot be postulated for languages diachronically (and unless there is very compelling evidence of an "accidental gap" in current synchronic data samples, we are not justified in assuming otherwise), then we can use current synchronic evidence to make predictions for possible and impossible relative orders of changes in the past.

There is an obvious moral here for all implicational universals when considered in a diachronic context. For example, any language that acquires a new relativization strategy, or expands (or diminishes) the relativization possibilities of an already existing strategy, can be expected to conform to the synchronic predictions of Keenan and Comrie's (1977) Accessiblity Hierarchy.

5.2 Some Finer Diachronic Predictions: The Doubling Acquisition Hypothesis and the Frequency Increase Hypothesis

The examples of Sections 5.1.2 and 5.1.3 are overly simple in one important respect. They make reference, like the implicational universals of Chapter 3, to basic word orders only, *P*, −*P*, *Q*, etc. But word order change proceeds via a process of doubling (Section 1.5.1). A language that is developing from OV to VO does not suddenly shift all its nominal objects from one side of the verb to the other. The incoming VO exists first for a long period as a minority structure alongside older OV and gains gradually in frequency and grammaticalization until it replaces OV as the basic, and perhaps eventually as the unique, order; that is, OV > OV/VO > VO. Now, as the implicational unversals are stated in terms of basic word orders they do not, strictly speaking, make any predictions about incoming minority word orders. Only when a minority *P* structure has achieved majority status does the predictive power of synchronic word order universals come into effect in requiring the co-occurrence of *Q* properties.

But if there is any reality to these synchronic word order dependencies, it is still possible that they will translate into historical predictions about incoming minority word order patterns in the course of change. If they do, then incoming minority *P* structures should be accompanied by incoming minority *Q* structures; or else, minority *P* structures will develop only after *Q* structures are already present (whether as doublets with −*Q* or not). Thus, minority *P* should be acquired either simultaneously with *Q* (−*P* & −*Q* > *P* & *Q*) or else after *Q* (−*P* & −*Q* > −*P* & *Q* > *P* & *Q*), but not before it, in order to avoid innovating *P* structures with no accompanying *Q* structures (−*P* & −*Q* > **P* & −*Q* > *P* & *Q*). Minority *P* structures will not arise in the total absence of *Q* structures, therefore:

THE DOUBLING ACQUISITION HYPOTHESIS (DAH): Given a set of synchronic universal implications of the form 'if *P* then *Q*', where *P* and *Q* are basic word orders of certain specified types; then, at two successive stages in the growth of a language,

IF: *P* is acquired as a doubling structure from the earlier uniquely −*P* stage;

THEN: EITHER *Q* must already be present at the earlier stage (whether as a doublet with $-Q$ or not), OR, if it is not present, *Q* must be acquired as a doubling structure simultaneously with *P*. But *P* will not be acquired in the total absence of *Q*.

This hypothesis refers to the first appearance of doubling structures at successive stages in a language. But it makes no claims about the way in which minority *P* and *Q* structures will develop further into basic structures. As we now have reasonably extensive frequency studies of competing word orders in evolving Indo-European languages, we might use these in order to test the following, stronger, hypothesis:

THE FREQUENCY INCREASE HYPOTHESIS (FIH): Given a set of synchronic universal implications of the form 'if *P* then *Q*', where *P* and *Q* are basic word orders of certain specified types; then, at two successive stages in the growth of a language,

IF: (*a*) there is an increase in the frequency of *P* structures relative to their doublets $-P$, and if (*b*) the frequency of the *Q* structures at the earlier stage, prior to the increase in *P*, was less than 100% (i.e., $-Q$ doublets existed);

THEN: the implied *Q* structures will also have gained in frequency along with *P* by the later stage.[1]

As it is formulated, the FIH predicts frequency increases both for newly acquired minority *P* and *Q* structures and for majority structures with less than 100% frequency at the earlier stage of comparison.

Notice that the DAH follows logically from the FIH, though not vice versa. Imagine, in the extreme case, that a language at some stage in its history has only $-P$ & $-Q$ structures, with no minority *P* or *Q* doublets. If, at the next stage, that language develops some *P* structures (and has, say, 10% *P* to 90% $-P$), then the FIH predicts that the percentage of *Q* structures can no longer be zero; that is, the acquisition of *P* doublets would imply in this case the acquisition of *Q* doublets, which is what the DAH requires as well. But imagine that, at the next historical stage of inspection, there are 25% *P* structures to 75% $-P$; then the FIH predicts that the percentage of *Q* structures must also have increased, whereas the DAH makes no predictions in this respect. The DAH is therefore just a specific instance of the more general FIH, and is entailed by it. As the FIH could still be false while the DAH is true, we shall continue to keep the two principles apart in our historical testing.

The DAH and FIH assume an extreme form of consistency with synchronic universal laws. The principle of UCH requires that languages in the past conform to the univesal laws of the present, and this enables us to make predictions for the relative ordering of changes in successive language states. As both earlier and later stages obey the universals, the DAH and FIH then make the more specific and not unreasonable claim that languages will innovate and increase only those minority word orders that do not result in $*P \& -Q$ co-occurrences for the corresponding basic word orders.

5.3 Testing the Diachronic Predictions of the UCH, DAH, and FIH

We shall now examine sample data from Indo-European, particularly from the Germanic family, in order to test whether diachronic developments from the earliest records are correctly predicted by our UCH, DAH, and FIH principles. Of particular importance will be adposition and noun modifier orders. We shall begin by testing UCH against the earliest records of all Indo-European languages (Section 5.3.1); diachronic developments in Avestan will then be considered which support the FIH (Section 5.3.2); and, finally, all three diachronic principles will be tested against data from Germanic.

5.3.1 SOME EARLY INDO-EUROPEAN DATA

The principle of Universal Consistency in History hypothesizes that the implicational universals of word order derived from currently attested languages will also be valid for all earlier stages of all languages. We begin by testing this against a small but important sample of historical data: the earliest records of the Indo-European languages. Are the earliest daughter languages of Indo-European consistent with the implicational universals of Chapter 3, or are they not? We will concentrate on our most adequately supported implicational word order universals—those derived from Greenberg's Appendix II (Section 3.2), in conjunction with the universals involving relative clauses. A handful of entries in Appendix II refer to languages existing prior to the twentieth century (e.g., Classical Arabic and Sumerian). But these in no way affect the formulation of the implicational universals. If they were removed from Appendix II, the universals would be exactly the same. Similarly, I have added some of the early IE dialects to the Expanded Sample of Chapter 8—but, again, not a single implicational universal derived from that sample would be altered if all non-twentieth-century linguistic data were removed.[2] The Appendix II universals (and those derived from the Expanded Sample) are therefore fully determined by twentieth-century linguistic data, and so enable us to test the correspondence with word order co-occurrences from earlier periods.

Friedrich (1975) gives a careful description of the Appendix II word orders and of relative clauses in the earliest IE dialects. There are many instances of doubling structures in these dialects (NAdj together with AdjN, NGen together with GenN, etc.); and Friedrich discusses both the relative frequencies and the grammatical diferences between competing orders before deciding which is basic. In a small number of cases, he concludes that two orders are equally basic. Friedrich's findings are summarized in Table 34 with the most important page references given for each entry. The Gothic data are taken from the more detailed study of J. Smith (1971) (see Table 36).

Consider, first, the relative orders of the noun modifiers: the adjective, genitive, and relative clause. Of the eight mathematically possible co-occurrences of these three modifiers, only four basic order co-occurrences are attested in Indo-European. It is significant that these are exactly the four permitted by the Prepositional Noun Modifier Hierarchy (see Sections 4.5.1, 7.5.1). Table 35 summarizes the four classes, ignoring the minority word orders for the sake of clarity.

Two entries from Table 34 are not listed in Table 35: Italic and Gathic Avestan.

Italic	*Gathic Avestan*
ADJ + N/	adj + n/n + adj
gen + n/n + gen	GEN + N/
/N + REL	/N + REL
SOV & PREP	SOV & PREP

Italic has no basic genitive order, and Gathic Avestan no basic adjective order. In effect, Italic is a mixture of Classes 2 and 3, since it has AdjN & NRel, while having both pre- and postnominal genitives. And Gathic Avestan is closest to Class 3, the only class having GenN & NRel. I shall consider these equally basic orders in relation to the synchronic predictions presently.

Let us now check each of the early IE dialects to see how they fare against the Appendix II-derived universals, plus Implications (IX′) and (XIII). I repeat the universals for convenience:

(I) SOV ⊃ (AN ⊃ GN)
(II) VSO ⊃ (NA ⊃ NG)
(III) Prep ⊃ (NA ⊃ NG) (= statistical)/ (III′) Prep & −SVO ⊃ (NA ⊃ NG)
(IV) Postp ⊃ (AN ⊃ GN)
(IX′) NG ⊃ NRel
(XIII) Prep ⊃ (−SOV ⊃ NRel)

TABLE 34 : Indo-European Word Order Data (from Friedrich 1975)

Celtic (pp. 58–59) /N + ADJ /N + GEN /N + REL /PREP /VSO	**Slavic** (p. 62) (adj + n)/N + ADJ (gen + n/N + GEN /N + REL /PREP sov/VSO	**Younger Avestan** (p. 45) adj + n/N + ADJ gen + n/N + GEN (rel + n)/N + REL (post)/PREP SOV/{svo, osv, ovs}
Albanian (pp. 25–26) ADJ + N/ /N + GEN /N + REL /PREP /SVO	**Old Armenian** (pp. 41–42) ADJ + N/n + adj gen + n/N + GEN /N + REL /PREP vso/SVO	**Homeric Greek** (pp. 23–26) ADJ + N/n + adj gen + n/N + GEN (rel + n)/N + REL /PREP sov/svo
Italic (pp. 52–58) ADJ + N/n + adj gen + n/n + gen (rel + n)/N + REL /PREP SOV/svo	**Old Persian** (p. 43) ADJ + N/n + adj GEN + N/n + gen (rel + n)/N + REL (post)/PREP SOV/svo	**Gothic** (cf. Table 36) ADJ + N/n + adj GEN + N/n + gen /N + REL /PREP SOV/{v-1, v-2}
Tocharian (pp. 49–50) ADJ + N/ GEN + N/ rel + n/N + REL POST/prep SOV/	**Gathic Avestan** (pp. 44–45) adj + n/n + adj GEN + N/n + gen rel + n/N + REL post/PREP SOV/{svo, osv, ovs}	**Sanskrit** (pp. 26,29,33,37) ADJ + N/n + adj GEN + N/n + gen REL + N/n + rel POST/prep SOV/
	Hittite (pp. 25,26,29,36) ADJ + N/ GEN + N/n + gen REL + N/n + rel POST/ SOV/	

Note: Capital letters refer to word orders that are basic or unique. Lower-case letters refer to nonbasic orders; those in parentheses designate word orders that are even more limited. This summary does not aim for completeness in presenting the minority word orders—the fact that some minority word order is not listed under a particular entry does not mean that it is totally unattested. Word orders written to the right of the slash are operand-before-operator orders; those to the left of the slash are operator-before-operand orders. For word orders involving the verb, the *basic* verb position has been situated according to this criterion; but any nonbasic verb positions are placed on the opposite side of the slash, regardless of their operator and operand ordering.

In what follows, I list alongside each IE language or subfamily all the relevant synchronic implications which contain implicational antecedent properties matching those of the entry in question. Consider Celtic, for example. Celtic has VSO. By Universal (II), because it has VSO, then if it has NA, it must have NG. It does have both NA and NG. Celtic also has

TABLE 35 : Indo-European Noun Modifier Classes

Class 1	Class 2	Class 3	Class 4
/N + ADJ /N + GEN /N + REL	ADJ + N/ /N + GEN /N + REL	ADJ + N/ GEN + N/ /N + REL	ADJ + N/ GEN + N/ REL + N/
Celtic (VSO & PREP)	Albanian (SVO & PREP)	Old Persian (SOV & PREP)	Sanskrit (SOV & POST)
Slavic (VSO & PREP)	Old Armenian (SVO & PREP)	Gothic (SOV & PREP)	Hittite (SOV & POST)
Younger Avestan (SOV & PREP)	Homeric Greek (sov/svo & PREP)	Tocharian (SOV & POST)	

Prep. By Universals (III) and (III′), it is again predicted to have NG, given that it has NA. By Universal (IX′), the presence of NG conditions the co-occurrence of NRel. This prediction is also fulfilled. And by Universal (XIII), a prepositional language with −SOV (which includes VSO) must again have NRel.

Consider first the Class 1 languages:

(3) Celtic and Slavic (VSO & PREP & N + ADJ & N + GEN & N + REL)
- (II): Consistency
- (III) & (III′): Consistency
- (IX′): Consistency
- (XIII): Consistency

(4) Younger Avestan (SOV & Prep & N + ADJ & N + GEN & N + REL)
- (I): Consistency (NA & NG is one of the three co-occurrences permitted by AN ⊃ GN)
- (III) & (III′): Consistency
- (IX′): Consistency
- (XIII): Consistency

Consider next the Class 2 languages:

(5) Albanian and Old Armenian (SVO & PREP & ADJ + N & N + GEN & N+ REL)
- (III): Consistency
- (IX′): Consistency
- (XIII): Consistency

(6) Homeric Greek (sov/svo & PREP & ADJ + N & N + GEN & N + REL)
- (III): Consistency

(IX′): Consistency
(XIII): Consistency

The Class 3 languages are as follows:

(7) Old Persian and Gothic (SOV & PREP & ADJ + N & GEN + N & N +REL)
(I): Consistency
(III) & (III′): Consistency
(IX′): Consistency
(XIII): Consistency

(8) Tocharian (SOV & POST & ADJ + N & GEN + N & N + REL)
(I): Consistency
(IV): Consistency
(IX′): Consistency

The Class 4 languages have identical basic word orders:

(9) Sanskrit and Hittite (SOV & POST & ADJ + N & GEN + N & REL +N)
(I): Consistency
(IV): Consistency
(IX′): Consistency

What emerges is that the basic word order co-occurrences of the 11 entries in Table 35 fall squarely within the parameters of variation defined by implicational universals for twentieth-century language samples.

Consider now Italic and Gathic Avestan. Italic was excluded from Table 35 because it has no basic genitive order, and Gathic Avestan because it has no basic adjective order. How are we to interpret these equally frequent genitive and adjective orders in the light of the implications? It is perhaps most plausible to argue that neither order is basic in these cases. With this interpretation, Italic does in fact exhibit an inconsistency, though Gathic does not:

(10) Italic (SOV & PREP & ADJ + N & gen + n/n + gen & N + REL)
(I): Inconsistency (since basic SOV & ADJ + N requires basic GEN + N, yet neither gen + n nor n + gen is basic)
(III) & (III′): Consistency (only basic N + ADJ requires basic N + GEN, and Italic has ADJ + N)
(IX′): Consistency (N + REL may occur whether a language has basic N + GEN or GEN + N)
(XIII): Consistency

(11) Gathic Avestan (SOV & PREP & adj + n/n + adj & GEN + N & N + REL)
(I): Consistency (SOV & GEN + N may co-occur with either prenominal or postnominal adjectives)
(III) & (III′): Consistency (since n + adj is not basic, N + GEN is not required)
(IX′): Consistency

However, the significance of the inconsistency of Italic with respect to one implication depends crucially on this interpretation of equally frequent word orders. If we were to adopt a different interpretation—allowing, for example, that any one of the equally frequent word orders could be regarded as basic—then neither Italic nor Gathic Avestan would exhibit any violation.[3]

Having presented data from the earliest IE dialects, we can now proceed to test the predictions of UCH, DAH, and FIH for subsequent word order changes in sample branches of IE.

5.3.2 AVESTAN

The FIH (and the DAH which it entails) predicts that doubling structures that are on the increase will obey the same regularities of co-occurrence that hold between basic word orders on synchronic evidence. The facts from Avestan (Iranian branch) are interesting in this regard (see Friedrich 1975:44–45 for data). Records of Gathic Avestan date from around 900 B.C., whereas records of Younger Avestan are probably from the fifth or fourth century B.C.—several hundred years later, at any rate. The quantities for competing word orders in Friedrich's sample are:

Gathic Avestan (SOV)		*Younger Avestan* (SOV)	
adj + n/n + adj		adj + n/N + ADJ	
21	20	28	38
GEN + N/n + gen		gen + n/N + GEN	
27	20	8	11
rel + n/N + REL		(rel + n)/N + REL	
11	20	2	13
postp/PREP		(postp)/PREP	
4	12	4	26

Consider Universals (III) and (IX′):

(III) Prep ⊃ (NA ⊃ NG)[4]
(IX′) NG ⊃ NRel

The increases from Gathic to Younger Avestan involve prepositions and all three postnominal modifiers. The ratio of Prep to Postp jumps from 3 : 1 to over 6 : 1. The equal distribution of adjective orders goes in favor of N + ADJ, the minority n + gen becomes the majority N + GEN, and the older dominant N + REL (by 2 :1) increases its dominance to 6 : 1, almost removing rel + n from the language.

This is important evidence for the FIH, which requires that, if there is a universal implication $P \supset Q$, then any increase in P (relative to $-P$ doublets) should be accompanied by increases in Q (relative to $-Q$ doublets, if any). Given that prepositions and postnominal adjectives increase in frequency from Gathic to Younger Avestan, it follows from the FIH in conjunction with Universal (III) that postnominal genitives must also increase in frequency. By Universal (IX′), a frequency increase for postnominal genitives must then be matched by an increase for postnominal relatives. Both predictions are fulfilled.[5]

5.3.3 THE EARLY GERMANIC DIALECTS

We shall now test all our diachronic principles against data from Germanic. The relevant synchronic universals are:

(I) SOV ⊃ (AN ⊃ GN)
(III) Prep ⊃ (NA ⊃ NG) (= statistical)/(III′) Prep & −SVO ⊃ (NA ⊃ NG)
(IX′) NG ⊃ NRel
(V′) NDem ⊃ NA
(XXI) NPoss ⊃ NA (= statistical)
(XIII) Prep ⊃ (−SOV ⊃ NRel)

The earliest records of Proto-Germanic are from runic inscriptions dating from A.D. 200–600, which J. Smith (1971) calls Late Common Germanic (LCGmc); and, though the evidence is sparse, he establishes the word order figures shown in Table 36.[6] Late Common Germanic is universally consistent (cf. UCH):

(12) Late Common Germanic (SOV & PREP & N + POSS & N + ADJ & gen + n/n + gen & N + REL)

(I):	Consistent
(III) & (III′):	Whether there is consistency depends on the interpretation of gen + n/n + gen
(IX′):	Consistent
(V′):	Consistent
(XXI):	Consistent
(XIII):	Consistent

From LCGmc to Gothic, the next oldest dialect, there are some interesting changes. Smith gives two sets of figures for Gothic (both taken from the Skeireins), which are also presented in Table 36.[7]

Compared to Late Common Germanic, Gothic has acquired two new word orders: ADJ + N as a basic structure, and poss + n as a minority structure. In addition, Gothic has increased the frequency of the following prenominal modifiers: GEN + N (from LCGcm 50% to Gothic 57 and 77%); ADJ + N (from LCGmc 0% to Gothic 73 and 83%); DEM + N (from LCGmc 33% to Gothic 100%); and poss + n (from LCGmc 0% to Gothic 27 and 14%).

Consider these figures in relation to the FIH and Universals (V′) and (XXI). Universal (V′) NDem ⊃ NA predicts, in conjunction with FIH, that if NDem increases in frequency, so must NA. In fact, it is the negation of the consequent property which has increased in Gothic: ADJ + N. As NDem ⊃ NA is logically equivalent to AN ⊃ DemN, the FIH requires that any increase in AN must be matched by an increase in DemN, and this does indeed happen. Similarly, (XXI) NPoss ⊃ NA is logically equivalent to AN ⊃ PossN, and so the increase in AN is predicted to be matched by an increase in PossN. This also holds.

TABLE 36 : Late Common Germanic and Gothic Word Order Data (from J. Smith 1971)

Late Common Germanic	Gothic (East Germanic daughter) (a)	Gothic (East Germanic daughter) (b)
/N + POSS 100%	poss + n/N + POSS 27% 73%	poss + n/N + POSS 14% 86%
dem + n/N + DEM 33% 67%	DEM + N/ 100%	DEM + N/ 100%
/N + ADJ 100%	ADJ + N/n + adj 73% 27%	ADJ + N/n + adj 83% 17%
gen + n/n + gen 50% 50%	GEN + N/n + gen 57% 43%	GEN + N/n + gen 77% 23%
/N + REL	/N + REL	/N + REL
/PREP	/PREP	/PREP
SOV/v-1, v-2	SOV/v-1, v-2	SOV/v-2, v-2

Note: Capital letters refer to word orders that are basic or unique. Lower-case letters refer to nonbasic orders; v-1 and v-2 designate verb-first and verb-second orders, as defined by Smith. Smith does not give relative clause and prepositional figures, and the figures for verb position are not relevant in the present context. The criterion for placing word orders to the right or left of the slash is the same as that used for Table 34. For Gothic, Column (a) gives figures averaged from the two texts of the Skeireins – a fourth-century Bible translation and a sixth-century commentary—and Column (b) gives figures from the commentary alone (see further Note 7).

Consider now Universal (IX′) NG ⊃ NRel. This time Gothic has increased the negation of the antecedent property, GEN + N. As GN occurs universally with both NRel and RelN (see Sections 3.3.4, 3.3.13), neither synchronic co-occurrence predictions nor diachronic frequency increase predictions are made for the relative clause.[8]

But the increase of GEN + N structures has consequences for adjective order, on account of Universal (III) Prep ⊃ (NA ⊃ NG). This universal is logically equivalent to Prep ⊃ (GN ⊃ AN). Gothic has basic, if not exclusive PREP. As GEN + N structures increase in frequency, so too must ADJ + N, and this latter in turn requires frequency increases for preposed demonstratives and possessives, as we have seen. All these predictions are fulfilled.[9]

The FIH therefore makes accurate predictions for Gothic. Consider now the predictions of the DAH. The new doublet ADJ + N (which is already a basic structure by the time of these figures) does not arise prior to the existence of structures that it logically entails: It arises at the same time as the new doublet poss + n (cf. AN ⊃ PossN), and after dem + n (cf. AN ⊃ DemN), which is already present in LCGmc (as a doublet); but it does not arise before either of these entailed properties. No other predictions are made by the DAH: The new doublet ADJ + N is not an implicational antecedent property in Universal (III); and, if the minority rel + n of Gothic is an innovation (cf. Note 8), it is significant that the consequent prenominal genitive property (RelN ⊃ GenN) is already present (as a doublet) in both LCGmc and Gothic. Thus, there is no instance in these data of a *P* structure arising in the total absence of a *Q* structure, where *P* ⊃ *Q*.

Gothic is also consistent with all nonstatistical universal implications (cf. UCH):

(13) Gothic (SOV & PREP & N + POSS & DEM+ N & ADJ + N & GEN + N & N + REL)
(I): Consistent
(III′): Consistent
(IX′): Consistent
(V′): Consistent
(XIII): Consistent

However, there is one slight anomaly in the Gothic data. Even though the DAH and FIH correctly predict the rise of a preposed possessive adjective, the postposed possessive is still in the majority, and this creates an exception to statistical implication (XXI) NPoss ⊃ NA, as N + POSS exists alongside ADJ + N. But this simply means that Gothic is one of the rare languages that are inconsistent with Implication (XXI). And it is significant that the one apparent case of an exception to UCH that we have found in our historical data involves one of the few statistical universals that we have proposed on current synchronic evidence. It is also significant that the DAH and FIH are still being obeyed, even in relation to this statistical universal. The extent of the increase of poss + n relative to LCGmc has simply not been sufficient to make it a basic word order.

Smith's figures for the early West Germanic dialects, shown in Table 37, reveal a development from LCGmc fundamentally similar to that which we have seen for Gothic. All the prenominal modifiers except for the relative clause have again increased in frequency, as predicted by the FIH in conjunction with Universals (V′), (XXI), (III), and (IX′). And the new doublets, ADJ + N and POSS + N, do not arise prior to the existence of structures that they logically entail: ADJ + N arises at the same time as POSS + N (cf. AN ⊃ PossN), and after DEM + N (cf. AN ⊃ DemN), in accordance with the DAH. The early West Germanic dialects are also consistent with all synchronic universals (cf. UCH). The PrNMH stipulates that if there is going to be only one basic postposed noun modifier in a prepositional language, that modifier must be the relative clause; that is, relative clauses are the last structures to prepose. This is the case in early West Germanic. The decline in SOV word orders (and hence the increase in non-SOV orders) is also compatible with—though not, of

TABLE 37 : Old Saxon, Old High German, and Old English Word Order Data (from J. Smith 1971)

Old Saxon (Heliand, ninth century AD)	Old High German (AD 750–1050)	Old English (Anglo-Saxon Chronicle entries for AD 1035)
POSS+ N/n + poss 85% 15%	POSS + N/n + poss 96% 4%	POSS + N/ 100%
DEM + N/n + dem 97% 3%	DEM + N/ 100%	DEM + N/ 100%
ADJ + N/n + adj 83% 17%	ADJ + N/n + adj 85% 15%	ADJ + N/n + adj 99% 1%
GEN + N/n + gen 65% 35%	GEN + N/n + gen 98% 2%	GEN + N/n + gen 87% 13%
/N + REL	/N + REL	/N + REL
/PREP	/PREP	/PREP
sov/v-1, v-2	sov/v-1, v-2	sov/v-1, V-2

Note: Capital letters refer to word orders that are basic or unique. Lower-case letters refer to nonbasic orders; v-1 and v-2 (or V-2) designate verb-first and verb-second orders, as defined by Smith. Smith does not give relative clause and prepositional figures, and the figures for verb position are not relevant in the present context. For relative clause data, see Weber (1971). The criterion for placing word orders to the right or left of the slash is the same as for Table 34.

course, required by—Universal (XIII) Prep ⊃ (−SOV ⊃ NRel), given the exclusive N + REL structures of these dialects (cf. Note 8; Weber 1971).

Finally, in contrast to Gothic, POSS + N is now a basic structure. As Gothic is an East Germanic daughter, whereas Old Saxon, Old High German, and Old English are West Germanic, we must compare both groups with their common immediately preceding stage, LCGmc, rather than with one another.[10]

5.3.4 A BRIEF LOOK AT MIDDLE ENGLISH AND MIDDLE HIGH GERMAN

English and German undergo similar noun modifier changes in their middle periods: Both postnominal adjectives and postnominal genitives increase in frequency. According to figures from Fries (1940), the Middle English postnominal genitive becomes basic and is used 84.5% of the time by A.D. 1300 (compared to 13% in 1035; cf. Table 37). Postnominal adjectives also increase in frequency in Middle English, and according to Lightfoot (1975) even become the "productive" pattern:[11]

> OE adjectival modifiers appeared characteristically in prenominal position, particularly for uncoordinated adjectives and participles. However, in ME postnominal adjectives become increasingly common. In this period most adjectives can occur as pre- and post-nominals, and the latter appear to represent the productive position, because all newly borrowed adjectives are introduced as post-nominals [p. 205].

Similarly, according to Barnes (1977), Middle High German postnominal genitives are just as frequent as prenominal genitives, which contrasts with the 2% figure for n + gen in Old High German (cf. Table 37). And, according to Lehmann (1971) and Lockwood (1968:39), postnominal adjectives are also more frequent in Middle High German than in Old High German, though prenominal adjectives still appear to be basic.

Consider these facts in relation to Universals (III) Prep ⊃ (NA ⊃ NG) and (IX′) NG ⊃ NRel. Middle English and Middle High German are exclusively prepositional. Since n + adj increases in frequency in both languages, the FIH in conjunction with Universal (III) predicts that n + gen will increase in both languages as well, which it does. And by the FIH and Universal (IX′), an increase in n + gen should be accompanied by an increase in N + REL, or else this structure must already be 100%. The latter is the case in both languages, and so this prediction is also satisfied.

Consider now the changes involving verb position. The old periods of all the West Germanic dialects contain a significant number of SOV structures: Some 30% (at least) of clauses in all dialects are SOV, according to J. Smith's (1971) figures:[12]

	Old Saxon	*Old High German*	*Old English*
V_1	25%	19%	9.5%
V_2	33%	40%	45.0%
V_3	10%	7%	16.0%
V-final	32%	34%	29.5%

In English, these SOV structures were soon eliminated. Canale (1978) uses frequency counts for verb positions in different types of clauses throughout Old English to argue for a base reanalysis, from SOV to SVO, in the twelfth century; that is, at the very end of the Old English period and the beginning of the Middle English period. Middle High German moved in a similar direction to English, though not nearly so far. Lehmann (1971) and Lockwood (1968:Chapter 11) document an increasing tendency in Middle High German to move the verb leftward in the sentence, compared to Old High German: Both prepositional phrases and NPs (including some direct objects) became increasingly frequent to the right of both finite and nonfinite verb forms in main and subordinate clauses, though Middle High German never became basic SVO.[13]

Given these increases in non-SOV structures (primarily V_2 and SVO), the FIH and Universal (XIII) Prep ⊃ (−SOV ⊃ NRel) predict an increase in N + REL, or else this structure must already be 100%. Again, this prediction regarding postnominal relatives is satisfied in both languages. The persistence of 100% N + REL may seem a rather weak test of the FIH, but as we shall see, rel + n emerges in later periods.

Thus, FIH predictions for the changes from Old English to Middle English, and from Old High German to Middle High German, are satisfied. The resulting basic word orders are also in accordance with UCH predictions. Middle English has the following co-occurrence array:

SVO/$^{v_1}_{v_2}$ & PREP & adj + n/N + ADJ & gen + n/N + GEN & N + REL;

which is fully consistent. The co-occurrence array for Middle High German is also consistent:

sov/$^{v_1}_{v_2}$ & PREP & ADJ + N/n + adj & gen + n/n + gen & N + REL.

Basic prenominal adjectives are compatible with either preposed or postposed genitives, and hence with both.

5.3.5 MODERN ENGLISH AND NEW HIGH GERMAN

In Modern English the prenominal genitive has gained ground again relative to Middle English, and prenominal adjectives have returned to their Old English status as the exclusive order (see Table 37). These increases are in accordance with the FIH and Universal (III) Prep ⊃ (NA ⊃ NG) [logically equivalent to: Prep ⊃ (GN ⊃ AN)]. Given the 100% prepositional nature of Modern English, an increase in prenominal genitives must be matched by an increase in prenominal adjectives, and this happens. Universals (V′) NDem ⊃ NA (equivalent to: AN ⊃ DemN) and (XXI) NPoss ⊃ NA (alias: AN ⊃ PossN) then lead to an FIH prediction that prenominal demonstrative determiners and possessive adjectives will also increase together with ADJ + N, or else these structures must also be 100%. The latter is the case, and hence these predictions also hold. Finally, an increase in prenominal genitives is negating the antecedent property of Universal (IX′) NG ⊃ NRel, and so no predictions are made: Either postnominal or prenominal relatives can increase. Middle English already has 100% postnominal relatives, and these are retained in the modern period. The resulting word order co-occurrence array for Modern English is set out in Table 38, given in what follows. Modern English exhibits no inconsistency with any independently motivated implicational universals for basic word orders.

The developments in New High German are fascinating in relation to our implicational universals. In the middle and late sixteenth century (Early New High German), there are six parallel developments in the word order of standard (written) German: (1) the language acquires a nonbasic prenominal relative clause strategy, operating on subjects and occasional direct objects; (2) the prenominal genitive increases in frequency relative to Middle High German; (3) the postnominal adjectives of Middle High German disappear, in favor of exclusive prenominal adjectives; (4) the rigid verb-final rule of the modern language becomes fixed, following the increasing tendency of Middle High German to move the verb leftward in the sentence (Note 13); (5) a number of postpositions develop alongside the (still predominant) prepositions; and (6) there is a significant increase in V + Aux structures. These changes are amply attested in the German linguistics literature (see in particular Lehmann, 1971, and Weber, 1971).[14]

Consider these facts in relation first to the universals of relevance for Modern English. Universal (III) Prep ⊃ (NA ⊃ NG) [alias: Prep ⊃ (GN ⊃ AN)] predicts, in conjunction with FIH, that an increase in both Prep and GN should be matched by an increase in AN. In fact, GN increases, though Prep does not [it actually declines; see (5) in the preceding paragraph]. Hence no predictions are made: The increase in GN and decline in Prep may or may not be matched by an increase in AN. The increase in AN, however, leads to an FIH prediction that prenominal demonstrative determiners and possessive adjectives will either increase or remain at 100%, on account of AN ⊃ DemN and AN ⊃ PossN [equivalent to: (V′) NDem ⊃ NA and (XXI) NPoss ⊃ NA respectively]. These predictions hold. Similarly, Universal (IX′) NG ⊃ NRel is equivalent to RelN ⊃ GN, and the increase (/acquisition) of German prenominal relative clauses must therefore be matched by an increase in prenominal genitives, which holds.

There are several additional implicational universals that make relevant FIH predictions for German. Universals (XI′) NDem ⊃ NRel and (XXIII) NPoss ⊃ NRel are logically equivalent to RelN ⊃ DemN and RelN ⊃ PossN respectively. The increase (/acquisition) in prenominal relatives must therefore be matched by an increase in DemN and PossN, or else these must both be 100%. This holds. Consider now Universal (XIII) Prep ⊃ (−SOV ⊃ NRel) (equivalent to: Prep & −SOV ⊃ NRel). Synchronically, a language that has prenominal relatives negates the ultimate consequent property of (XIII), NRel, and hence cannot have both Prep and −SOV. It may have either Postp with −SOV (e.g., SVO or VSO), or Prep with SOV, or both Postp and SOV. This last is by far the most frequent according to the principle of Cross-Category Harmony. Hence, by the FIH, the increase in prenominal relative structures must be accompanied by frequency increases in either postpositions, or SOV, or (most frequently) both. In fact, both postpositions and SOV do increase in frequency along with prenominal relatives in Early New High German.

The increase (/acquisition) of postpostions also activates FIH predictions in conjunction with Universals (IV) Postp ⊃ (AN ⊃ GN), (XV) Postp ⊃ (DemN ⊃ GN), and (XXII) Postp ⊃ (PossN ⊃ GN); and the increase in SOV structures activates (I) SOV ⊃ (AN ⊃ GN). In all these cases, the increase in Postp or SOV requires an increase in GN, if AN, DemN, and PossN increase as well, or are already 100%. The predictions hold in each case.

Finally, the significant increase in V + Aux structures, at the expense of Aux + V, is in conformity with Greenberg's 30-language sample data. Table 3 section H shows that all SOV languages in this sample have V + Aux, whereas almost all VO languages have Aux + V. This justifies the implication SOV ⊃ VAux. By the FIH, an increase in SOV therefore predicts an increase in V + Aux, given that this structure was not 100% hitherto.

All FIH predictions for Early New High German seem to be confirmed. Similarly, the DAH predicts that an antecedent *P* property will not arise in the total absence of the consequent *Q* property, where $P \supset Q$. Most of the changes in Early New High German involve frequency increases in already existing structures, except for postpositions and prenominal relatives, both of which are newly acquired. The relevant universals here are as follows. Universal (IX′) NG ⊃ NRel (alias: RelN ⊃ GN) requires that the new prenominal relative clause doublet cannot arise in the total absence of prenominal genitive structures. It does not. The acquisition of RelN also occurs after that of both DemN and PossN structures, in accordance with (XI′) NDem ⊃ NRel (alias: RelN ⊃ DemN), and (XXIII) NPoss ⊃ NRel (alias: RelN ⊃ PossN). And Universal (XIII) Prep ⊃ (−SOV ⊃ NRel) requires that prenominal relatives must arise after, or simultaneously with, either postpositions or SOV or both. This requirement is also met, as SOV structures exist prior to RelN (which is alone sufficient to satisfy the DAH), and postpositions arise at the same time.

The DAH predictions based on (IV) Postp ⊃ (AN ⊃ GN), (XV) Postp ⊃ (DemN ⊃ GN), and (XXII) Postp ⊃ (PossN ⊃ GN), are straightforwardly satisfied by the Early New High German data, as all these prenominal modifiers exist prior to the acquisition of postpositions. The DAH would have been falsified if both Postp and, for example, AN had arisen prior to GN.

All the Early New High German developments are therefore in accordance with both FIH and DAH predictions founded on the synchronic implicational universals of Chapter 3. The basic order co-occurrence array for Early New High German is also quite consistent (cf. UCH):

$$\text{sov}/{}^{\text{v}_1}_{\text{v}_2}\ \&\ \text{postp/PREP}\ \&\ \text{ADJ} + \text{N}\ \&\ \text{GEN} + \text{N/n} + \text{gen}\ \&\ \text{rel} + \text{n/N} + \text{REL}.$$

More recently, in New High German, prenominal relatives have declined in both frequency and grammatical relativization possibilities (cf. Note 14); and, according to Barnes (1977), postnominal genitives are more frequent and grammatically more productive than prenominal genitives in Modern German. As preposed and postposed genitives were approximately equal in Middle High German, and as prenominal genitives increased in Early New High German, this represents an increase in postnominal genitives in the modern period. Otherwise, noun modifier orders remain as in Early New High German. These developments are in accordance with Universal (IX′) NGen ⊃ NRel, in conjunction with the FIH: An increase in NGen must be matched by an increase in NRel, where this structure stands at less than 100%.[15]

The resulting word order co-occurrence array for New High German is set out in Table 38, along with that for Modern English. New High German, like Modern English, exhibits no inconsistency with independently motivated implicational universals.

A word finally to preempt two criticisms that have sometimes been made to me in connection with these predictions for German, namely, that the frequency increases are often slight and that they are possibly the result of Latin influence.

TABLE 38 : Modern English and New High German Word Order Data

Modern English	New High German
POSS + N/	POSS + N/
DEM + N/	DEM + N/
ADJ + N/	ADJ + N/
gen + n/n + gen	gen + n/N + GEN
/N + REL	rel + n/N + REL
/PREP	(postp)/PREP
v-1 (v-2)/SVO	sov/v-1 v-2

Note: Capital letters refer to word orders that are basic or unique. Lower-case letters refer to nonbasic orders; those in parentheses designate word orders that are even more limited. As in Tables 36 and 37, v-1 and v-2 designate verb-first and verb-second orders, except that for Modern English v-2 designates the non-SVO verb-second relics of the earlier more productive verb-second rule (e.g., *rarely does he play a wrong note;* see Hawkins, 1984). We take no stand here on the basicness of either genitive order in Modern English and German, or on the basicness of Modern German verb position, but are concerned to make predictions only for frequency increases and doubling acquisition through time. The criterion for placing word orders to the right or left of the slash is the same as for Table 34.

The first criticism is easy to dispose of, for the smaller the frequency increases from one historical stage to another, the greater, and more critical, is the test for our predictions. So, if these principles can make correct predictions for slight and subtle changes, as well as for wholesale rearrangments in basic word order, the likelihood increases that we are getting at something real.

As for Latin influence, there are numerous problems in invoking this which appear to have gone unnoticed hitherto; and even if there was Latin influence on New High German, this in no way undermines the validity of our predictions and results.

Latin was widely used prior to the sixteenth century in German-speaking territory. If the relevant constructions were borrowed, it is unclear why German should have waited till the sixteenth century in order to incorporate them. It is more likely (particularly in the light of our implicational universals) that the Early New High German developments were internally motivated, with any Latin influence merely supporting the appropriate structural changes at the appropriate time in the history of German. In addition, the Latin of this period had no native speakers, but was a lingua franca employed throughout Europe. It is therefore just as likely that Latin style was influenced by the native language(s) of the scribes who wrote it, rather than vice versa. In the case of the German prenominal relative, Weber (1971:141–148) provides evidence from Latin texts written by Germans which suggests that exactly this may have happened (though he does not himself consider the possibility of German influence on Latin). For in the sixteenth century, there is an observed change in Latin style: toward prenominal participial relatives (very similar to those of German), and away from postnominal participial relatives; that is, this change occurred during the precise period in which German itself was acquiring prenominal participial relative constructions (see Note 14).[16]

There is, therefore, a fundamental logical problem in invoking Latin influence on Early New High German. If similar structures were acquired *simultaneously* in the two written languages, it is much more likely that German was the donor, given the second language status of Latin. A necessary prerequisite for proving Latin influence is that the relevant structures existed in Latin *prior to* their acquisition in German. But even then, Latin influence is unconvincing, for why did German wait several centuries before borrowing the Latin structures? Either way, Latin influence is neither necessary nor sufficient to explain changes in German word order. At best, Latin supported internally motivated changes in the grammar of German, which is the conclusion that Weber (1971) argues for. My own suspicion is that, if any one language influenced the other, it was German that influenced Latin.

Finally, even if there was some supportive Latin influence on Early New High German word order changes, this in no way affects our synchronic and diachronic predictions. Whether change is exclusively internally motivated or contact induced, I predict (by UCH) that the receiving language will remain universally consistent; will acquire new doublets in accordance with DAH; and will effect frequency changes in accordance with FIH. In other words, languages cannot just change or borrow randomly. Which structures are acquired, and which are not, and when they are acquired, are subject to subtle constraints on the nature of human language, of the type that our universals define. And I expect borrowing to operate within these constraints as well (see also Notes 7 and 10 regarding Gothic).

5.3.6 OVERVIEW

We have seen that the Germanic languages, in their evolution from LCGmc, obey much finer predictions derived from synchronic implicational universals than are incorporated in UCH alone. The synchronic implications defined in terms of basic word order patterns can be translated into historical constraints on the acquisition and frequency increase of doubling structures, many of them minority word orders.

5.4 Trigger–Chain Theories: A Critique

The predictions for language history that we have just illustrated are founded on the predominantly nonstatistical implicational universals of Chapter 3. These universals project the co-occurrence regularities of (current) synchronically attested language types onto successive language stages in the past, and predict thereby the possible and impossible relative orders of changes in basic and nonbasic word orders.

There is, however, another view of the potential role of implicational universals within diachronic syntax, one that is founded on the statistical universals of Vennemann's Natural Serialization Principle (see Section 2.3.2). This theory is teleological. It views historical word order changes as gradual, goal-directed movements from one word order type to another, for example, from the operator-preposing (*X*V) to the operator-postposing (V*X*) type of the NSP. A change in type is "triggered" when a language evolves a word order inconsistent with that of its operator–operand type, and consistency is then reintroduced by acquiring the chain of implicationally dependent word orders consistent with the serialization of the trigger word order. This theory, which I shall call the "trigger–chain" theory, is most prominently associated with the work of Vennemann (1972, 1974a, 1974b, 1975) and Lehmann (1971, 1972b, 1973, 1974, 1978), though there are numerous other exponents as well.

In this section, I shall be offering a critique of such theories. But I should make it clear that there is a real insight that trigger–chain theories are attempting to capture which is, I believe, both important and correct: that certain word order co-occurrences are unstable and are under pressure to change; and that current language variation can make predictions (if only probabilistic ones) for the directionality of change in such cases. My critique will be directed at the manner in which trigger–chain theories attempt to capture this insight, rather than at the insight itself, which I will attempt to reformulate in a less problematic way. I have already argued against the adequacy of the synchronic universals upon which trigger–chain theories are based, the NSP (Section 2.4), so naturally I am not going to accept their predictive potential in this context. But I believe that trigger–chain theories are unworkable and internally contradictory from a purely historical perspective: statistical implications do not predict historical changes in the way that trigger–chain theorists argue they do.

Trigger–chain theories derive their attractiveness from the following two interrelated considerations: First, both the observed and the reconstructed word order changes among the daughter languages of diverse language families very often involve a plurality of cross-categorial word order changes; second, where historical records are available over several centuries — for example, for western Indo-European – word order changes do often move in a single direction by innovating consistent operator–operand or operand–operator word orders (though not invariably so, as shown by German which moved toward *VX* in its middle period, toward *XV* in its early new period, and which is now increasing its *VX* structures again; see Sections 5.3.4 and 5.3.5, Lehmann 1971, and Weber 1971). This universally based teleology has subsequently been used to account for Sapir's (1921) "drift," that is, for the fact that many languages have moved in the same or similar direction after their split from the parent language (cf. Vennemann 1975, Koch 1974). Drift is now equated with the gradual transition from one universal word order type to another over time.

More precisely, we can paraphrase the Lehmann–Vennemann trigger–chain theory as follows, letting property *P* stand for VO order, *Q* for the other properties of VO languages, $-P$ for OV order, and $-Q$ for the other properties of OV languages. A language that has, for example, $-P$ & $-Q$ at some stage in its history and then acquires *P*, thereby introducing inconsistency ($*P$ & $-Q$), is required by the implication 'if *P* then *Q*' to acquire *Q* later; that is, $-P$ & $-Q > *P$ & $-Q > P$ & Q [recall (1a) of Section 5.1.1]. Hence the change from OV to VO serves as a trigger which sets in motion the subsequent evolution of NAdj (from AdjN), of NGen (from GenN), of Prep (from Postp), etc., all of which are implicationally consequent upon VO.

This is a very appealing form of explanation. All that one needs to do is to explain why the trigger property, *P*, arose in the history of a language, and the statistical implicational universals will predict all the remaining changes. For Vennemann, the loss of case marking in an SOV language (through phonological reduction) brings about SOV/OSV ambiguities, which are resolved by developing the new basic word order SVO. The SVO (NP–V–NP) structures which arise are clearly distinguishable syntactically from object-topicalized OSV (NP–NP–V) structures. And SVO then serves as the trigger for the acquisition of the other *VX* word orders which are observed to co-occur on current synchronic evidence.

The trigger–chain theory exists in different forms. Most theorists assume some type of natural serialization principle in order to activate the chain, but the proposed trigger word orders vary according to author and language(s) under investigation, as does the type of explanation proposed for why the trigger word order arose in the first place. The major explanatory causes offered are disambiguation, grammatical reanalysis, afterthought, and perceptual ease. For Vennemann, SVO is the trigger structure, and its emergence is attributed to disambiguation, following morphological case leveling. Li and Thompson (1974) argue that the trigger word order in the reverse shift from SVO to SOV in Mandarin Chinese was not the object–verb order itself, but rather prepositional phrase in relation to verb. Grammatical reanalysis collapses complex SVOV(O) structures into simplex S + PP + V (+NP), as a result of the lexical change of a verb into a case marker and the creation of morphologically complex verbs. Hyman (1975) argues for adverbial and prepositional phrases constituting the trigger in the shift from SOV to SVO languages. In actual language use, speakers of (even rigid) SOV languages will sometimes add such phrases onto already completed sentences as afterthoughts, and these afterthought structures then provide the trigger for other V*X* word orders. The theory of Antinucci *et al.* (1979) proposes that the first property to change in an SOV language is not the position of the verb relative to its modifiers, but the relative clause. The prenominal relative clauses of SOV languages are perceptually difficult, and in order to ease this perceptual load, they shift into postnominal position. This then triggers the chain of V*X* structures.

We should now begin to appreciate why the precise logical status of the implicational universals constituting NSP is of crucial importance for trigger–chain theories. A word order change can only act as a trigger for a chain of related changes if the relevant properties are indeed consequent upon the trigger as antecedent, that is, if the chain is predictable given the trigger. The four types of triggers we have just illustrated are all valid triggers given a bilateral formulation of the implications. But, with a unilateral formulation, many of them would not be. For example, if we formulated Greenberg-type unilateral implications to permit threefold co-occurrences such as OV & AdvV, OV & VAdv, VO & VAdv, and OV & RelN, OV & NRel, VO & NRel (all of which are amply attested), the postposing of adverbials and relative clauses would no longer have trigger potential for verb–object order.[17]

5.4.1 SOME PROBLEMS FOR TRIGGER–CHAIN THEORIES

The first, and major, problem derives from the fact that the (statistical) implicational universals that constitute the NSP always make contradictory predictions when they are invoked in a trigger–chain context. Parker (1980) has drawn attention to this:

> Consider Basque, for example, a consistent OV language except that it has NA rather than AN order. If Basque were to become consistently OV by preposing

> its adjectives, this would be 'explained'. . . . That is, Basque became consistently OV because of its other OV characteristics. If on the other hand, Basque were to become consistently VO (or, for that matter, adopt any single VO characteristic in addition to the postposed adjectives), this too would be 'explained'. . . . That is, Basque became VO because it had NA order, a VO property. . . . [This theory] at once explains everything, yet explains nothing [p. 272].

We can paraphrase Parker's point as follows. Vennemann's NSP effectively consists of two implications of the form $P \supset Q$ and $-P \supset -Q$, where P and $-P$ are VO and OV respectively, and Q and $-Q$ the other properties of VO and OV languages respectively. A trigger–chain scenario is activated when a language has an inconsistent $*P$ & $-Q$ (e.g., VO & AN) or $*-P$ & Q (e.g., OV & NA) occurrence. The Basque situation is of the OV & NA type. But how is this inconsistency to be resolved? Either OV & AN or VO & NA are predicted; hence, either the verb position or the adjective position may change, and this indeterminacy reduces considerably the predictive potential of the trigger–chain theory.

But the logical problems are even worse than Parker's example suggests. Take Vennemann's paradigm case of a $-P$ & $-Q$ language that acquires (S)VO, becoming $*P$ & $-Q$. The implication $P \supset Q$ is supposed to predict the chain of subsequent changes. But $P \supset Q$ is logically equivalent to $-Q \supset -P$. So how could P arise in the first place at the $-P$ & $-Q$ stage, without contradicting the very implication that is supposed to be predicting subsequent changes? Any force that $P \supset Q$ exerts in explaining what is often a total restructuring in the syntax of a language must surely be equal to the force of the logically equivalent $-Q \supset -P$, and yet this latter should then prevent the whole sequence of events from getting started.

More precisely, the change from $-P$ to P necessarily proceeds via a doubling stage $-P > -P/P > P$. Any pull that P (VO) exerts in favor of the acquisition of Q structures at the $-P/P$ & $-Q$ stage will be offset first by the parallel implication $-P \supset -Q$ emanating from the coexisting (and initially basic) $-P$ (OV) in favor of the retention of $-Q$. And any attempted increase in the P structure, relative to $-P$, should be offset by the implication $-Q \supset -P$, forcing the co-occurrence and retention of $-P$. To claim, therefore, that the existence of $*P$ & $-Q$ co-occurrences explains the historical rise of positive Q word orders at the $-P/P$ & $-Q$ or P & $-Q$ stages is to invoke a single implication, $P \supset Q$, as a mechanism of change, when there are two other implications within the same theory, $-P \supset -Q$ and $-Q \supset -P$, which contradict this development and which should force a language to retain earlier consistent properties.

The second problem for trigger–chain theories derives from the statistical status of the implicational universals. Notice that this kind of historical theory is only possible with universals that are statistical: If the universals were exceptionless we would have no grounds for assuming the possibility of inconsistent $*P$ & $-Q$ co-occurrences in earlier periods. But the statistical status of the synchronic predictors puts trigger–chain theories in a double dilemma. First, there is a limit to the number of exceptions that a synchronic statistical implication can tolerate (cf. Section 4.3.3). One cannot claim that property P predicts the co-occurrence of Q if there are large numbers of languages with P that do not have Q. So, the fewer the synchronic exceptions are, the more adequate we judge our implicational statements to be. But, correspondingly, the fewer the synchronic exceptions, the less likely it is that individual languages will evolve inconsistent co-occurrences in their histories. Hence, the more adequate the synchronic universals are, the less likely it is that the triggering co-occurrences will ever arise, and the less plausible it becomes to invoke drag chains as *general* mechanisms of syntactic change. Conversely, it might be thought that the more synchronic exceptions there are, the more useful such universals will be for diachrony, even though their synchronic value is questionable. But this does not help either. For the more exceptions there are, the more likely it is that triggering co-occurrences will arise, but the less likely it is that the predicted chain of changes will follow suit. If there are many languages currently existing that do not obey the statistical implications in question, why should languages that evolve the relevant co-occurrences in earlier periods resolve inconsistencies any more than currently attested languages do?

Hence, the more adequate the synchronic universals are, the less likely the evolution of a triggering co-occurrence becomes; and the less adequate the synchronic universals are, the less likely it becomes that any chain of changes will follow suit. Either way, the trigger–chain theory is unsatisfactory.

Third, a crucial ingredient of the Lehmann–Vennemann theory seems to be the growth of SVO word order. But SVO is typologically ambivalent. In both Greenberg's implications (Sections 2.1, 2.2.4) and mine (Sections 3.2.1, 3.2.2), VSO and SOV can be implicationally antecedent properties, but not SVO. Nothing correlates with SVO in a unique and principled way, and hence SVO has no trigger potential in a historical context: There are no SVO word order universals to violate.

Fourth, because of the problem of contradictory predictions, there are no firm empirical predictions that NSP-based trigger–chain theories make. Nonetheless, even if we restrict ourselves to the frequently exemplified case of western Indo-European languages in their shift from OV to VO, and even if we were to succeed in limiting the predictions of the theory so that a drift toward greater consistency with the VX type is expected, the facts are much more complicated. In some cases the chain of changes triggered by the shift from OV to VO is fulfilled to quite an extent, as in the case of the Romance languages (cf., e.g., Harris 1978 for French). But in numerous cases it is not. We have already mentioned the to-ing and fro-ing in the acquisition of new word orders in German. The innovations are in accordance with the following typological drift: OHG *X*V > MHG V*X* > ENHG *X*V > NHG V*X* (see Sections 5.3.3, 5.3.4, 5.3.5). In addition, English has been a predominantly VO language since Old English. The Middle English increases in postnominal adjectives and genitives are in accordance with Vennemann's theory, but the subsequent increases in preposed adjectives, genitives, and also prenominal lexically compound adjectives are contrary to his predictions (see Section 5.3.5). So are the developments in Scandinavian. In their old periods, the Scandinavian languages were predominantly VO, with mixed pre- and postposed noun modifiers (cf. J. Smith 1971). But, instead of the predicted increase in postnominal modifiers, the reverse happens, giving the modern Scandinavian languages predominantly VO & modifier before noun co-occurrences, almost exactly as in Modern English.

Finally, in an earlier paper in which I discussed trigger–chain theories (Hawkins 1979), I used the Indo-European data of Section 5.3.1 as evidence against these theories, arguing that the consistency of the earlier records with current synchronic universals is a further nail in the coffin of the trigger–chain approach, as there is no motivation for inconsistency resolution as a mechanism of change. Since then, Mallinson and Blake (1981:407–417) have taken me to task for doing this. They point out that it is no argument against NSP-based trigger–chain theories to assert that there are improved, exceptionless universals, with whose predictions earlier language stages are fully consistent, when what is at issue is inconsistency with statistical implications. I accept Mallinson and Blake's point. But it should be clear both from this section and from my earlier paper that there are several other theoretical and empirical arguments against trigger–chain theories which make them unworkable, and that they are founded on synchronic universals which need to be improved.

At the same time, there is an important historical insight that trigger–chain theories are attempting to capture, and there is an important place for the operator–operand distinction within synchronic univerals. We have already reworked the operator–operand theory into an empirically more adequate set of (distributional) universals (CCH), and in Section 6.1 we shall attempt to capture the essential insight of the trigger–chain theory in a less problematic manner, avoiding its internal contradictions, by incorporating CCH as a synchronic predictor instead of statistical implications.

5.4.2 A PROBLEMATIC EXPLANATION FOR A TRIGGER WORD ORDER

It is important to appreciate that the explanations proposed for the emergence of the various trigger verb positions (Section 5.4) are logically independent of the trigger–chain theory itself. One could accept these explanations without committing oneself to the view that these new word orders had the status of a trigger converting "inconsistent" word orders into "consistent" ones. This is the position we shall take in Section 5.5. But there is one trigger explanation that is too problematic to be accepted in its present form: Vennemann's disambiguation motive for verb shift.

First, Vennemann's explanation requires that the verb–object reordering *precede* all other word order changes in the transition from one type to another. The other trigger–chain theories of Li and Thompson (1974), Hyman (1975), and Antinucci *et al.* (1979), however, present empirical and theoretical arguments to the effect that the verb–object reordering *follows* other word order changes. And Friedrich (1975) provides further examples of typological shifts that preceded the verb–object reordering in IE.

Second, it is true that the great majority of SOV languages have a case system distinguishing subject from object in some way [cf. Greenberg's (1966) universal (41-s): If in a language the verb follows both the nominal subject and nominal object as the dominant order, the language almost always has a case system]. But this, like all other unilateral implications, permits languages of three types:

(14)
a. OV & +Case (P & Q)
b. VO & +Case ($-P$ & Q)
c. VO & −Case ($-P$ & $-Q$)
d. *OV & −Case ($*P$ & $-Q$)

That is, although OV languages typically have a case system, VO languages occur both with and without one. Diachronically, it follows by UCH (Section 5.1.1) that an OV & +Case language (14a) has two pathways of change to reach VO & −Case (14c): It can acquire VO first, before it sheds its case system, (14a) > (14b) > (14c); or it can acquire VO and shed its case system at the same time, (14a) > (14c). But it cannot shed its case system before acquiring VO: (14a) > *(14d) > (14c). The existence of OV & +Case (14a) and VO & +Case (14b) languages thus results in the diachronic prediction that verb–object reordering can precede case syncretism, rather than follow it, as in Vennemann's trigger explanation. At best, this explanation must claim that verb–object reordering and case syncretism are simultaneous. But the fact that the synchronic data are compatible with verb–object reordering preceding case syncretism means that case syncretism is not a *necessary* cause of the OV > VO shift: This latter can occur independently.

The actual testing of these diachronic predictions is complicated by the paucity of records at crucial periods. Morphological changes are particularly slow moving. But the Baltic languages, especially Lithuanian, may provide evidence of the crucial shift (14a) > (14b). Lithuanian is currently SVO and has the most archaic case system of any contemporary IE language (Comrie 1981:208). But even relatively recently in its history it seems to have been predominantly OV (see Berneker 1900:56–58; Friedrich 1975:33). Hence, the OV > VO shift appears to have preceded the loss of subject/object case marking in this example.[18]

Although the absence of a case system is not a necessary cause of OV > VO (as this latter change can precede the loss of the case system), it may appear to be a sufficient one, given the logical equivalence of OV ⊃ +Case and −Case ⊃ VO. But the existence of exceptional *OV & −Case (14d) languages shows that even this does not hold. Ijo (SOV & −Case) is an example (Hyman 1975:117). The absence of subject/object case marking in Ijo has not caused verb–object reordering. Hence, the absence (or loss) of a case system is neither necessary, nor sufficient, to explain the shift from OV > VO.

A third argument against Vennemann's trigger explanation is discussed in Li and Thompson (1974). They attack the underlying assumption that change can be forced upon the syntactic system by independent phonological processes, especially given that a complete restructuring of the grammar is at stake:

> An essential step in [Vennemann's] argument is that phonological processes cause the obliteration of case systems in an SOV language. Such a step is highly questionable. If a case system is viable and phonological change begins to pose a threat to the system, the language can resort to some curative device such as paradigm borrowing to preserve the system. In other words, it is doubtful that phonological change will be the major factor in bringing about the decline of case systems and thus cause syntactic change, if there is no independent force within the syntactic system itself to induce a change in word order. Hence, if phonological change is to obliterate case systems at all, it is much more likely that the phonological obliteration occurs as a *result* rather than a *cause* of the degeneration of case systems [p. 212].

Dal (1962) gives convincing examples of exactly such paradigm borrowings in the history of Germanic. And Hawkins (1980b, 1981, 1984) provides some suggestions on what the "independent force" might be which results both in the syntactic changes and morphological leveling of Germanic.

Fourth, we can question, again with Li and Thompson (1974:211), the validity of "ambiguity avoidance" as a motive for word order change in this context. Not only could potential SOV/OSV ambiguities be resolved in numerous imaginable ways (e.g., through the development of object markers) without resorting to verb shift, but it is questionable to what extent such ambiguity needs to be resolved in the first place. Syntactic ambiguity is in general quite widespread in natural language, being "compensated for in actual performance by the redundancy of language as an information carrier and other perceptual cues in the environment [Li & Thompson 1974:211]." Even in German, a language whose evolution provides much of the data for Vennemann's theory, subject–object ambiguities are regularly tolerated at the sentence level, and disambiguated in context. Thus, *die Katze, die die Maus sah* can mean either 'the cat which saw the mouse' (cat = subject) or 'the cat which the mouse saw' (cat = object). Such ambiguities will always arise in German relative clauses unless a masculine singular noun is present (this being the unique bearer of a morphologically marked subject–object distinction) or unless one of the nouns is singular and the other plural (in which case the verb will disambiguate). Similar ambiguities are also possible in German main clauses. The sentence *die Maus hat die Katze gesehen* can mean either 'the mouse has seen the cat' or 'the cat has seen the mouse'.

5.5 On Understanding Word Order Change

5.5.1 CONCLUSIONS

Three conclusions can be drawn from our comparison of synchronic and diachronic data.

First, the trigger–chain theory is to be rejected. It can make historical predictions only in conjunction with a set of synchronic universals which are in need of improvement, and these predictions are internally contradictory and problematic.

Second, our predominantly nonstatistical universals make numerous predictions for historical changes—predictions that receive strong support from Avestan and Germanic. In effect, UCH and DAH predict the timing of word order changes relative to one another within a language. Given a synchronic implicational universal 'if P then Q', and a language with $-P \& -Q$, I claim that the acquistion of P must occur either after that of Q ($-P \& -Q > -P \& Q > P \& Q$), or simultaneously with it ($-P \& -Q > P \& Q$), but not before it, in order to avoid a $*P \& -Q$ co-occurrence ($-P \& -Q > *P \& -Q > P \& Q$). If P is acquired, therefore, this guarantees either the prior presence or the simultaneous acquisition of *Q*. And by the FIH, if *P* increases in frequency, so must *Q*, although *Q* may increase in frequency without *P*'s doing so.

However, the DAH and FIH make extremely strong claims, and it would not really surprise me if some counterexamples were found in other language families. I hope that a suitable modification will still be possible which preserves the essential insight that we have derived from the Avestan and Germanic data—their adherence to the DAH and FIH appears principled, given the extensive support for the basic word order universals from which the historical predictions are derived.

Third, the evidence against the trigger–chain theory calls for a new form of explanation for *why* word orders change, one that is consistent with more accurate synchronic universals, and with the diachronic principles of UCH, DAH, and FIH. We can no longer use implicational universals to explain the continued momentum for word order changes following some initial inconsistency. Instead, we must seek motivations for change within the parameters of synchronically attested variation. I shall conclude by briefly outlining an alternative framework for explaining change, one that operates within the constraints on word order variation defined by our implicational and distributional universals.

5.5.2 TOWARD AN ALTERNATIVE FRAMEWORK FOR EXPLAINING WORD ORDER CHANGE

The following two complementary issues need to be addressed when attempting to explain word order change: What is the set of possible word order co-occurrence types within which change can operate? And why should a language change from one of these types to another over time?

The first is a synchronic question. Why do our implicational universals define the range of permissible word order co-occurrences which they do? We have already offered an explanation (Section 3.4.2).

The second is the more relevant question in this context. If the majority of word order changes in a language are not a response to some initial universal inconsistency, what are they a response to, and why do they occur?

This diachronic question subdivides into two: Why should a language change any one of its word orders? Why is word order change frequently cross-categorial, involving a plurality of changes with similar directionality? It is this cross-categorial aspect, which has motivated the trigger-chain theory.

Recall that there is no shortage of explanations in the literature for individual word order changes in given languages. Some of these are proposed within the context of the trigger–chain theory, but as we pointed out in Section 5.4.2, explanations for the acquisition of so-called trigger word orders are logically independent of the trigger–chain theory itself. One can accept proposed explanations for a change in verb position, without accepting that the new verb position acquires the status of a trigger, converting inconsistent word orders into consistent ones.

The explanations offered for word order change are various. N. Smith (1981) argues for the importance of contact borrowing, that is, an external cause. Li and Thompson's (1974) explanation for the acquisition of S + PP + V structures in Mandarin Chinese (Section 5.4) views this word order change as a direct consequence of another change in the grammar: the lexical change of a verb into a case marker. There are numerous theories that seek motivations for change in terms of an analogical extension of one pattern over another, from among the variants permitted by the language as a whole. Parker (1980) points to competing word orders in matrix and relative clauses as a source for analogical extensions in all languages. Stockwell (1977) documents competing patterns in Old English verb position which could have led to the establishment of basic SVO order. Hyman's (1975) "afterthought" theory also involves an analogical extension of postverbal adverbials and prepositional phrases from a purely conversational structure into a syntactic norm. In contrast, Antinucci *et al.*'s (1979) perceptual difficulty explanation for the frequent postposing of relative clauses in SOV languages is a language-external, psychological explanation.

These explanations are in principle quite acceptable within the framework that I am advocating here, and are worthy of further refinement and testing. It seems eminently reasonable that there will be a multiplicity of change-inducing factors operating upon different languages, and even upon one and the same language—just as there are numerous factors that contribute to the explanation for synchronic universals (Section 3.4.2). The proposed explanations are therefore complementary rather than conflicting, and in all likelihood represent only a fraction of the total causes underlying word order change.

But having admitted the potential relevance of all these factors at a general level, it is extremely difficult to prove exactly which factor or factors is responsible for change in any one case. The identification of putative causes of change is as fraught with problems in the area of word order as it is elsewhere (cf. Lass 1980). Competing verb orders may be resolved in favor of SVO, as in Old English, but they do not have to be (witness German). Afterthoughts may turn into grammaticalized postverbal adverbs and prepositional phrases, but there are large numbers of languages in which they have not (all rigid SOV languages). The perceptual difficulty of prenominal relatives may indeed be real, but it has not caused change in a large number of SOV languages. Contact between languages has led to convincing instances of word order borrowing in some cases, but not others. And so on.

All of this should not cause undue despair. It simply means that explanations for diachrony are as complex, and as multifactored, as explanations for synchrony, which is what we would expect. And the explanations for language change that are generally proposed (see Lass, 1980, for discussion) are a little simplistic in invoking single causes for change, in isolation from other potentially relevant and interacting factors.

Consider an instructive analogy from synchrony. Imagine that someone were to propose that heaviness alone explained the noun modifier co-occurrences of Chapter 3. Clearly, this would explain a lot—but there would be counterexamples. This does not mean that heaviness is not a causal factor underlying synchronic universals. It means that it must be supplemented with other factors, such as mobility, which interact with it, and constrain its causality in predictable ways. Similarly, if I have evidence that contact borrowing has taken place between Languages *A* and *B*, but not between *C* and *D*, I should not dismiss a contact explanation out of hand in the former case. I should study *C* and *D* carefully to see what is different from the *A* and *B* case—for example, social differences, differences in the word orders involved (Chapter 6)—in order to refine the predicted effects of contact. What is wrong with most current explanations, therefore, is not that they fail to identify relevant causes of change—but that they fail to place these causes within a more general theory of mutually interacting explanatory forces, both synchronic and diachronic.

In effect, our synchronic implicational universals define an "upper bound" on historical changes (Lightfoot 1979:141). But I see no reason in principle why a historical theory cannot be developed which goes beyond the diachronic predictions of synchronic universals (Section 5.1) by specifying some at least of the lower bounds that Lightfoot's own approach eschews.[19] Such a theory would make more precise the role of analogy and contact, etc., their interaction with one another and with synchronic principles. Consider contact again. Some structures and areas of the grammar are more readily borrowed than others (cf. Weinreich 1953). By inspecting large numbers of languages in contact, in an attempt to determine when word order borrowing occurs and when it does not, it may be possible to establish a hierarchic ranking of ease of borrowing. Given such a ranking, given two languages in contact, and given a synchronic theory of word order, it should be possible to predict that if borrowing occurs (for social reasons, coupled with language-internal considerations of grammatical simplicity or complexity [Section 4.6; Chapter 6]), Structure *X* will be borrowed before Structure *Y*, or simultaneously with *Y*, etc., depending on the precise formulation of the contact borrowing heirarchy. Or consider again the Li and Thompson (1974) explanation for the evolution of S + PP + V structures in Mandarin Chinese. The S + PP + V structure appears to be a direct output of the change from one lexical category into another (verb into prepositional case marker). It may be possible to generalize such causality links: Given any language of the Chinese type, and a lexical change of the Chinese type, the new word order necessarily results. Similarly, a theory that specifies what are, and what are not, possible analogical extensions for languages of certain structural types (based on the kinds of considerations discussed in Parker 1980 and Stockwell 1977) does not seem to be wholly unattainable. All these predictions will clearly supplement the universal predictions for change of the form: Given an implicational universal 'if *P* then *Q*', and a language that acquires *P*, then *Q* must be acquired either simultaneously or antecedently.

There is an intermediate possibility for historical theories, which is in between these upper and lower bounds. The theory might delimit the set of available changes for languages of various types and assign probability weightings to each option. The principle of CCH is directly relevant for language history in this respect—as are all distributional universals, in fact—and we shall be discussing this aspect of the synchronic–diachronic relationship in the next chapter. We shall use CCH to explain why word order change is frequently cross-categorial and involves a plurality of changes with similar directionality.

The present chapter has been concerned with the role of implicational universals in language change. We have argued that implicational universals are not the appropriate device with which to explain any chain of word order changes following some independently motivated individual change. Instead, such universals are preferably exceptionless, and languages can be expected not to develop inconsistencies. As a result, implicational universals define an upper bound on language change, and constrain the timing of changes relative to one another in interesting ways. I have suggested that certain individual word order changes can be explained directly by a theory that specifies some of the lower bounds on word order change. And we will now see how distributional universals can predict, with varying degrees of probability, which other word order changes will accompany or follow such independently motivated individual changes.

Notes

1. Note that an increase in *P*'s frequency relative to $-P$ means, of course, a corresponding decrease in $-P$'s frequency. As a result, the FIH is equivalent to a requirement that any decrease in $-P$'s frequency must be matched by a decrease in $-Q$, where $-Q$ is more than 0%. However, although both the DAH and FIH make predictions for the relative timing of structures *acquired,* no predictions are being made by either hypothesis concerning structures *lost.* For example, if *P* increases to 100% (whereupon $-P$ decreases to 0% and is thereby lost altogether), the FIH requires only that Q should increase relative to $-Q$, not that *Q* should necessarily increase to 100% (and $-Q$ decrease to 0%). Thus it is possible that $-P$ could be lost before $-Q$, and equally that $-Q$ could be lost before $-P$. In the former case (i.e., P & $-Q/Q$), UCH would require that the $-Q$ structures co-existing with *Q* should not be basic, in order to avoid a $*P$ & $-Q$ co-occurrence. The laws of word order loss are thus claimed to be partly different from those of word order acquisition. This seems reasonable, as we know that archaic word orders are often retained in a language to perform certain grammatical functions (cf. Li and Thompson's, 1975, explanation for the retardation of the SVO > SOV shift in Chinese). By contrast, the actual innovation of a new word order pattern is here claimed to be deeply determined by the typological shape of the language at the historical stage in question, in the form of the prior availability (or simultaneous acquisition) of universally required *Q* structures as prerequisites for *P*'s acquisition (where $P \supset Q$).

2. Of course, this fact in itself illustrates the very correspondence between past and present that we are about to test. However, not all the early IE dialects have been placed in the Expanded Sample of Chapter 8, and not all the word order properties of early IE that we are about to test are listed in the Expanded Sample. A detailed investigation of early IE is therefore in order, particularly since these data will be important as a background to the testing of the DAH and FIH in Avestan and Germanic and to the discussion of Proto-Indo-European in Chapter 7.

3. Thus, if gen + n could count as a basic in Italic, this would save Implication (I) SOV ⊃ (AN ⊃ GN). And if either adj + n, or neither adj + n nor n + adj, count as basic in Gathic Avestan, this will save Implications (III) PREP ⊃ (NA ⊃ NG) and (III′). If n + adj were basic, this would create a $*P$ & $-Q$ co-occurrence with GEN + N. The major point about these early IE dialects, however, is that there is not a single clear counterexample in which a basic *P* structure co-occurs with a basic $-Q$ structure. These two instances of equally basic structures are the closest we get to a counterexample, and even then only for one implication in one language (Italic).

4. Universal (III) is actually statistical. We use it here instead of the more complicated (III′) Prep & −SVO ⊃ (NA ⊃ NG) in order to simplify the discussion of the diachronic predictions made by these universals. As both Avestan dialects are SOV (OV predominates over VO by a 2 : 1 ratio in both dialects; see Friedrich 1975:45), the implication NA ⊃ NG holds exceptionlessly for them.

5. Actually, the interpretation of FIH in relation to Universal (III) is slightly more complex than it is presented in the main text. This universal has the form $P \supset (Q \supset R)$. Yet the FIH formulates predictions only for implicational statements of the simple form $P \supset Q$. The consequent *Q* in Universal (III) is therefore complex, consisting of a further implication. Universal (III) is to be read: 'If a language has prepositions, then if it has NA, it will also have NG'. This permits prepositions to co-occur with NA & NG, AN & NG, or with AN & GN, but not with *NA & GN. Derivatively, the FIH requires that 'if a language increases its prepositions (relative to postpositions), then if it increases NA (relative to AN), it will also increase NG (relative to GN, if any)'. Thus, if prepositions increase, it does not necessarily follow that NA must increase; but if it does, NG must increase as well (if it stands at less than 100%). And if NA does not increase, NG may still increase, or it may not. If prepositions gain in frequency, therefore, there are three possibilities regarding frequency increases in the noun modifiers; and these possibilities correspond to the three noun modifier co-occurrences that are found for basic word orders in languages with prepositions:

(*a*) Both NA and NG increase (cf. Prep & NA & NG languages).
(*b*) NG increases while NA does not (cf. Prep & AN & NG languages).
(*c*) Neither NA nor NG increases (cf. Prep & AN & GN languages).

What is ruled out is:

(*d*) NA increases while NG does not (cf. *Prep & NA & GN).

We can therefore predict, on the basis of the impossibility of the co-occurrence *Prep & NA & GN for basic word orders, that there will be no increase in both prepositions and NA in a language that is not matched by an increase in NG. Where, as in the Avestan data, both Prep and NA do increase in frequency, NG must also increase. By parallel reasoning, a complex formula such as $P \supset (Q \;\&\; R)$ would predict, by the FIH, that 'if P increases in frequency, then both P and Q will increase'; and $P \supset (Q \vee R)$ would predict 'if P increases in frequency, then either Q or R (or both) will increase'. See also Note 9.

6. Although Smith's evidence is limited, the subsequent figures for East and West Germanic, presented in Tables 36 and 37, do make this state of affairs for LCGmc very plausible (see Notes 7 and 10).

7. The Skeireins consists of two texts: a late fourth-century Bible translation, and a sixth-century commentary. Smith gives two sets of figures—(a), averaged from both texts, and (b), from the commentary alone. His purpose is to avoid the possible effects of classical influence on Gothic word order in translation. However, the differences between the two sets of figures are not great; and the increased figures for GEN + N and ADJ + N in the commentary are plausibly accounted for by its later date. The preposing of noun modifiers has continued to a point where it is more in line with the early West Germanic dialects (except for the possessive adjective).

8. In fact, Gothic has N + REL, although some prenominal relatives are attested (see the example in Esau 1973:26, attributed to Vennemann). The existence of N + REL as a basic structure can be safely reconstructed for LCGmc on the basis of the earliest Germanic daughters, although no relative clauses are attested in these early inscriptions (A.D. 200–600) (see Section 7.3). Hence, we cannot know with certainty whether there were any minority prenominal relatives at this stage. Notice, however, that this indeterminacy does *not* undermine the precision of our FIH predictions. For in all the old periods of the East and West Germanic daughters (see also Table 37), it is GEN + N which has increased in frequency relative to LCGmc, which negates the antecedent property of (IX′) NG ⊃ NRel. The FIH is then compatible with all possibilities: If there were any prenominal relatives in LCGmc, either postnominal or prenominal relatives may have increased (cf. GN & NRel and GN & RelN languages); if there were exclusively postnominal relatives in LCGmc, the prenominal relatives of Gothic can have been acquired (cf. GN & RelN languages); and the relative clause situation may have remained exactly what it was, either in Gothic or early West Germanic, with no relative clause increases at all. All that is ruled out by the FIH is an increase in N + GEN structures that is not matched by an increase in N + REL structures (where these were previously less than 100%) or an increase in REL + N structures which is not matched by an increase in GEN + N. The increase of GEN + N structures in early Germanic guarantees that neither of these exceptional cases can have arisen.

9. Notice that the Gothic data (like the rest of the Germanic data to be considered) differ in a significant respect from the Avestan data of Section 5.3.2, against which Universal (III) and the FIH were also tested. Not only is the direction of change in Avestan toward increased modifier postposing rather than preposing but the ultimate antecedent property, PREP, does not increase in Germanic, although all the predicted noun modifiers do. Technically, given an implication of the form $P \supset (Q \supset R)$, an increase in both P and Q is required by FIH if an increase in R is to be guaranteed (as in the Avestan data). The reason for this can be seen most clearly by converting $P \supset (Q \supset R)$ into the logically equivalent $(P \mathbin{\&} Q) \supset R$, with a conjoined antecedent. A language that fails to have either P or Q is negating this conjunction [i.e., $-(P \mathbin{\&} Q)$], and hence nothing can be predicted for the consequent property R: A $-(P \mathbin{\&} Q)$ language may co-occur both with R and with $-R$. Diachronically, therefore, if just one member of the $(P \mathbin{\&} Q)$ conjunction increases and the other does not, no predictions are made for R, which may or may not increase. It is only when P and Q increase together that an increase in R is necessarily required. However, in all the Germanic dialects, PREP is already the overwhelmingly predominant, if not the exclusive, order (but cf. Early New High German, Section 5.3.5); hence it cannot reasonably increase further. As the property P cannot increase further, it is only natural to assume (as I do in the main text) that an increase in Q alone is sufficient to guarantee an increase in the R structures. In order to make this possibility fully explicit, and to illustrate the predictions of the FIH for formulae of the kind $P \supset (Q \supset R)$, let us redefine the FIH as follows:

Frequency Increase Hypothesis (Revised) (FIH):
Given a set of synchronic implicational universals of the form $P \supset (Q \supset R)$, where P, Q, and R are basic word orders of certain specified types; then, at two successive stages in the growth of a language,

IF: (*a*) there is an increase in the frequency of both P and Q structures relative to their doublets ($-P$ and $-Q$ respectively); *or* (*b*) there is an increase in the frequency of P structures relative to $-P$, with Q being already 100%; *or* (*c*) there is an increase in the frequency of Q structures relative to $-Q$, with P being 100%;
AND IF: (*d*) the frequency of the R structures at the earlier stage, prior to the increase in P or Q or both, was less than 100% (i.e., if $-R$ doublets existed);
THEN: the R structures will also have gained in frequency relative to $-R$, along with P or Q or both by the later stage.

Notice, finally, that we have again used the statistical implication (III), rather than the more complex nonstatistical (III′), for greater ease of exposition, as we did for Avestan. As Gothic is predominantly SOV (according to Smith's figures SOV far exceeds both v-1 and v-2), Universal (III) is again making exceptionless predictions for diachrony.

10. The trend to prepose noun modifiers in the early Germanic dialects has advanced further in West Germanic than in East Germanic. This is readily explainable in terms of the later date of the West Germanic records. The figures for Gothic are roughly what one would expect given the figures for LCGmc and early West Germanic. This preposing pattern lends further credibility to the LCGmc figures, and also to the reliability of the Gothic data. Whatever classical influences were exerted upon Gothic have not disrupted this development.

11. Importantly, Lightfoot (1975:Note 9) demonstrates that Middle English could not have borrowed the actual postnominal order from French (the source of most of the lexical borrowings), for the simple reason that the great majority of French adjectives in this period were prenominal. The postposing of adjectives in Middle English is, therefore, internally motivated.

12. See Stockwell (1977) for a critical discussion of J. Smith's criteria for distinguishing the non-verb-final structures from one another. The verb-final figures, however, can be taken as reasonably reliable indicators of the extent of verb-final retention from LCGmc. Smith's figures for LCGmc are:

	Late Common Germanic
v-1	16%
v-2	19%
v-3	3%
V-final	62%

13. An example of an SVO structure in MHG is *alse diu sunne an sich ziuhet den fiuhten luft* 'as the sun to itself draws the damp air' (Lockwood 1968:263). Object postposing affected heavier NPs before lighter ones (Section 3.4.1.1) in this period.

14. (1) Examples of prenominal relative clauses in Modern German are: *der die schöne Frau liebende Mann* 'the the beautiful woman loving man' (i.e., 'the man who loves the beautiful woman'); *die von Herrn Schmidt ausgewählten Paragraphen* 'the by Mr. Smith selected paragraphs'; *der mit uns zu schliessende Friedensvertrag* 'the with us to be signed peace treaty'. Weber (1971) refers to these constructions as "extended attributes," a label which he uses also for adverb + adjective attributes of the form *eine überraschend tiefe Stimme* 'a surprisingly deep voice'. The adverb + adjective constructions are attested before Early New High German. But the prenominal relatives proper arose only in the sixteenth century, and Weber (1971:93–137) gives detailed frequency counts for various styles of written German from the sixteenth to the twentieth century. In contemporary German, prenominal relatives are possible only on underlying subjects. But in the seventeenth and eighteenth centuries, they are also found on underlying direct objects (Weber 1971:158): *meine zu ihr tragende hefftige Liebe* 'my to her bearing passionate love' (i.e., 'the passionate love which I feel for her'). In the twentieth century the prenominal relative has undergone a sharp decline. It is interesting that before the sixteenth century, German employed lexical compounds as attributes, corresponding to the Modern English *heart-breaking, time-saving, tree-lined,* etc.: *sin minnesůchendes herze* 'his love-seeking heart'; *mit minneweinenden ogen* 'with love-crying eyes' (i.e., 'with eyes crying for/out of love') (see Weber 1971:88). The acquisition of the German prenominal relative can therefore be seen as the conversion of a lexical compounding rule into a transformational rule of the kind proposed in König (1971:39) (see also Hawkins 1980c:23–26, Wasow 1977). Lexical compounds of the type *heart-breaking* are essentially Modern English, according to Marchand (1960:91). The fact that lexically compound attributes precede prenominal relatives in the history of German, and arise in Modern English, does not justify the prediction that English will also move on to acquire German-type prenominal relatives. But it does suggest that lexical compounds of this type may be a prerequisite structure for prenominal relatives proper: A prepositional language that increases its noun modifier preposing to such an extent that even relative clauses become preposed (cf. PrNMH, 3.3.7) may have to acquire prenominal lexical compounds first.

(2) I have not seen or worked out any statistics on the genitive situation in Early New High German. My data are impressionistic only.

(3) There are some postnominal adjectives in OHG (see Table 37) and there is an increase in postnominal adjectives in MHG (Section 5.3.4); but thereafter single adjectives are exclusively preposed, as in Modern English (see Lockwood 1968:39).

(4) The rigid verb-final rule of Early New High German places nonfinite verb forms (infinitives, participles, particles, and other verbal satellites) at the end of main clauses (the finite verb being in second or first position), and both finite and nonfinite verb forms at the end of subordinate clauses. See Lehmann (1971), Lockwood (1968:260–265), and Weber (1971:131).

(5) See Lehmann (1971) regarding the acquisition of German postpositions of the type *das Ufer entlang* 'the bank along', *dem Haus gegenüber* 'the house opposite'.

(6) The significant increase of V + Aux structures in Early New High German, replacing Aux + V, is documented in Maurer (1926), using detailed frequency counts.

15. Universal (XIII) Prep ⊃ (−SOV ⊃ NRel) is also relevant for New High German. The increase in NRel in twentieth century German is documented in Weber (1971:125). Impressionistically, the rigid verb-final rule has also declined in favor of a more leftward positioning of the verb, as has the use of postpositions, though I have not seen relevant statistics. If both PREP and −SOV have increased, then the increase in NRel will also be predicted by (XIII). If one or the other has not increased, on the other hand, then no predictions are made.

16. The 1356 Golden Bull of Emperor Charles IV (composed in Latin) has frequent postnominal participial relatives, but only one isolated prenominal construction (Weber 1971:141–142). In a 1523 Latin text by Ulrich von Hutten, on the other hand, prenominal participial relatives are frequent (Weber 1971:144). And by 1648, prenominal participial relatives in the Westfalian peace treaties (composed in Latin) are just as frequent as their postnominal counterparts (Weber 1971:146). German translations of the 1648 text regularly employ prenominal relatives when rendering the prenominal relatives of Latin. Translations of the 1356 Golden Bull employ no prenominal relatives, of course. And although only a few prenominal relatives occur in a German translation of the 1523 text, dating from the same period, this can probably be attributed to the incipient and transitional nature of the construction in the early sixteenth century. The Latin style of German writers does, therefore, appear to initiate prenominal participial constructions at precisely the time that German itself acquires them.

17. The relevant implications would be AdvV ⊃ OV and RelN ⊃ OV respectively.

18. There is admittedly need for a more careful analysis of the historical facts in Baltic. Just as word order changes proceed via doubling, so case system leveling is also gradual, affecting some noun classes and cases before others. What is required is a precise quantification both of the OV and VO doublets and of the presence versus decline of the various morphological distinctions at the different historical stages. Greenberg's implicational universal (41-s) can then be tested in a more subtle manner, along the lines of DAH and FIH (Section 5.2). As a lot of morphological leveling took place in prerecorded periods, however, even this method is limited to attested historical stages. Despite these empirical difficulties with diachronic testing, it must be stressed that the synchronic co-occurrences alone [Example (14) in the main text] are sufficient to prove the independence of the OV > VO shift from case syncretism.

19. Lightfoot's (1979) historical theory is deliberately noncommittal about what changes a language will effect at a given point in time. At best, he argues, one can specify only *that* a change must occur in languages of certain types. His Transparency Principle is an example. When deep and surface structures become too opaque (i.e., sufficiently divergent that the language learner can no longer reconstruct deep from surface structures), a reanalysis occurs which brings deep structures more into line with surface structures. Exactly what this reanalysis is is left deliberately vague, since it is claimed to be unpredictable. I think this approach is reasonable for the kinds of examples that Lightfoot discusses. But it does not rule out a more ambitious historical theory in other cases, using multifactor and implicational predictions of the type we illustrate in the main text. There are going to be different types and strengths of predictions for historical change, and I would not want to elevate a whole historical theory around one such, as Lightfoot appears to do.

6 : *The Diachronic Predictions of Distributional Universals*

A major goal of universal grammar is to define parameters on language variation (Section 1.3). In the course of this book we have employed implicational universals for this purpose. We have also seen systematic differences in frequency among the attested language variants—differences which are theoretically revealing, and whose explanation involves intrinsically gradient rather than absolute causes. We shall now argue that the distributional principles which predict such relative frequencies can contribute to historical linguistics, by uncovering motives for change from one language type to another. These motives will enable us to supplement the theory of word order change outlined in Section 5.5.2.

Principled differences in language frequencies have been discussed in previous chapters for several areas of the grammar, and three types of explanatory gradients have been proposed: relative psycholinguistic processing difficulty (Section 3.4.2.1); relative complexity of cross-categorial word order rules (Section 4.6); and the relative strength of one principle in opposition to another (Section 4.3.1).

In Section 3.4.2.1 we attempted to explain the following frequency hierarchies in terms of relative processing difficulty:

Languages with clause-final S-complements > languages with clause-initial complements > languages with clause-medial complements
NRel languages > RelN languages
Languages without self-embedded relatives > languages with self-embedded relatives

The principle of CCH defines a whole set of frequency hierarchies, which we have explained in terms of different degrees of rule complexity, for example:

VSO & N_1 (N relative to Adj, Gen, and Rel) > VSO & N_2 > VSO & N_3 > VSO & N_4

And in Section 4.3.1 we appealed to the relative strength of Keenan's "Subjects Front" in explaining the following frequency hierarchy for VO languages:

SVO*X* > VSO*X* > VOS*X* > VO*X*S

The more that subjects front (for pragmatic reasons), and depart from the VO*X*S mirror image to S*X*OV (and hence from whatever syntactic-semantic principles explain the SXOV serialization in rigid verb-final languages and predict its simple mirror image for VO languages; (see, e.g., Section 3.6), the more languages there are. I gave no explanation for why the pragmatic principle should be the stronger one. But given the progressive increase in language frequencies as Subjects Front takes effect, it is clear that it is the stronger principle, and that this extra degree of strength is relative only, as alternative serialization principles are not entirely obliterated.

What do these language frequencies tell us about language history? Two (interrelated) conclusions can be drawn.

First, the further to the right a language occurs on one of the frequency hierarchies at some stage in time, the greater will be the pressure upon it to relieve the processing load, rule complexity, etc., by moving diachronically to the left. Infrequent language types have nonpreferred grammars. They are still possible and successful communication systems, so whatever difficulties underlie infrequency are clearly within the limits of tolerance. In all likelihood, languages with infrequent grammatical properties in some areas will have more frequent properties elsewhere, so that the overall simplicity and complexity of total grammatical systems is probably much the same throughout the world's languages. But these declining language frequencies suggest that there is an omnipresent structural pressure on languages to move diachronically to the left rather than to the right, and that the greater the infrequency, the greater is the pressure to do so. Independent considerations can lead a language to override the preferences we have documented by adopting an infrequent grammatical property, but the pressure on that language to initiate additional changes, either subsequently or simultaneously, turning it into a more frequent type will then be quantifiable on the basis of the frequency facts involved.

Second, logic dictates that there be a direct relation between language frequencies and the relative time amounts during which individual languages retain the relevant grammatical properties. Most of the properties in our frequency hierarchies involve word orders which, as we have seen, can be very variable over time. There are many language families that reveal extensive word order rearrangements among their daughters (e.g., Indo-European), and there is scarcely a language family, even in the limited time depth available to us for observation and reconstruction, which does not reveal at least some minor word order change(s). (Consult the typological and genetic classification of the Expanded Sample for confirmation of both these points.) Given that this is so, we would predict that the more frequent a word order type is on current synchronic evidence, the longer it will remain in the relevant word order state, and hence the more languages there are synchronically exemplifying this state.

The decreasing synchronic quantities of languages on our frequency hierarchies are therefore natural consequences of the fact that all languages, in the course of their evolution, have had preferred word order co-occurrences for greater periods of time than nonpreferred ones, with relative time amounts reflecting the varying degrees of preference (rule simplicity, etc.). I believe this is the only way of explaining these synchronic language quantities. If, on the other hand, historical time amounts were not in direct proportion to the preferences that underlie our frequency hierarchies, the chances of discovering widespread exceptions to principles such as CCH in synchronic samples (in the form of disproportionate numbers of disharmonic languages) would be almost inevitable.

6.1 Predictions for Cross-Categorial Word Order Changes

In Chapter 5 we discussed some explanations that have been proposed for individual word order changes (most of them involving verb position). Still in need of explanation, however, is the frequently cross-categorial nature of word order change, which, we argued, has motivated the trigger–chain theory. As we have rejected that theory, we must propose an alternative account of the facts that it was designed to explain. The alternative synchronic predictor that we offer is, of course, CCH.

CCH can make predictions for the extent to which word order changes involving one category will generalize to another. I would argue that the number of cross-category operator–operand deviations contained in each word order co-occurrence set defines not only relative quantities of the relevant languages on synchronic evidence, but also the relative probabilities with which languages will change from one word order type to another.

For example, if there is independent motivation for the verb to shift position, it is expected that this verb shift will be matched by cross-categorial readjustments. If a rigid SOV language becomes nonrigid, it is most expected that at least one noun operator will simultaneously move to the right of the noun. If a VSO language becomes SVO, at least one noun operator should simultaneously move to the left of the noun. Which noun operator or operators move will, in each case, conform to the PrNMH or PoNMH (Sections 3.3.7, 3.3.17). Similarly, if a (postpositional) SOV language develops into a (prepositional) VO language, the formerly non-preferred NA & NG co-occurrence (Po & V_3 & N_1 = 4 deviations; 7 languages in Appendix II, 11 languages in the Expanded Sample) becomes a much preferred co-occurrence with SVO or VSO (Pr & V_2 & N_1 = 2 deviations; 21 languages in Appendix II, 56 languages in the Expanded Sample; and Pr & V_1 & N_1 = 0 deviations; 19 languages in Appendix II, 38 languages in the Expanded Sample), and hence a most likely accompanying change. And in general, the extent of the probability of some change is quantifiable on the basis of the number of operator–operand ordering deviations (plus Subjects Front), and on the basis of the actual language quantities on current synchronic evidence. But to the extent that a reordering within one category is matched by reorderings that are less preferred by CCH, or by no reorderings at all, the language becomes a rarer and more complex type, and is under pressure to reintroduce cross-category harmony subsequently.

Furthermore, the nature of this pressure for change is now more readily understandable on the basis of our proposed explanation for CCH (Section 4.6). A language that effects word order changes involving individual categories only will be losing cross-categorial generalizations, unless there are word order adjustments in the other phrasal categories as well. To change verb position alone in a harmonic language type will be to complicate the serialization rules in one or more of the three ways that we outlined in Section 4.6.5: The grammar will be serializing identical categories at common bar levels to both left and right, rather than in a uniform direction; or the grammar will be introducing more conditions on rules; or the grammar will be reducing the generality of categories mentioned in its X-bar generalizations, thereby increasing the total number of serialization rules that the language requires. Pressure is not a loose metaphor in this context, therefore. It means that grammars of specified types are losing generalizations that they could be capturing if they had different word orders. And if we assume that languages do strive for greater rule simplifications in the wake of independently motivated changes that introduce complexity, then cross-categorial generalization is a natural form for such simplification to take.

The general explanatory framework for word order change which I would propose can therefore be set out as follows. As they evolve, all languages are constrained by implicational universals, and can change only relative to the co-occurrence possibilities that these permit. Some operator–operand reorderings, particularly involving the verb, can be explained directly, in terms of a variety of causal factors (within the context of a more sophisticated historical theory than we now have). Such categorial changes are then simultaneously or subsequently matched by cross-categorial word order readjustments which are explainable by CCH, and whose relative probabilities can also be predicted on the basis of this principle, as the rules of the grammar accommodate word order changes which are independently motivated for a single category.

Finally, it is important to make explicit how this account of word order change in relation to language universals differs from the trigger–chain theory. The two theories agree in the following two respects:

1. Both are founded on synchronic universal predictions that make crucial use of the operator–operand distinction.
2. Both attempt to describe the pressure on a language to change, and to make predictions for the directionality of change.

But they differ in the following two:

1. Our theory employs CCH in lieu of NSP as a synchronic predictor.
2. Our theory makes no use of drag-chains activated by statistical implicational universals in relation to inconsistent word order co-occurrences.

By not using statistical implicational universals, we avoid their contradictory predictions for diachrony (Section 5.4.1). And by using CCH to make predictions for the relative probabilities of different changes, we achieve a better match between current data and historical data: The possible and impossible states through which languages can pass diachronically are constrained by exceptionless synchronic implicational universals; the relative probabilities of transition from one state to the next are now determined by the composition of the earlier state, by independently motivated changes for individual word orders, and by current language quantities for the various word order co-occurrences of the independently explained word order innovations.

6.2 The Relative Time Hypothesis

At the beginning of this chapter, we suggested that the frequency hierarchies defined by distributional universals make two (interrelated) predictions for diachrony: There will be greater pressure for a language to move from right to left than vice versa; and there will be a direct relation between language frequencies and historical time amounts. We have made the notion "pressure for change" more precise, using CCH as an illustrative example for all distributional universals. We shall now discuss the relative time predictions, again using CCH as an illustrative example.

We can state the proposed relation between CCH and relative time amounts more precisely in the following way:

THE RELATIVE TIME HYPOTHESIS (RTH):

GIVEN: Two word order co-occurrence types, T and T', as defined for CCH in Section 4.2.8, with relative cross-category harmony measured as in Section 4.2.8 also.

PREDICTIONS: Whichever co-occurrence type, T or T', has more CCH (if any), the greater will be:

1. (Single language prediction) the relative amounts of time (if any) during which an arbitrary single language has exemplified either T or T' from its inception to the present;[1]
2. (Combined prediction) the relative combined time amounts during which all languages have exemplified either T or T' from their inceptions to the present.

Of the two predictions made by the RTH, the first is the stronger. The truth of the single language prediction guarantees the truth of the combined prediction, but the converse fails. If an arbitrary single language conforms with the RTH, then the combined time amounts of all languages together should conform. But these combined time amounts could conform, without the relative time amounts of an arbitrary single language necessarily conforming.

It is impossible to prove or disprove the RTH, as testing would require access to the total time period during which languages have been in existence. The strongest argument in its favor is, therefore, the indirect one in terms of language quantities. Those who wish to argue against the RTH must use this same indirect evidence, by demonstrating how synchronic language quantities could be the way they are at the same time that the RTH was false.[2]

Although the RTH is not testable, it does make a number of more specific, probabilistic predictions for the recent recorded past, which can be tested in a limited way against the records that we have. The available data cannot technically disconfirm these probabilistic predictions, yet they are worth enumerating, for the following reasons: They are derived from the RTH, which makes a precise historical prediction, with indirect synchronic support; the absence of direct historical support is no reason to dismiss the reality which underlies the RTH, in this or in any other field which attempts to uncover facts about the distant past; and because of the absence of sufficient historical data, it becomes the more urgent to appreciate the kinds of consequences that this current reality has for the past, so that we do not totally ignore the RTH in our historical theorizing, which is inevitably based on recent data.

These more specific, probabilistic predictions of the RTH include the following:

1. In attested historical records, the evolving daughter languages of some parent which are relatively harmonic by CCH will, all things being equal, retain their word order co-occurrences for longer periods of time than daughter languages with less harmonic orders.
2. In attested historical records, the daughter languages that introduce some common degree of disharmony first should, all things being equal, resolve it soonest.
3. In attested historical records, languages that are extremely disharmonic by CCH are predicted to relieve their disharmony within a short time span: specifically, within a time span which is less than that occupied by each of the more harmonic word order co-occurrences in the recorded history of that language—all things being equal.

To these three predictions we can add:

4. All things being equal, the more disharmonic a language's word order co-occurrence set, the more susceptible it is to contact borrowing from neighboring languages (on account of the relative complexity and internal instability of the grammar; Section 4.6).

These predictions are probabilistic for the simple reason that the small time slice of the recent past represents just a fraction of each language's total period of existence and gives us only part of the data needed to test the RTH. We are not predicting, and have no reason to expect, that the RTH will necessarily hold within each slice of 200, 500, or even 1000 years in a language's history, though this is more likely than not, and certainly the longer the time span under investigation, the greater the likelihood that RTH's predictions will be fulfilled within the relevant period. Thus, the RTH makes precise predictions for combined time amounts throughout a single language's total history, and for combined time amounts throughout the histories of all languages, with arbitrary time slices being expected to obey the RTH only with greater likelihood than not.

6.3 A Brief Illustration of the Relative Time Hypothesis' Predictions

I shall give only a brief, informal illustration of the RTH's Prediction (1). I have chosen to consider this prediction because it sheds some light on the fact that some of the Indo-European languages have undergone much greater word order fluctuations in their recorded histories than others.

The most stable Indo-European subfamily with respect to word order is probably Celtic (cf. Friedrich 1975:58–61), which has had throughout its recorded history almost maximal cross-category harmony: predominantly noun-initial, predominantly verb-initial, and prepositional orders. By contrast, Germanic has been one of the least stable branches. The earliest recorded stage, Late Common Germanic, was shown in Section 5.3.3 to have had word orders that are extremely disharmonic: predominantly noun initial, primarily verb final, and prepositional. This extreme disharmony between noun and verb position, and verb and adposition orders, was apparently short-lived. Gothic has primarily prenominal modifiers, matching SOV, both being, however, disharmonic with prepositions. The noun phrase clearly underwent significant change from LCGmc to Gothic, becoming more harmonic with verb position, but less harmonic with adposition order.

The earliest North Germanic records of A.D. 600–800 (see J. Smith 1971) also show a considerable alteration of LCGmc word order: predominantly verb-second, mixed preposed and postposed noun modifiers, and prepositions. The verb has now shifted position, matching prepositions, with noun position less initial than before (e.g., the adjective now precedes the noun, as in Gothic and early West Germanic).

The earliest West Germanic daughters have also radically abandoned the LCGmc word orders (see Table 36). In all of them the noun is now predominantly final within the NP, verb-final orders constitute only a third of all verb positions, with verb-second and verb-first being in the majority (see Section 5.3.4 for precise figures), and they are prepositional. Verb position and adposition order are therefore more harmonic than in LCGmc, though noun and adposition orders are much less so.

This stage is also short-lived. In the middle periods of English and German, there is considerable postposing of adjectives and genitives behind the noun (Section 5.3.4), making the noun more initial within the NP, matching prepositions, while the verb moves increasingly forward in the sentence (particularly in English where all verb-final orders are eliminated), a development that also matches prepositions.

This (relatively harmonic) stage is also short-lived. In the early modern periods the noun moves to the right of adjectives and numerous genitives in both English and German (Section 5.3.5). And German develops its prenominal relative clause strategy, and shifts the verb into a more rigidly final position. The result is that Modern English and German are both now extremely disharmonic by CCH:

Noun order & adposition order
English: Primarily noun-final & prepositional: extreme disharmony
German: Even more noun-final & prepositional (with a limited number of postpositions, cf. Section 5.3.5): extreme disharmony
Verb order & adposition order
English: SVO & prepositional: relative harmony
German: A majority of verb-final structures & prepositional (limited postpositions): disharmony
Noun order & verb order
English: Primarily noun-final & SVO: disharmony
German: Predominantly noun-final & a majority of verb-final structures: relative harmony

Two of the three pairs for each language exhibit quite considerable disharmony. I would predict that this present stage of disharmony will be short-lived, and that change is imminent. Across the languages of the world, this degree of disharmony is very rare, as the quantitative data of Chapter 4 will have shown.

The important point about Germanic, however, is that there has been considerable word order instability, following the extreme disharmony of both LCGmc and the earliest East and West Germanic daughters. These periods of extreme disharmony were short-lived, and there has been considerable fluctuation in basic word orders since then. The current stages of extreme disharmony in English and German can also be predicted to be short-lived. By contrast, the Celtic languages, which began their recorded lives with considerable CCH, have not undergone any such severe word order changes. And, whereas extreme harmony is matched by stability (Celtic) and extreme disharmony by sweeping changes (Germanic), it seems that more intermediate degrees of harmony throughout the attested stages of Indo-European (cf., e.g., Greek and the Romance languages) are matched by more modest word order changes, culminating in much more harmonic word order co-occurrences in the modern period (particularly in Romance).

Notes

1. As we trace individual languages back in time, it becomes necessary to use parent languages as the earlier stages of what are now separate individual languages. Thus, Latin is an earlier stage of both French and Spanish; Proto-Indo-European is an earlier stage again; and so on. Different members of the same language family will therefore share identical word order time amounts up to the point where the relevant daughters separate from the parent.

2. The trivial argument—that current synchronic language quantities just happen to be atypical—is, of course, inadmissible unless some justification can be given (which it cannot). We have no grounds for assuming that implicational and distributional universal constraints on languages were any different in the past from what they are today.

7 : *Language Universals and the Logic of Historical Reconstruction*

Chapters 5 and 6 explored the predictions made by implicational and distributional universals for word order change. Within historical linguistics, language universals are also productively employed in the methodologically quite distinct (and for some—e.g., Lightfoot 1979—quite questionable) task of reconstructing hypothesized protolanguages together with the putative changes which link these to their attested daughters; see, in particular, Lehmann (1974) and Friedrich (1975). As the synchronic universals that these authors employ are subject to some of the problems we have pointed out in Chapters 2–4, we shall formulate laws of reasoning for historical reconstruction that are derivable from our own implicational and distributional universals, and we shall illustrate the workings of these laws in relation to some problematic data in Indo-European and Bantu.

The chapter is organized as follows. Section 7.1 summarizes the major criteria that are generally employed in historical reconstruction. In sections 7.2–7.6 five laws of reasoning derived from synchronic universals are defined and illustrated: Universal Consistency in Reconstruction (Section 7.2); Deductive Inference (Section 7.3); The Reconstruction of Doubling Innovations (Section 7.4); The Logic of Competing Variants (Section 7.5); and Inductive Inference (Section 7.6).

7.1 The Method of Historical Reconstruction

Where the daughter languages of some parent all share a given property, *P*, there is no reconstruction problem. We deduce that *P* was a protolanguage property and that it has simply been inherited by all the daughters. Difficulties arise when the daughter languages vary with respect to some linguistic property. The selection of one (or very occasionally none) of the variants as the protolanguage property is then based on an inferencing procedure which draws on numerous reconstruction criteria. The major criteria are the following:

1. *Age:* All things being equal, the older some daughter language, *L*, the more it is considered to approximate to the protolanguage, as there is that much less time during which changes could have taken place. As a result, it is that much more likely that *L*'s version of some variant property (a phoneme, morpheme, word order, etc.) is that of the protolanguage.

2. *Quantities:* All things being equal, the more daughter languages and/or branches of a family there are with some shared variant property, P_i, the more likely it is that P_i was the protolanguage variant. (This is a weak criterion – when it is in conflict with other criteria, these generally take precedence.)

3. *Geographical location:* Where there are variants of a given property among daughter languages, geographical location may be able to explain some of these as a result of contact with, and borrowing from, neighboring languages. All things being equal, such variants are then eliminated from consideration as properties of the protolanguage.

4. *Morphological pointers:* The method of internal reconstruction uses frozen morphological patterns as pointers to earlier, more productive, rules and structures of the parent language (or of some stage intervening between the parent language and the attested daughter), for example, earlier phonological rules (Umlaut in Germanic), earlier more productive morphological variants (Ablaut), and earlier syntactic word order patterns (cf. Givón 1971). All things being equal, such internally reconstructed properties may be assigned to the protolanguage (age, etc., permitting).

5. *Compatibility with daughter language variants:* All things being equal, whichever variant is chosen as the protolanguage property from among competing variants should be that which is most compatible with all the attested variation in the daughter languages, that is, which best explains why the attested variants, rather than others, are the ones found in the different daughters, and which harmonizes best with other changes in the respective daughters.

6. *Protolanguage consistency:* Whichever variant is chosen as the protolanguage property from among competing variants must be consistent with the other properties that are independently reconstructible for the protolanguage.

7.2 Universal Consistency in Reconstruction (UCR)

Universal Consistency in Reconstruction (UCR) requires that reconstructed protolanguages be consistent with synchronic universal implications, as must all the intermediate language stages separating the protolanguage from the attested daughters.

This law is a special instance of UCH (Universal Consistency in History; cf. Section 5.1) within a reconstruction context, and it is supported by the same range of synchronic and diachronic evidence. It asserts that one can only reconstruct (in this context, word order) co-occurrence sets that are independently attested universally. By invoking language universals in this way, we contribute to the definition of Reconstruction Criterion (6), protolanguage consistency.

7.3 Deductive Inference (DI)

GIVEN: (*a*) a set of synchronic implicational universals of the form 'if *P* then *Q*', where *P* and *Q* represent one or more linguistic properties; and (*b*) a reconstructed partial protolanguage (or an incompletely attested dead language), *L*;

THEN: (1) if *L* can be independently reconstructed to have (/is attested with) property *P*, deduce the co-occurrence of *Q* (modus ponens); (2) if *L* can be independently reconstructed to have (/is attested with) property −*Q*, deduce the co-occurrence of −*P* (modus tollens); but (3) if *L* can be reconstructed to have (/is attested with) −*P* or *Q*, deduce nothing (as −*P* may co-occur with either *Q* or −*Q*, and *Q* may co-occur with either *P* or −*P*).

Consider as an illustration of this reasoning the data of the incompletely attested dead language, Late Common Germanic (see J. Smith 1971; Janda 1980; Section 5.3.3). There are no relative clauses attested in these early inscriptions (see Chapter 5, Note 8), but possessive adjectives, demonstrative determiners, and descriptive adjectives all follow the noun as the basic or only order, and LCGmc is prepositional (see Table 36). In Chapter 3 we established the following synchronic implicational universals, which are relevant in this context:

(XXI)	NPoss ⊃ NA (statistical)	(3.4.2.2)
(V′)	NDem ⊃ NA	(3.3.11)
(X)	Prep ⊃ (NA ⊃ NRel)	(3.3.5)

(XI′)	NDem ⊃ NRel	(3.3.14)
(XXIII)	NPoss ⊃ NRel	(3.4.2.2)

Late Common Germanic is consistent in its possessive adjective, demonstrative determiner, and descriptive adjective orders with (XXI) and (V′). But from Universals (X), (XI′), and (XXIII) we can now infer, via DI, that it had postnominal (rather than prenominal) relative clauses. All three universals conspire in this case to produce the same result. And we see hereby that DI can provide evidence about unattested linguistic properties in protolanguages and incompletely attested dead languages, by locating the known properties of, in this case, LCGmc in the universal co-occurrence sets in which they are well formed, and surveying the necessary accompanying properties.

7.4 The Reconstruction of Doubling Innovations (RDI)

The UCR and DI are laws of reconstruction founded on Universal Consistency in History (Section 5.1). We can also exploit the Doubling Acquisition Hypothesis and the Frequency Increase Hypothesis within a reconstruction context, by inferring which member of a pair of competing word order doublets was the more recently innovated (either acquired or increased). Our inferencing procedure assumes that word order changes in prerecorded periods obey both the DAH and the FIH. It can be adopted only for some word order doublets, however, as follows:

GIVEN: (*a*) a set of synchronic implicational universals of the form 'if *P* then *Q*', where *P* and *Q* represent one or more linguistic properties; and (*b*) the earliest records of a language, *L* (*L* may be extinct, or else a contemporary language with no recorded history);

THEN: (1) if *L* has exclusive *P* word orders and doubling on *Q* (i.e., *P* & $-Q/Q$), deduce that *Q* is the more recent innovating doublet, and $-Q$ the historical relic; (2) if *L* has doubling on *P* and exclusive $-Q$ word orders (i.e., $-P/P$ & $-Q$), deduce that $-P$ is the more recent innovating doublet, and *P* the historical relic; (3) if *L* has doubling on *P* and exclusive *Q* word orders (i.e., $-P/P$ & *Q*), or exclusive $-P$ word orders and doubling on *Q* (i.e., $-P$ & $-Q/Q$), deduce nothing.

Consider Case (1). Imagine that a *P* & $-Q/Q$ language had innovated $-Q$ more recently than *Q*. Then, whether *P* was the exclusive order before the first records, or whether some $-P$ doublets existed and *P* became the exclusive order by the time of the first records, makes no difference. This language has innovated a $*P \& -Q$ co-occurrence, which violates $P \supset Q$, and is forbidden by the FIH (and DAH). Hence, Q must be the innovating doublet, and $-Q$ the earlier historical relic. We have seen in Section 5.2 (see in particular Note 1 of Chapter 5) that the DAH and FIH are defined in terms of doubling structures *acquired* rather than *lost,* and permit relic doublets of the $P \& -Q/Q$ type to remain in a language for a certain period (as long as $-Q$ is not the basic doublet).

Case (2) is explainable in a similar way. If P were the more recently innovated doubling structure in a $-P/P \& -Q$ language ($-Q$ being 100% in the first records, and either being or becoming 100% just prior to these), the language would have innovated a $*P \& -Q$ co-occurrence. Only if $-P$ is the more recent innovation, and P the relic, is this avoided.

The Case (3) co-occurrences represent the synchronically most frequent types of doubling, in which languages exhibit a plurality of implicationally permitted word order co-occurrences, in combination (see Section 3.3.8). Thus, the co-occurrence $-P/P \& Q$ combines $P \& Q$ and $-P \& Q$, both of which are permitted by $P \supset Q$, while $-P \& -Q/Q$ combines $-P \& Q$ and $-P \& -Q$, both of which are again permitted by $P \supset Q$. As there is no potential $*P \& -Q$ co-occurrence in these cases, we can draw no inferences for reconstruction: Either P or $-P$ could be the most recent innovator in $-P/P \& Q$, and either $-Q$ or Q in $-P \& -Q/Q$.

Consider LCGmc again as illustration of the RDI. Late Common Germanic has 100% N + POSS and 100% N + ADJ, but doubling on the genitive: gen + n (50%)/n + gen (50%) (cf. Table 36). LCGmc provides us with a Case (1) co-occurrence, $P \& -Q/Q$, in relation to the universals NPoss ⊃ NG (Section 3.4.2.2) and (III) Prep ⊃ (NA ⊃ NG) (Section 3.2.3). By RDI reasoning, gen + n cannot be the innovating doublet, as this would result in increases in the forbidden co-occurrences *NPoss & GN and *Prep & NA & GN. Hence, n + gen must be the more recent innovator, with the gen + n structures relics of an earlier modifier before noun ordering, harmonic with SOV but disharmonic with prepositions.

7.5 The Logic of Competing Variants (LCV)

Before defining this law of reconstruction (Section 7.5.7), I shall illustrate its workings. The general purpose of the LCV is to reconstruct plausible typological features for a protolanguage which are most compatible with the attested daughter language variation. As a result, it contributes to the definition of Reconstruction Criterion (5), compatibility with daughter language variants (Section 7.1.5).

We argued in Section 3.5 that the notion of a "language type" does not mean that all operator–operand pairs are serialized in a uniform manner throughout a language. It means, instead, that languages of each given type exemplify one of a restricted and predictable number of co-occurrence sets defined by our implicational universals, subject to predicted distributional preferences. The major typological indicators are the "operand-peripheral" word orders, Prep/Postp, and VSO/SOV. By examining the word order co-occurrences found in the earliest daughter languages, it becomes possible to determine the synchronic compatibility of one or another typological indicator with all the attested daughter language variation, to reconstruct this property for the protolanguage, and to devise a diachronically plausible progression of events leading to the attested daughters.

We shall illustrate our method with respect to adposition, verb, and noun orders in Proto-Indo-European.

7.5.1 ADPOSITION ORDER IN PROTO-INDO-EUROPEAN

The implications of the PrNMH (Section 3.3.7) define the following four noun modifier co-occurrence sets (ignoring the smaller modifiers—demonstratives, numerals, and possessive adjectives):

(1) Subtype 1 (Prep) NAdj & NGen & NRel
Subtype 2 (Prep) AdjN NGen NRel
Subtype 3 (Prep) AdjN GenN NRel
Subtype 4 (Prep) AdjN GenN RelN

We pointed out in Section 5.3.1 that the earliest IE daughters appear to exemplify exactly these four noun modifier co-occurrences. We repeat the relevant table (Table 35′) for convenience (adding to it the Latin of Tacitus for greater completeness; see Friedrich 1975:56). What is remarkable about this correspondence between the noun modifier classes of IE and the four subtypes of (1) is that not all IE daughters have prepositions. Tocharian, Sanskrit, and Hittite are postpositional, and hence the noun modifier co-occurrences of these postpositional languages overlap with those permitted in prepositional languages, and there are no uniquely postpositional noun modifier co-occurrence types in early IE. Examples would be (cf. the PoNMH, Section 3.3.17):

(2) a. (Postp) NAdj & GenN & RelN
b. (Postp) NAdj & GenN & NRel

The total absence of Co-occurrences (2a) and (2b) in early IE is surprising, as some 44% (35) of 79 postpositional languages in Greenberg's Appendix

TABLE 35′ : Indo-European Noun Modifier Classes (Basic Word Orders Only)

Class 1: N_1	Class 2: N_2	Class 3: N_3	Class 4: N_4
/NAdj /NGen /NRel	AdjN/ /NGen /NRel	AdjN/ GenN/ /NRel	AdjN/ GenN/ RelN/
Celtic (VSO & Prep)	Albanian (SVO & Prep)	Old Persian (SOV & Prep)	Sanskrit (SOV & Postp)
Slavic (VSO & Prep)	Old Armenian (SVO & Prep)	Italic (Tacitus) (SOV & Prep)	Hittite (SOV & Postp)
Younger Avestan (SOV & Prep)	Homeric Greek (sov/svo & Prep)	Gothic (SOV & Prep)	
		Tocharian (SOV & Postp)	

II have either (2a) or (2b) as their noun modifier co-occurrences (i.e., NAdj & GenN), while another 44% have the overlapping noun modifier co-occurrences of Subtypes 3 and 4 in (1) for prepositional languages (i.e., AdjN & GenN). (The remaining postpositional languages in Appendix II have NAdj & NGen.) Hence, based on this synchronic evidence, there is an equal chance that the early postpositional IE daughters could have had (2a) or (2b) in lieu of Subtypes 3 and 4 of (1), and there is an almost 1-in-2 chance that any postpositional language will have either (2a) or (2b)—yet *none* of the IE languages do. They exhibit only those noun modifier co-occurrences which are also found in prepositional languages.[1]

7.5.2 PRELIMINARY INFERENCES

We can account for the facts of Section 7.5.1 in the following way:

Let us reconstruct prepositions (rather than postpositions, as in Lehmann 1974) for Proto-Indo-European. The evolving daughter languages will then have inherited prepositions, and these will have shaped the permitted noun modifier co-occurrences as the daughters divided themselves up into the available noun modifier classes, with increasing operator preposing down subtypes 1 through 4 of (1). The early IE noun modifier variation is therefore most simply explained as a reflex of the typological indicator, Prep, existing prior to the first records in *all* IE daughters. And though the typological indicator itself has changed in some branches (a minority), the co-occurrences of the first records provide a typological clue to PIE, which outlasts the typological indicator itself in some branches.

Those IE daughters that have changed prepositions to postpositions have done so at a point in their evolution when their noun modifier co-occurrences were logically compatible with both Prep and Postp. In this way consistency with all synchronic implicational universals is preserved (cf. UCR). As the postpositional languages grew out of prepositional languages (at some presumably recent stage between PIE and the first records), they exhibit no noun modifier co-occurrences of a uniquely postpositional nature, but only those which overlap with, and are properly included in, the prepositional co-occurrences. If PIE had been, conversely, postpositional, we might have expected to see the prepositional noun modifier co-occurrences properly included in those for postpositional languages.

The postpositional IE daughters are all SOV, and are either exclusively operator preposing within the NP (i.e., noun final) or predominantly so. It is precisely such extreme operator preposing relative to V and N which motivates the shift from prepositions to postpositions within the adposition phrase, by the principle of Cross-Category Harmony, as we shall now illustrate.

7.5.3 CROSS-LANGUAGE DISTRIBUTIONAL SUPPORT FOR PREPOSITIONS IN PIE

Early IE is heavily skewed toward prepositions, both in the relative quantities of its prepositional daughters and in the composition of its co-occurrence sets. Table 35′ reveals that 100% of IE VSO and SVO daughters are prepositional, as are 4 out of 7 SOV daughters (57%), 3 being postpositional (43%). By contrast, Table 39 shows that only 63% of SVO languages in Greenberg's Appendix II sample (77% of the Expanded Sample) have Prep, and only 8% of SOV languages in Appendix II (7% of the Expanded Sample) have Prep. The VSO co-occurrence figures are effectively the same in IE and the universal samples. Similarly, Table 35′ reveals that 100% of N_1 and N_2 orders in early IE co-occur with Prep, as do 75% of N_3 orders. Yet, Table 40 shows that only 60% of N_2 orders in the 30-language sample (59% in the Expanded Sample) co-occur with Prep, as do only 14% of N_3 orders (52% in the Expanded Sample). The N_1 and N_4 co-occurrence figures agree in IE and the universal samples. This skewing toward prepositions in early IE is readily explainable on the assumption that PIE was prepositional. If we assume original prepositions, then postpositions are the innovators, and they have been acquired in co-occurrence with all and only the word orders for which there is strong universal pressure in favor of postpositions: SOV, N_3, and N_4. By contrast, assume that PIE had postpositions. The innovation of prepositions now flies in the face of the synchronic evidence. Indo-European prepositions certainly occur in word order co-occurrences where they are to be expected (with VSO, SVO, and N_1)—but they have also been massively

TABLE 39 : Distribution of Adposition and Verb Co-occurrences

Early IE daughters (cf. Table 35′)		Greenberg's Appendix II (cf. Table 2)		Expanded Sample (cf. Table 41)	
VSO:	Pr/VSO = 2/2 = 100%	*VSO:*	Pr/VSO = 25/26 = 96%	*V-1:*	Pr/V-1 = 52/53 = 98%
	Po/VSO = 0/2 = 0%		Po/VSO = 1/26 = 4%		Po/V-1 = 1/53 = 2%
SVO:	Pr/SVO = 2/2 = 100%	*SVO:*	Pr/SVO = 33/52 = 63%	*SVO:*	Pr/SVO = 84/109 = 77%
	Po/SVO = 0/2 = 0%		Po/SVO = 19/52 = 37%		Po/SVO = 25/109 = 23%
SOV:	Pr/SOV = 4/7 = 57%	*SOV:*	Pr/SOV = 5/64 = 8%	*SOV:*	Pr/SOV = 12/174 = 7%
	Po/SOV = 3/7 = 43%		Po/SOV = 59/64 = 92%		Po/SOV = 162/174 = 93%

Note: Pr/SOV = 4/7 = 57% means '4 out of 7 SOV languages, or 57%, have Prep', etc.

TABLE 40 : Distribution of Adposition and Noun Co-occurrences

Early IE daughters (cf. Table 35′)	Greenberg's 30-language sample (cf. Table 15)	Expanded Sample (cf. Language Index)
N_1: $Pr/N_1 = 3/3 = 100\%$	N_1: $Pr/N_1 = 12/12 = 100\%$	N_1: $Pr/N_1 = 65/68 = 96\%$
$Po/N_1 = 0/3 = 0\%$	$Po/N_1 = 0/12 = 0\%$	$Po/N_1 = 3/68 = 4\%$
N_2: $Pr/N_2 = 3/3 = 100\%$	N_2: $Pr/N_2 = 3/5 = 60\%$	N_2: $Pr/N_2 = 19/32 = 59\%$
$Po/N_2 = 0/3 = 0\%$	$Po/N_2 = 2/5 = 40\%$	$Po/N_2 = 13/32 = 41\%$
N_3: $Pr/N_3 = 3/4 = 75\%$	N_3: $Pr/N_3 = 1/7 = 14\%$	N_3: $Pr/N_3 = 11/21 = 52\%$
$Po/N_3 = 1/4 = 25\%$	$Po/N_3 = 6/7 = 86\%$	$Po/N_3 = 10/21 = 48\%$
N_4: $Pr/N_4 = 0/2 = 0\%$	N_4: $Pr/N_4 = 0/4 = 0\%$	N_4: $Pr/N_4 = 1/29 = 3\%$
$Po/N_4 = 2/2 = 100\%$	$Po/N_4 = 4/4 = 100\%$	$Po/N_4 = 28/29 = 97\%$

Note: $Pr/N_3 = 3/4 = 75\%$ means '3 out of 4 N_3 languages, or 75%, have Prep' (N relative to Adj, Gen, and Rel in these calculations).

innovated in co-occurrence with SOV, although only 8%/7% of SOV languages are prepositional in current synchronic samples. Prepositions have also gone overboard with N_3 (75% versus 14%/52% on universal evidence), and with N_2 (100% versus 60%/59%). The reconstruction of postpositions for Proto-Indo-European necessarily leads to the unfortunate conclusion that prepositions were innovated not only in the majority of IE daughters, but in numerous co-occurrences for which all other languages of the world demonstrate an overwhelming preference for, or strong tolerance of, postpositions rather than prepositions.

Thus, the percentage figures from Greenberg's samples and the Expanded Sample are quantifying different degrees of structural pressure in favor of Prep or Postp, as a function of the co-occurring N and V positions. If we assume that PIE had Prep, we can say that only those daughters changed Prep > Postp whose N and V positions introduced a very strong structural pressure to do so. Such strength is presumably needed to counteract the conservative pressure against change (why change unless there is good reason?) and explains why not all the relevant daughter languages have changed Prep > Postp.

One final piece of evidence against assuming Postp > Prep as an early innovation comes from the fact that there are no good reasons why adposition order should spearhead the drive toward operator preposing (as it would in the co-occurrences Pr & SOV, Pr & N_3, in early IE, given the Postp > Prep reconstruction). All the attempts to motivate individual early word order changes discussed in Section 5.4 involve the modifiers of the verb and of the noun (with the exception of serial verb and adposition reanalyses, which are not relevant for IE).

7.5.4 VERB ORDER IN PROTO-INDO-EUROPEAN

7.5.4.1 Distributional Evidence

If Proto-Indo-European was prepositional, then SOV is a most unlikely co-occurrence. Only 8% of prepositional languages in Greenberg's Appendix II and the Expanded Sample are SOV (5 out of 63 in Appendix II; 12 out of 148 in the Expanded Sample). By contrast, 40% of Appendix II prepositional languages are VSO (VSO/Pr = $^{25}/_{63}$ = 40%), and 35% of the Expanded Sample prepositional languages are V-1 (V-1/Pr = $^{52}/_{148}$ = 35%). Furthermore, 52% of Appendix II prepositional languages are SVO (SVO/Pr = $^{33}/_{63}$ = 52%), and 57% of the Expanded Sample prepositional languages are SVO (SVO/Pr = $^{84}/_{148}$ = 57%). Either VSO (/V-1) or SVO are therefore much more likely PIE verb positions than SOV, with SVO being preferred.

7.5.4.2 Implicational Evidence

Universals (I) SOV ⊃ (AN ⊃ GN) and (II) VSO ⊃ (NA ⊃ NG) define the following co-occurrence sets respectively (Sections 3.2.1, 3.2.2):

(3) Subtype 1 (SOV) AdjN & GenN
Subtype 2 (SOV) NAdj GenN
Subtype 3 (SOV) NAdj NGen

(4) Subtype 1 (VSO) NAdj & NGen
Subtype 2 (VSO) AdjN NGen
Subtype 3 (VSO) AdjN GenN

Universal (I) defines the same set of adjective and genitive co-occurrences as does Universal (IV) Postp ⊃ (AN ⊃ GN) (Section 3.2.4), and (II) matches (III) Prep ⊃ (NA ⊃ NG) (Section 3.2.3). No comparable implications are possible for SVO, which co-occurs with all possible combinations of adjective and genitive orders.

Once again, the attested co-occurrences of early IE are exactly those which are permitted by the implication NA ⊃ NG in Universals (II) and (III), whereas AN ⊃ GN in (I) and (IV) makes different predictions. Specifically, VSO is compatible with all and only the IE noun modifier co-occurrences of Table 35′. SVO is compatible with all, but not only, the IE noun modifier co-occurrences (as SVO can co-occur universally with NAdj & GenN, which is unattested in IE). But SOV is compatible neither with all nor with only the IE noun modifier co-occurrences (SOV is universally compatible with the unattested NAdj & GenN, and is not compatible with the attested AdjN & NGen).

Nor can the total absence in early IE of NAdj & GenN with SOV [i.e., Subtype 2 of (3)] be attributed to the rarity of this co-occurrence universally. I calculate that 41% of SOV & Po languages in Greenberg's Appendix II (24 out of 59) have it (35% for the Expanded Sample: 56 out of 162), whereas 47% (28 out of 59) have AdjN & GenN, that is, Subtype 1 of (3), corresponding to IE noun modifier classes 3 and 4 in Table 35′ (59% for the Expanded Sample: 95 out of 162). The co-occurrence NAdj & GenN is therefore found in over one-third of all SOV & Po languages, whereas AdjN & GenN is found in over one-half. But this difference in distribution is not so great that one would expect all SOV & Po languages in IE to be of the latter type. And the total absence of SOV & Po & NA & GN is therefore in need of explanation.

The SOV noun modifier co-occurrences of IE are thus properly included in those permitted in VSO and SVO languages universally. Following the reasoning of Section 7.5.2, I see this as evidence for PIE being either VSO or SVO, with SOV arising in those dialects only whose noun modifier co-occurrences overlap with those of the earlier verb position (thereby obeying UCH). The absence of uniquely SOV-type noun modifier co-occurrences in early IE, despite some distributional pressure in their favor, then follows from the fact that SOV grew (relatively recently) out of VSO/SVO, rather than vice versa.

The implicational evidence thus supports the distributional evidence that PIE had either VSO or SVO, but not SOV.

7.5.5 NOUN MODIFIER ORDERS IN PROTO-INDO-EUROPEAN

Let us assume on the basis of the foregoing that PIE was prepositional, and either VSO or SVO. If PIE was VSO, then the most likely noun modifier co-occurrence class to reconstruct from Table 35′ for the parent language is N_1 (i.e., NAdj & NGen & NRel). Of VSO & Pr languages in Greenberg's 30-language sample, 100% (6 out of 6) are N_1; of VSO & Pr languages in Appendix II, 76% (19 out of 25) are N_1, with 20% (5 out of 25) being N_2 (i.e., AdjN & NGen & NRel); in the Expanded Sample, 73% of V-1 & Pr languages (38 out of 52) are N_1, with 25% N_2 (13 out of 52). If PIE was SVO, the most likely co-occurrence is again N_1, as 64% of SVO & Pr languages in Appendix II are N_1 (21 out of 33), with 24% N_2 (8 out of 33), and 67% of SVO & Pr languages in the Expanded Sample have N_1 (56 out of 84), with 20% N_2 (17 out of 84). With either VSO & SVO, therefore, we are led to reconstruct NGen & NRel for the parent language, and we prefer a reconstruction of NAdj over AdjN.

It is interesting that the N and V positions in early IE are well balanced and almost exactly what the universal synchronic distributions would predict, in contrast to the adposition orders of Section 7.5.3. The N_1 IE languages of Table 35′ are predominantly VSO (V_1), the N_2 languages are predominantly SVO (V_2), the N_3 languages are exclusively SOV (mostly nonrigid V_3, in fact), and the N_4 languages are that much more rigidly verb final (V_4), (compare Section 4.5).

I conclude that PIE was prepositional, either VSO or SVO, and most likely N_1 (NAdj & NGen & NRel) although possibly N_2 (AdjN & NGen & NRel). And I would rule out the following reconstructions on universal grounds: Postp, SOV, GenN, and RelN.

7.5.6 UNIVERSAL EVIDENCE AND OTHER RECONSTRUCTION CRITERIA

Before defining LCV precisely, it should be stressed that the reasoning employed here does not definitely prove that PIE had the word orders for which I have argued, as these results must be seen alongside the other reconstruction criteria of Section 7.1. For example, the age criterion appears to argue against it, as the oldest attested dialects have SOV, Postp, etc. What my argumentation does reveal is the evidence of synchronic universals for the reconstruction process. What weight is to be given to this evidence must then depend on the other reconstruction criteria.

But having mentioned this important qualification, it should be added that any kind of language-universal evidence is by definition very strong, and the conclusions of this section cannot be dismissed lightly. In the present instance the universal evidence is particularly important, for two reasons.

First, given the extreme word order variation within early IE, and given the very uneven recorded time depth across the different branches, it does not follow that the dialects which are recorded earliest are necessarily the most conservative. Our universal evidence suggests that, if we had comparable recorded time depths for all IE families, the oldest records of a great number of them would be more in line with the word orders which we have proposed for PIE. And, given the relative rapidity of word order change, it is very possible that significant word order changes occurred between the break-up of the parent language (3000 BC) and the first attested records (1700 BC).

Second, the other reconstruction criteria do not yield unambiguous results when applied to Indo-European. There is currently a stalemate between the two major authors on this topic: Lehmann (1974) and Friedrich (1975). Lehmann stresses the antiquity of the OV dialects, their quantity, and also morphological pointers, in reconstructing the operator-before-operand (OV) type for PIE. Friedrich (1975), on the other hand, disputes the strength of the quantitative and age evidence (asserting the frequent occurrence of VO in many dialects, plus the strength of VO in the early attested Homeric Greek), and appeals to geographical location (the proximity of non-IE OV languages to the OV IE daughters) as the source of a possible contact borrowing of OV features. For Friedrich a VO reconstruction is therefore just as likely.

The universal evidence of this section argues in favor of operand-before-operator orders in PIE more in line with the reconstruction of Friedrich (1975). And I see in the earliest IE daughters evidence for an increasing preposing of operators relative to the noun and the verb, with the Prep > Postp change occurring only in those dialects which underwent extreme operator preposing, and in which there existed the strongest pressure to harmonize the adposition phrase with noun and verb orders (Section 7.5.3).

7.5.7 THE LOGIC OF COMPETING VARIANTS (LCV): DEFINITION

GIVEN:

(*a*) a set of properties (in this context, word orders) which vary throughout the attested daughters of some language family, F, such that the attested co-occurrences are, for example: Q, R, S; $-Q$, R, S; $-Q$, $-R$, S; $-Q$, $-R$, $-S$; and only these;[2]

(*b*) a further (word order) property, P_i, and its converse, P_j, both of which are attested in the daughter languages of F;

(*c*) a synchronic implicational universal, U_i, which permits P_i to co-occur in current synchronic language samples with all (and possibly only) the co-occurrences of F (Q, R, S; $-Q$, R, S; etc.); and an implicational universal, U_j, permitting P_j to co-occur in current synchronic language samples with some, but not all, of the co-occurrences of F, and also with co-occurrences not attested in F; P_i and P_j having thereby the status of "typological indicators" for the co-occurrence sets defined by U_i and U_j respectively;[3]

(*d*) a distributional universal (CCH) which can motivate the acquisition of P_j from P_i in all and only those co-occurrences of F that have it, on the basis of strong preferences for the presence of P_j in the appropriate co-occurrences universally; whereas the acquisition of P_i from P_j would involve a widespread innovation of P_i in co-occurrences of F in which P_i is universally very rare or nonpreferred.

THEN: Reconstruct P_i, rather than P_j, as the protolanguage typological indicator, on the following grounds:

(1) P_i is logically compatible with all the attested variation in all the daughter languages of F (in the sense that P_i is found universally together with all the co-occurrences of F, as defined by the implication U_i).

(2) The co-occurrences with typological indicator P_j in F are properly included in the set defined for type P_i languages universally by U_i; but the co-occurrences with P_i in F are not properly included in the set defined for type P_j languages universally by U_j.[4]

[Thus, (1) and (2) suggest that property P_i shaped the permissible co-occurrences in all the daughters of F until shortly before the first records, whereupon some daughters shifted $P_i > P_j$. But the combined co-occurrence sets of all the daughters act as a pointer to a preceding, undocumented stage, in which they were all type P_i.]

(3) The acquisition of P_j from P_i can be universally motivated by CCH in the relevant daughter languages of F, but the reverse innovation ($P_j > P_i$) cannot be so motivated.

7.6 Inductive Inference (II)

GIVEN: A universal of language distribution (CCH) defining the relative cross-category harmony of numerous word order co-occurrence pairs *A* & *B* versus *A′* & *B′* (see Sections 4.2.3 and 4.2.5), for example, Pr & N_1 versus Pr & N_2, Pr & N_2 versus Pr & N_3, etc.; and predicting derivatively the relative frequencies of whole co-occurrence sets across the languages of the world (see Section 4.2.8). For example, CCH predicts a declining frequency for Subtypes 1–4 of the prepositional languages of (1). Greenberg's 30-language sample quantities confirm CCH's prediction (Expanded Sample quantities in parentheses):

(1′) Subtype 1 Prep & NAdj & NGen & NRel = Pr & N_1
12 languages (65)
Subtype 2 Prep AdjN NGen NRel = Pr & N_2
3 languages (19)
Subtype 3 Prep AdjN GenN NRel = Pr & N_3
1 language (11)
Subtype 4 Prep AdjN GenN RelN = Pr & N_4
0 languages (1)

THEN:

(1) *Relative Probability* (RP): All things being equal, the less the cross-category harmony of *A* & *B* or *A′* & *B′*, the less likely it is that the relevant co-occurrence set was that of the protolanguage. For example, if Prep can be independently reconstructed for some protolanguage, *L*, then the co-occurrences of Subtypes 1 through 4 in (1′) can be reconstructed with decreasing likelihood.

(2) *Relative Quantities* (RQ): All things being equal, the less the cross-category harmony of *A* & *B* or *A′* & *B′*, the fewer the number of daughter languages that should be assumed to have had the relevant co-occurrences in their histories.

(3) *Relative Time* (RT): All things being equal, the less the cross-category harmony of *A* & *B* or *A′* & *B′*, the less should be the total time period both for each single daughter language and for all daughter languages combined, during which the relevant co-occurrences are postulated.

Notice that RT is founded on the assumption that there is a correlation between language quantities on current synchronic evidence and relative time amounts for the relevant co-occurrence sets in language history, in accordance with the Relative Time Hypothesis (6.2).

7.6.1 EXAMPLE: THE RECONSTRUCTION OF PROTO-BANTU WORD ORDER

The basic word order of almost all Bantu languages is SVO & Pr & NAdj & NGen & NRel [i.e., Prepositional Type 1—cf. (1′)—with SVO]. But Larry Hyman (personal communication) informs me that there are two Bantu languages, Tunen and Bandem, which are Type 1 with SOV.

(9)	*Type A: Tunen and Bandem*	*Type B: All other Bantu languages*
	SOV	SVO
	Pr	Pr
	NAdj	NAdj
	NGen	NGen
	NRel	NRel

What then was the verb order of Proto-Bantu?

By Reconstruction Criterion 2 (quantities), Type B clearly wins. But, by Reconstruction Criterion 3 (geographical location), Type A is considered by Hyman to be at the very least a serious contender: Tunen and Bandem are spoken in the Cameroon grasslands, at the source of Bantu radiation and spread to east and south; and they are isolated communities which may have been less susceptible to contact influence by other (predominantly SVO) languages of Africa.[5]

However, the universal evidence clearly supports Type B, by Inductive Inference:

Relative Probability (RP): Type B is a more harmonic co-occurrence set by CCH, a fact that is reflected in our synchronic samples: Appendix II contains 21 Type B languages, but only 4 Type A languages; the Expanded Sample contains 56 Type B languages, and 10 Type A languages. Type B is therefore a more probable Proto-Bantu co-occurrence.

Relative Quantities (RQ): If Type A is reconstructed, all the daughters will have inherited it, and all but Tunen and Bandem will have changed it into Type B. If Type B is reconstructed, only Tunen and Bandem need be assumed to have ever had a universally rare co-occurrence. The quantity of Bantu daughters for which a universally rare co-occurrence set needs to be postulated is, therefore, much greater for a Type A than for a Type B reconstruction.

Relative Time (RT): If Type A is reconstructed, Tunen and Bandem will have retained this universally rare co-occurrence set throughout their histories, and all the other daughters will have inherited it, kept it for a certain period, and changed it prior to the first records. But if we reconstruct Type B, none of the Bantu languages except Tunen and Bandem need ever have had the universally rare Type A co-occurrence, and even Tunen and Bandem can have acquired it fairly recently. The total time periods both for Tunen and Bandem and for all daughter languages during which the universally rare co-occurrence set needs to be postulated is therefore much less with Type B.

7.7 Conclusions

The major purpose of this chapter has been to propose some laws of historical reconstruction derived from a different set of synchronic universals from that which is usually employed. The chief novelty of our approach lies in the fact that a language "type" is defined as the set-theoretic union of a restricted and predictable number of co-occurrence sets (or subtypes), each of which contains a typological indicator for that type, such as Prepositions, Postpositions, SOV, etc. The members of these sets are determined by implicational universals, and the relative frequency and distribution of the various permitted co-occurrence sets is predicted by the principle of Cross-Category Harmony. By matching these universal co-occurrence sets against the earliest attested co-occurrences of the relevant properties in the daughter languages of some family, and against the partially attested or reconstructed data of dead languages, we can reason our way to reconstructed language systems, and we can fill in missing details from dead languages.

Crucial to my approach is the recognition that there is a large discrepancy synchronically between the small number of co-occurrence sets which are attested, and the very much larger number of mathematically possible co-occurrences of linguistic properties which are unattested.

In the area of historical change (see Chapter 5) this discrepancy enables us to predict the relative ordering of numerous individual changes in the transition from one language stage to another, by locating the acquired properties within the set(s) of co-occurrences in which they are well-formed, and surveying the necessarily accompanying properties (here word orders) within these sets. We predict that these latter must have been acquired prior to, or simultaneously with, the former.

And in the area of reconstruction we can use the attested and permitted co-occurrence sets (together with their relative frequencies) to argue for the compatibility (cf. Criterion 5, Section 7.1) of one reconstruction property versus another with all the variant subtypes of the daughters; we can define protolanguage consistency (cf. Criterion 6, Section 7.1) and use this consistency to deduce the details of totally reconstructed or partially attested dead languages; and we can exploit relative language frequencies in making inductive inferences about parent language word order co-occurrences, with degrees of probability reflecting current language quantities.

Notes

1. This quantitative argument is weakened by the figures from the Expanded Sample: Of postpositional languages, 36.2% have either (2a) or (2b) (68 out of 188 postpositional languages), whereas 58% (109 out of 188) have the AdjN & GenN co-occurrence corresponding to Subtypes 3 and 4 of (1). There is therefore a greater chance that a postpositional language will have AdjN & GenN. However, whereas Appendix II would lead us to expect that half of the postpositional IE languages would have either (2a) or (2b), we still expect that at least one-third should. All things being equal, we do not expect all of the IE postpositional languages to have the AdjN & GenN co-occurrence. See also Section 7.5.4.

2. In the examples of Sections 7.5.1 and 7.5.4, *Q*, *R*, and *S* represent word orders comprising a head (operand) category and a single modifier (operator) category, and $-Q$, $-R$, etc., represent the (unique) opposite order for each head and modifier pair.

3. P_i and P_j represent word orders comprising an identical operand plus one or more identical operators, with different relative orderings of operand and operator(s) in the two cases. In the example of Section 7.5.1, P_i represents adposition before NP, that is, prepositions (co-occurring universally with all and only the co-occurrences of *F*); and P_j represents adposition after NP, that is, postpositions (co-occurring universally neither with all nor with only *F*'s co-occurrences). In Section 7.5.4, P_i represents either VSO (co-occurring universally with all and only the co-occurrences of *F*) or SVO (co-occurring universally with all but not only the co-occurrences of *F*); and P_j represents SOV (co-occurring universally neither with all nor with only *F*'s co-occurrences).

4. That is, the co-occurrences with postpositions in *F* are properly included in those with prepositions universally; and the co-occurrences with SOV in *F* are properly included in those with either VSO or SVO universally.

5. Cf. Givón (1975) for the reconstruction of SOV for Niger-Congo generally.

8 : *The Expanded Sample*

In this chapter we present the Expanded Sample. We have already considered Expanded Sample data in the presentation of both the implicational universals of Chapter 3 and the distributional universal of Chapter 4. We must now classify the Expanded Sample itself.

The Expanded Sample is primarily an extension of Greenberg's Appendix II, though with additional word order data collected for as many languages as possible. In a seminar on word order which I organized at the University of Southern California in the Spring of 1978, one of the collective projects was to check Greenberg's entries, as far as possible, and to add both languages and word orders to the sample. Some additional data were also collected between 1974 and 1976 in seminars on universal grammar held at Cambridge University (organized by Ed Keenan) and at Essex University (organized by David Kilby and myself). Since 1978 I have added numerous languages to the sample, working on an individual basis. Despite these additions, the Expanded Sample is still a convenience sample, with choice of languages reflecting the interests and expertise of the contributors, the availability of sources of information, and the original Greenberg sample. No attempt was made to collect fixed numbers of languages from the various language families, from the various geographical regions, or from the various language types. But contributors were encouraged not to work on the same language family or group wherever possible, in order to maximize genetic diversity.

The Expanded Sample is given in Section 8.1, and is classified both typologically and genetically. Only the Appendix II word orders and types are listed here. All the other word orders researched for each language are given in the Language Index, together with the source(s) of information.

8.1 The Expanded Sample: Typological and Genetic Classification

The typological classification of the Expanded Sample divides languages into essentially the same 24 possible types as in Greenberg's Appendix II, though with V-1 (Verb-first) replacing VSO, for reasons discussed in Section 3.2.2. Where a language is VOS or V-initial, this is indicated in parentheses. Where no such indication is given, the language is VSO. The sources of information on the basis of which typological classification has been made are various. They include previous classifications, such as Greenberg (1966) or Ultan (1978); individual descriptive studies and grammars; native informant work (conducted either by myself or by a collaborator); and occasionally personal information from a knowledgeable and reliable linguist. The Language Index lists the precise source for each language. Obviously, the reliability of the classification will be no greater than the adequacy and informativeness of the source.

The genetic classification is based primarily on Ruhlen (1976). The sytem of presentation is as follows. Within each of the 24 language types, genetic affiliations of the exemplifying languages are listed in parentheses. Language families are written in capital letters, for example, (AFRO–ASIATIC), and listed in alphabetic order. Within each language family, the major genetic subgroupings are given, also in alphabetical order, and in descending order of inclusion, for example, (Semitic:North). To the right of each such genetic subgrouping are listed the exemplifying languages of that word order type. Each subgrouping begins on a separate line, and is closed off with a "/". Occasionally, no subgrouping is given beyond the overall language family itself.

A number of classificational changes have been made relative to Greenberg's Appendix II. These are summarized in Note 2 of Chapter 2.

Type 1 V-1/Pr/NG/NA

(AFRO-ASIATIC): (Semitic:North) Aramaic, Biblical Hebrew/
(Semitic:South:Ethiopic) Ge'ez/
(Semitic:South:Southwest) Ancient Egyptian, Iraqi Arabic, Syrian Arabic/
Berber/
(ANDEAN-EQUATORIAL): (Equatorial:Arawakan:Maipuran:Southern) Baure (VOS)/
(AUSTRO-TAI: AUSTRONESIAN): (Indonesian:East) Wolio/
(Indonesian:West) Malagasay (VOS), Toba Batak (VOS)/
(Oceanic) Fijian (V-initial)/
(Oceanic:Eastern:Micronesian) Gilbertese (VOS)/
(Oceanic:Eastern:Polynesian) Polynesian languages, Easter Island, Hawaiian, Maori, Nieuan, Samoan (V-initial), Tahitian, Tongan (V-initial)/
(INDO-EUROPEAN): Celtic languages/
(Celtic:Goidelic) Modern Irish, Old Irish, Scots Gaelic/
(Celtic:Brythonic) Welsh/
(NILO-SAHARAN): (Chari-Nile:Sudanic:Eastern) Didinga, Lotuko, Masai, Nandi, Turkana/
(OTO-MANGUEAN): (Chinantecan) Chinantec/
(Mixtecan) Mixtec/
(Zapotecan) Zapotec/
(PENUTIAN): (Mayan:Kanjobalan) Jacaltec/
Chinook/
Tsimshian/
(SALISH): (Interior:South) Coeur d'Alene (VOS)/

Type 2 V-1/Pr/NG/AN

(AUSTRO-TAI: AUSTRONESIAN): (Indonesian:North:Philippine) Bukidnon, Cebuano, Hiligaynon, Kampangan, Tagabili/
(MACRO-ALGONQUIAN): Quileute/
(MACRO-CHIBCHAN): Xinca/
(OTO-MANGUEAN): (Otomian) Otomi (VOS)/
(PENUTIAN): Classical Mayan (VOS)/
(Mayan:Cholan) Chontol/
(Mayan:Tzeltalan) Tzeltal (VOS)/
(SALISH): (Coast:Central) Squamish (V-initial)/
(WAKASHAN): (Kwakiutlan) Kwakiutl/

Type 3 V-1/Pr/GN/AN

(AZTEC-TANOAN): (Uto-Aztecan:Aztecan) Milpa-Alta-Nahuatl/

Type 4 V-1/Pr/GN/NA

No examples

Type 5 V-1/Po/NG/NA

No examples

Type 6 V-1/Po/NG/AN

No Examples

Type 7 V-1/Po/GN/AN

(AZTEC-TANOAN): (Uto-Aztecan:Sonoran) Pima-Papago/

Type 8 V-1/Po/GN/NA

No examples

Type 9 SVO/Pr/NG/NA
(AFRO-ASIATIC): (Chadic) most Chadic languages but not Hausa/
(Semitic:North) Modern Israeli Hebrew, Neo-Syriac/
(AUSTRO-ASIATIC): (Mon-Khmer) Khasi, Khmer (=Cambodian), Sre/
(Mon-Khmer:Bahnaric:South)Chrau/
(Mon-Khmer:Viet-Muong) Vietnamese/
Nicobarese/
(AUSTRO-TAI: AUSTRONESIAN): (Indonesian:West) Bahasa Indonesian, Indonesian, Macassarese, Malay, Sundanese/
(Oceanic:Buka) Halian/
(Oceanic:Eastern) Rotuman/
(Oceanic:Eastern:Micronesian) Marshallese, Mokilese, Ulithian/
(Oceanic:Eastern:Polynesian) Luangiua/
(Oceanic:Eastern:San Cristobal) Arosi/
(AUSTRO-TAI: KAM-TAI): (Tai-Kam-Sui:Tai:Southwest) Lao, Thai, all Thai languages, Yuan/
(HOKAN): (Tlapanecan) Subtiaba/
(INDO-EUROPEAN): Albanian/
Romance languages/
(Romance:West) French, Italian, Portuguese, Spanish/
(Romance:East) Rumanian/
(NIGER-KORDOFANIAN): (Niger-Congo), most Benue Congo languages/
(Niger-Congo:Benue-Congo:Bantu) almost all Bantu languages (not Tunen and Bandem), Aghem, Douala, Ewondo, Haya, Luganda, Shona, Swahili, Xhosa, Zulu/
(Niger-Congo:Kwa) Edo Group, Ekpeye, Igbo, Ikwere, Ogbah, Yoruba/
(Niger-Congo:West Atlantic) West Atlantic languages, Dyola, Fulani/
(NILO-SAHARAN): (Eastern Sudanic) Acholi, Bari, Shilluk/

Type 10 SVO/Pr/NG/AN
(AFRO-ASIATIC): (Chadic) Hausa/
(AUSTRO-TAI: AUSTRONESIAN): (Oceanic) Chamorro/
(INDO-EUROPEAN): (Germanic:North) Icelandic/
(Germanic:West) Dutch/
Modern Greek/
Old Armenian/
(Romance) Papiamento/
Slavic languages/
(Slavic:East) Russian/
(Slavic:West) Czech/
(Slavic:South) Serbian/
(NIGER-KORDOFANIAN): (Niger-Congo:Adamawa-Eastern) Kredj, Gbeya, Sango/
(Niger-Congo:Benue-Congo:Cross River) Efik/
(Niger-Congo:Kwa) Abua/
(PENUTIAN): (Mayan:Mamean) Maya/

Type 11 SVO/Pr/GN/AN
(AUSTRALIAN): (Iwaidjan) Maung/
(Tiwian) Tiwi/
(AUSTRO-TAI: AUSTRONESIAN): (Oceanic:Melanesian) Kiriwinan/
(INDO-EUROPEAN): (Baltic) Lithuanian/
(Germanic:North) Danish, Swedish/
(PALEOSIBERIAN): (Chuckchi-Kamchatkan) Kamchadel (=Iteljmen)/

Type 12 SVO/Pr/GN/NA
(AUSTRO-TAI: AUSTRONESIAN): (Oceanic:New Britain) Kaliai-Kove/
(INDO-PACIFIC): Arapesh, Gitua/
(SINO-TIBETAN): (Tibeto-Burman) Karen/

Type 13 SVO/Po/NG/NA
No examples

Type 14 SVO/Po/NG/AN
No examples

Type 15 SVO/Po/GN/AN
(CAUCASIAN): (Northeast:Avaro-Andi-Dido) Tsez, Khvarsh/
(Northeast:Lezghian) Rutul, Udi/
(MACRO-ALGONQUIAN): Algonquian/
(Algonquian:Central) Ojibwa/
(PALEOSIBERIAN): (Chuckchi-Kamchatkan) Chuckchi, Kerek, Koryak/
(PENUTIAN): (Mixe-Zoque) Zoque/
(URALIC): (Finnic) Estonian, Finnish/

Type 16 SVO/Po/GN/NA
(ANDEAN-EQUATORIAL): (Equatorial:Tupi) Guarani, Kokama/
MACRO-ALGONQUIAN): Tonkawa/
(NIGER-KORDOFANIAN): (Niger-Congo) most Mande languages, most Gur (=Voltaic) languages/
(Niger-Congo:Kwa) Ewe, Fante, Gã, Guang, Kru, Twi/
(NILO-SAHARAN): Songhai, Zarma/

Type 17 SOV/Pr/NG/NA
(AFRO-ASIATIC): (Cushitic:Southern) Iraqw/
(Semitic:North) Akkadian, Neo-Aramaic/
(AUSTRALIAN): (Gunwingguan) Gunwinggu/
(AUSTRO-TAI: KAM-TAI): (Tai-Kam-Sui:Tai:Southwest) Khamti/
(INDO-EUROPEAN): (Iranian) Younger Avestan/
(Iranian:Western) Persian (Tajik), Persian (Tehran)/
(NIGER-KORDOFANIAN): (Niger-Congo:Benue-Congo:Bantu) Bandem, Tunen/

Type 18 SOV/Pr/NG/AN
No examples

Type 19 SOV/Pr/GN/AN
(AFRO-ASIATIC): (Semitic:South:Ethiopic) Amharic/
(INDO-EUROPEAN): (Iranian:Western) Old Persian/

Type 20 SOV/Pr/GN/NA
No examples

Type 21 SOV/Po/NG/NA
(AFRO-ASIATIC): (Cushitic:Eastern) Galla/
Elamite/
Sumerian/
(AUSTRALIAN): Aranda/
(Djingili-Wambayan:Djingilic) Djingili/
Kamilaroi and other southeastern Australian languages/
(Pama-Nyungan:Southwest:Ngarga) Walbiri/
(NILO-SAHARAN): (Saharan) Kanuri, Teda/
(SINO-TIBETAN): (Tibeto-Burman-Tibetan) Ladakhi/

Type 22 SOV/Po/NG/AN
No examples

Type 23 SOV/Po/GN/AN
(AFRO-ASIATIC): (Cushitic:Central) Chamir/
(Cushitic:Eastern) Sidamo/
(Cushitic:Northern) Bedauye (=Beja)/
(Semitic:South) Gafat, Harari/
(ALTAIC): Korean/
(Japanese) Japanese, Ryukyuan/
(Mongol) Buryat, Dagur, Kalmyk (=Oirat), Khalkha, Moghol, Monguor, Pao-An, Tung-Hsiang/
(Tungus:Northern) Evenki, Lamut (=Even)/
(Tungus:Southern) Manchu, Nanay, Udege/
(Turkic:Bulgar) Chuvash/
(Turkic:Common Turkish:Central) Kazakh/
(Turkic:Common Turkish:Eastern) Uygur, Uzbek/
(Turkic:Common Turkish:Northern) Altay, Khakas, Tuva, Yakut/
(Turkic:Common Turkish:Southern) Ancient Turkish, Osmanli (Turkish)/
(Turkic:Common Turkish:Western) Bashkir, Tatar/
(ANDEAN-EQUATORIAL): (Andean:Quechumaran) Quechua/
(Equatorial:Arawakan:Maipuran:Pre-Andine) Piro/
(AZTEC-TANOAN): (Uto-Aztecan:Sonoran) Yaqui/
(CAUCASIAN): (Northeast:Avaro-Andi-Dido) Andi, Avar, Akhvakh, Botlikh Godoberi, Gunzib, Karata, Tindi/
(Northeast:Lak-Dargwa) Dargwa, Lak/
(Northeast:Lezghian) Budukh, Kryz, Lezgi, Tabasaran, Khinalug/
(Northeast:Vejnax) Bats, Chechen, Ingush/
(South) Gruzin, Laz, Svan/
(DRAVIDIAN): Dravidian languages/
(Dravidian:Central) Pengo, Telugu/
(Dravidian:North) Brahui/
(Dravidian:South) Kannada, Sri Lanka Tamil, Tamil/
(INDO-EUROPEAN): Hittite/
Modern Armenian/
(Indo-Iranian:Iranian:Eastern) Ossetic/
(Indo-Iranian:Indic) Assamese, Bengali, Gujarati, Hindi, Punjabi, Sanskrit, and other Aryan languages of India/
Tocharian/
(INDO-PACIFIC): (Central New Guinea:East New Guinea Highlands) Fore, Hua, Usarufa/
(Southwest New Guinea) Marind-Anim/
(KHOISAN): (Central) Nama Hottentot/
(NA-DENE): (Athapaskan-Eyak:Athapaskan) Navajo/
(NIGER-KORDOFANIAN): (Niger-Congo:Kwa) Ijo, Izon/
(PALEOSIBERIAN): Gilyak (=Nivkh), Ket, Yukaghir/
(PENUTIAN): (Maidu) Maidu/
(SINO-TIBETAN): Newari and other Sino-Tibetan languages/
(Tibeto-Burman:Bodo-Naga-Kachin) Garo/

(URALIC): (Finno-Ugric) Finno-Ugric languages except for Finnic Group/
(Finno-Ugric:Ugric) Hungarian, Vogul/
(Finno-Ugric:Volgaic) Kurku-mari/
(Isolates): Ainu, Burushaski/

Type 24 SOV/Po/GN/NA
(AFRO-ASIATIC): Hurrian/
Urartian/
(AUSTRALIAN): most Australian languages/
(Daly) Maranungku/
Loritja/
(Pama-Nyungan:Southwest:Wati) Gugada, Western Desert/
(AUSTRO-TAI:AUSTRONESIAN): (Melanesian:Massim:Wedauic) Wedauan/
(New Guinea) Motu/
(CAUCASIAN) (Northwest) Abkhazian, Adyge, Kabardian, Ubykh/
(HOKAN): Chitimacha/
(Yuman:Delta-Californian) Cocopa, Diegueño/
(Yuman:Pai) Havasupai, Paipai, Walapai/
(Yuman:River) Mojave, Yuma/
(INDO-PACIFIC): (Central New Guinea) Kate/
(Central New Guinea:Huon Finisterre) Selepet/
(Central New Guinea:Madang-Adalbert Range) Waskia/
(Milne Bay and Central Districts) Daga/
(Mount Bosave) Kaluli/
(Rai Coast:Kabenau) Siroi/
(West New Guinea) Asmat, Bunak, Makasai/
(KHOISAN): Sandawe/
(MACRO-ALGONQUIAN): Tunica/
(MACRO-CHIBCHAN): Lenca, Matagalpa, Warao/
(Eastern Chibchan) Chibcha/
(Western Chibchan) Cuna/
(MACRO-SIOUAN): (Siouan) Assiniboine (= Dakota), Biloxi/
(NA-DENE): Haida, Tlingit/
(NIGER-KORDOFANIAN): (Niger-Congo:Gur) Wara/
(Niger-Congo:Mande:Western) Bambara, Kpelle/
(NILO-SAHARAN): (Chari-Nile) Kunama/
(Chari-Nile:Sudanic:Eastern) Nubian/
Fur/
(PENUTIAN): Zuni/
(SINO-TIBETAN): (Tibeto-Burman:Bodo-Naga-Kachin) Chingpaw (Kachin), Tsang/
(Tibeto-Burman:Burmese-Lolo) Burmese, Lisu/
(Tibeto-Burman:Naga-Kuchi-Chin) Lushei/
(Tibeto-Burman:Tibetan) Classical Tibetan/
(Isolate): Basque/

8.2 Expanded Sample Quantities

In Table 41, I summarize the quantities of languages of each of the 24 types given in Section 8.1.The Expanded Sample contains a total of 336 entries. The language families and groups listed in Greenberg's original sample are retained in the Expanded Sample, and I estimate that these effectively add 1000+ languages to the sample, which increases its numerical significance.[1] If 336 + 1000 languages do indeed occupy the relevant co-occurrence cells of the Expanded Sample, they will thereby be conforming with the implicational predictions of Chapter 3, which increases the likely universality of these implications. For distributional purposes I shall continue to count families and groups as individual entries only, as in Table 2 (Chapter 2): Not all the members of these groups have been checked directly, and where they have they are listed as single entries. The purpose of keeping the groups as such is simply to make some concession

TABLE 41 : Expanded Sample Quantities: Typological

1.	V-1/Pr/NG/NA	38
2.	V-1/Pr/NG/AN	13
3.	V-1/Pr/GN/AN	1
4.	V-1/Pr/GN/NA	0
5.	V-1/Po/NG/NA	0
6.	V-1/Po/NG/AN	0
7.	V-1/Po/GN/AN	1
8.	V-1/Po/GN/NA	0
9.	SVO/Pr/NG/NA	56
10.	SVO/Pr/NG/AN	17
11.	SVO/Pr/GN/AN	7
12.	SVO/Pr/GN/NA	4
13.	SVO/Po/NG/NA	0
14.	SVO/Po/NG/AN	0
15.	SVO/Po/GN/AN	12
16.	SVO/Po/GN/NA	13
17.	SOV/Pr/NG/NA	10
18.	SOV/Pr/NG/AN	0
19.	SOV/Pr/GN/AN	2
20.	SOV/Pr/GN/NA	0
21.	SOV/Po/NG/NA	11
22.	SOV/Po/NG/AN	0
23.	SOV/Po/GN/AN	96
24.	SOV/Po/GN/NA	55

Note: Total number of languages = 336. Number with V-1 = 53; SVO = 109; SOV = 174. Number with Pr = 148; Po = 188. Number with N_1 = 115; N_2 = 102; N_3 = 119.

TABLE 42 : Expanded Sample Quantities: Genetic

Language family	Languages in sample	Percentage of family (estimated)
Afro-Asiatic	25	10
Altaic	28	80
Andean-Equatorial	5	.5
Australian	13	6.5
Austro-Asiatic	6	4
Austro-Tai:Austronesian	35	7
Austro-Tai:Kam-Tai	5	10
Aztec-Tanoan	3	10
Caucasian	29	83
Dravidian	7	30
Eskimo-Aleut	0	0
Ge-Pano-Carib	0	0
Hokan	9	35
Indo-European	39	39
Indo-Pacific	15	2
Khoisan	2	13
Macro-Algonquian	5	22
Macro-Chibchan	6	.6
Macro-Siouan	2	11
Na-Dene	3	14
Niger-Kordofanian	40	5
Nilo-Saharan	15	13
Oto-Manguean	4	13
Paleosiberian	7	87
Penutian	10	17
Salish	2	13
Sino-Tibetan	11	4
Uralic	6	30
Wakashan	1	17
Isolates	3	

to the existence of other languages of the relevant groups in the relevant co-occurrence cells.

Table 42 provides a genetic quantification. For each language family, I give the number of entries listed in the Expanded Sample, followed by a percentage estimate of the proportion of the total family that these account for (using primarily the language quantities given in Ruhlen 1976). The purpose of this genetic quantification is to indicate where the sample is well or badly represented, in the hope that future research will be directed to the appropriate linguistic areas.

Notes

1. The estimated ADDITIONAL language quantities subsumed by the group entries in the Expanded Sample (i.e., over and above the individually listed members of the respective groups) are as follows. These estimates are based primarily on Ruhlen's (1976) figures for language totals in the respective groups.

Type 1 V-1/Pr/NG/NA
Polynesian languages (Austro-Tai: Austronesian): 9
Celtic languages (Indo-European): 1

Type 9 SVO/Pr/NG/NA
Most Chadic languages (Afro-Asiatic): ?72
Thai languages (Austro-Tai:Kam-Tai): 40
Romance languages (Indo-European): 6
Most Benue-Congo languages (Niger-Kordofanian) }
Almost all Bantu languages (Niger-Kordofanian:Benue-Congo) } ?450
Edo languages (Niger-Kordofanian:Kwa): 5
West Atlantic languages (Niger-Kordofanian): 21

Type 10 SVO/Pr/NG/AN
Slavic languages (Indo-European): 8

Type 15 SVO/Po/GN/AN
Algonquian languages (Macro-Algonquian): 10

Type 16 SVO/Po/GN/NA
Most Mande languages (Niger-Kordofanian): 20
Most Gur languages (Niger-Kordofanian): 40

Type 21 SOV/Po/NG/NA
Other southeastern Australian languages: ?15

Type 23 SOV/Po/GN/AN
Dravidian languages: 16
Other Aryan languages of India (Indo-European): 28
Other Sino-Tibetan languages: ?200
Finno-Ugric languages minus Finnic (Uralic): 7

Type 24 SOV/Po/GN/NA
Most Australian languages: ?150

The estimated total number of these additional languages is 1098.

Conclusions

This book has attempted to justify a number of conclusions, which we shall summarize very briefly. We present the conclusions for a theory of universal grammar first, followed by those for diachrony, and those for typology. We end with a comment about innateness and language acquisition.

We pointed out in Section 1.4 that there were two variables in our cross-language data that could inform the construction of a theory of word order universals: The first involved the distinction between attested and nonattested word order combinations; the second, language frequencies. For the first we need to set up explanations of an absolute kind, setting parameters on possible and impossible grammars. The second is the result of more gradient causes, involving different degrees of rule complexity, or involving the relative strength of one principle in relation to an opposing one. The existence of all and only the attested word order co-occurrence types with their associated frequencies is therefore the product of several interacting explanatory principles. And it has been the goal of this study to try and factor out some of these principles, and describe their interaction.

Chapter 2 summarized the major descriptive universals and explanatory principles currently available (those associated with Greenberg, Lehmann, Vennemann, and Keenan). It was argued that these principles did not distinguish attested from unattested word order co-occurrences in a satisfactory manner, and that some interesting differences in relative language frequencies had gone unnoticed. Chapters 3 and 4 build on the descriptive statements and theoretical notions of Chapter 2, in the attempt to refine their predictive power, and to take the explanatory process further.

Chapter 3 proposed some principles which are designed to explain the Prepositional Noun Modifier Hierarchy (Section 3.3.7) and the Postpositional Noun Modifier Hierarchy (Section 3.3.17), that is, all and only the attested co-occurrences of adposition order in relation to NP, and noun order in relation to noun modifiers. The first of these was the Heaviness Serialization Principle (HSP) (see Sections 3.4.1.1, 3.4.2.1):

$$\text{Rel} \geqslant_{R} \text{Gen} \geqslant_{R} \text{Adj} \geqslant_{R} \begin{Bmatrix} \text{Dem} \\ \text{Num} \end{Bmatrix},$$

where $\geqslant_R$ means "exhibits more or equal rightward positioning relative to the head noun across languages," the second, the Mobility Principle (MP) (Sections 3.4.1.2, 3.4.2.2):

$$\begin{Bmatrix} \text{Adj} \\ \text{Dem} \\ \text{Num} \end{Bmatrix} \geqslant_{M} \begin{Bmatrix} \text{Rel} \\ \text{Gen} \end{Bmatrix},$$

where $\geqslant_M$ means "exhibits greater or equal mobility away from the adposition + NP serialization," and the third, the modifier–head principle (Section 3.4.1.3), whereby a head of phrase (N, V, Adp, and Adj) retains category constancy when a modifier is added. A fourth principle, the Mobility and Heaviness Interaction Principle (MHIP), does exactly what its name suggests (Section 3.4.1.2).

It is argued (Section 3.4.2.1) that there is ultimately a psycholinguistic explanation for the HSP involving language processing, and that the "heaviness" effects in the noun phrase are to be linked explanatorily to heaviness effects that have been documented in other areas of word order data. The MP is explained in part syntactically, and in part as a consequence of a general principle of historical change, namely, gradualness. The MP incorporates a grammatical distinction between nonphrasal and nonbranching nodes on the left, and phrasal and branching nodes on the right. The prior movement of the former away from the co-occurring adposition serialization, before the latter, is required by gradualness: If phrasal and branching nodes departed from the adposition serialization first, a major and more inclusive realignment in surface structure would be effected before a minor one (Section 3.4.2.2). The modifier–head principle (Section 3.4.1.3) is claimed to be a valid cross-categorial generalization about language. Like all major generalizations, it unifies a number of phenomena under a higher regularity: The categories N, V, Adp, and Adj are assigned the common status "head" within their respective phrasal categories, and all other constituents within these are assigned the status "modifier of the head."

Chapter 4 motivated the principle of Cross-Category Harmony (CCH), defining the relative frequencies of the attested word order co-occurrences. The principle predicts that the more similar the position of the head relative to its respective modifiers across all the phrasal categories, the more languages there are. It is argued (Section 4.6) that CCH is a consequence of different degrees of syntactic rule complexity correlating with decreasing language numbers. Our data are too limited for us to be able to provide a comprehensive theory of complexity for word order rules, but a clear general correspondence is demonstrated between rule complexity and markedness, as these are defined by some current X-bar theories, and frequency differences between language types. It is suggested that grammars incorporate cross-categorial word order generalizations to a greater or lesser extent (by using single rules which span a plurality of phrasal categories), and that the more such generalizations there are, the more exemplifying languages we find. An outline theory of a set of cross-categorial word order rules is presented, identifying some of the features that make for added complexity in word order rules (Section 4.6.5).

We are now in a position to answer the general methodological question that we posed in Section 1.3.3, namely, What exactly does large-scale language comparison yield for a theory of universal grammar that single-language analysis does not? To paraphrase, What general insights do we claim to have derived from the cross-language perspective of this study that we could not have derived from an in-depth analysis of English alone, or from English in conjunction with a handful of other languages?

Four general points can be made. But it must be stressed that I see the single-language and multilanguage approaches to universal grammar as complementary rather than opposed. The massive literature on English reveals clearly the explanatory insights into language in general that can be gained using this in-depth methodology. My concern is to articulate what I consider to be the complementary benefits of cross-language comparison for explanation in universal grammar.

The first advantage involves the distinction between attested and nonattested word order combinations. This distinction can only be convincingly motivated on the basis of large language samples (see Section 3.1.1). What we have seen is that the descriptive statements that define this distinction in some grammatical area typically reveal patterns about language (e.g., the noun modifier preposing pattern of the PrNMH), and these patterns in turn suggest explanations (the HSP, MP, etc.) and constrain theory construction. But these particular patterns can be seen only when one considers a plurality of languages. A single language provides insufficient data, and so underdetermines theory construction in these areas.

Take the example of the demonstrative determiner in English: *This man* is grammatical; **man this* is ungrammatical. Why? More generally: Why do all determiners precede the head in English? This question can scarcely be answered on the basis of English alone. Either the data suggest no solution or the range of possibilities is so unconstrained that speculation is idle. The X-bar theory has picked on a solution that is as plausible as any, given English data only. *This* is argued to be a specifier in the phrase *this man,* just as *have* is a specifier in *have seen.* Given the assumption of common ordering for common X-bar macrocategories (Section 4.6.4), the grammaticality facts are explained. However, the value of this particular explanation is immediately contradicted by cross-language comparison, as the majority of languages in which there are inflected auxiliaries corresponding to English *have* in *have seen* place auxiliary and main verb in an order that is opposite to that of demonstrative determiner and head noun (giving, e.g., *this man* and *seen have*). And we have suggested (Section 4.6.4) that there is no specifier macrocategory in universal grammar.

Instead, we explain the data of English in two steps. First, we discover and explain the PrNMH, that is, the constraints on and principles underlying noun modifier co-occurrences in all languages, including English. Second, we consider the particular data of English in relation to the PrNMH and its causes. English has AdjN and some GenN too—hence in accordance with the universal data and their proposed explanation, it has to have DemN. More generally, this example shows that the observed parameters on cross-language word orders can reveal and constrain explanations for all and only the grammatical sentences in the relevant languages, in areas where these are not revealed or constrained by single-language data alone.

Second, the principle of CCH is built on a set of declining frequencies between language types. These frequencies provide, in this case, a set of data that can inform the construction of a theory of rule complexity (and markedness), by providing a complementary perspective to the single-language approach. They enable us to make certain general theoretical decisions which are left unresolved by data from a single language (or even from a handful of languages).

Third, certain other frequency differences between languages as well as cross-language combinatorial restrictions on certain word orders (cf. Section 3.4.2.1) have led us to reassess the role of processing difficulty in linguistic theory. The same kinds of processing considerations that

Chomsky used to motivate the irrelevance of performance to the competence grammar of English are now being used to explain the form and functioning of numerous grammatical rules across the world's languages, for example, PS-rules for S-complements, cross-categorial word order serialization rules, filters on self-embedded structures, rightward-moving T-rules, etc.

Fourth, a large plurality of languages can reveal the nature of the interaction between explanatory principles in universal grammar, particularly when these are in partial conflict with one another. We saw an example in the discussion of Keenan's Subjects Front (SF) principle (Section 4.3.1), whereby VO languages obey the frequency hierarchy SVO*X* > (= more numerous than) VSO*X* > VOS*X* > VO*X*S. Subjects Front contradicts both Keenan's predicted VO*X*S order (the mirror image of S*X*OV), and also the CCH prediction that VSO & Pr & N_1 languages should be more frequent than SVO & Pr & N_1. Evidently, the more that SF applies, the more VO languages there are. What we see in the combinatorial and frequency data in this example is the interplay and relative strength of opposing principles. A single language cannot reveal this particular interaction, as each language has selected its position on the frequency hierarchy, and has resolved the conflict, in some cases (English) by obeying SF in its entirety and obliterating contrary principles.

In the diachronic chapters of this book (Chapter 5–7), the synchronic universals of Chapters 3 and 4 are considered in relation to historical change and linguistic reconstruction. Chapter 5 shows how implicational universals can predict the relative timing of changes, as languages move from one word order type to another, preserving consistency with currently attested variation data (cf. Universal Consistency in History [UCH], Section 5.1). It is also proposed that synchronic implicational universals can be converted into diachronic predictions for the acquisition and frequency increase of word order doublets (e.g., AdjN coexisting with NAdj), as follows. Given an 'if *P* then *Q*' universal, a language will not acquire a word order doublet *P* (coexisting with $-P$), in the total absence of *Q* word orders. And if *P* gains in frequency at successive historical stages, relative to its doublet $-P$, then *Q* will also gain in frequency, relative to $-Q$, or else *Q* must already be the exclusive order (i.e., there must be no $-Q$ doublets). These principles are formulated as the Doubling Acquisition Hypothesis (DAH) and the Frequency Increase Hypothesis (FIH) respectively (Section 5.2), and are tested against some Indo-European (particularly Germanic) data in Section 5.3. The results are surprisingly good (surprisingly since the DAH and FIH are strong principles, and do not follow strictly from a set of synchronic principles made in terms of cross-language *basic* word orders only). An alternative use of implicational universals in diachrony, the trigger–chain theory, is criticized (Section 5.4).

Chapter 6 proposes that there is a correspondence between synchronic quantities of languages with the different word order types and the relative time amounts during which all languages remain in the corresponding states (cf. the Relative Time Hypothesis [RTH], Section 6.2). And, in both Chapters 5 and 6, an alternative model of word order change is outlined, which preserves the essential insights of the trigger–chain theory, while avoiding some of the logical problems discussed in Section 5.4. It is claimed that numerous factors can effect and explain changes involving single word orders, such as verb–object or relative clause–head noun reordering (Section 5.5.2). But these single changes do not then act as triggers converting inconsistent into consistent co-occurrences, in accordance with a set of (statistical) implicational universals. Rather, a reordering in one phrasal category has consequences for word orders in the other phrasal categories, because of the common cross-categorial rules linking these. These word order readjustments elsewhere will accompany independently motivated changes within a single category to the extent and with the probability predicted by current language frequency data, and the associated synchronic principles explaining these, such as CCH. The result is a closer fit between current data and historical theorizing.

Chapter 7 formulates and implements several laws of historical reconstruction, derived from our synchronic universals. For example, implicational universals enable us to fill in missing details from partially reconstructed protolanguages and from dead languages (cf. Deductive Inference [DI], Section 7.3). And, by matching our universal data against the observed variation in the earliest attested daughters of some language family, it is possible to infer the major typological features of the parent —by assessing the compatibility of one or other typological indicator with the various word order co-occurrence sets of the daughter languages (cf. the Logic of Competing Variants [LCV], Section 7.5). When our synchronic universals are used in conjunction with this reconstruction methodogy, the most likely word orders for Proto-Indo-European turn out to be: Prep, VO, NGen, and NRel; that is, just the opposite of what is most commonly assumed.

There is one major conclusion for typology that emerges from this study. It concerns the notion of a "language type" itself. The predominant current view is that a type is defined by a set of properties, each of which is present (at least with more than chance frequency) in all exemplifying languages, and one member of which (a particularly salient one) serves as the typological indicator (e.g., VO versus OV). But we have argued (3.5) that a type is really a family of subtypes, each of which may differ from one another in certain ways, but all of which will obey certain general regularities and have some typological indicator property in common. At least some of these subtypes must also be uniquely representative of the type in question.

As a result, the notion of a type becomes more abstract. The subtypes of the PrNMH constitute just such a family, with Prep the typological indicator. The permitted co-occurrences of the PrNMH are highly constrained and patterned, and most of them are unique to prepositional languages. By separating prepositional from postpositional languages, we are able to capture universal patterns and typological regularities which would otherwise be obscured. And, by pursuing this method, it transpires that verb position is of limited use as a typological indicator, so we suggest the abandonment of the Greenbergian VSO/SVO/SOV trichotomy. Languages with these and other basic verb positions clearly exist—but Prep and Postp are more general typological indicators. I also reject Vennemann's recent strict separation of typologies and universals (see Section 2.5.2).

Finally, I have said very little in this book about the role of innate grammatical knowledge in the explanation of word order universals. This has been deliberate. It seems to me quite reasonable to assume that *some* form of grammatical knowledge is innate within the human species, and that this knowledge contributes to the task of language acquisition. But I find it equally reasonable to believe that many of our linguistic abilities are particular instantiations of more general cognitive abilities, which find expression in other domains as well (see Swinney & Smith 1982). And, conversely, I consider it undeniable that many language universals are to be explained in noninnateness terms, for example, as consequences of the functions that language has to perform, or of constraints on language change, or of processing limitations (see Section 1.3.2).

Methodologically, therefore, it is simply unhelpful to invoke innate grammatical knowledge as an explanation for language universals when no attempt is made to eliminate these more general cognitive or alternative linguistic explanations, as it typically is not in the generative literature. What I have attempted to do in this book is to propose, first, the most general grammatical principles I can which are compatible with my word order data. And second, I have offered some noninnateness linguistic explanations for these where there is independent evidence for such further principles (involving language processing and language change). For some grammatical principles, however, I can find no such further explanation. These are the residue cases, and innateness now becomes a serious candidate. For example, we have seen a lot of evidence for some form of modifier–head theory. Is knowledge of the modifier–head regularity innately represented, and does this knowledge structure the formulation of language-particular hypotheses in acquisition? It may well. But, even here, it is not implausible to argue that the modifer–head distinction exists in grammars simply because there are genuine linguistic generalizations underlying such a binary division. And the child's learning of this distinction between categories could be activated by general pattern recognition abilities, rather than by any innately specified grammatical knowledge. The assignment of different categories to a binary division on the basis of shared commonalities has numerous parallels outside of language, so why should we assume that innate and language-specific knowledge is being activated in this particular case? And the recognition of complexity in the ordering of these abstract linguistic categories might be no different from the recognition of behavioral differences between otherwise similar members of nonlinguistic categories.

The fields of linguistics and cognitive science are currently proceeding to the point where these kinds of questions can be seriously pursued. In the meantime, to answer the question, Why do all languages behave in such and such a way? by invoking innateness is to add very little to the narrowly grammatical explanations that one comes up with in the first place.

I have taken my data and explanatory principles as far as I am prepared to go at the present time. I hereby donate them to those who can take them further.

References

Abdullaev, Z. G. (1967) "Darginskij Jazyk." *Jazki Narodov SSSR* 4, 508–523.

Abega, P. (1970) *Grammaire Ewondo,* The Federal University of Cameroon.

Ades, A. E., & M. J. Steedman (1982) "On the Order of Words." *Linguistics and Philosophy* 4, 517–558.

Agard, F. B. (1958) *Structural Sketch of Rumanian.* Language Monograph 26.

Allen, J., & J. Allen (1965) *Halia Language Course.* Department of Information and Extension Services, Port Moresby.

Allwood, J., L.-G. Andersson, & Ö. Dahl (1977) *Logic in Linguistics.* Cambridge: Cambridge University Press.

Anceaux, J. C. (1952) *The Wolio Language.* The Hague: Smits.

Anderson, J. M., & C. Jones, eds. (1974) *Historical Linguistics, 1.* Amsterdam: North Holland.

Anderson, S. R., & S. Chung (1977) "On Grammatical Relations and Clause Structure in Verb-Initial Languages." In P. Cole & J. M. Sadock, eds., 1977. *Syntax and Semantics, 8: Grammatical Relations.* New York: Academic Press.

Antinucci, F., A. Duranti, & L. Gebert (1979) "Relative Clause Structure, Relative Clause Perception, and the Change from SOV to SVO." *Cognition* 7, 145–176.

Ashton, E. O., E. M. K. Mulira, E. G. M. Ndawula, & A. N. Tucker (1954) *A Luganda Grammar.* London: Longmans.

Avrorin, V. A. (1959–1961) *Grammatika Nanajskogo Jazyka,* 2 vols. Moscow.

Bamgbose, A. (1967) *A Short Yoruba Grammar.* Ibadan and London: Heinemann Educational Books.

Barnes, M. R. (1977) "German Word Order and Word Order Typology." Paper presented at the meeting of The Modern Language Association, December 1977.

Baskakov, N. A. (1958) *Altajskij Jazyk.* Moscow.

Baskakov, N. A. (1975) *Grammatika Khaksskogo Jazyka.* Moscow.

Bee, D. (1973) "Usarufa: A Descriptive Grammar." In H. McKaughan, ed., *The Languages of the Eastern Family of the East New Guinea Highland Stock* (Vol. 1). Seattle: University of Washington Press.

Behagel, O. (1932) *Deutsche Syntax: Eine Geschichtliche Darstellung. Band IV Wortstellung, Periodenbau.* Heidelberg: Carl Winter.

Bender, B. W. (1969) *Spoken Marshallese.* Honolulu: University of Hawaii Press.

Bender, B. W. (1971) "Micronesian Languages." In *Current Trends in Linguistics* 8, 426–465.
Benton, R. (1971) *Pangasinan Reference Grammar.* Honolulu: University of Hawaii Press.
Benzing, J. (1943) *Kleine Einführung in die Tschuwasch Sprache.* Berlin.
Berneker, E. (1900) *Die Wortfolge in den Slavischen Sprachen.* Berlin: Behr's Verlag.
Bever, T. G. (1970) "The Influence of Speech Performance on Linguistic Structures." In G. B. Flores d'Arcais & W. J. M. Levelt, eds., *Advances in Psycholinguistics.* Amsterdam: North Holland.
Bever, T. G. (1974) "The Ascent of the Specious Or, There's a Lot We Don't Know About Mirrors." In D. Cohen, ed., *Explaining Linguistic Phenomena.* Washington, D.C.: Hemisphere Publishing Corporation.
Bierwisch, M. (1963) *Grammatik des Deutschen Verbs.* Studia Grammatika 2. Berlin: Akademieverlag.
Bloch, J. (1946) *Structure Grammaticale des Langues Dravidiennes.* Translated by Ramkrishna Ganesh Harshe in *Decan College Series* 3, Poona, 1954.
Bloomfield, L. (1956) *Eastern Ojibwa.* Ann Arbor: University of Michigan Press.
Böhtlingk, O. (1964) *Über die Sprache der Jakuten.* Uralic and Altaic Series, Vol. 35, Bloomington.
Bokarev, E. A. *et al.*, eds., (1967a) *Jazki Narodov SSSR 4: Iberiysko-Kaukazskuye Jazki.* Moscow.
Bokarev, E. A. (1967b) "Tsezskij Jazyk." *Jazki Narodov SSSR* 4, 404–420.
Bokarev, E. A. (1967c) "Khvarshinskij Jazyk." *Jazki Narodov SSSR* 4, 421–435.
Bokarev, E. A. (1967d) "Gunzibskij Jazyk." *Jazki Narodov SSSR* 4, 472–487.
Bolinger, D. (1972) "Linear Modification." In F. W. Householder, ed., *Syntactic Theory, 1: Structuralist.* Harmondsworth, England: Penguin Books.
Bowen, J. T., & J. J. Rhys Jones (1970) *Welsh.* London: The England Universities Press.
Bray, D. de S. (1909) *The Brahui Language, Part 1.* Calcutta.
Bredsdorff, E. (1970) *Danish: An Elementary Grammar and Reader.* Cambridge: Cambridge University Press.
Bresnan, J. (1976) "On the Form and Functioning of Transformations." *Linguistic Inquiry* 7, 3–40.
Briggs, E. (1961) *Milta Zapotec Grammar.* Instituto Lingüístico de Verano, Mexico.
Bright, W. (1958) *An Outline of Colloquial Kannada.* Indian Linguistic Monograph Series I, 8, Poona.
Burling, R. (1961) *A Garo Grammar.* Deccan College, Poona.
Burrow, T., & S. Bhattacharya (1970) *The Pengo Language.* Oxford: Clarendon Press.
Byarushengo, E., A. Duranti, & L. Hyman, eds., (1977) *Haya Grammatical Structure.* Southern California Occasional Papers in Linguistics, No. 6, University of Southern California.
Campbell, S., & C. Shaweevongse (1962) *The Fundamentals of the Thai Language* (2nd ed.). New York.
Canale, M. (1978) *Word Order Change in Old English: Base Reanalysis in Generative Grammar.* Doctoral dissertation, McGill University.
Capell, A. (1969) *A Survey of New Guinea Languages.* Sydney: Sydney University Press.
Capell, A. (1971) *Arosi Grammar.* Pacific Linguistics Series B, No. 20.
Capell, A., & H. E. Hinch (1970) *Maung Grammar.* The Hague: Mouton.
Cardona, G. (1965) *A Gujarati Reference Grammar.* Philadelphia: University of Pennsylvania Press.
Chadwick, N. (1975) *A Descriptive Study of the Djingili Language.* Australian Institute of Aboriginal Studies, Canberra.
Chapin, P. G. (1978) "Easter Island: A Characteristic VSO Language." In W. P. Lehmann, ed., 1978.

Chomsky, N. (1965) *Aspects of the Theory of Syntax.* Cambridge, Mass.: MIT Press.
Chomsky, N. (1970) "Remarks on Nominalization." In R. A. Jacobs & P. S. Rosenbaum, eds., 1970, *Readings in English Transformational Grammar.* Waltham, Mass.: Blaisdell.
Chomsky, N. (1972) *Language and Mind.* New York: Harcourt Brace Jovanovich.
Chomsky, N. (1981) *Lectures on Government and Binding.* Dordrecht: Foris Publications.
Churchward, C. M. (1940) *Rotuman Grammar and Dictionary.* Sydney: Sydney University Press.
Churchward, C. M. (1953) *Tongan Grammar.* Oxford: Oxford University Press.
Clark, H. H., & E. V. Clark (1977) *Psychology and Language: An Introduction to Psycholinguistics.* New York: Harcourt Brace Jovanovich.
Cole, P., & J. M. Sadock, eds., (1977) *Syntax and Semantics, 8: Grammatical Relations.* New York: Academic Press.
Comrie, B. (1978) "Ergativity." In W. P. Lehmann, ed., 1978.
Comrie, B. (1981) *Language Universals and Linguistic Typology.* Chicago & Oxford: University of Chicago Press.
Comrie, B., & E. L. Keenan (1979) "Noun Phrase Accessibility Revisited." *Language* 55, 649–664.
Cornyn, W., & D. H. Roop (1968) *Beginning Burmese.* New Haven: Yale University Press.
Counts, D. R. (1969) *A Grammar of Kaliai-Kove.* Oceanic Linguistics Special Publication, 6, Honolulu.
Cowan, D. (1964) *Modern Literary Arabic.* Cambridge: Cambridge University Press.
Cowell, M. W. (1964) *A Reference Grammar of Syrian Arabic.* Arabic Series 7, Washington, D.C.: Georgetown University Press.
Cowell, R. (1951) *The Structure of Gilbertese.* Beru, Gilbert Islands: Rongorongo Press.
Craig, C. G. (1977) *The Structure of Jacaltec.* Austin: University of Texas Press.
Culicover, P. W., & K. Wexler (1974) "The Invariance Principle and Universals of Grammar." *Social Sciences Working Papers* 55, University of California, Irvine.
Dal, I. (1962) "Systemerhaltende Tendenzen in der Deutschen Kasusmorphologie." In H. Moser, ed., *Das Ringen um eine Neue Deutsche Grammatik. Aufsätze aus Drei Jahrzehnten (1929–59).* Darmstadt: Wissenschaftliche Bibliothek.
Danusugondo, P. (1975) *Bahasa Indonesia: Indonesian for Beginners.* Sydney: Sydney University Press.
Defrancis, J. (1963) *Beginning Chinese.* New Haven: Yale University Press.
Derbyshire, D. C. (1977) "Word Order Universals and the Existence of OVS Languages." *Linguistic Inquiry* 8, 590–599.
Derbyshire, D. C. (1979) *Hixkaryana.* Lingua Descriptive Series 1, Amsterdam: North Holland.
Derbyshire, D. C., & G. K. Pullum (1979) "Object Initial Languages." *Work Papers of the Summer Institute of Linguistics, University of North Dakota Session* 23, 1–34. (A slightly revised version appears in *International Journal of American Linguistics* 47).
Desheriev, J. D. (1967a) "Chechenskij Jazyk." *Jazki Narodov SSSR* 4, 190–209.
Desheriev, J. D. (1967b) "Batsijskij Jazyk." *Jazki Narodov SSSR* 4, 228–246.
Desheriev, J. D. (1967c) "Budukhskij Jazyk." *Jazki Narodov SSSR* 4, 643–658.
Desheriev, J. D. (1967d) "Khinalugskij Jazyk." *Jazki Narodov SSSR* 4, 659–675.
Doke, C. M. (1961) *Textbook of Zulu Grammar.* Cape Town: Longmans.
Dolakova, P. I. (1967) "Ingushskij Jazyk." *Jazki Narodov SSSR* 4, 210–227.
Douglas, W. H. (1958) *An Introduction to the Western Desert Language of Australia.* Oceania Linguistic Monographs 4, Sydney: Sydney University Press.
Drake, J. (1903) *A Grammar of the Kurku Language.* Calcutta.
Dryer, M. S. (1980) "The Positional Tendencies of Sentential Noun Phrases in Universal Grammar." *The Canadian Journal of Linguistics* 25.2, 123–195.

Dugast, I. (1971) *Grammaire du Tunen.* Paris: Éditions de Klincksieck.

Dzhejranishvili, E. F. (1967a) "Rutulskij Jazyk." *Jazki Narodov SSSR* 4, 580–590.

Dzhejranishvili, E. F. (1967b) "Udinskij Jazyk." *Jazki Narodov SSSR* 4, 676–688.

Einandi, P. F. (1976) *A Grammar of Biloxi.* New York: Garland Publishers.

Elkins, R. E. (1970) *Major Grammatical Patterns of Western Bukidnon Manobo.* Norman, Okla.: Summer Institute of Linguistics.

Emonds, J. (1976) *A Transformational Approach to English Syntax: Root, Structure-Preserving, and Local Transformations.* New York: Academic Press.

Emonds, J. (1980) "Word Order in Generative Grammar." *Journal of Linguistic Research* 1.1, 33–54.

Erguvanli, E. E. (1979) *The Function of Word Order in Turkish Grammar.* Doctoral dissertation, University of California, Los Angeles.

Erwin, W. M. (1963) *A Short Reference Grammar of Iraqi Arabic.* Arabic Series 4, Washington, D.C.: Georgetown University Press.

Esau, H. (1973) "Order of Elements in the German Verb Constellation." *Linguistics* 98, 20–40.

Faust, W. N. (1972) *Gramática Cocama: Lecciones para el Aprendizaje del Idioma Cocoma.* Instituto Lingüístico de Verano, bajo convenio con el Ministerio de Educación, Yarinacocha, Perú.

Firbas, J. (1971) "On the Concept of Communicative Dynamism in the Theory of Functional Sentence Perspective." *Sbornik Praci Filosoficke Fakulty Brnenske University* A-19, 135–144.

Flynn, M. (1982) "A Categorial Theory of Structure Building." In: G. Gazdar, G. Pullum & E. Klein, eds., *Order, Concord and Constituency.* Dordrecht: Foris Publications.

Fodor, J. A., T. G. Bever, & M. F. Garrett (1974) *The Psychology of Language: An Introduction to Psycholinguistics and Generative Grammar.* New York: McGraw Hill.

Fodor, J. D. (1978) "Parsing Strategies and Constraints on Transformations." *Linguistic Inquiry* 9, 427–473.

Fodor, J. D. (1979) "Superstrategy." In W. E. Cooper & E. C. T. Walker, eds., *Sentence Processing: Psycholinguistic Studies Presented to Merrill F. Garrett.* Hillsdale, N.J.: Lawrence Erlbaum.

Forbes, N. (1964) *Russian Grammar* (2nd ed.). Melbourne.

Forman, M. L. (1971) *Kampangan Grammar Notes.* Honolulu: University of Hawaii Press.

Fortune, G. (1955) *An Analytical Grammar of Shona.* London: Longmans.

Francke, A. (1901) *Sketch of Ladakhi Grammar.* Calcutta: Asiatic Society.

Friedrich, P. (1975) *Proto-Indo-European Syntax.* Journal of Indo-European Studies, Monograph 1. Montana College of Mineral Science and Technology, Butte.

Fries, C. C. (1940) "On the Development of the Structural Use of Word Order in Modern English." *Language* 16, 199–208.

Gabain, von A. (1950) *Alttürkische Grammatik* (2nd ed.). Leipzig: VEB Verlag Enzyklopädie.

Garbell, I. (1965) *The Jewish Neo-Aramaic Dialect of Persian Azerbaijan.* Janua Linguarum, Series Practica 3, The Hague.

Gazdar, G. (1981) "On Syntactic Categories." In *The Psychological Mechanisms of Language.* London: The Royal Society and the British Academy.

Gikobara, A. C. (1967) "Gruzinskij Jazyk." *Jazki Narodov SSSR* 4, 22–61.

Gill, H. S. & H. A. Gleason, Jr. (1963) *A Reference Grammar of Panjabi.* Hartford Studies in Linguistics 3, Hartford.

Givón, T. (1971) "Historical Syntax and Synchronic Morphology: An Archaeologist's Field Trip." *Papers from the Seventh Regional Meeting of the Chicago Linguistic Society.* Chicago: Chicago Linguistic Society.

Givón, T. (1975) "Serial Verbs and Syntactic Change: Niger-Congo." In C. N. Li, ed., 1975.

Givón, T. (1977) "The Drift from VSO to SVO in Biblical Hebrew: The Pragmatics of Tense-Aspect." In C. N. Li, ed., 1977.

Gorgonijev, Y. A. (1965) *The Khmer Language.* Moscow: Nauka.

Gragg, G. B. (1972) "Sumerian and Selected Afro-Asiatic Languages." In P. M. Peranteau et al., eds., 1972.

Green, M., & G. E. Igwe (1963) *A Descriptive Grammar of Igbo.* London: Oxford University Press.

Greenberg, J. H. (1966) "Some Universals of Grammar with Particular Reference to the Order of Meaningful Elements." In J. H. Greenberg, ed., *Universals of Language* (2nd ed.). Cambridge, Mass.: MIT Press.

Greenberg, J. H., C. A. Ferguson, & E. A. Moravcsik, eds., (1978) *Universals of Human Language, 4: Syntax.* Stanford: Stanford University Press.

Gregores, E., & J. A. Suarez (1967) *A Description of Colloquial Guarani.* The Hague: Mouton.

Grosu, A., & S. Thompson (1977) "Constraints on the Distribution of NP Clauses." *Language* 53, 104–151.

Gudava, T. E. (1967a) "Botlikhskij Jazyk." *Jazki Narodov SSSR* 4, 293–306.

Gudava, T. E. (1967b) "Godoberijskij Jazyk." *Jazki Narodov SSSR* 4, 307–321.

Gudava, T. E. (1967c) "Tindinskij Jazyk." *Jazki Narodov SSSR* 4, 368–383.

Haas, M. R. (1940) *Tunica.* New York: J. J. Augustin.

Haenisch, E. (1961) *Mandschu-Grammatik.* Leipzig: VEB Verlag Enzyklopädie.

Haiman, J. (1980) *Hua: A Papuan Language of the Eastern Highlands of New Guinea.* Amsterdam: Benjamins.

Hale, K. (1978) "On the Position of Walbiri in a Typology of the Base." Unpublished paper, MIT.

Hale, K. (1982) "Preliminary Remarks on Configurationality." Unpublished paper, MIT.

Halitsky, D. (1975) "Left-Branch S's and NP's in English: A Bar Notation Analysis." *Linguistic Analysis* 1, 279–296.

Harkins, W. E. (1953) *A Modern Czech Grammar.* New York: King's Crown Press.

Harris, M. B. (1978) *The Evolution of French Syntax: A Comparative Approach.* London: Longmans.

Harrison, S. P. (1976) *Mokilese Reference Grammar.* Honolulu: University of Hawaii Press.

Hawkins, J. A. (1978) "Theoretically Significant Word Order Patterns in Greenberg's (1966) Appendix II." *University of Essex Department of Language and Linguistics Occasional Papers No. 20: Universal Grammar,* 87–150.

Hawkins, J. A. (1979) "Implicational Universals as Predictors of Word Order Change." *Language* 55, 618–648.

Hawkins, J. A. (1980a) "On Implicational and Distributional Universals of Word Order." *Journal of Linguistics* 16.2, 193–235.

Hawkins, J. A. (1980b) "Semantic Generalisations Uniting Contrasting Syntactic Rules in English and German." L.A.U.T. (Linguistics Agency Universität Trier) No. 73. (Also appears in W. F. W. Lohnes & E. A. Hopkins, eds., 1982, *The Constrastive Grammar of English and German,* Ann Arbor: Karoma Press).

Hawkins, J. A. (1980c) "On the Theoretical Significance of English/German Syntactic Contrasts." Paper presented at the International Contrastive Grammar Conference, Stanford University, March 1980.

Hawkins, J. A. (1981) "The Semantic Diversity of Basic Grammatical Relations in English and German." *Linguistische Berichte* 75, 1–25.

Hawkins, J. A. (1982a) "Cross-Category Harmony, X-bar and the Predictions of Markedness." *Journal of Linguistics* 18.1, 1–35.

Hawkins, J. A. (1982b) "Constraints on Modelling Real-Time Language Processes: Assessing the Contributions of Linguistics." Paper presented at the Conference on Constraints on Modelling Real-Time Language Processes, Port Camargue, France, June 1982.

Hawkins, J. A. (1984) "*The Unity of English/German Contrasts: A Case Study in Language Variation.* London: Croom Helm.

Hawkins, S., & E. L. Keenan (1974) "The Psychological Validity of the Accessibility Hierarchy." Paper presented at the summer meeting of the Linguistic Society of America, 1974.

Heny, F., ed. (1981) *Binding and Filtering.* London: Croom Helm; Cambridge, Mass.: MIT Press.

Hertz, B. (1954) *Practical Handbook of the Kachin or Chingpaw Language.*

Hohepa, P. W. (1967) *A Profile Generative Grammar of Maori.* Supplement to *International Journal of American Linguistics,* Vol. 33 No. 2.

Hope, E. R. (1974) *The Deep Syntax of Lisu Sentences: A Transformational Case Grammar.* Pacific Linguistics Series B, No. 34, Australian National University, Canberra.

Hou, J. Y. (1979) Grammatical Relations in Chinese. Doctoral dissertation, University of Southern California, Los Angeles.

Hsieh, Hsin-I. (1976) "Reconstructability and Predictability in Syntactic Change." Paper read at the Symposium on the Mechanisms of Syntactic Change, Santa Barbara.

Huber, W., & W. Kummer (1974) *Transformationelle Syntax des Deutschen, I.* Munich: Fink Verlag.

Hutton, J. H. (1929) *Outline of Chang Grammar.* Journal of the Asiatic Society of Bengal, Vol. 25.

Hyman, L. M. (1975) "On the Change from SOV to SVO: Evidence from Niger-Congo." In C. N. Li, ed., 1975.

Hyman, L. M. (1978) "On Reconstructing the Object Properties of Proto-Bantu." Paper presented at the 9th Annual Conference on African Linguistics, Michigan State University, April 1978.

Hyman, L. M., ed., (1979) *Aghem Grammatical Structure.* Southern California Occasional papers in Linguistics, No. 7, University of Southern California, Los Angeles.

Hyman, L. M. (1981) *Noni Grammatical Structure.* Southern California Occasional Papers in Linguistics, No. 9, University of Southern California, Los Angeles.

Iskhakov, F. G., & A. A. Paljmbakh (1961) *Grammatika Tuvinskogo Jazyk.* Moscow.

Jackendoff, R. (1977) *$\bar{X}$ Syntax: a Study of Phrase Structure.* Linguistic Inquiry Monograph 2.

Janda, R. (1980) "The Runic Inscriptions of Late Common Germanic." Paper presented to the UCLA Historical Seminar, December 1980.

Jones, R. B. (1961) *Karen Linguistic Studies: Description, Comparison, and Texts.* Berkeley: University of California Press.

Jónsson, S. (1966) *A Primer of Modern Icelandic.* London: Oxford University Press.

Kahanunui, D. M., & A. P. Anthony (1970) *Let's Speak Hawaiian.* Honolulu: University of Hawaii Press.

Kalman, B. (1965) *Vogul Chrestomathy.* Uralic and Altaic Series, 46, Indiana University Publications, Bloomington.

Karlsson, F. (1972) "Relative Clauses in Finnish." In P. M. Peranteau, et al., eds., 1972.

Keenan, E. L. (1972) "Relative Clause Formation in Malagasay (and some related and some not so related languages)." In P. M. Peranteau, et al, eds., 1972.

Keenan, E. L. (1973) "Logical Expressive Power and Syntactic Variation in Natural Languages." In E. L. Keenan, ed., *Formal Semantics of Natural Language.* Cambridge: Cambridge University Press.

Keenan, E. L. (1974) "The Functional Principle: Generalizing the Notion of Subject-of." In *Papers from the 10th Regional Meeting of the Chicago Linguistic Society.* Chicago: Chicago Linguistic Society.

Keenan, E. L. (1976a) "Remarkable Subjects in Malagasay." In C. N. Li, ed., 1976.
Keenan, E. L. (1976b) "Towards a Universal Definition of Subject." In C. N. Li, ed., 1976.
Keenan, E. L. (1978a) "Language Variation and the Logical Structure of Universal Grammar." In H. Seiler, ed., *Language Universals.* Tübingen: Gunter Narr Verlag.
Keenan, E. L. (1978b) "The Syntax of Subject-Final Languages." In W. P. Lehmann, ed., 1978.
Keenan, E. L. (1979) "On Surface Form and Logical Form." *Studies in the Linguistic Sciences,* Special Issue, Vol. 8, no. 2, 1–41.
Keenan, E. L., & B. Comrie (1972) "Noun Phrase Accessibility and Universal Grammar." Paper presented at the Winter meeting of the Linguistic Society of America.
Keenan, E. L., & B. Comrie (1977) "Noun Phrase Accessibility and Universal Grammar." *Linguistic Inquiry* 8, 63–99.
Keenan, E. L., & L. M. Faltz (1978) "Logical Types for Natural Language." *UCLA Occasional Papers in Linguistics* 3.
Khanmagomedov, B. G. (1967) "Tabasaranskij Jazyk." *Jazki Naradov SSSR* 4, 545–561.
Kimball, J., ed., (1972) *Syntax and Semantics, volume 1.* New York: Academic Press.
Kimball, J. (1973) "Seven Principles of Surface Structure Parsing in Natural Language." *Cognition* 2, 15–47.
King, C. (1901) *A Grammar and Dictionary of the Wedau Language.* Sydney: Pepperday & Co.
Knorozov, Y. V. (1963) *Pismennost Indeytsev Maya.* Moscow.
Koch, M. (1974) "A Demystification of Syntactic Drift." *Montréal Working Papers in Linguistics* 3.
Kolesnikova, V. D. (1966) *Sintaksis Evenkijskogo Jazyka.* Moscow.
König, E. (1971) *Adjectival Constructions in English and German: A Contrastive Analysis.* Heidelberg: Julius Groos Verlag.
Kratochvil, P. (1968) *The Chinese Language Today.* London: Hutchinson.
Krejnovich, J. A. (1958) *Jukagirskij Jazyk.* Moscow.
Krejnovich, J. A. (1968) "Ketskij Jazyk." *Jazyki Narodov SSSR* 5, 453–473.
Krueger, J. R. (1961) *Chuvash Manual.* Uralic and Altaic Series, Vol. 7, Indiana University, Bloomington.
Kuipers, A. H. (1967) *The Squamish Language.* Janua Linguarum, Series Practica 73, The Hague.
Kumakhov, M. A. (1967a) "Adygejskij Jazyk." *Jazki Narodov SSSR* 4, 145–164.
Kumakhov, M. A. (1967b) "Ubykhskij Jazyk." *Jazki Narodov SSSR* 4, 689–704.
Kuno, S. (1974) "The Position of Relative Clauses and Conjunctions." *Linguistic Inquiry* 5, 117–136.
Kuno, S. (1978) *Japanese: A Characteristic OV Language.* In W. P. Lehmann, ed., 1978.
Lafitte, P. (1944) *Grammaire Basque.* Bayonne: Le Livre.
Langdon, M. (1977) "Syntactic Change and SOV Structure: The Yuman Case." In C. N. Li, ed., 1977.
Lanyon-Orgill, P. A. (1944) *A Study of the Leuangiua Language.* London: Luzac.
Lass, R. (1980) *On Explaining Language Change.* Cambridge: Cambridge University Press.
Lawes, W. G. (1896) *Grammar and Vocabulary of Language Spoken by Motu Tribe.* Sydney: Charles Potter.
Lehmann, W. P. (1971) "On the Rise of SOV Patterns in New High German." In K. G. Schweisthal, ed., *Grammatik, Kybernetik, Kommunikation (Festschrift für Alfred Hoppe).* Bonn: Dümmler.
Lehmann, W. P. (1972a) "Proto-Germanic Syntax." In F. van Coetsem & H. L. Kufner, eds., *Toward a Grammar of Proto-Germanic.* Tübingen: Max Niemeyer.
Lehmann, W. P. (1972b) "Contemporary Linguistics and Indo-European Studies." *Publications of the Modern Language Association* 87, 976–993.

Lehmann, W. P. (1973) "A Structural Principle of Language and its Implications." *Language* 49, 47–66.
Lehmann, W. P. (1974) *Proto-Indo-European Syntax.* Austin: University of Texas Press.
Lehmann, W. P., ed., (1978) *Syntactic Typology: Studies in the Phenomenology of Language.* Austin: University of Texas Press.
Lehtinen, M. (1963) *Basic Course in Finnish.* Uralic and Altaic Series 27, Indiana University, Bloomington.
Leslau, W. (1968) *Amharic Textbook.* Berkeley: University of California Press.
Levin, N. B. (1964) *The Assiniboine Language.* Bloomington: Indiana University Press.
Lewis, G. L. (1967) *Turkish Grammar.* Oxford: Oxford University Press.
Lewis, M. B. (1969) *Sentence Analysis in Modern Malay.* Cambridge: Cambridge University Press.
Li, C. N., ed., (1975) *Word Order and Word Order Change.* Austin: University of Texas Press.
Li, C. N., ed., (1976) *Subject and Topic.* New York: Academic Press.
Li, C. N., ed., (1977) *Mechanisms of Syntactic Change.* Austin: University of Texas Press.
Li, C. N., & S. A. Thompson (1974) "Historical Change of Word Order: A Case Study of Chinese and Its Implications." In J. M. Anderson & C. Jones, eds., 1974.
Li, C. N., & S. A. Thompson (1975) "The Semantic Function of Word Order: A Case Study in Mandarin." In C. N. Li, ed., 1975.
Lightfoot, D. W. (1975) "Diachronic Syntax: Extraposition and Deep Structure Reanalysis." *Proceedings of the 5th Annual Meeting, N.E. Linguistic Society,* 200–214.
Lightfoot, D. W. (1979) *Principles of Diachronic Syntax.* Cambridge: Cambridge University Press.
Lightfoot, D. W. (1980) "Constraining Phrase Structure Rules." Lecture given in the Department of Linguistics, University of Southern California, March 1980.
Lindenfeld, J. (1973) *Yaqui Syntax.* University of California Publications in Linguistics 76, Berkeley.
Lisker, L. (1963) *Introduction to Spoken Telugu.* New York: American Council of Learned Societies.
Little, G. D. (1977) "Linguistic Typology and Syntactic Change in Amharic." Paper presented at the meeting of the Modern Language Association, December 1977.
Lockwood, W. B. (1968) *Historical German Syntax.* London: Oxford University Press.
Lomtatidze, K. V. (1967) "Abkhazskij Jazyk." *Jazki Narodov SSSR* 4, 101–122.
Macdonald, R. R. (1976) *Indonesian Reference Grammar.* Washington, D.C.: Georgetown University Press.
Madieva, G. I. (1967) "Avarskij Jazyk." *Jazki Narodov SSSR* 4, 255–271.
Magomedbekova, Z. M. (1967a) "Karatinskij Jazyk." *Jazki Narodov SSSR* 4, 322–335.
Magomedbekova, Z. M. (1967b) "Akhvakhskij Jazyk." *Jazki Narodov SSSR* 4, 336–350.
Makhmudov, K. (1954) "Kratkij Ocherk Grammatika Kazakhskogo Jazyka." In K. Makhmudov & G. Musabajev, *Kazakijsko-Russkij Slovarj.* Alma-Ata.
Mallinson, G., & B. J. Blake (1981) *Language Typology: Cross-Linguistic Studies in Syntax.* Amsterdam: North Holland.
Malov, S. E. (1957) *Jazyk Zheltykh Ujgurov.* Alma-Ata.
Manley, T. (1972) *Outline of Sre Structures.* Honolulu: University of Hawaii Press.
Marchand , H. (1960) *The Categories and Types of Present-Day English Word-Formation.* Wiesbaden: Otto Harrassowitz.
Mardirussian, G. (1978) "The Change from SVO to SOV: The Case of Eastern Armenian." Paper presented at the Conference on Historical Linguistics, University of Michigan, Ann Arbor.
Marsack, C. C. (1962) *Teach Yourself Samoan.* London: The English Universities Press.

Martin, S. E. (1961) *Dagur Mongolian.* Uralic and Altaic Series, Vol. 4, Indiana University, Bloomington.

Matteson, E. (1965) *The Piro (Arawakan) Language.* University of California Publications in Linguistics 42, Berkeley.

Maurer, F. (1926) *Untersuchungen über die Deutsche Verbstellung in Ihrer Geschichtlichen Entwicklung.* Heidelberg.

McCawley, J. D. (1975) "Review of Chomsky, *Studies on Semantics in Generative Grammar.*" *Studies in English Linguistics* 3, 209–311.

McCawley, J. D. (1982a) "Parentheticals and Discontinuous Constituent Structure." *Linguistic Inquiry* 13, 91–106.

McCawley, J. D. (1982b) *Thirty Million Theories of Grammar.* London: Croom Helm.

McClean, R. J. (1969) *Teach Yourself Swedish.* London: The English Universities Press.

McElhanon, K. A. (1972) *Selepet Grammar Part 1: From Root to Phrase.* Pacific Linguistics Series B, No. 21, Australian National University, Canberra.

McGregor, R. S. (1972) *Outline of Hindi Grammar.* Oxford: Clarendon Press.

Mejlanova, U. A. (1967) "Lezginskij Jazyk." *Jazki Narodov SSSR* 4, 528–544.

Mintz, M. W. (1971) *Bikol Grammar Notes.* Honolulu: University of Hawaii Press.

Moore, T. E. (1972) "Speeded Recognition of Ungrammaticality." *Journal of Verbal Learning and Verbal Behavior* 11, 550–560.

Murane, E. (1974) *Daga Grammar: From Morpheme to Discourse.* Norman, Okla.: Summer Institute of Linguistics.

Murkelinskij, G. B. (1967) "Lakskij Jazyk." *Jazki Narodov SSSR* 4, 488–507.

Newman, S. (1965) *Zuni Grammar.* Albuquerque: University of New Mexico Press.

Newmark, L. (1957) *Structural Grammar of Albanian.* International Journal of American Linguistics 23.4, Part II.

Novikova, K. A. (1960) *Ocherki Dialektov Evenskogo Jazyka.* Moscow.

Oates, L. F. (1964) *A Tentative Description of the Gunwinggu Language (of Western Arnhem Land).* Oceania Linguistic Monographs 10, Sydney.

Obolensky, S., K. Y. Panah, & F. K. Nouri (1963) *Persian Basic Course.* Washington, D.C.: Center for Applied Linguistics.

Osborne, C. R. (1974) *The Tiwi Language.* Canberra: Australian Institute of Aboriginal Studies.

Panfilov, V. Z. (1968) "Nivkhskij Jazyk." *Jazki Narodov SSSR* 5, 408–434.

Parker, F. (1980) "Typology and Word Order Change." *Linguistics* 18, 269–288.

Peranteau, P. M., J. N. Levi, & G. C. Phares (1972) *The Chicago Which Hunt.* Chicago: Chicago Linguistic Society.

Platt, J. T. (1972) *An Outline Grammar of the Gugada Dialect: South Australia.* Canberra: Australian Institute of Aboriginal Studies.

Polomé, E. C. (1967) *Swahili Language Handbook.* Washington, D.C.: Center for Applied Linguistics.

Poppe, N. (1960) *Buriat Grammar.* Uralic and Altaic Series, Vol. 2, Indiana University, Bloomington.

Poppe, N. (1964) *Bashkir Manual.* Uralic and Altaic Series Vol. 36, Indiana University, Bloomington.

Posch, U. (1964) "Das Kalmükische und Verwandte Dialekte." In *Handbuch der Orientalistik,* Bd. 5.2. *Mongolistik.* Leiden.

Postal, P. (1974) *On Raising.* Cambridge, Mass.: MIT Press.

Pritsak, O. (1959) "Das Altaitürkische." In: J. Deny *et al.,* eds., *Philologiae Turcicae Fundamenta.* Wiesbaden.

Pritsak, O. (1964) "Das Mogholische." In *Handbuch der Orientalistik,* Bd. 5.2, *Mongolistik.* Leiden.

Pullum, G. K. (1981) "Languages with Object before Subject: A Comment and a Catalogue." *Linguistics* 19, 147–155.

Rabel, L. (1961) *Khasi, a Language of Assam.* Baton Rouge: Louisiana State University Press.

Rastorgueva, V. S. (1963) *A Short Sketch of Tajik Grammar. IJAL* 29.4, pub. 28.

Rastorgueva, V. S. (1964) *A Short Sketch of the Grammar of Persian. IJAL* 30.1, pub. 29.

Raun, A. (1969) *Basic Course in Uzbek.* Uralic and Altaic Series, Vol. 59, Indiana University, Bloomington.

Ray, P. S., M. Hai, & L. Ray (1966) *Bengali Language Handbook.* Washington, D.C.: Center for Applied Linguistics.

Redden, J. E. *et al.* (1963) *Twi Basic Course.* Washington, D.C.: Foreign Service Institute.

Reece, L. (1970) *Grammar of the Walbiri Language of Central Australia.* Oceania Linguistic Monographs, No. 13.

Reinhart, T. (1981) "Definite NP Anaphora and C-Command Domains." *Linguistic Inquiry* 12, 605–635.

Rijksbaron, A. (1981) "Relative Clause Formation in Ancient Greek." In Bolkestein *et al.*, eds., *Predication and Expression in Functional Grammar.* London: Academic Press.

Rosenthal, J. M. (1972) "On the Relative Clauses of Classical Nahuatl." In P. M. Peranteau, eds., 1972.

Ross, J. R. (1967) "Constraints on Variables in Syntax." Doctoral dissertation, Massachusetts Institute of Technology.

Ross, M., & J. N. Paol (1978) *A Waskia Grammar Sketch and Vocabulary.* Pacific Linguistics Series B, No. 56., Australian National University, Canberra.

Ruhlen, M. (1976) *A Guide to the Languages of the World.* Language Universals Project, Stanford University.

Saadiev, S. M. (1967) "Kryskij Jazyk." *Jazki Narodov SSSR* 4, 627–642.

Salmond, A. (1974) *A Generative Syntax of Luangiua.* The Hague: Mouton.

Samarin, W. J. (1966) *The Gbeya Language.* University of California Publications in Linguistics 44, Berkeley.

Samarin, W. J. (1967) *A Grammar of Sango.* The Hague: Mouton.

Sapir, E. (1921) *Language: An Introduction to the Study of Speech.* New York: Harcourt Brace.

Sauvageot, A. (1951) *Esquisse de la Langage Hongroise.* Paris: Librairie C. Klircksieck.

Schachter, P. & F. T. Otanes (1972) *Tagalog Reference Grammar.* Berkeley: University of California Press.

Schieffelin, B. (1979) "A Developmental Study on the Interaction between Discourse and Syntax: Word Order and Case Marking in an Ergative Language (Kaluli)." Paper presented to the Department of Linguistics, University of Southern California.

Schmidt, P. W. (1926) *Die Sprachfamilien und Sprachenkreise der Erde.* Hamburg: Buske.

Schwartz, A. (1972) "The VP-Constituent of SVO Languages." In J. Kimball, ed., *Syntax and Semantics, vol. 1.* New York: Academic Press.

Scott, G. (1978) *The Fore Language of Papua, New Guinea.* Pacific Linguistics Series B, No. 47, Australian National University, Canberra.

Seiter, W. J. (1980) *Studies in Niuean Syntax.* New York: Garland Publishing Inc.

Senn, A. (1966) *Handbuch der Litauischen Sprache (Band I: Grammatik).* Heidelberg.

Shagirov, A. K. (1967) "Kabardinskij Jazyk." *Jazki Narodov SSSR* 4, 165–183.

Shetter, W. Z. (1958) *Introduction to Dutch.* The Hague: Martinus Nijhoff.

Silva-Corvalan, C. (1982) "Subject Expression and Placement in Mexican-American Spanish." In. J. Amastae & L. Elias-Olivares, eds., *Spanish in the United States: Sociological Aspects.* Cambridge: Cambridge University Press.

Sjoberg, A. F. (1963) *Uzbek Structural Grammar.* Uralic and Altaic Series, Vol. 18, Indiana State University, Bloomington.

Skorik, P. I. (1968a) "Chukotskij Jazyk." *Jazki Narodov SSSR* 5, 248–270.

Skorik, P. I. (1968b) "Kerekskij Jazyk." *Jazki Narodov SSSR* 5, 310–333.

Smith, C. (1961) "A Class of Complex Modifiers in English." *Language* 37, 342–365.

Smith, D. L. (1978) "Mirror Images in Japanese and English." *Language* 54, 78–122.

Smith, J. R. (1971) *Word Order in the Older Germanic Dialects.* Doctoral dissertation, University of Illinois.

Smith, N. V. (1981) "Consistency, Markedness and Language Change: On the Notion 'Consistent Language'." *Journal of Linguistics* 17.1, 39–54.

Sohn, H. & B. W. Bender (1973) *A Ulithian Grammar.* Pacific Linguistics Series C, No. 27, Australian National University, Canberra.

Steele, S. (1978) "Word Order Variation: A Typological Study." In J. H. Greenberg, C. A. Ferguson, & E. Moravcsik, eds., (1978).

Stennes, L. H. (1961) *An Introduction to Fulani Syntax.* Hartford Studies in Linguistics, 2.

Stockwell, R. P. (1977) "Motivations for Exbraciation in Old English." In C. N. Li, ed., 1977.

Street, J. C. (1963) *Khalkha Structure.* Uralic and Altaic Series, Vol. 24, Indiana University, Bloomington.

Strehlow, T. G. H. (1942–1944) *Aranda Phonetics and Grammar.* Oceania Linguistic Monographs 7, Sydney.

Sunik, O. P. (1968) "Udegejskij Jazyk." In *Jazki Narodov SSSR* 5.

Svelmoe, G., & T. Svelmoe (1974) *Notes on Mansaka Grammar.* Asian-Pacific Series No. 6, SIL, Huntington Beach, Calif.

Swadesh, M. (1946) "Chitimacha." In C. Osgood, ed., *Linguistic Structures of Native America.* Viking Fund Publications in Anthropology 6, 312–336.

Swift, L. B. (1963) *A Reference Grammar of Modern Turkish.* Uralic and Altaic Series 19, Indiana University, Bloomington.

Swinney, D., & E. E. Smith (1982) "Cognitive Issues in Understanding Language Processes." Paper presented at the Conference on Constraints on Modelling Real-Time Language Processes, Port Camargue, France, June 1982.

Taylor, F. W. (1923) *A Practical Hausa Grammar with Exercises, Vocabularies and Specimen Examination Papers.* Oxford: Oxford University Press.

Tenishev, E. R. (1976) *Ctroj Saryg-Jugurskogo Jazyka.* Moscow.

Thomas, D. D. (1971) *Chrau Grammar.* Oceanic Linguistics Special Publication No. 7, Honolulu: University of Hawaii Press.

Thompson, L. C. (1965) *A Vietnamese Grammar.* Seattle: University of Washington Press.

Thompson, S. A. (1978) "Modern English from a Typological Point of View: Some Implications of the Function of Word Order." *Linguistische Berichte* 54, 19–35.

Thomsen, K. (1959) "Das Kasantatarische und die Westsibirischen Dialekte." In J. Deny *et al.*, eds., *Philologiae Turcicae Fundamenta,* Wiesbaden: Franz Steiner.

Todajeva, B. K. (1961) *Dunsjanskij Jazyk.* Moscow.

Todajeva, B. K. (1964) *Baoanjskij Jazyk.* Moscow.

Todajeva, B. K. (1973) *Mongorsksij Jazyk.* Moscow.

Togeby, K. (1965) *Structure Immanente de la Langue Française Contemporaine.* Paris: Libraire Larousse.

Tomlin, R. (1977) "Toward an Explanation of the Basic Word Order Typology." Unpublished paper, University of Michigan.

Topping, D. M. (1973) *Chamorro Reference Grammar.* Honolulu: University of Hawaii Press.

Topuria, V. T. (1967) "Svanskij Jazyk." *Jazki Narodov SSSR* 4, 77–94.

Tryon, D. T. (1970a) *Conversational Tahitian.* Berkeley: University of California Press.

Tryon, D. T. (1970b) *An Introduction to Maranungku.* Pacific Linguistics Series B, No. 15, Australian National University, Canberra.

Tsertsvadze, I. I. (1967) "Andijskij Jazyk." *Jazki Narodov SSSR* 4, 276–292.

Ultan, R. (1978) "Some General Characteristics of Interrogative Systems." In J. H. Greenberg, C. A. Ferguson, & E. A. Moravcsik, eds., (1978).

Vaquero, A. (1965) *Idioma Warao: Morfologia, Sintaxis, Literatura.* Estudios Venezolanos Indigenas, Caracas.

Vennemann, T. (1972) "Analogy in Generative Grammar: The Origin of Word Order." Paper presented at the 11th International Congress of Linguists, Bologna.

Vennemann, T. (1974a) "Theoretical Word Order Studies: Results and Problems." *Papiere zur Linguistik* 7, 5–25.

Vennemann, T. (1974b) "Topics, Subjects and Word Order: From SXV to SVX via TVX." In J. M. Anderson & C. Jones, eds., 1974.

Vennemann, T. (1975) "An Explanation of Drift." In C. N. Li, ed., 1975.

Vennemann, T. (1976) "Categorial Grammar and the Order of Meaningful Elements." In A. Juilland, ed., *Linguistic Studies Offered to Joseph Greenberg on the Occasion of His Sixtieth Birthday.* Saratoga, Calif.: Anma Libri.

Vennemann, T. (1977) "Konstituenz und Dependenz in einigen neueren Grammatiktheorien." *Sprachwissenschaft* 2, 259–301.

Vennemann, T. (1981) "Typology, Universals and Change of Language." Paper presented at the International Conference on Historical Syntax, Poznan, March 1981.

Vennemann, T., & R. Harlow (1977) "Categorial Grammar and Consistent Basic *VX* Serialization." *Theoretical Linguistics* 4, 227–254.

Volodin, A. P. (1976) *Iteljmenskij Jazyk.* Leningrad.

Voorhoeve, C. L. (1965) *The Flamingo Bay Dialect of the Asmat Language.* The Hague: Mouton.

Wasow, T. (1977) "Transformations and the Lexicon." In P. Culicover, T. Wasow, & A. Akmajian, eds., *Formal Syntax.* New York: Academic Press.

Waterhouse, V. (1962) *The Grammatical Structure of Oaxaca Chontol. IJAL* 28.2, part II, pub. 19.

Weber, H. (1971) *Das Erweiterte Adjektiv–und Partizipialattribut im Deutschen.* Munich: Hueber.

Weinreich, U. (1953) *Languages in Contact: Findings and Problems.* Publications of the Linguistic Circle of New York, 1. (Reprinted by Mouton, The Hague).

Wells, M. A. (1979) *Siroi Grammar.* Pacific Linguistics Series B, No. 51, Australian National University, Canberra.

Welmers, W. E. (1946) *A Grammar of Fanti.* Language Dissertation, 39.

Whitman, J. (1981) "The Internal Structure of NP in Verb Final Languages." *Papers from the Seventeenth Regional Meeting of the Chicago Linguistic Society.* Chicago: Chicago Linguistic Society.

Williams, R. J. (1967) *Hebrew Syntax.* Toronto: University of Toronto Press.

Wolfendon, E. F. (1971) *Hiligaynon Reference Grammar.* Honolulu: University of Hawaii Press.

Wolff, J. U. (1966) *Beginning Cebuano.* New Haven: Yale University Press.

Wurm, S. A., & D. C. Laycock (1970) "Embedding, Deletion and Gapping in Maori Narrative Texts." In *Pacific Linguistic Studies in Honour of Arthur Capell,* 255–282.

Yamamoto, K. (1955) "Manshu Bungo Keitai Ron." In S. Ichikawa & S. Hattori, eds., *Gengo Gaisetsu, vol. 2,* Tokyo.

Yates, K. M. (1954) *Essentials of Biblical Hebrew.* New York: Harper & Row.

Yates, W. G., & S. Sayasithsena (1970) *Lao Basic Course, vol. 1.* Washington, D.C.: Foreign Service Institute.

Yngve, V. H. (1960) "A Model and an Hypothesis for Language Structures." *Proceedings of the American Philosophical Society* 104, 444–466.

Zhukova, A. N. (1968) "Korjakskij Jazyk." *Jazki Narodov SSSR* 5, 271–293.

Author Index

The following index lists authors cited in the main text and footnotes, but not those cited in the Language Index or References.

T

U

V

W

Y

Subject Index

V

W

X

Language Index

The following Language Index lists the languages and language groups that have been referred to in this book. Each entry contains a genetic classification (given in parentheses), a word order summary, a typological classification, the reference(s) consulted for word order information, and any additional citations within the main text, in that order. The genetic classification is based primarily on Ruhlen (1976) and follows a similar method of presentation to that employed in Chapter 8. The major language family is given first, followed by genetic subgroupings in descending order of inclusion (e.g., Afro-Asiatic:Semitic:North). In summarizing the word orders, modifier and head categories whose initial letters are capitalized (e.g., NumN, GN, etc.) designate basic or unique orders. Categories that are written entirely in lower-case letters (numn, gn, etc.) refer to non-basic orders. Word orders written to the right of a slash are head-before-modifier orders, those to the left are modifier-before-head orders (e.g., an/NA). Where two capitalized entries are given for the same modifier-head pair (e.g., AN/NA), the two orders are of equal (or undecidable) basicness. The typological classification is that of the Expanded Sample, abbreviated ES type 1, ES type 2, etc. The Language Index contains a total of 357 entries (excluding 29 cross-references), 336 of which constitute the Expanded Sample of Chapter 8. The additional 21 entries in the Language Index are either languages with undecidable basic word order for at least one of the word orders of the Expanded Sample typology, or languages with OVS word order, or else successive historical stages of one and the same language. The two former cases are not readily classifiable in terms of the basic word orders of the Expanded Sample, and many of the historical stages have been excluded in order not to overrepresent one particular language. All the entries of the Language Index have been used in testing the validity of the implicational universals of Chapter 3.

A

C

D

E

F

G

Gugada (Australian:Pama-Nyungan:Southwest:Wati) SOV; Po; NNum,ND,NPoss,NA,GN; ES type 24; Platt (1972).
Gujarati (Indo-European:Indo-Iranian:Indic) SOV; Po; AN,GN; ES type 23; Cardona (1965), Ultan (1978).
Gunwinggu (Australian:Gunwigguan) SOV; Pr; NA,NG; ES type 17; Oates (1964), Ultan (1978).
Gunzib (Caucasian:Northeast:Avaro-Andi-Dido) SOV; Po; NumN,DN,AN,GN; ES type 23; Bokarev (1967d).
Gur languages (= Voltaic languages) (Niger-Kordofanian) most = ES type 16 (SVO; Po; GN,NA); Greenberg (1966).

H

Haida (Na-Dene) SOV; Po; NA,GN; ES type 24; Greenberg (1966).
Halian (Austro-Tai:Austronesian:Oceanic:Buka) SVO; Pr; NA,NG; ES type 9; Allen & Allen (1965), Ruhlen (1976).
Harari (Afro-Asiatic:Semitic:South) SOV;Po; AN,GN; ES type 23; Greenberg (1966).
Hausa (Afro-Asiatic:Chadic) SVO; Pr; DemN/NDem,AN,NG,NRel; ES type 10; Greenberg (1966), Ruhlen (1976), Taylor (1923).
Havasupai (Hokan:Yuman:Pai) SOV; Po; NNum,ND,NA,GN; ES type 24; Langdon (1977).
Hawaiian (Austro-Tai:Austronesian:Oceanic:Eastern:Polynesian) VSO; Pr; NA,NG,NRel; ES type 1; Kahananui & Anthony (1970), Ruhlen (1976).
Haya (Niger-Kordofanian:Niger-Congo:Benue-Congo:Bantu) SVO; Pr; NNum,ND,NPoss,NA,NG,NRel; ES type 9; Byarashengo *et al.* (1977), Hyman (1978).
Hebrew cf. Biblical Hebrew, Modern Israeli Hebrew
Hiligaynon (Austro-Tai:Austronesian:Indonesian:North:Philippine) VSO; Pr; NumN,DN,PossN,AN,NG,NRel; ES type 2; Wolfendon (1971).
Hindi (Indo-European:Indic) SOVr; Po; NumN,DN,AN,GN,NRel/RelNRel; AdvAdj,SMAdj; ES type 23; Greenberg (1966), Keenan & Comrie (1977), McGregor (1972), native informant work; Additional word orders, 24–25; Doubling along adjacent subtypes of the PoNMH, 87; Re Vennemann's NSP, 56n; Sequencing (noun phrase), 119.
Hittite (Indo-European) SOV; Po; AN,GN/ng,RelN/nrel; ES type 23; Friedrich (1975); In relation to synchronic implicational universals, 217–219; In relation to the Logic of Competing Variants, 266–267.
Hixkaryana (Ge-Pano-Carib:Macro-Carib:Carib:North) OVS; Po; NA,GN; Derbyshire (1977,1979); Noun position, 127n; Typological classification, 64; Verb position, 1, 22, 64.
Homeric Greek (Indo-European) SOV/SVO; Pr; AN/na,gn/NG,NRel; Friedrich (1975); In relation to synchronic implicational universals, 217–219; In relation to the Logic of Competing Variants, 267; Re Cross-Category Harmony, 259; Verb position, 274.

I

J

K

Khalkha (Altaic:Mongol) SOV; Po; AN,GN; ES type 23; Street (1963).
Khamti (Austro-Tai:Kam-Tai:Tai-Kam-Sui:Tai:Southwest) SOV; Pr; NA,NG; ES type 17; Greenberg (1966).
Khasi (Austro-Asiatic:Mon-Khmer) SVO; Pr; ND,NA,NG; ES type 9; Greenberg (1966), Rabel (1961), Ultan (1978).
Khinalug (Caucasian:Northeast:Lezghian) SOV; Po; NumN,DN,AN,GN,RelN; SMAdj; ES type 23; Desheriev (1967d).
Khmer (= Cambodian) (Austro-Asiatic:Mon-Khmer) SVO; Pr; NNum,ND,NA,NG,NRel; ES type 9; Gorgonijev (1965), Greenberg (1966), Ruhlen (1976), informant work.
Khvarsh (Caucasian:Northeast:Avaro-Andi-Dido) SVO; Po; NumN,DN,AN,GN,RelN; ES type 15; Bokarev (1967c).
Kiriwinan (Austro-Tai:Austronesian:Oceanic:Melanesian) SVO; Pr; DN,AN,GN,NRel; ES type 11; Pullum (pers. comm.).
Kokama (Andean-Equatorial:Equatorial:Tupi) osv/SVO; Po; NumN,DN,PossN,an/NA,GN,NRel; ES type 16; Faust (1972); Doubling along adjacent subtypes of the PoNMH, 87.
Korean (Altaic) SOVr; Po; NumN,DN,PossN,AN,GN,RelN; ES type 23; Greenberg (1966), Ruhlen (1976), informant work.
Koryak (Paleosiberian:Chuckchi-Kamchatkan) sov/SVO; Po; AN,GN; ES type 15; Zhukova (1968).
Kpelle (Niger-Kordofanian:Niger-Congo:Mande:Western) SOVnr; Po; NA,GN; ES type 24; Givón (1975).
Kredj (Niger-Kordofanian:Niger-Congo:Adamawa-Eastern) SVO; Pr; AN,NG; ES type 10; Greenberg (1966).
Kru (Niger-Kordofanian:Niger-Congo:Kwa) SVO; Po; NA,GN; ES type 16; Givón (1975), Greenberg (1966).
Kryz (= Kryts) (Caucasian:Northeast:Lezghian) SOV; Po; NumN,DN,AN,GN; SMAdj; ES type 23; Saadiev (1967).
Kunama (Nilo-Saharan:Chari-Nile) SOV; Po; NA,GN; ES type 24; Greenberg (1966), Ruhlen (1976).
Kurku-mari (Uralic:Finno-Ugric:Volgaic) SOV; Po; AN,GN; ES type 23; Drake (1903), Ultan (1978).
Kwakiutl (Wakashan:Kwakiutlan) VSO; Pr; AN,NG; ES type 2; Greenberg (1966).

L

Ladakhi (Sino-Tibetan:Tibeto-Burman:Tibetan) SOV; Po; NA,NG; ES type 21; Francke (1901).
Lak (Caucasian:Northeast:Lak-Dargwa) SOV/svo; Po; NumN,DN,AN,GN,RelN; ES type 23; Murkelinskij (1967).
Lamut (= Even) (Altaic:Tungus:Northern) SOV; Po; AN,GN; ES type 23; Novikova (1960).
Lao (Austro-Tai:Kam-Tai:Kam-Sui:Tai:Southwest) SVO; Pr; NA,NG; ES type 9; Ruhlen (1976), Yates & Sayasithsena (1970).

M

Mojave (Hokan:Yuman:River) SOV; Po; ND,NA,GN,NRel; ES type 24; Langdon (1977).

Mokilese (Austro-Tai:Austronesian:Oceanic:Eastern:Micronesian) SVO; Pr; NNum,ND,NA,NG; ES type 9; Harrison (1976).

Mongour (Altaic:Mongol) SOV; Po; AN,GN; ES type 23; Todajeva (1973).

Motu (Austro-Tai:Austronesian:New Guinea) SOV; Po; DN,PossN/NPoss,NA,GN,RelN; ES type 24; Capell (1969), Lawes (1896); Doubling along adjacent subtypes of the PoNMH, 85.

N

Nahuatl cf. Milpa

Nama Hottentot (Khoisan:Central) SOV; Po; AN,GN; ES type 23; Greenberg (1966).

Nanay (Altaic:Tungus:Southern) SOV; Po; AN,GN; ES type 23; Avrorin (1959–1961).

Nandi (Nilo-Saharan:Chari-Nile:Sudanic:Eastern) VSO; Pr; NA,NG; ES type 1; Greenberg (1966), Ruhlen (1976).

Navajo (Na-Dene:Athapaskan-Eyak:Athapaskan) SVO; Po; AN,GN; ES type 23; Greenberg (1966), Ruhlen (1976).

Neo-Aramic (Afro-Asiatic:Semitic:North) SOV; Pr; NA,NG; ES type 17; Garbell (1965), Ultan (1978).

Newari (Sino-Tibetan) SOV; Po; AN,GN; ES type 23; Greenberg (1966).

Nicobarese (Austro-Asiatic) SVO; Pr; NA,NG; ES type 9; Greenberg (1966).

Niuean (Austro-Tai:Austronesian:Oceanic:Eastern:Polynesian) VSO; Pr; NNum,ND,NPoss,NA,NG,NRel; ES type 1; Seiter (1980).

Nivkh cf. Gilyak

Noni (Niger-Kordofanian:Niger-Congo:Benue-Congo:Bantu) SVO; Pr; NNum,ND,NPoss,NA,NG,NRel; ES type 9; Hyman (1981); Sequencing (noun phrase), 119.

North Germanic languages cf. Danish, Icelandic, Norwegian, Swedish; Cross-Category Harmony in the earliest records, 258; Word orders in the earliest records, 258.

Norwegian (Indo-European:Germanic:North) SVO; Pr; NumN,DN,AN,GN/NG,NRel;AdvAdj,AdjMS; Greenberg (1966); Additional word orders, 24–25; Re Vennemann's NSP, 56n.

Nubian (Nilo-Saharan:Chari-Nile:Sudanic:Eastern) SOVnr; Po; NNum,DN,NA,GN,RelN/NRel; SMAdj; ES type 24; Greenberg (1966); Additional word orders, 24–25; Re Vennemann's NSP, 56n, 127n.

Nupe (Niger-Kordofanian:Niger-Congo:Kwa:Nupe-Gbari) SVO; Pr/Po; NA,GN; L. Hyman (pers. comm.); Typological classification, 53n.

O

P

Q

R

S

T

U

V

Y

Z